A Census of Autograph Music Manuscripts of European Composers in American Libraries

A Census of Autograph
Music Manuscripts of European
Composers in American Libraries

By Otto E. Albrecht

Philadelphia
UNIVERSITY OF PENNSYLVANIA PRESS
1953

FOREWORD

The present Census was begun in 1938 under the sponsorship of the Oberlaender Trust. That it has required a little less than fifteen years for its completion is due to several factors. Except for a few periods of perhaps two months at a time it was never a full-time project, and more serious still, the hegira of our library treasures to the American equivalent of the salt mines was an effectual bar to progress during the war years. Almost coincident with the return of the manuscripts to their accustomed places was the writer's departure for Germany for several years' service with Military Government. This sojourn, which in normal times would have been of considerable assistance to the Census, was, because of the chaotic condition of German libraries immediately after the war, unable to contribute to its progress. Many of the inconsistencies inevitable to such piecemeal composition have been rectified as the copy went to the printer, but some will unhappily subsist. The problem of migration of manuscripts, too, was serious, but it has been possible not only to record the movement of some autographs from one individual to another, or to a library, after the item was originally examined, but also to include many of the manuscripts which have come to these shores in the last few years.

Some comment on the principles governing inclusion of manuscripts in the Census and on the descriptive details furnished may not be amiss. Although the original suggestion of the trustees of the Oberlaender Trust was to catalogue autograph manuscripts of German masters only, from Bach to Brahms, they acquiesced readily in the view that a comprehensive survey, without chronological or qualitative limitations, would be of greater service to musical scholars. At the outset, then, the only criterion for inclusion was whether the manuscript was in the autograph of a European composer. However, as the number of entries increased to formidable proportions it became necessary to exclude several hundred items of lesser importance, mostly by composers not known to biographical dictionaries. With 571 composers still represented after these excisions, it was manifestly impossible to be assured that all the 2017 manuscripts listed were authentic autographs. In many cases of lesser-known composers no autographs were accessible for comparison. Even where the manuscripts could be confronted with undoubted originals or facsimiles there were many where it was impossible to guarantee authenticity. In general, for the larger music libraries, it was deemed advisable to accept their classification as autographs unless it was obviously in error. In a few cases where manuscripts have recently been shown to be not in the composer's autograph, the entries were retained with a statement to that effect (see nos. 54, 894, 1354).

If the determination of autographs was not always simple, neither was the simple-looking matter of the European composer. This is complicated by the western migration of a fair number of the species during the last forty years. Should the autograph compositions of contemporary European who settled permanently in the United States, at whatever period, be included? If so, should their works composed after their arrival in this country be included, although no works by native-born Americans were accepted? Should political events be allowed to exclude from the Census the autographs of significant modern works such as the Bartók quartets, *Pierrot lunaire,* and the *Symphony of Psalms,* while the scores of *Wozzeck,* of the *Turangalîla* symphony, or of Malipiero's chamber music remained? Advice was widely sought and received, but it was largely contradictory. At last a formula was evolved which has been followed with but few exceptions. The autographs of European composers who settled permanently in the United States have been included, but only of those works composed before their final settlement in this country. The two major exceptions are Bartók and Rachmaninoff. In the former case the fact that about 95 per cent of all Bartók's manuscripts are in this country made it seem important to list them all together, rather than to exclude the relatively few works composed in the last years of his life. As for Rachmaninoff, although he did indeed become an American citizen the month before his death, he also maintained a residence abroad and could just as well be considered a European almost to the end of his life. Needless to say, the works of European composers written while visiting this country or composed as commissions from American groups or individuals have been included without any hesitation.

For each entry is given the title, scrupulously copied from the manuscript, omitting besides the dedication, which is indicated in the descriptive notes, only unimportant or repetitive details. A very few dedications are left in their original position in the title. A conventional title in brackets is used either to supplement the information given in the mansucript title, or to permit grouping together items which would otherwise be separated alphabetically from each other.

The collation gives the number of pages or leaves (or volumes, in the case of large works that are unpaged) and the dimensions in centimeters, height preceding width. The descriptive notes following the collation aim to identify as completely as possible both the composition and the manuscript, if the former is not adequately identified in the title. Fragments and sketches by the more important composers have been included and identified where possible, but with less complete descriptive notes. In the case of complete works, the notes state the medium of performance, the person to whom the work is dedicated (if indicated in the manuscript), the author and first line of the text for songs, the author of the libretto for operas, oratorios, or cantatas, and any indication of place and date of composition. Except for operas, where the place and date of the first performance are cited, the publisher and date of the first edition is given, although practical considerations prevented furnishing this information in many cases, especially for minor composers. Where "complete" critical editions exist, reference is also given to the proper volume and page. Works are still further identified by the serial number in catalogues of the works of composers such as Bach, Donizetti, Liszt, Milhaud, Mozart, Schubert, and Weber. Such critical editions and catalogues are listed in the bibliography at the end of the volume. Published facsimiles are also indicated, whether complete or partial, and references to articles or books are generally given when they bear upon the manuscript in question.

Where the information was readily ascertainable, the previous owners of the autographs have been noted. For too many, however, the provenience could not be traced within the time at the compiler's disposal. A list of former owners at the end of the volume permits the reader to note those items that have come to this country from well-known collections abroad such as those of Mrs. Burrell, William H. Cummings, Wilhelm Heyer, Edward Speyer, and Jerome Stonborough. The curious may also discover that the musicologists are more numerous than composers among the ex-owners (of other composers' scores!); to match the names of Friedländer, Alois Fuchs, Otto Jahn, Kiesewetter, Sonneck, Spitta, Stumpff, and Thayer one finds only Brahms, Cherubini, Mendelssohn, and Schumann. However, the honor of the species *musicus* is upheld by the galaxy of distinguished performers and conductors, from Farinelli to Kreisler.

The final note for each entry is the name of the present owner. These are also alphabetically listed at the end of the volume, with the serial numbers of the manuscripts owned by each, permitting a quick reference to the entries in the body of the Census. In a few cases where the manuscript changed hands after the entry had been prepared, and the new owner preferred not to be listed, the entry has been retained with the notation "private collector." No apology is made for including some fifty manuscripts in the hands of dealers. These may of course sooner or later leave the United States for a permanent home elsewhere, but so may any of the autographs owned by some seventy-two individuals. The information given in the Census may continue to be of service even when the autographs are no longer in this country, particularly if they are inaccessible in their new home.

The bibliography at the very end of the Census does not attempt to serve as a reading list for those interested in the subject of musical autographs nor as a record of the hundreds of volumes that have been consulted in the course of this undertaking, but merely as a convenient reference to those works referred to in the text: complete editions, thematic and other catalogues of composers and collections, and studies bearing on specific manuscripts.

In the course of his investigations the census-taker has had the opportunity of inspecting, albeit sometimes too briefly, all but about 150 of the autographs enumerated in the Census. But of more than two thousand manuscripts listed, fewer than one hundred were adequately described or identified in published catalogues or card catalogues. Indeed, some of the most interesting and valuable manuscripts were located in libraries which had replied to the first questionnaire that they possessed no autograph musical manuscripts. No one knows better than the compiler of this Census, however, that there are omissions, both numerous and serious. Nor would it surprise him very much if some of those who let repeated letters go unanswered were among the first to protest the omission of their treasures. Some, it is hoped, may even recant their firm assertion that the value of their manuscripts would depreciate if their location were known, and release news of their autograph holdings. And if one ponders the various unrelated happy accidents that resulted in the inclusion of certain items in the Census, some of which were described by the writer in the *Musical Quarterly*, it must be obvious that there were many more accidents that never befell him at all. Since it is quite likely that there will be addenda and corrigenda bobbing up from various quarters, it is hoped that they will be forwarded direct to the writer so that supplements may be issued as required.

Finally it is a particular pleasure, the greater for being so long delayed, to acknowledge the assistance extended over many years to the author by librarians, musicologists, dealers and collectors, in facilitating access to manuscripts and in giving generously of the fruits of their knowledge and experience. Special appreciation is due Dr. Harold Spivacke, Mr. Edward N. Waters, and Mr. Richard S. Hill of the Music Division of the Library of Congress, and Dr. Carleton Sprague Smith, Mr. Philip L. Miller, and Mr. Sidney Beck of the Music Division of the New York Public Library, indeed to the whole staff of both these Music Divisions, for it was in these two splendid music libraries that not only more than half of the autographs listed in the Census were found, but that a great deal of the work on the descriptive notes on other manuscripts was done as well. Dr. Richard G. Appel of the Boston Public Library and Dr. Nathan van Patten of the Memorial Library of Music at Stanford University greatly eased the labor incident to the cataloguing of the large collections under their care. At various times the special knowledge of the late Dr. Alfred Einstein, and of Dr. Otto Erich Deutsch, Dr. Antony von Hoboken, and Dr. Curt Sachs was freely given in the solution of special problems. The Oberlaender Trust deserves special gratitude not only for originating the project, but also for assuming the financial burden of its progress and eventual publication, through dark days where patience was sorely strained. Last of all, the author wishes to thank the staff of the University of Pennsylvania Press, and particularly Mr. Robert Dear, for his understanding coöperation in seeing the work through the press.

OTTO E. ALBRECHT

University of Pennsylvania
January 1, 1953

INTRODUCTION

Carleton Sprague Smith

When one thinks of manuscripts, the average person envisages a document which has never been published or perhaps a carefully copied text bound in vellum with illuminated miniatures. The case of music is somewhat different. True, there are many unpublished works, but printing being expensive, there were thousands and thousands of copies made for performance purposes—for use rather than esthetic pleasure. Composers themselves preferred a nice calligraphic copy or a printed edition to their own script, much as businessmen today favor a stenographic presentation of their thoughts to their own handwritten drafts.

Some presentation copies of music manuscripts were made in the later Middle Ages and the Renaissance and there are a few with illuminated decorations. The *Liber Amicorum,* for instance, were often beautifully written, and Mendelssohn decorated a few of his manuscripts with romantic water colors at the top of the page in order to give the "Stimmung" of the piece. This is, however, rare, and the printed music page from the time of Petrucci in 1501 was usually clearer and easier to read and play from than any but the finest manuscripts. The composer's holograph was not accorded any particular importance either by musicians or the authors themselves until the nineteenth century, and as late as 1848, Schubert's scores could be used in Vienna for lighting an oven!

*   *   *

As a result of this attitude, manuscripts were scattered to the four winds and, even when they were valued, were like as not given as mementos to admirers of the deceased. Even in our own day, the widow of a well-known composer cut pieces out of her husband's compositions and gave them to his friends. Fortunately libraries, conservatories, state archives, and collectors have made successful efforts to pick up holographs by distinguished creators, but all too often the family held on to the pieces for a generation or two and then the papers slipped away, were thrown out or disappeared.

The performer and the composer are apt to have a different approach to music. The former generally plays what is on the music stand before him, giving the matter little further thought. The composer, on the other hand, is interested in the inner content and is attentive to every phase and the structure of the work. In the old days, composers often copied dozens of compositions which interested them and we have manuscripts of Vivaldi's works in Bach's handwriting and compositions of Bach copied by Mozart. Today composers consult printed and black line print scores without being forced to copy them out. Some time is gained by this; familiarity with the work is not generally so thorough.

With the recent development of musicology in our universities and conservatories and the rounded training of our composers, the analysis of the creative process is receiving more and more importance and, studying the great composers, we naturally turn to their holographs. Reading a music manuscript is not as easy as perusing a letter because the symbols must be heard in the former and not one sound only but many at the same time. More people can extract the full meaning from a manuscript poem or novel than from a string quartet or a symphony. To transfer the habit of reading printed scores to manuscript sources requires special training, but it is most rewarding and worth the effort.

*　　*　　*

A knowledge of paleography is needed to read any body of manuscripts, since the handwriting of individuals varies tremendously. Each country and each century has certain characteristics and the abbreviations, letters, and symbols change over the years. We are still rather ill informed about handwriting and are learning more every day.

In recent years, graphological analyses have come to play a part in our study of manuscripts and frequently unusual insight is obtained thereby. Graphology can often explain the intellectual and moral personality of an individual, for handwriting is an index to the manner in which a person thinks. There are many elements to analyze which the average reader casually looking at a score might ignore. A music student examines the writing for size, form, direction, spacing, and neatness. Then there are factors such as intensity, heavy or light shading, fast or slow strokes. Sometimes there are many abbreviations. Continuity is another element and the writing can be unequal in height and width and some of the letters may be of different sizes. Certain composers write up and down, others incline to the right or left; some are stiff, their opposites supple. We find separated and run together scores—some clear as crystal, others confused. There is nothing quite like a manuscript to divulge the workings of a creator's mind.

One of the remarkable differences between a normal literary manuscript and a music manuscript is the indication of *tempo* in the latter. Sir Walter

Scott's *Ivanhoe* does not indicate whether it is to be read at top speed or a leisurely pace, but some of Vachel Lindsay's poems have stage directions. A musical score, of course, is completely dependent on speed, and the old Italian words *adagio, andante, allegro* and *presto* are still accepted by most musicians, although French, German, and English equivalents are used.

Music notation is a less exact science than our written language made up of various alphabets and constantly evolving. From neumes, the European musician went to four and then to five-line notation and tablature. Modern electric instruments and quarter-tone compositions require still other symbols. Composers have struggled with notation from the beginning and probably always will. Sometimes they have made mistakes which time has corrected. Part of the creative process is making the symbols do what one wants, and Martin Luther, speaking of Josquin des Prés, said: "He is the master of the notes; the others are mastered by them."

*   *   *

The struggle with the notes is best illustrated in Beethoven, who worked his compositions over and over again and sometimes made as many as five different endings. His sketch books are full of fragments showing how he changed and remodeled. For the student, it is often more important to see what a composer crossed out than what has remained.

In contrast to Beethoven, Mozart devised pieces completely in his head and then simply wrote them down. His powers of concentration were so great that he could write out one of his compositions with all sorts of noise going on around him and, in a letter to his sister, he tells of composing a prelude in his head while copying out a fugue (April 20, 1782). When Georges Enesco wrote a long violin sonata in two days, he explained to some astonished friends: "Yes, I wrote it down in two days, but I'd been thinking about it for two years."

There are many different ways of composing. Some musicians regard every note which they have written as sacred, others do not care if players change their ideas slightly. Bach's handwriting has a baroque solidity to it and his ornamentation is written out in great detail. He was one of the first composers to take the trouble to indicate exactly what he wanted, while others, notably Handel, left the ornamentation to the imagination of the performer. In Bach's manuscripts, the angle of the notes often indicates tempo and design of the phrase and the concentration and force of his personality is mirrored in his holographs. Even in the *Clavier-Uebung* and the first part of the *Kunst der Fuge*, which were engraved on copper by the Leipzig Cantor, we feel this force and expressiveness. Haydn, like Bach an extremely religious man, often put *Laus Deo* at the top of his scores. His writing is clear and a little bourgeois, but he was very sure of himself, and the father of the modern symphony and the string quartet

⋖{ xiii }⋗

wrote with consummate taste. Schubert's manuscripts have a Biedermeier quality, Chopin possessed an almost feminine tenderness, while Brahms was energetic and manly. The calculating genius Richard Wagner had a very neat hand and he even made lithographs of *The Flying Dutchman* and *Tannhäuser*.

*   *   *

This brings us to the whole question of facsimiles and microfilm. It is of course impractical to let everyone handle rare scores and for that reason, photostats, facsimiles and microfilm copies are highly to be recommended. Certain libraries make a point of giving the readers reproductions rather than originals and this is an excellent idea if the institution can afford it. Several hundred classical works have been reprinted in facsimile form although the editions have nearly all been small. The benefit of these copies should be made available to thousands, not hundreds of musicians throughout the world. That they are not is due partly to ignorance of their value. What amateur or serious student, however, would not be delighted to have a facsimile of *The Messiah*, the *Ninth Symphony* or a Schubert song?

Playing a piece with which one is familiar from a reproduction of the composer's holograph, always supposing that it is legible (some of course are not), gives a performer an entirely different sense. If we follow a recording with the facsimile before us, a similar sensation is experienced. Becoming acquainted wth the manuscript is a rewarding and instructive pleasure and a personal element is added which contributes both an esthetic and a psychological understanding.

A manuscript gives one a view into the workshop of the composer, showing how he creates and thinks. There are naturally several types of manuscripts. The initial sketch, the reduced score, the full score, the first finished version, the final version which goes to the engraver and so forth. For many students, the earlier versions have a greater interest than the final copies which can be quite impersonal. There is a danger of course in reading too much into a manuscript and deducing things which are not so. A few years ago, a musician who was examining a symphony by a well-known composer, concluded that the first movement, which was copied in a restrained style, showed the author in a relaxed mood, while the other movements, written with nervous haste, found him warming to his task. The idea was logical, the only trouble being that the first movement was written out by a copyist. Let not the uninitiated scoff too much. Frequently the amanuenses imitated the handwriting of the composers they were working for and we have the well-known case of Bach's second wife who could write very much as her husband, and Mozart's pupil, Süssmayer, who reproduced the Salzburg master's hand amazingly.

In modern times, many musicians have followed Wagner's lead and there are thousands of photolithographed pieces available, particularly orchestral scores and operas, in the handwriting of the authors. Their legibility sometimes puts them into the class of professional calligraphic writing, or even works of art, in which case they may or may not reveal as much about the composer as an earlier draft. Undoubtedly the legible photo-offset reproduction or black line print is psychologically preferable to most printed scores.

*　　*　　*

Perhaps a word should be said about music collecting in the United States. One of the first collectors was Joseph Drexel, who came from Austria as a young boy. His fine library formed the basis of the present music division of the New York Public Library in the 1880's. Despite this beginning, there has never been the same interest in music manuscripts in the United States as in their literary counterparts. The Library of Congress is a notable exception; the late Oscar G. Sonneck, first chief of its Music Division, acquired for it significant manuscripts from the Heyer and Cummings collections, and those holdings have been swelled in recent years by the treasures of the Coolidge, Whittall, and Koussevitzky Foundations, giving our national library a distinguished place among the great music libraries of the world. The public libraries of New York and Boston and the Newberry Library in Chicago have in their smaller collections a number of important items. Some of our well-known universities, Harvard, Yale, Rochester, and Stanford, have likewise formed collections of interest. Curiously enough, outstanding private collections are few in number, and the most important have been given to public or institutional libraries.

Scholars searching for manuscripts in America have not found it easy in the past, as many who consult this Census can testify. Who for instance would expect to find the first draft of Wagner's *Das Rheingold* in Titusville, Pennsylvania, the Schubert *Impromptus*, op. 90, in Newark, Delaware, Beethoven's *Rage over the Lost Penny* in Providence, or the violin concerto of Alban Berg in Syracuse? Three of Massenet's operas (including *Thaïs* and *Werther*) are in a private collection in Yonkers, and so it goes. Dr. Albrecht has had a most interesting time tracking down material and he could surely write a book of his adventures. Manuscripts tend to become more valuable with the years and it is ironic perhaps to think that a few of the scores of Schubert and Mozart would bring more today than the composers ever earned in their lifetime.

A manuscript means nothing to many—and, in a way, it comes to life only when the music sounds within the inner ear. It is of course only a wehicle, for the music itself must be recreated by performers. Once written, how-

⊰ xv ⊱

ever, the ideas are condensed and crystallized in a way that enables posterity to look behind the scenes, and studying a manuscript in the quiet of a library is, to the initiated, one of the world's supreme pleasures. An important holograph can be the materialized pattern of the composer's thought, a guide to the understanding of the science and practice of music. A manuscript is not an absolute source but an invaluable one.

As Robert Schumann so well observed: "Die Musiken mancher Komponisten gleichen ihren Handschriften: schwierig zu lesen, seltsam anzuschauen; hat man's heraus aber, so ist's als könne es gar nicht anders sein; manche Handschrift gehört zum Gedanken, der Gedanke zum Charakter."

*   *   *

In 1937 a number of librarians and music scholars, realizing that there was no good list of European music manuscripts in the United States, outlined a project to remedy this situation. The Oberlaender Trust, which was set up to further German and Austro-American relations, became interested in the scheme, since fully three-quarters of the manuscripts came from composers born in those countries. Professor Otto E. Albrecht of the University of Pennsylvania was selected to undertake the task, owing to his unusual knowledge of music, languages, and manuscripts and his meticulous care as a bibliographer.

It is not an easy task to cover so large a territory. For one thing, many of our large libraries are not always sure of their holdings. Sometimes a piece is catalogued under the name of the composer but not under the heading *Manuscripts*. In this way, unless one looks under the name of the musician, the manuscript may be ignored. This study actually is concerned with holographs rather than manuscripts and some libraries do not distinguish between them. A holograph is a manuscript written entirely in the author's hand. A manuscript, of course, can be by anyone. There are thousands of handwritten copies in our libraries which are not the work of the composers. In order to judge the authenticity of a manuscript, a knowledge of paleography is necessary and here, too, a great deal of skill is required, since a good many forgeries have come upon the scene during the past fifty years.

The migratory propensities of people in America sometimes make it difficult to give the exact location of a manuscript, as the owner may move from New York to San Francisco or even Florence with his collection. Certain buyers are given to trading and their collections do not stay the same from year to year. Still other owners refuse to give any information whatsoever about their holdings and unless the manuscript is well known or described in a sale catalogue one can only conjecture what the particular individual possesses.

Dr. Albrecht has traveled the length and breadth of the land and seen most of the manuscripts he describes. This is no mean feat and, having looked at nearly two thousand holographs, he really knows whereof he writes. Inevitably there will be errors, and a census is soon out of date as new material is discovered in archives and additions made to important collections. Notwithstanding these facts, this catalogue will be of tremendous benefit to all. Serious musicians and music lovers must be grateful to Dr. Albrecht and to the Oberlaender Trust for making the publication possible.

Abeille, (Johann Christian) Ludwig, 1761-1838

1. III sonates pour le clavecin ou forte piano par Louis Abeille. Opera III à Heilbronn chez I. Andre.

    1, [20]p. 16½ x 20½ cm.

    No. 1 in F; no. 2 in G; no. 3 in B flat.

    Former owner: Mrs. William A. Sullivan

    UNIVERSITY OF PENNSYLVANIA LIBRARY

Abel, Carl Friedrich, 1723-1787

2. [Quartet, strings, A major]

    Quartetto, di C. F. Abel. No. 6 . . .

    [11]p. 24 x 29½ cm.

    Score.

    Former owners: T. B. Cramer, Alois Fuchs, William H. Cummings (catalogue no. 70).

    LIBRARY OF CONGRESS

Abt, Franz, 1819-1885

3. [Autograph sketch book]

    [64]p. 13½ x 21 cm.

    Contains about 64 more or less finished sketches, mostly of part-songs.

    LIBRARY OF CONGRESS

4. . . . Lebwohl, du schöne Stunde. Franz Abt. Gedicht von Jul. Altmann.

    [1]p. 17 x 27 cm.

    Four-part song for men's voices unaccompanied.

    At end: Braunschweig, 1. März 1871.

    LIBRARY OF CONGRESS

5. Sweet angel, dream of me (George Cooper).

    [2]p. 27 x 35 cm.

    Song with piano accpt.

    At end: Franz Abt, New York, 30 mai 72.

    Former owner: Joseph Muller.

    NEW YORK PUBLIC LIBRARY

Adam, Adolphe (Charles), 1803-1856

6. Chant de victoire à Jeanne d'Arc; paroles d'Alph. Garalle; mus. d'Ad. Adam.

    [4]p. 27 x 34½ cm.

    For 4-part men's chorus unaccompanied.

    At end: 10 mars 1855. Ad. Adam.

    First line: Vierge de Domrémy, porte haut ta bannière.

    MEMORIAL LIBRARY OF MUSIC, STANFORD UNIVERSITY

7. [Ma balancelle]

    fol. 21v-22r. 18 x 25½ cm.

    In Demidov, Album of autographs.

    Song with piano accpt.

    First line: Ma balancelle au vent du soir chancelle.

    At end: Adolphe Adam, 7 février 1838.

    LIBRARY OF CONGRESS

Adam, Adolphe (Charles)—*continued*

8. [Le postillon de Longjumeau. Oui, des choristes du théâtre]
   [3]p. 26 x 34½ cm.
   Piano-vocal score of Alcindor's aria, no. 7.
   MEMORIAL LIBRARY OF MUSIC, STANFORD UNIVERSITY

9. Le rêve du bonheur, romance composée pour Ed. Teyssoire par Ad.
   Adam.
   [3]p. 27½ x 35 cm.
   Song with piano accpt.
   At end: Mars 1845.
   First line: Déjà la nuit silencieuse.   LIBRARY OF CONGRESS

Alary, Giulio Eugenio Abramo, 1814-1891

10. L'amitié. Poésie de Millevoye.
    fol. 4v. 18 x 25½ cm.
    In Demidov, Album of autographs.
    Song with piano accpt.
    First line: Toi que d'amour j'aimerais pour la vie.
    At end: . . . Giulio Alary. Paris ce 26 mars 1853.
    LIBRARY OF CONGRESS

11. La fleur du souvenir. Poésie de Millevoye.
    fol. 3v-4r. 18 x 25½ cm.
    In Demidov, Album of autographs.
    Song with piano accpt.
    First line: On m'a conté qu'en Helvétie.
    At end: . . . Giulio Alary. Paris ce 26 may 1853.
    LIBRARY OF CONGRESS

Albert, of Saxe-Coburg-Gotha, prince consort of Victoria, queen of Great Britain, 1819-1861

12. [Invocazione alla armonia]
    [55]p. 28 x 37 cm.
    Full score (chorus and orchestra).   BOSTON PUBLIC LIBRARY

Alfano, Franco, 1876-

13. Sonata per pianoforte e violoncello. Franco Alfano (1925) . . .
    [66]p. 35 x 27 cm.
    Score.
    Dedication to Mrs. E. S. Coolidge, Oxford, 29 mai 1926.
    LIBRARY OF CONGRESS, COOLIDGE FOUNDATION

Alvars, Elias Parish, 1806-1849

14. Parish Alvars' first harp concerto. Full score . . .
    [228]p. 23 x 30 cm.   LIBRARY OF CONGRESS

Anderton, Thomas, 1836-?

15. [Trio, alto, tenor & bass, unacc.]
       Trio composed for 24th April 1865 by Thomas Anderton . . .
       [2]p. 30 x 23½ cm.
     Text from Shakespeare's *Antony and Cleopatra*.
     First line: Come, thou monarch of the vine.
     THE FOLGER SHAKESPEARE LIBRARY

Antalffy, Dezsö, 1885-

16. Canon (en réflection) pour 4 voix (quartette à cordes) composé par
       Dezsö d'Antalffy. Partition (pour 2 violons, viola et v.cello).
       [8]p. 34 x 26½ cm.
     Former owner: Oscar G. Sonneck.   LIBRARY OF CONGRESS

Arditi, Luigi, 1822-1903

17. Amelia ed Ermanno. Operetta in un sol atto composta . . . dal sigr.
       Luigi Arditi . . .
       113 leaves. 22 x 30 cm.
     Full score, Italian text.
     Dated on fol. 2: 16 settembre 1841.
     Former owner: Miroslav Weber, Jr.   LIBRARY OF CONGRESS

18. [Overture]
       Originale. Sinfonia eseguita . . . in Milano . . . 18 agosto 1841.
       1 leaf, [58]p. 32½ x 22 cm.
     Full score.   MEMORIAL LIBRARY OF MUSIC, STANFORD UNIVERSITY

19. "Se saran rose" (Rosebuds). Waltz for piano composed by Luigi
       Arditi.
       [3]p. 27 x 38 cm.
     Former owner: Mrs. Mary Louise Zimbalist.
     CURTIS INSTITUTE OF MUSIC

Arne, Thomas Augustine, 1710-1778

20. [Miss in her teens. No ice so hard, so cold as I]
       Song in Miss in her teens. Set by Dr. Arne. Js. Dodd.
       12, [4]p. 24 x 28 cm.
     Full score, first 12 p. only in Arne's autograph.
     Former owner: William H. Cummings (catalogue, no. 75).
     LIBRARY OF CONGRESS

21. Whittington's feast; a new parody on Alexander's Feast. Written by
       a college wag. The overture, songs, &c, with all the grand choruses
       new composed by Thomas Augustine Arne . . . London, printed
       for the author, 1776.
       [12]p. 32 x 23 cm. 154, 99 [i.e. 98]p. 23 x 29 cm.
     Full score.
     Former owners: W. Goodwin; Society of British Musicians.
     LIBRARY OF CONGRESS

Arnim, Bettine von, 1785-1859

22. [Album of musical compositions and sketches]
  134 p. 21 x 27½ cm.
  Some 97 p. contain musical settings by Bettine of poems by her brother, Achim, by her husband, Clemens Brentano, and by Goethe and Hölderlin. In addition there are 30 loose leaves in the hand of Bettine, Achim, Reichardt and others.
             HEINEMAN FOUNDATION

Arnold, Samuel, 1740-1802

23. Elegy, on the death of Mr. Shenstone, performed Ap. 28, 1778 at the Theatre Royal in the Haymarket for the benefit of the widow of Dr. Arne . . . The vocal parts by Dr. Arne, the instrumental by Dr. Arnold . . .
  [15]p. 24 x 30 cm.
  Full score.
  Former owner: William H. Cummings (catalogue, no. 77).
             LIBRARY OF CONGRESS

Ashton, Algernon (Bennet Langton), 1859-1937

24. My God, oh, look upon me. Anthem by Algernon Ashton.
  13 p. 35 x 27 cm.
  Score for 4 part mixed chorus & organ. LIBRARY OF CONGRESS

Atterbury, Luffmann, d. 1796

25. [O harmony. Glee for alto, 2 tenors & bass]
  [4]p. 24 x 29½ cm.
  At end: L. A. Feby 13 - 96.
  Former owners: Earl of Stanford; Clinton, earl of Lincoln; Dr. Randall of Dulwich; Julian Marshall. BOSTON PUBLIC LIBRARY

26. [See the blooming spring. Round for 3 voices]
  [1]p. 24 x 29½ cm.
  At end: L. Atterbury. Jany. 1795. BOSTON PUBLIC LIBRARY

Auber, Daniel François Esprit, 1782-1871

27. [Quel pouvoir peut à cette fête]
  [3]p. 35½ x 27 cm.
  Fragment of piano-vocal score, presumably from an opera.
    MEMORIAL LIBRARY OF MUSIC, STANFORD UNIVERSITY

Audran, Edmond, 1840-1901

28. Frou-frou waltz from "Miss Helyett." Audran.
  [1]p. 34 x 25½ cm.
  For piano.
  Former owner: Hugo Riesenfeld. NEW YORK PUBLIC LIBRARY

Bach, August Wilhelm, 1796-1869

29. Praeludium für die Orgel. A. W. Bach (1828).
    [2]p. 21 x 30 cm.
    On p. 2 a *Postludium.*
    Former owners: Alois Fuchs; Joseph Muller.

    NEW YORK PUBLIC LIBRARY

30. Bonifacius. Oratorium in 3 Abtheilungen von A. W. Bach. Klavier-
    auszug.
    55 [i.e. 52], 54, 59 p. 21 x 27½ cm.   BOSTON PUBLIC LIBRARY

Bach, Carl Philipp Emanuel, 1714-1788

31. Fantasia, allegretto. Von mir, C. P. E. Bach. No. 208.
    [4]p. 34 x 21½ cm.
    Wotquenne, no. 61.
    Published in his *Clavier Sonaten und freye Fantasien . . . Sechste
    Sammlung,* Leipzig, 1787.   LIBRARY OF CONGRESS

32. [Ich hoff auf Gott mit festem Muth]
    [8]p. 10 x 16 cm.
    Song with piano accpt.
    Wotquenne, no. 200.
    At end: Hamburg, den ersten November 1785.
    Published in his *Neue Lieder-Melodien,* Lübeck, 1789.

    MR. RUDOLF F. KALLIR

Bach, Johann Christian, 1735-1782

33. Allessandro nell' Indie. Atto terzo.
    71 p. 22 x 31 cm.
    Full score, but lacking "two songs and the chorus."
    Text by Metastasio.
    First performed at Naples, Jan. 20, 1762.

    ESTATE OF MR. FRANK A. TAFT

34. Cefalo e Procri. Cantata a tre voci del sigr. G. C. Bach. Londra 1776.
    [155]p. 23½ x 29 cm.
    Full score, Italian text.
    Former owner: William H. Cummings (catalogue, no. 215).

    LIBRARY OF CONGRESS

Bach, Johann Christoph Friedrich, 1732-1795

35. Sonaten für cembalo von Joh. Christoph Friedrich Bach . . .
    32 p. 30½ x 23 cm.
    Pp. 9-12 and 23-26 lacking.
    Caption title of Sonate I: *Sonata I per il cembalo solo o piano
    forte . . .*
    Former owner: George B. Weston.   HARVARD UNIVERSITY LIBRARY

Bach, Johann Sebastian, 1685-1750

The numbers at the end of the bracketed conventional title refer to the serial numbers in Wolfgang Schmieder's *Thematisches Verzeichnis der Werke Johann Sebastian Bachs*, Leipzig, Breitkopf & Härtel, 1950. The notes further refer to publication in Bach's *Werke*, 60 vols., Leipzig, Breitkopf & Härtel, 1851-1926 (reprinted Ann Arbor, Edwards Bros., 1947).

36. [Cantata no. 7. Christ unser Herr zum Jordan kam. S. 7]
    [4]p. 36 x 21 cm.
    Continuo part only.   MR. JOHN G. MC CULLOUGH

37. [Cantata no. 9. Es ist das Heil uns kommen her. S. 9]
    Doica 6 post Trinitatis. Es ist das Heyl uns kommen her a 4 voci.
    1 trav. 1 hautb. 2 violini. viola e cemb.
    [17]p. 35½ x 22 cm.
    Full score.
    Werke, Jahrgang I, p. 245.
    Cf. *Katalog des musikhistorischen Museums von Wilhelm Heyer*,
    IV, 99, and *Report of the Librarian of Congress*, 1931, p. 205-207,
    (with two facsimiles).
    Former owner: Werner Wolffheim.   LIBRARY OF CONGRESS

38. [Cantata no. 10. Meine Seel' erhebt den Herrn. S. 10]
    In festo Visitationis Mariae. Meine Seele erhebt den Herrn.
    2 leaves, [17]p. 36 x 21½ cm.
    Full score.
    Cover title (in another hand): *Festo Visitationis Mariae Meine Seel
    erhebt den Herren a 4 voc. tromba 2 hautbois 2 violini viola e
    continuo di sign. J. S. Bach.*
    Werke: Jahrgang I, p. 277.
    Former owners: Ernst Rudorff, Paul Wittgenstein.
                        LIBRARY OF CONGRESS, WHITTALL COLLECTION

39. [Cantata no. 97. In allen meinen Taten. S. 97]
    In allen meinen Thaten à 4 voci, 2 hautb., 2 violini, viola e
    continuo.
    [20]p. 34½ x 22 cm.
    Full score.
    At end: Fine SDG1. 1734.
    Werke: Jahrgang XXII, p. 187.
    Former owners: J. A. Stumpff, Frederick Locker-Lampson, Lillie
    Bliss, Dr. Christian A. Herter.   NEW YORK PUBLIC LIBRARY

40. [Cantata no. 117. Sei Lob und Ehr' dem höchsten Gut. S. 117]
    J. J. Sey Lob und Ehr dem höchsten Guth, à 4 Voci. 2 Trav:
    2 Hautb: 2 Violini Viola e Cont di Bach.
    [20]p. 35 x 22 cm.
    Full score.

Bach, Johann Sebastian—*continued*

Werke: Jahrgang XXIV, p. 161.
Former owner: Breitkopf & Härtel.
Facsimile of first and last pages in W. Schmieder, *Musikerhand-schriften in drei Jahrhunderten,* Leipzig, 1939, p. 6-7.

PRIVATE COLLECTOR

41. [Cantata no. 118. O Jesu Christ, mein's Lebens Licht. S. 118]
Motetto à 4 Voci. 2 Litui. 2 Violini, Viola, 2 Oboe e Bassano se piace e Continuo. Bach.
[4]p. 34 x 22 cm.
Full score.
Werke: Jahrgang XXIV, p. 185.
Former owner: Breitkopf & Härtel. PRIVATE COLLECTOR

42. [Cantata no. 118. O Jesu Christ, mein's Lebens Licht. S. 118]
J. J. Motetto a 4 Voci. due Litui. 1 Cornet. 3 Trombone.
[4]p. 34 x 22 cm.
Full score.
Former owner: Breitkopf & Härtel. PRIVATE COLLECTOR

43. [Cantata no. 131. Aus der Tiefe ruf' ich. S. 131]
Aus der Tieffen ruff ich Herr zu dir, a una obboe, uno violino, doi viola e fagotto. S. A. T. B. e fondo da Gio: Bast: Bach.
15 p. 33 x 30 cm.
Full score.
At end: Auff Begehr tit Herrn Dr. Georg Christ: Eilmar in die Music gebracht von Joh: Seb: Bach Org. Molhusino.
Werke: Jahrgang XXVIII, p. 3.
Former owners: Alois Fuchs, Wilhelm Rust. MR. RUDOLF F. KALLIR

44. [Cantata no. 174. Ich liebe den Höchsten. S. 174]
[2]p. 32 x 21 cm.
Voice part of the aria for bass, no. 4, beginning: Greifet zu! fasst das Heyl!
Former owners: Alfred Bovet de Valentigny, Edward Speyer, George T. Keating.
MEMORIAL LIBRARY OF MUSIC, STANFORD UNIVERSITY

45. [Cantata no. 174. Ich liebe den Höchsten. S. 174]
Viola 2 concertato.
[4]p. 35½ x 22 cm.
Second viola part only.
Former owner: Christian Zabriskie. LIBRARY OF CONGRESS

46. [Cantata no. 180. Schmücke dich, o liebe Seele. S. 180]
Concerto. Dominica 20 post Trinit: Schmücke dich o liebe Seele p à 4 voci. Traversiere 2 Flauti. 2 Hautbois. 2 Violini Viola. Continuo di Sig: Joh: Seb: Bach.
1 leaf, 20 p. 36 x 21½ cm.
Full score.

Bach, Johann Sebastian—*continued*

> Caption title: *J. J. Doica 20 post Trinit. Schmücke dich o liebe Seele p.*
> At end: SDG Fine.
> Werke: Jahrgang XXXV, p. 295.
> Former owners: Felix Mendelssohn-Bartholdy, Julius Rietz, Pauline Viardot-Garcia.   MRS. MARY LOUISE ZIMBALIST

47.   [Cantata no. 188. Ich habe mein Zuversicht. S. 188]
>   [2]p. 32½ x 19½ cm.
>   Fragment of score of the aria: *Wenn alles bricht und alles fällt,* and the following recitative.   LIBRARY OF CONGRESS

48.   [Cantata-fragment. Ehre sei Gott in der Höhe. S. 197a]
>   [4]p. 33 x 20 cm.
>   Full score of the only extant fragment of a cantata written for Christmas, 1728. Contains closing portion of an alto aria: *O du angenehmer Schatz*; a bass recitative: *Das Kind ist mein*; a bass aria: *Ich lasse dich nicht*; and the final chorale: *Wohlan! so will ich mich.*
>   Werke: Jahrgang XLI, p. 109.
>   Facsimile of one page in *Notes*, VII (1949-50), p. 197.
>   Former owner: Julius Epstein, Frau Conrat Horn.
>   HEINEMAN FOUNDATION

49.   Clavier-Büchlein vor Wilhelm Friedemann Bach angefangen in Cöthen den 22. Januar Ao. 1720.
>   2 leaves, [138]p. 17 x 19½ cm.
>   About two-thirds of the book in J. S. Bach's autograph.
>   Contents listed in Schmieder, *Thematisches Verzeichnis*, p. 659.
>   Former owners: Johann Christian Bach, J. Koetschau, Siegfried Krug.   YALE UNIVERSITY SCHOOL OF MUSIC

50.   [Fantasia, harpsichord, C minor. S. 906]
>   Fantasia per il cembalo di G. S. Bach.
>   [2]p. 35 x 21 cm.
>   Werke, Jahrgang XXXVI, p. 145.
>   Former owner: Max Friedländer.
>   Facsimile in Musical Quarterly, XXXI (1945), opp. p. 492.
>   MR. FRANZ ROEHN

51.   [Prelude, organ, no. 1, C major. S. 531]
>   Praeludium pedaliter di Joh. Bach.
>   [4]p. 36 x 21 cm.
>   Werke, Jahrgang XV, p. 81.
>   Followed on p. 2 by an unidentified *Fuga da G* and on p. 4, by a *Marche de Sign Triflich*, equally unidentified.
>   Former owner: William H. Cummings (catalogue, no. 82).
>   LIBRARY OF CONGRESS

Bach, Johann Sebastian—*continued*

52. [Suite, keyboard, F major. S. Anh. 80]
   [4]p. 33 x 19½ cm.
   Contents: *Allemanda, Courante, Sarabanda, Gigue.*
   Unpublished.
   Facsimile of p. 1 in Van Patten, *Catalogue*, p. 8.
   Former owner: Manfred Gorke.
                    MEMORIAL LIBRARY OF MUSIC, STANFORD UNIVERSITY

53. [Suites, harpsichord (French suites) S. 812-817]
   Six suites bestehend in Allemanden, Couranten, Sarabanden,
   Giguen, Menuetten, Boureen, und andere Galantr. Denen
   Liebhabern zur Gemüthsergötzung verfertigt von Johann
   Sebastian Bach . . .
   [64]p. 17 x 20 cm.
   This ms. was believed by Spitta to be Bach's autograph, but the
   correctness of this assumption remains to be proved.
   Former owners: S. W. Dehn, A. W. Dohn.   LIBRARY OF CONGRESS

54. [Das wohltemperirte Klavier. Part II, no. 23, B major. S. 892]
   Fuga à 4.
   [4]p. 33 x 21 cm.
   This ms. has recently been proved not to be the autograph of J. S.
   Bach. See R. S. Hill, "A mistempered Bach manuscript," *Notes,*
   VII (1949-50), 377-86.   NEWBERRY LIBRARY

Bach, Wilhelm Friedemann, 1710-1784
55. Bach, Johann Sebastian, 1685-1750
   [Cantata no. 80. Ein' feste Burg. S. 80]
   [25]p. 33 x 20 cm.
   Full score of a revised version of the chorale: *Und wenn die Welt
   voll Teufel wär*, with Latin words: *Manebit verbum Domini*
   instead of Luther's original text. See *Library of Congress Quarterly Journal*, V, no. 1 (Nov. 1947), 44-45, with facsimile.
                                        LIBRARY OF CONGRESS

56. [Fragment of an unidentified cantata]
   [2]p. 33½ x 20½ cm.
   Fragment of the cembalo part, including 3 recitatives and an aria.
   Former owner: George B. Weston.   HARVARD UNIVERSITY LIBRARY

57. Zelenka, Johann Dismas, 1679-1745.
   Magnificat à 4. C.A.T.B. J.D.Z.
   10 numbered leaves. 34½ x 21½ cm.
   Full score in the autograph of W. F. Bach.
   Former owners: Werner Wolffheim (sale catalogue, II, no. 79);
   George B. Weston.   HARVARD UNIVERSITY LIBRARY

Bach, Wilhelm Friedemann—*continued*

58. [Sonata, harpsichord, D major]
        II, no. 153. Sonata pel cembalo . . . dal sig. il cavaliere W. F. Bach.
        [11]p. 35½ x 21 cm.
     Former owner: William H. Cummings (catalogue, no. 83).
                                                    LIBRARY OF CONGRESS

Baillot, Pierre Marie François de Sales, 1771-1842
59. Canon à l'unisson à 4 voix égales. Composé par Baillot pour son
        ami Cherubini, Paris, 28 mars 1841.
        [1]p. 23 x 18½ cm.
     First line: Cantiamo, cantiamo sempre il gran maestro.
     Former owners: Luigi Cherubini, Julian Marshall.
                                                    LIBRARY OF CONGRESS

Balakirev, Miliĭ, Alekseevich, 1837-1910
60. Rêverie pour le piano par Mili Balakirew.
        7 p. 36 x 26½ cm.
     Dated April 10, 1903.
     Published ca. 1903 by Zimmermann in St. Petersburg.
     Former owner: Michel D. Calvocoressi.
                                MEMORIAL LIBRARY OF MUSIC, STANFORD UNIVERSITY

Baldenecker, Conrad, 1828-
61. Wilhelm Tell. Melodrama von Conrad Baldenecker. Partitur.
        18 leaves. 29 x 23½ cm.
     Full score of the second part only.
     Former owner: H. Henkel.   LIBRARY OF CONGRESS

Balfe, Michael William, 1808-1870
62. . . . The echoes of the heart. Words, R. Tyler, Music, Balfe . . .
        [4]p. 33 x 25 cm.
     Song with piano accpt.
     First line: When roaming through this world.
     At end: Composed expressly for Madame Sala by her friend
        M. W. B.
     Former owner: William H. Cummings (catalogue, no. 88).
                                                    LIBRARY OF CONGRESS

63. The young soldier. Words by Edward Fitzball, Esqr. Music by M. W.
        Balfe. No. 4.
        [6]p. 30½ x 23 cm.
     Song with piano accpt.
     First line: Calm is the sleep of the young soldier.
                                MEMORIAL LIBRARY OF MUSIC, STANFORD UNIVERSITY

Bantock, Granville, 1868-1946

64. Overture to a Greek tragedy "Oedipus at Colonos" (Sophocles) for
      orchestra by Granville Bantock . . .
      77 p. 35 x 27 cm.
      Full score.
      At end: G. B. 4/8/11 Lyme Regis.
      Published in 1912 by F. E. C. Leuckart in Berlin.
                                                    LIBRARY OF CONGRESS

Barbier, Frédéric Etienne, 1829-1889

65. Le docteur Tam-Tam (opérette) par F. Barbier.
      [85]p. 24 x 32 cm.
      Full score.
      Libretto by Francis Tourte.
      First performed in Paris in 1859.   LIBRARY OF CONGRESS

Barnett, John, 1802-1890

66. Abraham on the altar of his son. 1823.
      1 leaf, [13]p. 28½ x 24½ cm.
      Full score for voice and orchestra.   BOSTON PUBLIC LIBRARY

67. Before breakfast; operetta. The music composed by John Barnett.
      1826.
      1 leaf, [62]p. 28½ x 22½ cm.
      Full score.
      Text by Richard Peake.
      First performed in 1828 at the Lyceum Theatre, London.
                                                    BOSTON PUBLIC LIBRARY

68. Daniel in the den of lions, an oratorio.
      [158]p. 35 x 34 cm.
      Full score; unfinished.
      Composed in 1841.   BOSTON PUBLIC LIBRARY

69. [Fair Rosamond]
      858 p. 24 x 24 cm.
      Full score.
      Text by C. Z. Barnett.
      First performed February 28, 1837 at the Drury Lane Theatre
      in London.   BOSTON PUBLIC LIBRARY

70. [Fair Rosamond. Overture]
      Overture to Fair Rosamond; an opera in 4 acts . . .
      1 leaf, 162 p. 22 x 22 cm.
      Full score.   BOSTON PUBLIC LIBRARY

71. [Farinelli. Opera in 2 acts]
      3 vols. (118, 140, 186 p.) 35 x 34 cm.
      Full score.
      On page 1: October 1837. John Barnett.
      Text by C. Z. Barnett.
      First performed February 8, 1839, at the Drury Lane Theatre
      in London.   BOSTON PUBLIC LIBRARY

Barnett, John—*continued*

72. Farinelli. Overture.
    41 p. 35 x 34 cm.
    Full score.

73. L'Ipocondria. Characteristic symphonia. John Barnett. 1839.
    78 p. 36 x 26½ cm.
    Full score.

74. Kathleen. Opera in 2 acts.
    Score (312, 308 p.) and parts. 35 x 34 cm.
    Full score.
    Text by James Sheridan Knowles.
    At end: John Barnett. Sepr. 1840.
    This opera was never produced or published.

75. [Mass, no. 1, G minor]
    Mass no. 1. John Barnett. 1823.
    114 p. 24 x 29½ cm.
    Full score.

76. [Miscellaneous orchestral compositions]
    2 vols. 28 x 36 cm.

77. [Miscellaneous vocal compositions]
    1 vol. 28 x 36 cm.

78. Monsieur Mallet.
    [165]p. 28½ x 22½ cm.
    Full score of the opera.
    Text by Thomas Moncrieff.
    First performed in 1828 at the Adelphia Theatre in London.

79. [The Mountain sylph. Opera in 3 acts]
    2 vols. (263, 283 p.) 26½ x 27 cm.
    Full score.
    Text by T. J. Thackeray.
    Some instrumental parts inserted, as well as 43 loose leaves, mostly
        from the same opera.
    First performed August 25, 1834 at the Lyceum Theatre in London.

80. [The Mountain sylph. Overture]
    Overture to the Mountain sylph.
    43 p. 25 x 36 cm.
    Full score.

81. [The Mountain sylph. Finale]
    Finale. The Mountain sylph.
    36 p. 24½ x 34 cm.
    Full score; incomplete.

Barnett, John—*continued*

82. The Omnipresence of the Deity; an oratorio in 1 part composed by
    John Barnett. 1829.
        100 p. 29½ x 24 cm.
    Piano-vocal score.
    Never performed; published in 1829.   <small>BOSTON PUBLIC LIBRARY</small>

83. [Overture, orchestra, A major]
        Overture. New piece. J. Barnett. 1821.
        42 p. 24 x 29½ cm.
    Full score.   <small>BOSTON PUBLIC LIBRARY</small>

84. [Overture, orchestra, C major]
        Overture. John Barnett. 1821 [or 1826?]
        44 p. 24 x 29½ cm.
    Full score.   <small>BOSTON PUBLIC LIBRARY</small>

85. [Quartet, strings, C major]
        Quartetto, 2 violins, viola and violoncello. John Barnett. 1835.
        Score (1 leaf, [33]p. 19 x 25 cm. and parts. 34 x 24 cm.
            <small>BOSTON PUBLIC LIBRARY</small>

86. [Quartet, strings, D major]
        Quartuor [!] pour 2 violons, alto et violoncello composé par Jean
            Barnett. 1836 à Paris.
        Score (1 leaf, [48]p.) and parts. 24 x 31 cm.
    Violin I part lacking.   <small>BOSTON PUBLIC LIBRARY</small>

87. Queen Mab. A scena written by Percy Bysshe Shelley. Composed by
    John Barnett. 1831. Partitura.
        43 p. 24 x 30½ cm.
    Full score (for tenor voice and orchestra).   <small>BOSTON PUBLIC LIBRARY</small>

88. Robert the Devil.
        [270]p. 29 x 22 cm.
    Full score of the musical drama.
    Separate numbers signed: John Barnett. 1829.
    Title added after completion; most numbers bear title: *New drama,*
    or *New piece.*
    First performed February 2, 1830 at Covent Garden in London.
            <small>BOSTON PUBLIC LIBRARY</small>

89. [Sonata, piano, C minor]
        Sonata for pianoforte composed by J. Barnett.
        23 p. 25½ x 30½ cm.   <small>BOSTON PUBLIC LIBRARY</small>

90. Song of the exiled knight. English Romances no. 3. John Barnett.
    1827.
        [4]p. 24 x 30 cm.
    Song with piano accpt.
    First line: Afar, afar from my own bright land.
            <small>MRS. EUGENE ALLEN NOBLE</small>

Barnett, John—*continued*

91. [Win her and wear her. Opera in 3 acts]
    [286]p. 29½ x 22 cm.
    Full score.
    First performed in 1839 at the Drury Lane Theatre in London.

Barnett, Joseph Alfred, 1811-1898

92. [Throwing the hatchet. Carnival song]
    The carnival song in Throwing the hatchet, composed by Joseph
    Alfred Barnett.
    Full score.

Barthélemon, François Hippolyte, 1741-1808

93. Jefte, oratorio in due parti, a 4 voci e cori; poesia dell' sigr. abbate
    Semplici; musica dell' sigr. Franco. Ipolito Barthelemon. Parte
    prima. Rappresentato nel teatro di via del Coromero nell autunno
    dell'anno 1776. Firenze anno 1776.
    [314]p. 22½ x 29½ cm.
    Full score.
    Former owner: William H. Cummings (catalogue, no. 253).

Bartók, Béla, 1881-1945

94. [Bagatelles, piano, op. 6]
    14 Bagatellen (Klavier).
    [33]p. 35 x 27 cm.
    Published in 1909 by Rozsnyai in Budapest.

95. [Barley song. Kecske dal]
    2 leaves. 35 x 27 cm.
    Ukrainian folk-song for voice and piano, Hungarian and English
    text. Composed 1945.

96. [Burlesque, orchestra, op. 2]
    "Wuth über den unterbrochenen Besuch" vagy Rondoletto à ca-
    priccio vagy "A boszú édes" vagy "Játszd ha tudod" vagy
    November 27.
    [8]p. 34 x 26 cm.
    Full score, composed 1904.
    Unpublished.

97. Cantata profana. Partitur ...
    1 leaf, [67]p. 34 x 27 cm.
    Full score, Hungarian text.
    At end: Budapest, 1930. sept. 8.
    Published in 1934 by Universal Edition in Vienna.
    Another copy on tissues, 70 leaves.

Bartók, Béla—*continued*

98. [Cantata profana]
    36 leaves. 35 x 24½ cm.
    Tissues, music on recto only.
    Piano-vocal score.
    Published in 1934 by Universal Edition in Vienna.

99. Cantata profana (Konzept).
    [30]p. 34 x 27 cm.
    First draft.

100. [Choruses for 2 or 3 voices]
    Kinder und Frauenchöre; "Aus allen Zeiten" (Männerchor) . . .
    [38]p. 34 x 26 cm.
    Sketches for the 27 choruses for children's and women's voices and
        for the 3 choruses for 3-part male chorus (*From times past*), both
        sets published ca. 1935 by Magyar Kórus in Budapest.

101. [Choruses for 2 or 3 voices]
    [16]p. 34 x 27 cm.
    The composer's orchestration of the accompaniment for 5 of these
        choruses.

102. [Concerto, orchestra]
    Concerto per orchestra written for the Koussevitzky Foundation
        in memory of Mrs. Natalie Koussevitzky.
    [2], 92 [i.e. 93]p. 34 x 27 cm.
    Full score.
    At end: 1943. okt. 8.
    On p. [2], instrumentation and exceptionally detailed timing of 46
        passages in the composer's autograph.
    Published in 1946 by Boosey and Hawkes in London.

103. [Concerto, orchestra]
    Concerto for orchestra, reduction for piano solo. Béla Bartók.
    43 leaves. 34½ x 28 cm.
    Tissues, music on recto only.
    Published in 1944 by Boosey and Hawkes in London.

104. [Concerto, orchestra]
    [98]p. 12 x 17 cm.
    Originally used for a field note-book for collecting Anatolian folk-
        songs in 1937, this ms. contains on all pages not occupied by these
        melodies, and on empty lines between them, complete sketches
        in pencil for the concerto. The sketches occupy altogether 52 p.
        and fill completely p. 75-98.

Bartók, Béla—*continued*

105. [Concerto, orchestra]
      [4]p. 35 x 27 cm.
      Full score of bars 602-625 only.   ESTATE OF BÉLA BARTÓK

106. [Concerto, piano, no. 1]
      I. Klavierkonzert (Partitur).
      [2], 73 p. 34 x 26½ cm.
      Full score.
      Also sketches, [30]p. At end: 1926. nov. 12.
      Published in 1927 by Universal Edition in Vienna.
                                                 ESTATE OF BÉLA BARTÓK

107. [Concerto, piano, no. 1]
      I. Klavierkonzert (Einrichtung für 2 Klaviere).
      1 leaf, 42 p. 34 x 26½ cm.
      Reduction of orchestra accpt. for a 2nd piano.
      Published in 1927 by Universal Edition in Vienna.
                                                 ESTATE OF BÉLA BARTÓK

108. [Concerto, piano, no. 2]
      2. Concert pour piano et orchestra. Béla Bartók.
      98 leaves. 32 x 25 cm.
      Tissues, music on recto only.
      Full score.
      At end: Budapest, 1930 X., 1931. IX. X.
      Published in 1932 by Universal Edition in Vienna.
                                                 ESTATE OF BÉLA BARTÓK

109. [Concerto, piano, no. 2]
      40 leaves. 32 x 25 cm.
      Tissues, music on recto only.
      Composer's reduction of orchestra accpt. for a 2nd piano.
      Published in 1941 by Universal Edition in Vienna.
                                                 ESTATE OF BÉLA BARTÓK

110. [Concerto, piano. no. 2]
      2. Klavierkonzert (Konzept).
      [77]p. 33½ x 27 cm.
      First draft.   ESTATE OF BÉLA BARTÓK

111. [Concerto, piano, no. 3]
      62 leaves. 38 x 28 cm.
      Tissues, music on recto only.
      Full score.
      Published (for 2 pianos) in 1947 by Hawkes and Son in London.
                                                 ESTATE OF BÉLA BARTÓK

112. [Concerto, piano. no. 3]
      [20]p. 34½ x 27½ cm.
      Sketches.   ESTATE OF BÉLA BARTÓK

Bartók, Béla—*continued*

113. [Concerto, 2 pianos & percussion]
    42 leaves. 34 x 27 cm.
    Tissues, music on recto only.
    Full score.
    This is the orchestral version of the *Sonata for 2 pianos and percussion.*
    At end: Budapest, 1937. jul.-aug.
    Published in 1942 by Boosey & Hawkes in London.
    ESTATE OF BÉLA BARTÓK

114. [Concerto, 2 pianos & percussion]
    [29]p. 34 x 26½ cm.
    First draft of the orchestral accpt.   ESTATE OF BÉLA BARTÓK

115. [Concerto, 2 pianos & percussion]
    11 p. 34 x 27 cm.
    Tissues, music on recto only.
    Score of percussion parts only.   ESTATE OF BÉLA BARTÓK

116. [Concerto, viola]
    [15]p. 35 x 27 cm.
    Sketches, left incomplete at the composer's death.
    Published (as completed by Tibor Serly) in 1950 by Boosey & Hawkes in London.   ESTATE OF BÉLA BARTÓK

117. [Concerto, violin]
    98 leaves. 34½ x 25½ cm.
    Tissues, music on recto only.
    Full score.
    At end: Budapest, 1937 aug. - 1938. dec. 31.
    Published in 1946 by Boosey and Hawkes in London.
    ESTATE OF BÉLA BARTÓK

118. [Concerto, violin]
    35 leaves. 33 x 27 cm.
    Tissues, music on recto only.
    Composer's reduction for violin and piano.
    At end: Budapest, 1937 aug. - 1938. dec. 31.
    Published in 1941 by Hawkes and Son in London.
    ESTATE OF BÉLA BARTÓK

119. [Concerto, violin]
    [36]p. 34 x 27 cm.
    First draft.   ESTATE OF BÉLA BARTÓK

120. [Contrasts. Clarinet, violin & piano]
    18 leaves. 33 x 24½ cm.
    Tissues, music on recto only.
    Score.

Bartók, Béla—*continued*

At end: Budapest. 1938. sept. 24.
Published in 1942 by Boosey & Hawkes in New York.

121. [Contrasts. Clarinet, violin & piano]
Three pieces for clar. viol. & piano (brouillon).
[16]p. 33½ x 27 cm.
Sketches.
After title, in another hand: Trio for Szigeti, Goodman and Bartok.

122. [Dance suite, orchestra]
Tanzsuite (Skizze).
2 leaves, [10]p. 35 x 27 cm.
Sketches.
Published in 1923 by Universal Edition in Vienna.

123. [Danses de Transylvanie]
Tänze aus Siebenbürgen. Béla Bartók (1915).
11, [2]p. 34 x 26 cm.
Full score of the composer's orchestration of his *Sonatina* for piano.
Published as *Tänze aus Siebenbürgen (Erdelyi tancok)* in 1932
by Rózsavölgyi in Budapest.

124. [Dirges, piano]
4 Nénies et Esquisses.
1 leaf, [14]p. 34 x 26 cm.
Published as *4 Nénies* in 1912 by Rózsavölgyi in Budapest and as
7 *Esquisses,* op. 9, in 1912 by Rozsnyai in Budapest.

125. Divertimento. Béla Bartók.
26 leaves. 33 x 27 cm.
Tissues, music on recto only.
Full score, for string orchestra.
At end: Saanen, 1939. aug. 2.-17.
Published in 1940 by Hawkes & Son in London.

126. [Divertimento]
[23]p. 34 x 27 cm.
First draft.
At end: Saanen, 1939, aug. 2.-17.

127. [Duos, 2 violins]
44 duo (népi dallamokkal). Béla Bartók.
27 leaves. 33 x 27 cm.
Tissues, music on recto only.
Published in 1933 by Universal Edition in Vienna.

Bartók, Béla—*continued*

128. [Duos, 2 violins]
    44 duos . . . für 2 Viol. (Konzept).
    [26]p. 33½ x 27 cm.
    First draft.
ESTATE OF BÉLA BARTÓK

129. [Ten easy piano pieces]
    10 Klavierstücke. Béla Bartók.
    [22]p. 34 x 26 cm.
    Nos. 3 and 5 lacking.
    At end of no. 9: Budapest 1908 juni.
    Published in 1909 by Rozsnyai in Budapest.
ESTATE OF BÉLA BARTÓK

130. [Folk-songs, Hungarian, mixed chorus]
    19 leaves. 35 x 27 cm.
    Tissues, music on recto only.
    At end: Budapest, 1930. V.
    Published in 1932 by Universal Edition in Vienna as *Vier ungarische Volkslieder für gemischten Chor.*
ESTATE OF BÉLA BARTÓK

131. [Folk-songs, Hungarian, mixed chorus]
    Ungarische Volkslieder für gemischten Chor . . .
    [10]p. 34 x 27 cm.
    Sketches, Hungarian text, for the preceding collection.
ESTATE OF BÉLA BARTÓK

132. [Folk-songs, Hungarian, male chorus]
    Ungarische Volkslieder für Männerchor.
    [3]p. 34 x 26 cm.
    Published as *Négy régi magyar népdal férfikarre; Vier altungarische Volkslieder* in 1928 by Universal Edition in Vienna.
ESTATE OF BÉLA BARTÓK

133. [Folk-songs, Slovak, mixed chorus]
    Slowakische Volkslieder für gemischtes Chor mit Klavierbegleitung.
    1 leaf, [8]p. 34 x 26 cm.
    Published in 1918 by Universal Edition in Vienna.
ESTATE OF BÉLA BARTÓK

134. [Folk-songs, voice and piano]
    [36]p. 34½ x 26½ cm.
    Songs with Hungarian or Rumanian text, apparently unpublished.
ESTATE OF BÉLA BARTÓK

135. [Folk-songs, Hungarian, voice and piano]
    8 Ungarische Volkslieder (Klavier und Singstimme).
    14 p. 27 x 35 cm.
    Published in 1922 by Universal Edition in Vienna.
ESTATE OF BÉLA BARTÓK

Bartók, Béla—*continued*

136. [Folk-songs, Hungarian, voice and piano]
    41 leaves. 26½ x 34 and 33½ x 27 cm.
    Music on one side of leaf only.
    Published as *Zwanzig ungarische Volkslieder* in 1932 by Universal
    Edition in Vienna.　　　　　　　　　　　　　ESTATE OF BÉLA BARTÓK

137. [Folk-songs, Hungarian, voice and piano]
    [29]p. 33½ x 27 cm. and 10 leaves. 27 x 34 cm.
    Sketches for the preceding collection.　　　ESTATE OF BÉLA BARTÓK

138. [Folk-songs, Hungarian, voice and orchestra]
    Ot magyar népdal (ének és zenekar). 5 ungarische Volkslieder
        (Singstimme und Orchester).
    2 leaves, 24 p. 34 x 27 cm.
    Full score, Hungarian text.
    Arranged, in 1933, from his *Zwanzig ungarische Volkslieder*.
    Published in 1937 by Magyar Kórus in Budapest.
    　　　　　　　　　　　　　　　　　　　　　ESTATE OF BÉLA BARTÓK

139. [Folk-songs, Rumanian]
    25 leaves. 13 x 19 cm.
    Melody and text only.　　　　　　　　　　ESTATE OF BÉLA BARTÓK

140. [Folk-songs, Slovak, male chorus]
    Slowakische Volkslieder für Männerchor.
    [5]p. 34 x 26 cm.
    Published in 1918 by Universal Edition in Vienna.
    　　　　　　　　　　　　　　　　　　　　　ESTATE OF BÉLA BARTÓK

141. [For children, 85 pieces for piano]
    Für Kinder (I. II. Heft). Gyermekeknek . . .
    1 leaf, [42]p. 35 x 27 cm.
    Published as *Für Kinder, kleine Stücke für Anfänger (ohne
        Oktavenspannung) mit Benutzung ungarländischer Kinder- und
        Volkslieder,* in 1909 by Rozsnyai in Budapest.
    　　　　　　　　　　　　　　　　　　　　　ESTATE OF BÉLA BARTÓK

142. [For children, 85 pieces for piano]
    Für Kinder (III. IV. Heft) (20 Stücke fehlen; hiervon sind 2
        überhaupt nicht von mir). Tót gyerekdalok.
    1 leaf, [17]p. 35 x 27 cm.
    Published in 1911 by Rozsnyai in Budapest.
    　　　　　　　　　　　　　　　　　　　　　ESTATE OF BÉLA BARTÓK

143. [For children]
    Transkription aus "Für Kinder". I. II Heft für Viol. und Klavier.
    1 leaf, [10]p. 35 x 27 cm.
    Published in 1947 by Rózsavölgyi in Budapest.
    　　　　　　　　　　　　　　　　　　　　　ESTATE OF BÉLA BARTÓK

144. [Hungarian peasant songs, orchestra]
    Ungarische Bauernlieder.
    p. 3-29. 34 x 26 cm.
    Tissues, music on recto only.
    Full score, arranged from the piano version of 1914-17.
    Published in 1933 by Universal Edition in Vienna.
    ESTATE OF BÉLA BARTÓK

145. [Hungarian sketches, orchestra]
    Ungarische Bilder für Orchester.
    [2], 22 p. 34 x 26 cm.
    Full score, arranged from various early piano pieces.
    At end: Mondsee 1931. VIII.
    Published as *Bilder aus Ungarn; Magyar kepek* in 1932 by
    Rózsavölgyi in Budapest. ESTATE OF BÉLA BARTÓK

146. [Images, orchestra, op. 10]
    Deux images.
    1 leaf, 15, 30 p. 34 x 26 cm.
    Full score.
    At end: Budapest 1910 VIII.
    Published in 1912 by Rózsavölgyi in Budapest.
    ESTATE OF BÉLA BARTÓK

147. [Images, orchestra, op. 10]
    15 [i.e. 16]p. 34 x 26 cm.
    Reduction for piano 2 hands.
    Published in 1912 by Rózsavölgyi in Budapest.
    ESTATE OF BÉLA BARTÓK

148. [Improvisations, piano, op. 20]
    Improvisationen (für Klavier).
    1 leaf, [13]p. 35 x 27 cm.
    Published in 1922 by Universal Edition in Vienna.
    ESTATE OF BÉLA BARTÓK

149. [Kossuth, symphonic poem]
    "Kossuth." Szimfóniai költemény. Nagy zenekarra irta Bartók
    Béla (1903. ápr. 2.—1903. aug. 18).
    [2], 89 p. 34½ x 26 cm.
    Full score.
    At end: (Vége) 1903. aug. 18 én.
    Only the *Funeral March* has been published, as *Marche funèbre
    pour piano,* in 1910 by Rozsnyai in Budapest.
    ESTATE OF BÉLA BARTÓK

150. [Little pieces, piano]
    9 kleine Klavierstücke (Skizzen) (einige Skizzen zu Mikro-
    kosmos, "Im Freien" & Klavierkonzert).
    1 leaf, [28]p. 35 x 27 cm.
    Sketches for the piano works indicated. ESTATE OF BÉLA BARTÓK

Bartók, Béla—*continued*

151. [Mikrokosmos, piano]
    74 leaves. 33½ x 24½ cm.
    Tissues, music on recto only.
    Published in 1940 by Hawkes and Son in London.
ESTATE OF BÉLA BARTÓK

152. Mikrokosmos (Klavierstücke. Brouillon).
    [64]p. 34 x 26 cm.
    Sketches.
ESTATE OF BÉLA BARTÓK

153. [Mikrokosmos, piano]
    [28]p. 11½ x 21, 35 x 27, and 21½ x 27 cm.
    First draft.
ESTATE OF BÉLA BARTÓK

154. [Mikrokosmos, piano]
    7 leaves. 38 x 28 cm.
    Tissues, music on recto only.
    Selected pieces arranged for 2 pianos.   ESTATE OF BÉLA BARTÓK

155. [The miraculous mandarin, pantomime, op. 19]
    A csodálatos mandarin. Bartók Béla.
    127 p. 35 x 27 cm.
    Full score, also a *Neuer Schluss* in two copies of [8] and [9]p., and
    sketches for the whole work [40]p.
    Published in 1927 by Universal Edition in Vienna.
ESTATE OF BÉLA BARTÓK

156. [The miraculous mandarin, pantomime, op. 19]
    [64]p. 35 x 27 cm.
    Reduction for piano 4 hands.
    Published in 1925 by Universal Edition in Vienna.
ESTATE OF BÉLA BARTÓK

157. [Music for strings, percussion and celesta]
    Musik für Streichinstrumente. Béla Bartók.
    71 p. 34 x 26 cm.
    Full score.
    At end: Budapest. 1936. sept. 7.
    Also sketches for the work, [12]p.
    Published in 1937 by Universal Edition in Vienna.
ESTATE OF BÉLA BARTÓK

158. [Orchestra pieces, op. 12]
    4 Orchesterstücke. Op. 12.
    1 leaf, [25]p. 34 x 26 cm.
    First draft.
    Note on fly-leaf: Partitur verschollen.
    Published in 1923 by Universal Edition in Vienna.
ESTATE OF BÉLA BARTÓK

Bartók, Béla—*continued*

159. [Out of doors, five pieces for piano]
     Im Freien. (Klavierstücke) . . .
     [11]p. 35 x 27 cm.
     Also sketches for the work, [9]p.
     Published in 1927 by Universal Edition in Vienna.
                                        ESTATE OF BÉLA BARTÓK

160. [Portraits, orchestra, op. 5]
     2 Portraits.
     11, 9 p. 35 x 27 cm.
     Full score.
     Published in 1912 by Rozsnyai in Budapest.
                                        ESTATE OF BÉLA BARTÓK

161. [Prince Bluebeard's castle, op. 11]
     118 [i.e. 122]p. 34½ x 26½ cm.
     Full score.
     At end: 1911 sept. 20.
     Libretto by Béla Balasz.
     Published in 1925 by Universal Edition in Vienna.
                                        ESTATE OF BÉLA BARTÓK

162. [Quartet, strings, no. 1]
     1. Streichquartett. I. Vonósnégyes.
     2 leaves, 23 p. 35 x 26½ cm.
     Score.
     At end: Budán. 1909 jan. 27.
     Published in 1911 by Rózsavölgyi in Budapest.
                                        ESTATE OF BÉLA BARTÓK

163. [Quartet, strings, no. 2]
     II. Quatuor à cordes.
     [28]p. 34 x 26 cm.
     Score.
     At end: 1917. okt.
     Published in 1920 by Universal Edition in Vienna.
                                        ESTATE OF BÉLA BARTÓK

164. [Quartet, strings, no. 3]
     3. Streichquartett (Konzept).
     [18]p. 35 x 27 cm.
     First draft.
     Published in 1929 by Universal Edition in Vienna.
                                        ESTATE OF BÉLA BARTÓK

165. [Quartet, strings, no. 4]
     4. Streichquartett (Reinschrift).
     1 leaf, 39 p. 35 x 27 cm.
     Score.
     At end: Budapest, 1928., VII-IX.
     Published in 1929 by Universal Edition in Vienna.
                                        ESTATE OF BÉLA BARTÓK

Bartók, Béla—*continued*

166. [Quartet, strings, no. 4]
      IV. Streichquartett (Konzept).
      1 leaf, [38]p. 35 x 27 cm.
      First draft.   ESTATE OF BÉLA BARTÓK

167. [Quartet, strings, no. 5]
      . . . 5. stringquartette (manuscript), Budapest, IX, 1934.
      50 leaves, 35½ x 27 cm.
      Music on recto only.
      Score.
      First performed in the Library of Congress, April 8, 1935 (com-
      missioned by the Coolidge Foundation).
      Published in 1936 by Universal Edition in Vienna.
                              LIBRARY OF CONGRESS, COOLIDGE FOUNDATION

168. [Quartet, strings, no. 5]
      5. quatuor à cordes (brouillon).
      [63]p. 33½ x 27 cm.
      First draft.   ESTATE OF BÉLA BARTÓK

169. [Quartet, strings, no. 6]
      VI. vonósnégyes. Bartók Béla.
      25 leaves. 33 x 27 cm.
      Tissues, music on recto only.
      Score.
      At end: Saanen-Budapest 1939. VIII-XI.
      Published in 1941 by Hawkes & Son in London.
                                                     ESTATE OF BÉLA BARTÓK

170. [Quartet, strings, no. 6]
      [21]p. 34 x 27 cm.
      First draft.   ESTATE OF BÉLA BARTÓK

171. [Rhapsody, piano, op. 1]
      Rhapsodie pour le piano et l'orchestre.
      1 leaf, 43 p. 34 x 26 cm.
      Full score of the transcription for piano and orchestra.
      Published as *Morceaux de concert pour piano avec orchestre* in 1910
      by Rózsavölgyi in Budapest.   ESTATE OF BÉLA BARTÓK

172. [Rhapsody, piano, op. 1]
      Morceaux de concert par Béla Bartók. (La transcription des
      parties d'orchestre pour un second piano).
      17 p. 34 x 26 cm.
      Reduction of the orchestral accpt. of the preceding number for a
      2nd piano.
      Published in 1911 by Rózsavölgyi in Budapest.
                                                     ESTATE OF BÉLA BARTÓK

Bartók, Béla—*continued*

173. [Rhapsody, violin and piano, no. 1]
    [23]p. 35 x 27 cm.
    Published in 1930 by Universal Edition in Vienna.
    ESTATE OF BÉLA BARTÓK

174. [Rhapsody, violin and piano, no. 1]
    I. Rhapsodie für Viol. & Orch. . . . .
    [1], 40 p. 35 x 27 cm.
    Full score of the composer's arrangement for violin and orchestra.
    Published in 1931 by Universal Edition in Vienna.
    ESTATE OF BÉLA BARTÓK

175. [Rhapsody, violin and piano, no. 2]
    1 leaf, [18]p. 34½ x 27 cm.
    Published in 1930 by Universal Edition in Vienna.
    ESTATE OF BÉLA BARTÓK

176. [Rhapsody, violin and piano, no. 2]
    II. Rhapsodie.
    1 leaf, 39 p. 34½ x 27 cm.
    Full score of the composer's arrangement for violin and orchestra.
    Published in 1931 by Universal Edition in Vienna.
    ESTATE OF BÉLA BARTÓK

177. [Rhapsody, violin and piano, no. 2]
    Aenderungen zur II. Rhapsodie für Viol. & Orch.
    [25]p. 34½ x 27 cm.
    Corrections in the full score.
    Also 12 leaves of corrections, 33 x 24 cm.   ESTATE OF BÉLA BARTÓK

178. [Rumanian Christmas songs, piano]
    [5]p. 34 x 26 cm.
    Published as *Rumänische Volkstänze aus Ungarn* in 1918 by Universal Edition in Vienna.   ESTATE OF BÉLA BARTÓK

179. [Rumanian dances, piano, op. 8a]
    [7]p. 35 x 27 cm.
    Published as *Deux danses roumaines* in 1910 by Rózsavölgyi in Budapest.   ESTATE OF BÉLA BARTÓK

180. [Rumanian dances, piano, op. 8a]
    I. Rumänischer Tanz für Orch. instrumentiert (Partition). I. Román tánc (op. 8 bis).
    [2], 13 p. 35 x 27 cm.
    Full score of the arrangement of the first of the dances.
    ESTATE OF BÉLA BARTÓK

181. [Rumanian folk-dances, piano]
    Rumänische Volkslieder.
    12 p. 34 x 26 cm.
    Published as *Rumänische Volkstänze aus Ungarn* in 1918 by Universal Edition in Vienna.   ESTATE OF BÉLA BARTÓK

Bartók, Béla—*continued*

182. [Sonata, piano]
     [11]p. 35 x 27 cm.
     Sketches.
     Published in 1927 by Universal Edition in Vienna.
                              ESTATE OF BÉLA BARTÓK

183. [Sonata, 2 pianos and percussion]
     Sonate pour 2 pianos et percussion (brouillon).
     [35]p. 33½ x 27 cm.
     First draft.
     Published in 1942 by Hawkes and Son in London.
                              ESTATE OF BÉLA BARTÓK

184. [Sonata, violin and piano, no. 1]
     I. Klavier-Violinsonate.
     1 leaf, [37]p. 35 x 27 cm.
     At end: 1921. dec. 12.
     Published in 1923 by Universal Edition in Vienna.
                              ESTATE OF BÉLA BARTÓK

185. [Sonata, violin and piano, no. 2, op. 21]
     2. Klavier-Violinsonate.
     1 leaf. [22]p. 35 x 27 cm.
     Published in 1923 by Universal Edition in Vienna.
                              ESTATE OF BÉLA BARTÓK

186. [Sonata, violin solo]
     10 leaves. 34½ x 28 cm.
     Tissues, music on recto only.
     At end: 1944. márc. 14.
     Published in 1947 by Hawkes & Son in London.
                              ESTATE OF BÉLA BARTÓK

187. [Songs, op. 16]
     5 Lieder (Ady) op. 16. Klavier & Singstimme.
     [18]p. 34 x 26 cm.
     At end of no. 2: 1916 febr.
     Published in 1923 by Universal Edition in Vienna.
                              ESTATE OF BÉLA BARTÓK

188. Studie für die linke Hand allein (Klavier).
     [9]p. 35 x 27 cm.
     Published as no. 1 of *Quatre morceaux* in 1903 by F. Bárd et frère
     in Budapest.   ESTATE OF BÉLA BARTÓK

189. [Studies, piano, op. 18]
     3 Etudes (piano).
     1 leaf, [15]p. 35 x 27 cm.
     Published in 1920 by Universal Edition in Vienna.
                              ESTATE OF BÉLA BARTÓK

Bartók, Béla—*continued*

190. [Suite, orchestra, no. 1, op. 3]
    I. Suite (für grosses Orchester) von Béla Bartók.
    [2], 160 p. 34 x 26 cm.
    Full score.
    Published in 1915 by Rózsavölgyi in Budapest.
    ESTATE OF BÉLA BARTÓK

191. [Suite, orchestra, no. 2, op. 4]
    II. Suite (für kleines Orchester) von Béla Bartók.
    [71]p. 35 x 27 cm.
    Full score.
    At end: Bécs 1905 nov.—Rákospalota 1907 sept. 1.
    Published in 1908 by the composer in Budapest.
    ESTATE OF BÉLA BARTÓK

192. [Suite, orchestra, no. 2, op. 4]
    Serenade.
    31 leaves. 38 x 28 cm.
    Tissues, music on recto only.
    Composer's arrangement for 2 pianos (1943).
    ESTATE OF BÉLA BARTÓK

193. [Suite, orchestra, no. 2, op. 4]
    [12]p. 35 x 27 cm.
    Fragment of first draft of composer's arrangement for 2 pianos.
    ESTATE OF BÉLA BARTÓK

194. [Suite, piano, op. 14]
    Suite op. 14 für Klavier.
    [15]p. 34 x 26 cm.
    Published in 1918 by Universal Edition in Vienna.
    ESTATE OF BÉLA BARTÓK

195. [Székely songs, male chorus]
    Székely dalok. Siebenbürgisch ungarische Lieder. Bartók Béla.
    9 leaves. 33 x 24 cm.
    Tissues, music on recto only.
    Nos. 3-5 published in the *Schweizerische Sängerzeitung;* nos. 1-2
    unpublished.   ESTATE OF BÉLA BARTÓK

196. [Village scenes, voice and piano]
    Dorfszenen (Slowakische Volkslieder). Klav. & Singstimme.
    1 leaf, [14]p. 35 x 27 cm.
    Published in 1927 by Universal Edition in Vienna.
    ESTATE OF BÉLA BARTÓK

197. [Village scenes, chorus and orchestra]
    54 p. 35 x 26½ cm.
    Full score, Hungarian text, for women's chorus and chamber orches-
    tra, of nos. 3-5 of the preceding number.

Bartók, Béla—*continued*

Commissioned by the League of Composers, New York.
Published in 1927 by Universal Edition in Vienna.

ESTATE OF BÉLA BARTÓK

198. [The wooden prince, ballet, op. 13]
Der holzgeschnittene Prinz (Skizzen).
[43]p. 34 x 26 cm.
Published in 1921 (piano 2 hands) and 1924 (full score) by Universal Edition in Vienna. ESTATE OF BÉLA BARTÓK

Bartolucci, Ernesto
199. . . . String quartette in A by Ernesto Bartolucci. Op. 25 . . .
[59]p. 34 x 27 cm.
Score.
At end: Ernesto Bartolucci. Porto-Saïd 1945.
Dedication to Mrs. E. S. Coolidge.

LIBRARY OF CONGRESS, COOLIDGE FOUNDATION

Basily, Francesco, 1767-1850
200. Achille all'assedio di Troja, dramma composto da Francesco Basily nel regio Teatro della Pergola in Firenze il Carnevale nel 1798.
2 vols. (209, 213 p.) 11½ x 16 cm.
Full score.
Former owner: Natale Gallini (catalogue, no. 23).

MEMORIAL LIBRARY OF MUSIC, STANFORD UNIVERSITY

Bassani, Giovanni Battista, 1657-1716
201. Suonate a due, tre instrumenti, col basso continuo per l'organo da Gio. Battista Bassani . . . Opera quinta, 1691.
24 p. 37 x 24 cm.
Score.
At end: Finis. Mr. Battista Bassani.
Former owners: John Holmes, William H. Cummings (catalogue, no. 262). LIBRARY OF CONGRESS

Bax, *Sir* Arnold Edward Trevor, 1883-
202. [Octet. Horn, piano, 2 violins, 2 violas, violoncello & double bass]
. . . Octet. Arnold Bax.
35 p. 36 x 26½ cm.
Score.
At end: London, Oct. 31st, 1934.
Dedication to Mrs. E. S. Coolidge.

LIBRARY OF CONGRESS, COOLIDGE FOUNDATION

203. Saga—fragment. Arnold Bax.
33 p. 35 x 26 cm.
Full score for piano and chamber orchestra.
Former owner: Harriet Cohen. LIBRARY OF CONGRESS

Beauharnais, Hortense Eugénie de, 1763-1814

204. [Songs with piano accpt.]
 [6]p. various sizes, in a scrap-book.
 The songs are: *Cri de guerre et d'amour; L'émigré un proscrit; M'oublieras-tu?* The text of all 3 songs is by Auguste Louis Charles de Messence, comte de Lagarde-Chambonne.
 M'oublieras-tu? published in the *Album artistique de la reine Hortense* ca. 1860 by Heugel et Cie. in Paris.
HENRY E. HUNTINGTON LIBRARY

Beck, Conrad, 1901-

205. Concert für Streichquartett und Orchester. Dättlikon Sommer 29. Partitur.
 1 leaf, 81 p. 34½ x 25½ cm.
 Dedication to Mrs. E. S. Coolidge.
 Published in 1929 by B. Schott's Söhne in Mainz.
LIBRARY OF CONGRESS, COOLIDGE FOUNDATION

Becker, Reinhold, 1842-1924

206. Liebesleben. Dichtung von Carl Albanus. Cyclus in vier Gesängen componirt von Reinhold Becker.
 1 leaf, [5]p. 35 x 27 cm.
 Songs with piano accpt., German and English text.
 Published as op. 76 in 1893 by Arthur P. Schmidt in Boston.
LIBRARY OF CONGRESS

Bedford, Herbert, 1867-1945

207. Meditation among the trees, poem by Frederick William Harvey, music by Herbert Bedford.
 [1]p. 47½ x 30 cm.
 Song unaccompanied.
 First line: Sweetness of birdsong shall fall upon my heart.
 Published in 1922 by J. Curwen & Sons in London.
LIBRARY OF CONGRESS

208. Lyrical interlude: Pathways of the moon, for flute, oboe, violin, viola and pianoforte. Herbert Bedford (opus 50) . . .
 [1], 26 p. 33½ x 30 cm.
 Score.
 Dedication to Mrs. E. S. Coolidge, dated September 1929.
LIBRARY OF CONGRESS, COOLIDGE FOUNDATION

Beer-Walbrunn, Anton, 1864-1929

209. Quintet für 2 Violinen, Viola, Violoncello u. Klavier, von A. Beer-Walbrunn, op. 17.
 1 leaf, [118]p. 32½ x 25 cm.
 Score.
 Former owner: Oscar G. Sonneck. 　　　LIBRARY OF CONGRESS

[Allegretto, piano]
See his *Wonne der Wehmut*

210. Allegretto quasi andante.
[1]p. 26 x 21 cm.
An unpublished composition of 13 bars for piano, in G minor.
At end: Comme un souvenir à Sarah Burney Payne par Louis van Beethoven le 27 septembre 1825.
Former owner: Herr Alsager. MR. LOUIS KRASNER

211. An die Hoffnung aus Tiedge's Urania.
[10]p. 35½ x 24½ cm.
Song with piano accpt.
First line: Die du so gern in heil'gen Nächten.
Published as op. 94 in 1816 by S. A. Steiner in Vienna.
Another setting published as op. 32 in 1805.
Werke, series XXIII, no. 9.
First page cancelled; title from p. 2.
Former owner: Amy Lowell. HARVARD UNIVERSITY LIBRARY

212. [Canon. Da ist das Werk]
[1]p. 23 x 30½ cm.
This canon, addressed to Carl Holz, accompanied the ms. of Beethoven's arrangement of his *Grosse Fuge* (op. 133) for piano 4 hands (op. 134), and demanded payment of 12 ducats (from the publisher Artaria).
Published by O. E. Albrecht in *Musical Quarterly*, XXXI (1945), opp. p. 497 (facsimile) and in *Musica*, II (1948), p. 134.
PEABODY CONSERVATORY OF MUSIC

213. [Canon. Kurz ist das Schmerz]
[2]p. 10 x 11½ cm.
At end: Für Hr. Naue zum Andenken. Wien am 23ten November 1813.
Another setting of the same text was made for Spohr in 1815.
Werke, series XXIII, no. 256 (3a).
Former owners: Johann Friedrich Naue, Mrs. Charles Albert, W. C. South. MR. KENNETH ROSE

[Cavatina]
See his *Wonne der Wehmut*

214. [Concerto, piano, op. 73, E flat major]
[2]p. 29 x 35 cm.
Sketches for the two main themes of the first movement, and for the main theme of the finale. HEINEMAN FOUNDATION

215. [Counterpoint exercises]
[2]p. 23 x 29½ cm.
The second of two missing leaves from a book of instructions on

Beethoven, Ludwig van—*continued*

double counterpoint written about 1809 and probably for Arch-
duke Rudolph. See Nottebohm, *Beethoveniana*, p. 190 ff. The
examples are from Fux, *Gradus ad Parnassum*.
Former owners: Tobias Haslinger, Mrs. Tillie Israel.

LIBRARY OF CONGRESS

216. Mozart, Wolfgang Amadeus, 1756-1791.
[Don Giovanni. K. 527]
[7]p. 23 x 32 cm.
Fragments in Beethoven's autograph, containing the *Terzett* (death
of the Commendatore, end of no. 1) and the *Quartet: Non ti
fidar* (no. 9).
Former owner: Max Friedländer.   MR. FRANZ ROEHN

217. [Egmont. No. 1. Die Trommel gerühret]
[2]p. 23 x 31½ cm.
Sketches for Clärchens song.
On p. 2, sketches for no. 4, *Freudvoll und leidvoll*.
Not mentioned in G. Kinsky, *Die Handschriften von Beethoven's
Egmont-Musik,* Vienna, 1933. See O. Jonas, "An unknown
sketch by Beethoven" (with facsimile of this ms.), *Musical
Quarterly*, XXVI (1940), 186-191.
Former owner: Alexander Lambert.   NEW YORK PUBLIC LIBRARY

218. [Egmont. No. 7. Clärchens Tod bezeichnend]
[2]p. 23 x 32½ cm.
The last leaf of this number, lacking in the autograph in the Koch
Collection. Facsimile in the catalogue of Yale University Library,
Speck Collection, vol. I, plate 11.

YALE UNIVERSITY LIBRARY, SPECK COLLECTION

[Fughetta]
See his *Wonne der Wehmut*

219. [In questa tomba oscura]
[3]p. 24 x 32 cm.
Song with piano accpt.
Text by Giuseppe Carpani.
Published as no. 63 of *In questa tomba oscura, arietta con accom-
pagnamento di piano-forte, composta in diverse manieri da molti
autori* in 1808 by T. Mollo in Vienna.
Werke, series XXIII, no. 39.
Former owners: Domenico Artaria, Max Friedländer.
Facsimile in Van Patten, *Catalogue*, p. 12.

MEMORIAL LIBRARY OF MUSIC, STANFORD UNIVERSITY

220. Lied aus der Ferne, von . . . Ludwig van Beethoven. 1809.
[4]p. 23½ x 32 cm.
Song with piano accpt.
Text by C. L. Reissig.

Beethoven, Ludwig van—*continued*

First line: Als mir noch die Träne.
A different setting from that published in 1810 (Werke, series XXIII, no. 22).
Unpublished.
On p. 1, sketches for an unidentified work.
Former owners: August Artaria, H. L. S. Mortier de Fontaine, la Tolstoi (?), M. Katenn, Jerome Stonborough.

LIBRARY OF CONGRESS, WHITTALL FOUNDATION

221.   Handel, George Frederic, 1685-1759.
       [Messiah. And with his stripes we are healed]
       [4]p. 25 x 30 cm.
   A copy in Beethoven's autograph of the voice parts of the fughetta.
   Former owner: Bronislaw Huberman.   MR. ARTURO TOSCANINI

222.   [Missa solemnis]
       [2]p. 23 x 30 cm.
   Sketches, apparently for the *Benedictus.*
   Former owner: Hugo Neuburger.   MR. WALTER SLEZAK

223.   [Missa solemnis, op. 123]
       pp. 46-47. 23 x 28 cm.
   Sketches for the *Quoniam* of the *Gloria,* from a sketch-book of 80 p. for the *Missa solemnis* once the property of Mendelssohn. The remainder of the book was sold by Liepmannssohn in 1911.

SIBLEY MUSICAL LIBRARY

224.   [Quartet, strings, op. 18, no. 2. G major]
       [2]p. 23 x 32 cm.
       Sketches for the last movement.   NEW YORK PUBLIC LIBRARY

225.   [Quartet, strings, op. 95, F minor]
       [8]p. 23½ x 33 cm.
   Sketches.
   Former owner: Oscar Bondy.   LIBRARY OF CONGRESS

226.   [Quartet, strings, op. 130, B flat major]
       [11]p. 24½ x 31½ cm.
   Score of the second movement (presto) only, with some corrections and 4 cancelled bars.
   Former owners: Hans Woerz, Jerome Stonborough.

LIBRARY OF CONGRESS, WHITTALL FOUNDATION

227.   [Quartet, strings, op. 131, C sharp minor]
       [2]p. 24 x 27½ cm.
   Sketches for the last movement.
   Former owner: Ferdinand Hiller.

LIBRARY OF CONGRESS, WHITTALL FOUNDATION

Beethoven, Ludwig van—*continued*

228. [Quintet, strings, op. 29, C major]
      [2]p. 22 x 30 cm.
    Sketches for the first movement.
    Former owner: George T. Keating.
                  MEMORIAL LIBRARY OF MUSIC, STANFORD UNIVERSITY

229. [Romance, violin and orchestra, op. 50, F major]
      Romance.
      [24]p. 24 x 34 cm.
    Full score.
    Published in 1805 by the Bureau d'Arts et d'Industrie in Vienna.
    Werke, series IV, no. 3.
    Facsimile of first page in *Library of Congress Quarterly Journal,*
      IX, no. 1 (Nov. 1951), opp. p. 34.
    Former owners: Franz Amerling, Joseph Joachim, Hermine
    Wittgenstein.   LIBRARY OF CONGRESS, WHITTALL FOUNDATION

230. [Rondo a capriccio, piano, op. 129]
      [8]p. 25 x 32 cm.
    Title (apparently in Schindler's hand) on p. 1: *Die Wuth über den*
    verlorenen Groschen ausgetobt in einer Caprice. Title in Bee-
    thoven's hand on p. 2: *Alla ungharese quasi un capriccio.*
    On p. 1 sketches for this work and on p. 8 sketches "related to the
    finale of the *First Symphony* and the first movement of the
    C major Piano Concerto." See E. Hertzmann, "The newly dis-
    covered autograph of Beethoven's *Rondo a capriccio,* op. 129,"
    Musical Quarterly, XXXII (1946), 171-195. See also R. S. Hill
    in *Notes,* VII (1949-50), 441-42.
    Facsimile of p. 1 and 8 in Hertzmann's article, and of p. 2 in
    Musical Quarterly, XXXI (1945), opp. p. 496.
    Published in 1848 by A. Diabelli in Vienna, and (correct edition
    from this ms.) in 1949 by G. Schirmer in New York.
    Composed between 1795 and 1798, according to Hertzmann.
    Werke, series XVIII, no. 191.   MRS. EUGENE ALLEN NOBLE

231. [Sonata, piano, op. 27, no. 2. C sharp minor]
      [2]p. 20 x 28 cm.
    Sketches for the last movement.
    Former owner: Robert Schumann.   MR. HAROLD HUTCHESON

232. [Sonata, piano, op. 106, B flat major]
      [12]p. 32 x 24 cm.
    Sketches.
    Former owner: J. A. Stumpff.   LIBRARY OF MR. JOHN H. SCHEIDE

233. [Sonata, piano, op. 106, B flat major]
      [8]p. 24 x 32 cm.
    Sketches for the fugue.
    Former owner: Jerome Stonborough.
              LIBRARY OF CONGRESS, WHITTALL FOUNDATION

Beethoven, Ludwig van—*continued*

234. [Sonata, piano, op. 109, E major]
     Sonate für das Hammerklavier von L. van Beethoven.
     1 leaf, [36]p. 24 x 31½ cm.
     Facsimile of one page in *Library of Congress Quarterly Journal,*
     VI, no. 1 (Nov. 1948), 29.
     Published in 1821 by Schlesinger in Berlin and Artaria in Vienna.
     Werke, series XVI, no. 153.
     Former owner: Hermine Wittgenstein.
                    LIBRARY OF CONGRESS, WHITTALL FOUNDATION

235. [Sonata, violin and piano, op. 23, A minor]
     [4]p. 23 x 34 cm.
     Sketches.
     Former owner: Bronislaw Hubermann.   MR. ARTURO TOSCANINI

236. [Sonata, violin and piano, op. 96, G major]
     Sonata. Im Februar 1812 oder 13.
     [44]p. 35½ x 24 cm.
     Score.
     Published in 1816 by S. A. Steiner und Comp. in Vienna.
     Werke, series XII, no. 10.   THE PIERPONT MORGAN LIBRARY

237. [Symphony, no. 7, op. 92, A major]
     [2]p. 11 x 29½ cm.
     Sketches.   MR. GEORGE DARMSTADT

238. [Trio, piano and strings, op. 70, no. 1. D major]
     Trio.
     [65]p. 24 x 31 cm.
     Score.
     The first 2 p. of the 2nd movement in another hand.
     Published in 1809 by Breitkopf & Härtel in Leipzig.
     Werke, series XI, no. 82.
     Former owner: Max Friedländer.   PRIVATE COLLECTOR

239. [Trio, piano and strings, op. 97, B flat major]
     [2]p. 23 x 32 cm.
     First draft of part of the *Scherzo.*
     Former owners: Felix Mendelssohn-Bartholdy, Robert Schumann,
     Carl Friedberg, Walter Damrosch.   NEW YORK PUBLIC LIBRARY

240. [Trio, piano and strings, op. 97, B flat major]
     [8]p. 22½ x 32 cm.
     Sketches.
     Former owners: Frederick Locker-Lampson, Dr. Christian A.
     Herter.   NEW YORK PUBLIC LIBRARY

Beethoven, Ludwig van—*continued*

241. [Trio, strings, op. 3, E flat major]
     Finale.
     10 p. 22½ x 31 cm.
     Score of the last movement in an earlier version than the printed
     version.
     Cf. Carl Engel, "Beethoven's Op. 3 an *envoi de Vienne?*", *Musical
     Quarterly*, XIII (1927), 261-279.
     Published in 1796 by Artaria et Comp. in Vienna.
     Werke, series VII, no. 54.
     Former owner: William H. Cummings (catalogue, no. 94).
                                              LIBRARY OF CONGRESS

242. [Tu mi traffigi il cor]
     [4]p. 22½ x 30½ cm.
     Sketch for a song with orchestra accpt.
     According to Heinrich Schenker, this ms. belongs to the studies
     which Beethoven wrote while studying with Salieri.
     Unpublished.
             MEMORIAL LIBRARY OF MUSIC, STANFORD UNIVERSITY

243. [Unidentified fragment]
     [1]p. 14 x 30½ cm.
     At foot of page: L. Van Beethoven's own handwriting, written on
     his death-bed for me. J. A. Stumpff.
     Cf. R. F. Kallir, "A Beethoven relic," *Music Review*, IX (1949),
     173-177, with facsimile, and letter from E. H. W. Meyerstein,
     ibid., 327-8.   MR. RUDOLF F. KALLIR

244. [Unidentified sketches]
     [2]p. 23½ x 30½ cm.   WALTER R. BENJAMIN

245. [Unidentified sketches]
     [4]p. 23 x 30½ cm.   MR. EMIL HEERMANN

246. [Unidentified sketches]
     [2]p. 17 x 29 cm.
     Former owners: Carl Czerny, Theodor Leschetizky.
                                   MR. CHRISTIAN ZABRISKIE

247. [Unidentified sketches]
     2 leaves. 24 x 31½ cm.
     On leaf, in ink, with sketches on both sides; the other in pencil,
     with sketches on one side only.   MR. GREGOR PIATIGORSKY

248. [Unidentified sketches]
     [2]p. 23 x 32 cm.
     One of the sketches entitled: *Marsch,* in D major.
     Former owner: Alexander Posonyi.   HENRY E. HUNTINGTON LIBRARY

249. [Unidentified sketches]
     [2]p. 21 x 27½ cm.   MRS. EUGENE ALLEN NOBLE

Beethoven, Ludwig van—*continued*

250. [Unidentified sketches]
[2]p. 22 x 30 cm.
Fragment of an orchestral composition in C major.

251. [Unidentified sketches]
[2]p. 24½ x 31 cm.

252. [Wonne der Wehmut]
[2]p. 23½ x 31½ cm.
Sketch (melody, partly with figured bass), of a different setting of
Goethe's poem from that published in 1811 as no. 1 of op. 83.
The ms. also contains sketches of an *Allegretto* for piano (facsimile of the opening bars in Liepmannssohn's catalogue no. 184);
a *Fughetta* and a *Cavatina*.

Belcke, Christian Gottlieb, 1796-1875
253. "Des Sängers Vaterland." Gedicht von E. Müller für Solostimmen,
Chor und Orchester componirt von C. G. Belcke. Opus 30.
1 leaf, 26 p. 24 x 29½ cm.
Full score with piano reduction beneath.
At end: den 6. 2. 49.

Bellermann, Johann Gottfried Heinrich, 1832-1903
254. Der Fremdling auf Golgotha. Cantate nach Herder. H. Bellermann.
1 leaf, 176 p. 27½ x 33½ cm.
Full score, German text.
On front cover: 22 August 1852.

255. "In Monte Oliveti oravit," für Chor mit Instrumentalbegleitung von
Heinrich Bellermann. Berlin d. 1 Sept. 1854.
69 p. 33 x 24 cm.
For chorus of mixed voices, Latin text.

256. Mahomets Gesang, von Goethe. Musik von Heinrich Bellermann.
2 leaves, 114 p. 33 x 26½ cm.
Full score (mixed chorus and orchestra).
At end: Berlin d. 20 April 57.

257. Sophokleous Oidipous Turannos. Die Chöre zu König Oedipus
des Sophokles in Musik gesetzt von Heinrich Bellermann. (Berlin
im Sommer 1856, Verbesserungen u. Zusätze im December 1857).
1 leaf, 179 p. 25 x 33½ cm.
Full score, Greek and German text.

Bellini, Vincenzo, 1801-1835

258. Mozart, Wolfgang Amadeus, 1756-1791.
[Davidde penitente. K. 469, no. 9]
La cantata di Davide pentito [sic]—Tutte le mie speranze, terzetto del sig: maestro Amadeo Mozart's. Bellini.
1 leaf, 18 p. 21 x 28 cm.
Full score of the terzetto in Bellini's hand.
MEMORIAL LIBRARY OF MUSIC, STANFORD UNIVERSITY

259. Mancar mi sento il cor. Canzonetta.
[2]p. 19½ x 25 cm.
Voice part with cues for accpt.
Former owner: Antonietta Pozzoni Anastasi.
MR. ARTURO TOSCANINI

260. La ricordanza, sonetto di C. Repoli con musica di Bellini.
fol. 25r-26v. 18 x 25½ cm.
In Demidov, Album of autographs.
Song with piano accpt.
First line: Era la notte e presso di colei.
At end: . . . V. Bellini, Parigi 15 aprile 1834.
LIBRARY OF CONGRESS

261. Tantum ergo 3. Prima voce sola. Bellini 3.
[3]p. 22 x 30 cm.
Voice part only.
At head of title, in another hand: 1811. Fratello Carmelo Bellini. Mo. Vincenzo Bellini.
Former owner: Charles Sumner (a note in his hand: G. S. said this was Bellini's earliest production). HARVARD UNIVERSITY LIBRARY

262. [Vanne, o voga fortunata]
[3]p. 22 x 30 cm.
Song with piano accpt. (piano part incomplete).
First line as above.
In another hand: 1835 Fratello Carmelo Bellini. Mo. Vincenzo Bellini.
Former owner: Charles Sumner (a note in his hand: . . . said this was Bellini's latest work, found on his desk at his death).
HARVARD UNIVERSITY LIBRARY

Benda, Georg, 1721-1795

263. Festo Annunciationis Mariae a 2 violini, viola, canto, alto, tenore e basso con il fondamento di G. Benda. 1754. No. 1.
[8]p. 34 x 20 cm.
Full score, German text. LIBRARY OF CONGRESS

Bennett, William Sterndale, 1816-1875

264. [His salvation is nigh unto them that fear Him]
[4]p. 30 x 24 cm.
Song with piano accpt.
Former owner: William H. Cummings (catalogue, no. 96).

Berg, Alban, 1885-1935

265. [Concerto, violin]
. . . Violinkonzert von Alban Berg. Partitur . . .
39, [2]p. 44 x 33 cm.
Full score.
Dedicated to Louis Krasner.
Published in 1936 by Universal Edition in Vienna.

266. [Two songs]
[1], 4 p. 32½ x 25 cm.
Songs with piano accpt.
On cover: Berghof 1904. Alban Berg.
Caption titles: No. 1: *Grabschrift* (Text von Jakobowski). No. 2:
Traum (Text von Frida Semler).
First lines: No. 1. "Dem Auge fern, dem Herzen nah!" No. 2. Der
Mondschein lag auf dem Wasser.
Unpublished.
Former owner: Mrs. Mortimer A. (Frida Semler) Seabury.

267. Viel Träume. Rob. Hamerling. Op. 7, no. 2.
[1], 2 p. 34½ x 26½ cm.
Duet with piano accpt.
First line: Viele Vögel sind geflogen.
Unpublished.
On cover: Fräulein Frida Semler zugeeignet. Alban Berg. 1903.
Op. 7 is *Wozzeck*; this is an earlier numbering.

268. [Wozzeck. Op. 7]
Georg Büchners Wozzecks; Oper in 3 Akten (15 Scenen) von
Alban Berg. Op. 7.
3 vols. (165, 187, 100 p.) 34½ x 27½ cm.
Full score.
Published in 1923 by Universal Edition in Vienna.

269. [Wozzeck. Op. 7]
Georg Büchners Wozzeck (in der Fassung von Karl Emil Franzos).
Oper in drei Akten (15 Scenen) von Alban Berg. Op. 7
(Particell).
1 leaf, 193 p. 34 x 26 cm.
Short score.
At end: Sonntag. 16/7/22.

Berger, Ludwig, 1777-1839

270. [Prelude and fugue, piano, D minor]
Prélude et fugue composées par L. Berger.
[6]p. 29½ x 23 cm.
Former owner: Max Friedländer.   MR. FRANZ ROEHN

Bergt, Christian Gottlob August, 1772-1837

271. Preis des sterbenden Erlösers für 2 Tenöre u. Bass mit instr.
Begleitung v. Aug. Bergt.
30 p. 22½ x 35½ cm.
Full score.   BOSTON PUBLIC LIBRARY

Berlioz, Louis Hector, 1803-1869

272. La captive. Orientale de Victor Hugo, musique de Hector Berlioz.
2 inside p. 22 x 29 cm.
Song with piano accpt.
First line: Si je n'étais captive.
This first version was published in his Werke, vol. XVII, no. 12a
in 1904 by Breitkopf & Härtel in Leipzig.
A version for voice, violoncello and piano was published in 1834
and one for voice and orchestra (as op. 12), ca. 1850 (a reduction of this version for voice and piano had been published in
1849, arr. by Stephen Heller).
Hopkinson, *Bibliography*, no. 16A.   MR. RUDOLF F. KALLIR

273. [Le temple universel, op. 28]
[2]p. 35 x 26½ cm.
Fragment of score for two 4-part men's choruses and organ.
Published in 1861 by L'Orphéon in Paris.
Hopkinson, *Bibliography*, no. 62a.
Facsimile in Van Patten, *Catalogue*, p. 21.
MEMORIAL LIBRARY OF MUSIC, STANFORD UNIVERSITY

Bertin, Louise Angélique, 1805-1877

274. Guy Mannering. Opéra-comique en trois actes. Paroles et musique
de Louise Bertin.
3 v. (1 leaf, 334, 169, 247 p.) 35 x 26 cm.
Full score.   BOSTON PUBLIC LIBRARY

Bertini, Benôit Auguste, 1780-ca. 1830

275. Una visita a Bedlam. Opera buffa in due atti. Musica di A. Bertini.
2 v. (742 p.) 22 x 29 cm.
Full score.
First performed January 20, 1824.   BOSTON PUBLIC LIBRARY

Bettingen, Balthasar, 1889-

276. [Concerto, viola da gamba, op. 34]
Konzert für Viola da gamba und Orchester. B. Bettingen.
[34]p. 36 x 26 cm.
Full score.
At end: Köln 28. 3. 1931.

LIBRARY OF CONGRESS, COOLIDGE FOUNDATION

Bishop, *Sir* Henry Rowley, 1786-1855

277. Caractacus: a grand serious ballet of action, with choruses, performed at the Theatre Royal, Drury Lane, the ballet by Mr. d'Egville, the whole of the music by Henry R. Bishop. March 1808. Originale.
[1], 270 p. 23½ x 28½ cm.
Full score.
In another hand: The words by T. Sheridan.
First performed April 22, 1808, at Drury Lane Theatre in London.

LIBRARY OF CONGRESS

278. Clari, or the maid of Milan. Opera in three acts, performed at the Theatre Royal Covent Garden May 8, 1823. Composed by Henry R. Bishop. Originale. 1823.
[1], 437 p. 24½ x 28½ cm.
Full score.
Cf. B. Duncan, " 'Home, sweet home,' " *University of Rochester Library Bulletin*, IV (1948-49), 21-25, with facsimile of title-page and of *Home, sweet home*.
Former owners: Julian Marshall, Mrs. Luther Livingston.

SIBLEY MUSICAL LIBRARY

279. Concertante in F for violino, flauto, oboe, fagotto & contra basso with accompaniments for a full orchestra composed by Henry R. Bishop. Originale. November 1807.
139 p. 26 x 30½ cm.
Full score, with added parts for timpani and trombone on 6 additional pages at the end.

SIBLEY MUSICAL LIBRARY

280. The departure from Paradise. Cantata a voce sola from Milton's Paradise Lost, Book XI, composed expressly for the Philharmonic Society, London, by Henry R. Bishop. May, 1836.
1 leaf, [1], 43 p. 30 x 24 cm.
Full score.
First performed June 6, 1836.
Former owner: William H. Cummings (catalogue, no. 302).

LIBRARY OF CONGRESS

281. Epicedium. Henry R. Bishop.
[9]p. 23½ x 29½ cm.
Full score.
Dated on cover: 1820.

LIBRARY OF CONGRESS

282. The fallen angel, oratorio composed by Henry R. Bishop.
    1 leaf, 406 p. 30½ x 24 cm.
    Full score.
    Apparently never performed and unpublished.
    Presumably from the William H. Cummings collection (catalogue,
    no. 303).   MEMORIAL LIBRARY OF MUSIC, STANFORD UNIVERSITY

283. The grand alliance, an interlude (or allegorical festival) performed,
    in compliment to the illustrious visitors at that time at the
    British court, viz. Alexander, emperor of Russia, Frederick, king
    of Prussia &c &c at the Theatre Royal Covent Garden, June 13th
    1814. The musick, selected, composed, & arranged by Henry R.
    Bishop . . . 1814. Originale.
    [1], 45 p. 23½ x 29½ cm.
    Full score.
    The music is selected from Handel, Arne, Mozart, Haydn, and
    from various national airs.
    Former owner: William H. Cummings (catalogue, no. 307).
                                                LIBRARY OF CONGRESS

284. John of Paris. Opera in 2 acts . . . the music partly selected from
    A. Boieldieu, & the rest composed (and the whole adapted and
    arranged) by Henry R. Bishop.
    [120]p. 24 x 29 cm.
    Full score.
    First performed November 12, 1814 at Covent Garden Theatre
    in London.   BOSTON PUBLIC LIBRARY

285. Let not a bell be toll'd. The poetry by C. C. Clarke. Composed . . .
    by Henry R. Bishop, April, 1834.
    1 leaf, 6 p. 24 x 30 cm.
    Song with piano accpt.
    Dedicated to Miss Clara Novello.
                  MEMORIAL LIBRARY OF MUSIC, STANFORD UNIVERSITY

286. The magpie or the maid? Melo-drama, the whole of the musick
    (with the exception of one air) composed by Henry R. Bishop.
    [114]p. 24 x 29½ cm.
    Full score.
    First performed September 15, 1815 at Covent Garden Theatre in
    London.   BOSTON PUBLIC LIBRARY

287. [My pretty Jane]
    The bloom is on the rye. Sir H. R. Bishop.
    [2]p. 24½ x 30½ cm.
    Score for voice and small orchestra, without text.
    Text by Edward Fitz-Ball.
                  MEMORIAL LIBRARY OF MUSIC, STANFORD UNIVERSITY

Bishop, *Sir* Henry Rowley—*continued*

288. Sadak and Kalasrade; or the waters of oblivion. A grand Asiatick
     spectacle: performed at the Theatre Royal, Covent Garden
     April 11th, 1814. Composed by Henry R. Bishop . . . Originale
     April 1814. NB. The music to the 2nd act of this piece was
     composed by Mr. Ware.
     225 p. 24½ x 29½ cm.
     Full score   LIBRARY OF CONGRESS

289. The virgin of the sun! a grand operatick drama in three acts, per-
     formed at the Theatre Royal Covent Garden January 31th 1812.
     The whole composed by Henry Rowley Bishop, . . . 1811-12.
     Written by Frederick Reynolds Esqr. Originale.
     2 vols. (169, 247 p.) 24 x 29½ cm.
     Full score.
     Former owner: William H. Cummings (catalogue, no. 307).
                                                  LIBRARY OF CONGRESS

290. [Waltz, piano, A flat major]
     Waltz.
     [1]p. 23½ x 19 cm.
     Former owner: Jules Planché.   HENRY E. HUNTINGTON LIBRARY

     Bizet, Georges (Alexandre César Léopold), 1838-1875
291. La fuite. Duo. Poésie de Théophile Gautier. Musique de Georges
     Bizet.
     5 p. 35 x 27 cm.
     Duet (for Kadidja and Ahmid) with piano accpt.
     First line: Au firmament sans étoiles.
     Published in 1872 by Choudens in Paris.   LIBRARY OF CONGRESS

     Blangini, Giuseppe Marco Maria Felice, 1781-1841
292. Trajano in Dacia. Dramma lirico in due atti posto in musica . . .
     G. Blangini . . .
     2 vols. 22 x 29 cm.
     Full score, Italian text.
     First performed at Munich, 1814.   LIBRARY OF CONGRESS

     Bliss, Arthur Edward Drummond, 1891-
293. Music for oboe and four strings. Arthur Bliss.
     [56]p. in 3 vols. 36½ x 27 cm.
     Score.
     Dedication to Mrs. E. S. Coolidge.
     Published in 1927 by Oxford University Press in London.
                            LIBRARY OF CONGRESS, COOLIDGE FOUNDATION

Bliss, Arthur Edward Drummond—*continued*

294. Nature moods (1).
  [7]p. 34½ x 27½ cm.
  Dedication to Mrs. E. S. Coolidge.
  Published as no. 1 of his *Two interludes for the pianoforte* in 1925
  by J. & W. Chester in London.

295. [Quartet, strings]
  Quartet. Arthur Bliss . . .
  [26]p. 34 x 27½ cm.
  Score.
  At end: Arthur Bliss. Feb. 1941.
  On Jan. 13, 1941, the first 3 movements were performed by the
  Coolidge Quartet in New York; on April 9, 1941, the complete
  quartet (the first 3 movements revised and the 4th movement
  added) was performed by the Pro Arte Quartet in Berkeley,
  California.

296. . . . Symphony, Bliss.
  1 leaf, 22 p. 45½ x 31 cm.
  Full score of the first movement of his *Color Symphony*.
  Dedicated to Adrian Boult.
  Published in 1924 by J. Curwen in London.

Bloch, Ernest, 1880-

297. . . . Israël. Symphonie pour grand orchestre par Ernest Bloch.
  12, 99 p. 35 x 27 cm.
  Full score.
  Dedicated to Harriet Lamer.
  At end: Geneva, Switzerland, 1912-1916. Ernest Bloch.
  Published in 1924 by G. Schirmer in New York.

298. [Israël]
  Voix. Israël—symphonie—(IIe partie). Ernest Bloch.
  13 p. 34 x 26 cm.
  Piano-vocal score of choral portion.

299. . . . Prélude et Psaume 114 pour soprano solo et grand orchestre.
  Poème adapté de l'hébreu par Edmond Fleg. Musique de Ernest
  Bloch.
  8, 21 p. 35½ x 27 cm.
  Full score.
  At end of Prelude: Ernest Bloch. Satigny. 20 octobre, 1912.
  At end of Psalm: Satigny, 14 septembre, 1912. Ernest Bloch.
  Dedicated to Edmond Fleg.
  Published in 1921 by G. Schirmer in New York (with *Psalm 137*).

Bloch, Ernest—*continued*

300. [Prélude et Psaume 114]
> Chant et piano. Psaume 114 pour soprano solo et grand orchestre.
> Poème adapté de l'hébreu par Edmond Fleg. Musique de
> Ernest Bloch.
>
> 11 p. 36 x 27 cm.

Piano-vocal score (the psalm only).
At end: Ernest Bloch. 1912.
A dedication at the top of the title-page has been deleted.
Published in 1919 by G. Schirmer in New York.

301. [Psalm 22]
> Partition. Psaume 22 pour baryton solo et grand orchestra[!].
> Adaptation d'Edmond Fleg. Musique de Ernest Bloch.
>
> 37 p. 36 x 27 cm.

Full score.
At end: Satigny, 16 avril, 1914. Ernest Bloch.
Published in 1921 by G. Schirmer in New York.

302. [Psalm 22]
> . . . Psaume 22 pour baryton solo et grand orchestre. Réduction
> chant et piano. Adaptation d'Edmond Fleg. Musique de
> Ernest Bloch.
>
> 18 p. 37 x 28 cm.

Piano-vocal score.
At end: Satigny, le 16 avril, 1914. Ernest Bloch.
Dedicated to Romain Rolland.
Published in 1919 by G. Schirmer in New York.

303. [Psalm 137]
> Psaume 137 pour soprano et grand orchestre par Ernest Bloch.
>
> 24 p. 36 x 27½ cm.

Full score.
At end: Satigny, le 15 mai, 1914.
Published in 1921 by G. Schirmer in New York (with *Prélude
et Psaume 114*).

304. [Psalm 137]
> . . . Chant et piano. Psaume 137 pour soprano et grand orchestre.
> Adaptation d'Edmond Fleg. Musique de Ernest Bloch.
>
> 37 p. 35 x 27 cm.

Piano-vocal score.
At end: Satigny, 16 avril, 1914. Ernest Bloch.
Dedicated to Edmond and Madeleine Fleg.
Published in 1919 by G. Schirmer in New York.

305. [Quartet, strings, G major]
     . . . Quatuor à cordes par Ernest Bloch.
     [83]p. 35 x 28 cm.
     Score, each movement paged separately.
     At end of first 3 movements: Ernest Bloch. Genève. Juillet, 1916.
     At end of 4th movement: Ernest Bloch. New York, 27 août—5
     sept., 1916.
     Published in 1919 by G. Schirmer in New York.
     UNIVERSITY OF CALIFORNIA LIBRARY (BERKELEY)

306. [Symphony, C sharp minor]
     . . . Symphonie en ut ♯ mineur pour grand orchestre par Ernest
     Bloch. . . .
     [295]p. 40 x 30 cm.
     Full score.
     Dedicated to Robert Godet.
     Each movement paged separately.
     Signed and dated at end of each movement as follows: [I]: Ernest
     Bloch. Composé à Munich en octobre, 1901. Orchestré en octobre,
     1902. [II]: Composé à Munich en février, 1902. Orchestré en
     novembre. Ernest Bloch. [III]: Munich, mars 1902. Orchestré
     en décembre. [IV]: Composé à Munich, avril, 1902. Orchestré
     en février, 1903. Ernest Bloch.
     Published in 1925 by F. E. C. Leuckart in Leipzig.
     UNIVERSITY OF CALIFORNIA LIBRARY (BERKELEY)

Blow, John, 1649-1708

307. Anthems with introductory symphony.
     [27]p. 32 x 20½ cm.
     Full score (of the symphony); the anthems unaccompanied.
     Facsimile of one page in Van Patten, *Catalogue*, p. 29.
     MEMORIAL LIBRARY OF MUSIC, STANFORD UNIVERSITY

308. Full anthem a 4 and 6 voices.
     [4]p. 33 x 20½ cm.
     Score (incomplete).
     First line: O Lord God of my salvation.   LIBRARY OF CONGRESS

309. O how amiable.
     [4]p. 33 x 20½ cm.
     Score for 4 voices and bass; incomplete.
     First line: O how amiable are Thy dwellings. LIBRARY OF CONGRESS

310. A song for New Year's Day 1683 for the king, composed by Dr. Blow.
     [19]p. 32 x 20½ cm.
     Full score (orchestra and chorus).
     First line: Arise, great monarch, arise.   MR. NATHAN VAN PATTEN

Blum, Karl Ludwig, 1786-1844

311. Ein Stündchen vor dem Potsdamer Thore. Vaudeville in einem Act von Blum. Clavierauszug.

[22]p. 30 x 26 cm.

First performed February 23, 1829, at Breslau.

Boieldieu, François Adrien, 1775-1834

312. [Galop]

Premier [!] intention du galop pour l'Opéra, no. 16.

[1]p. 12½ x 26½ cm.

Compressed score, incomplete.

Published in *Recueil de six galops composés pour les bals de l'Opéra par MM. Auber, Boieldieu, Carafa, Halévy, Herz et Labarre* in 1834 by Troupenas in Paris.

313. Ni larmes ni regrets! Romance, paroles de mr. Emile de Barateau, musique d'Adrien Boieldieu.

[3]p. 35 x 27½ cm.

Song with piano accpt.

First line: Humble toit de bruyère.

314. Romance composée . . . par Boieldieu.

fol. 5v-6r, 18 x 25½ cm.

In Demidov, Album of autographs.

Song with piano accpt.

First line: Quand je te vois et qu'un malin sourire.

At end: Paris ce 28 avril 1834.

Boisdeffre, Charles Henri René de, 1838-1906

315. Dianora. Partition piano et chant.

vi, 64 p. 35½ x 26½ cm.

Piano-vocal score, French text.

316. Ewa la folle. Légende norwégienne, poésie de Paul Collin, musique de René Boisdeffre.

1 leaf, 68 p. 36 x 26½ cm.

Full score (soli, chorus and orchestra).

At end: le 30 octobre 1884. René de Boisdeffre.

Boito, Arrigo, 1842-1918

317. [La-do-mi]

[4]p. 24 x 33 cm.

Song with piano accpt.

First line: L'armonia del vostro viso.

At end: Arrigo Boito. 1865.

Published in 1926 by La Bottega di poesia in Milan.

Bononcini, Giovanni Battista, 1672- after 1748

318. Musique pastorale pour le 23 novembre 1730, jour de la naissance de Lady Mary Godolphin: Le triomphe, la marche, dance de nimphes, une gigue, menuet gay, menuet doux, la follette, autre menuet.
   1 leaf, 31 p. 27 x 22½ and 30 x 23½ cm.
   Score and parts for 2 violins and bass.
   Former owner: Arthur F. Hill.
   Facsimile of one page in Van Patten, *Catalogue*, p. 32.
   MEMORIAL LIBRARY OF MUSIC, STANFORD UNIVERSITY

319. [Suite]
   For the birthday of the sweet angel, November the 23rd, 1731; Vivace, andante, gavotte, marche, sarabande, gigue, 1-menuet, 2-menuet.
   1 leaf, 16 p. 30 x 23½ cm.
   Score and parts for 2 violins and bass.
   Former owner: Arthur F. Hill.
   MEMORIAL LIBRARY OF MUSIC, STANFORD UNIVERSITY

Bordes, Charles, 1863-1909

320. Chanson d'automne. Mélodie. Paul Verlaine (Poème saturnien). Ch. Bordes (Automne 1886) (Paysages tristes no. 2).
   [3]p. 30 x 23 cm.
   Song with piano accpt.
   First line: Les sanglots longs des violons.
   At end: Paris le 27 8bre 1886. Ch. Bordes.
   Published as no. 2 of his *Paysages tristes* by J. Hamelle in Paris.
   MR. CARL H. TOLLEFSEN

Borodin, Aleksandr Porfir'evich, 1834-1887

321. [Bogatyry]
   [1]p. 24 x 25½ cm.
   Sketch for the tavern scene from the opera-farce.
   MEMORIAL LIBRARY OF MUSIC, STANFORD UNIVERSITY

322. [Kniaz' Igor']
   6 leaves. 38 x 26 cm.
   Sketches (mostly in full score) of 5 passages from the opera.
   LIBRARY OF CONGRESS

Bossi, Renzo, 1883-

323. [Trio, piano and strings, op. 16, C major]
   Trio in 4 tempi concatenati (in do maggiore). Renzo Bossi.
   Score (60 p.) and string parts. 32 x 25 cm.
   Composed 1907-08; honorable mention, Berkshire Festival, 1921.
   Published as *Laude in 4 tempi concatenati* by G. Ricordi & Co. in Milan.   LIBRARY OF CONGRESS, COOLIDGE FOUNDATION

Bottesini, Giovanni, 1821-1889

324. Duetto per violoncello e contrabasso. Piatti e Bottesini. London 12 Nov. 1851.

    40 p. 24 x 30½ cm.

Full score (violoncello, double bass and orchestra).

Former owner: Natale Gallini (catalogue, no. 53).

The Gallini and Van Patten catalogues agree in giving the date 1831, which is manifestly incorrect since the performers were 9 and 10 years old respectively, and Bottesini did not appear in London until 1849.

MEMORIAL LIBRARY OF MUSIC, STANFORD UNIVERSITY

Boughton, Rutland, 1878-

325. Alcestis, a choral drama adapted from the play of Euripides. Englished by Gilbert Murray, musicked by Rutland Boughton.

    202 p. 37½ x 23½ cm.

Piano-vocal score.

At end: Finished June 3, 1922.

Published in 1923 by Goodwin and Tabb in London.

MEMORIAL LIBRARY OF MUSIC, STANFORD UNIVERSITY

Bourgault-Ducoudray, Louis Albert, 1840-1910

326. La conjuration des fleurs. Partition orchestre.

    3 vols. 35½ x 27 cm.

Full score of the *petit drame satirique*.

Published (piano-vocal score) in 1883 by Heugel in Paris.

BOSTON PUBLIC LIBRARY

327. Stabat mater pour voix et orgue par A. Bourgault.

    [73]p. 26 x 37 cm.

Score (4-part mixed chorus and organ).   LIBRARY OF CONGRESS

Boyce, William, 1710-1779

328. Anthem from I. Kings by Dr. Boyce. Organo.

    [7]p. 24½ x 30½ cm.

Organ part.

First line: I have surely built thee an house.   LIBRARY OF CONGRESS

329. Monumental inscription to the memory of Dr. Gostling, late minor canon of the cathedral of Canterbury. The music by Dr. Boyce. The words by Sir John Hawkins.

    4 leaves. 24 x 30 cm.

Score for 4-part chorus and figured bass.

Original title read: *Elegy on Mr. Gostling,* etc.

First line: Hither, ye sons of harmony repair.

Former owners: Vincent Novello, Musical Antiquarian Society, Anthony J. Drexel.   NEW YORK PUBLIC LIBRARY

Boyce, William—*continued*

330. Ode.
    [102]p. 30 x 24 cm.
    Full score (soli, chorus and orchestra).
    First line: Lo, on the thorny bed of care.
    Former owner: William H. Cummings (catalogue, no. 340).
                                 LIBRARY OF CONGRESS

331. Ode for St. Cecilia's Day. Dr. Boyce.
    86 [i.e. 88] numbered leaves. 23 x 29 cm.
    Full score.
    Text by John Lockman.
    Former owners: M. Peck, George Hodges.   LIBRARY OF CONGRESS

332. Solomon.
    200 [i.e. 204], 59 p. 29 x 22½ cm.
    Full score of the serenata (oratorio).
    Pp. 17-20 in second series of paging lacking.
    Text by Edward Moore.
    Published in 1743 by J. Walsh in London.
    Former owner: William H. Cummings (catalogue, no. 340).
                                 LIBRARY OF CONGRESS

Bradsky, Wenzel Theodor, 1833-1881

333. Christine, Königin von Schweden. Drama von George Conrad.
    Musik componirt von Theodor Bradsky. Clavierauszug.
    2 vols. 27 x 34 and 33½ x 26 cm.
    The overture is arranged for 4 hands.   BOSTON PUBLIC LIBRARY

Brahms, Johannes, 1833-1897

334. Abenddämmerung. Adolf Friedr. von Schack.
    [4]p. 25½ x 33 cm.
    Song with piano accpt.
    At end: den 6ten Mai 67.
    First line: Sei willkommen, Zwielichtstunde.
    Published as no. 5 of op. 49, *Fünf Lieder,* in 1868 by N. Simrock in Berlin.
    Werke, vol. 24, p. 74.   LIBRARY OF CONGRESS

335. Ade. Siegfried Kapper (nach dem Böhmischen).
    [2]p. 25½ x 33 cm.
    Song with piano accpt.
    First line: Wie schienen die Sternlein so hell.
    Published as no. 4 of op. 85, *Sechs Lieder,* in 1882 by N. Simrock in Berlin.
    Werke, vol. 25, p. 106.
    Former owners: Ottilie von Balassa, Jerome Stonborough.
        LIBRARY OF CONGRESS, WHITTALL FOUNDATION

336. Ave Maria für Frauenchor mit Orchester- oder Orgel-Begleitung
von Johannes Brahms. Op. 12.
10 p. 25 x 34 cm.
Full score, Latin text.
Published in 1861 by J. Rieter-Biedermann in Winterthur.
Werke, vol. 19, p. 113.
Former owner: Jerome Stonborough.
LIBRARY OF CONGRESS, WHITTALL FOUNDATION

337. Ave Maria. Johannes Brahms. Op. 12.
[4]p. 25 x 34 cm.
Piano-vocal score.
Op. 16 has been cancelled in caption title.
Only the piano part in Brahms' autograph.
Former owner: Jerome Stonborough.
LIBRARY OF CONGRESS, WHITTALL FOUNDATION

338. [Begräbnisgesang. Op. 13]
Gesang zum Begräbnis.
[18]p. 24½ x 33½ cm.
Full score (chorus and wind instruments).
Part of the text not in Brahms' autograph.
Published in 1861 by J. Rieter-Biedermann in Winterthur.
Werke, vol. 19, p. 124.
Former owner: Jerome Stonborough.
LIBRARY OF CONGRESS, WHITTALL FOUNDATION

339. [Begräbnisgesang. Op. 13]
Begräbnis-Gesang für Chor und Blas-instrumente von Joh.
Brahms. Op. 13. (Klavierauszug).
[10]p. 24½ x 33½ cm.
Brahms' original title: *Gesang zum Begräbniss* has been cancelled
and the above title written in another hand. The caption-title
Begräbniss-Gesang has been altered to *Grab-Gesang*.
Former owner: Max Friedländer.   PRIVATE COLLECTOR

340. Benedictus. Joh. Brahms.
[2]p. 22 x 18 cm.
Score (soprano I-II, alto and tenor), Latin text.
This is presumably the F major *Benedictus* (part of a *Mass* for five
voices) which Brahms sent to Joachim in June, 1856, as mentioned in *Brahms-Joachim Briefwechsel*, I, p. 147. Kalbeck knew
the work only from a 2nd soprano part.
Soprano II and alto parts of an arrangement of this work for Brahms'
women's chorus in Hamburg, in a part-book in the hand of Marie
Völckers, are in the possession of Mr. and Mrs. Henry S. Drinker
of Merion, Penna.
This work is unpublished except for a complete facsimile in *Notes,*

Brahms, Johannes—*continued*

VII (1949-50), p. 199-200. However, Brahms used the first 10 bars for the 2nd part of his Motet, op. 74, *Warum ist das Licht gegeben den Mühseligen.*
Former owner: Mary Sefton Thomas Lux.   HEINEMAN FOUNDATION

Bitteres zu sagen denkst du.
See his *Lieder und Gesänge von Platen und Daumer*

341. Blinde Kuh, nach dem Italienischen v. Kopisch.
[2]p. 25½ x 32½ cm.
Song with piano accpt.
First line: Im Finstern geh ich suchen.
Published as no. 1 of op. 58, *Lieder und Gesänge,* in 1871 by J. Rieter-Biedermann in Leipzig.
Werke, vol. 24, p. 109.
Former owners: Ottilie von Balassa, Jerome Stonborough.
LIBRARY OF CONGRESS, WHITTALL FOUNDATION

342. Botschaft, op. 47, no. 1. Daumer nach Hafiz.
[3]p. 25 x 32 cm.
Song with piano accpt.
First line: Wehe, Lüftchen, lind und lieblich.
At end: Juni 68.
Published as no. 1 of op. 47, *Fünf Lieder,* in 1868 by N. Simrock in Berlin.
Werke, vol. 24, p. 32.   PRIVATE COLLECTOR

343. [Cadenza for the last movement of J. S. Bach's piano concerto in D minor]
[1]p. 21 x 17½ cm.
Werke, vol. 15, p. 101.
Former owner: Jerome Stonborough.
LIBRARY OF CONGRESS, WHITTALL FOUNDATION

344. [Cadenza for the first movement of Mozart's piano concerto in C minor, K. 491]
[2]p. 33 x 24 cm.
Werke, vol. 15, p. 109.
Former owner: Jerome Stonborough.
LIBRARY OF CONGRESS, WHITTALL FOUNDATION

345. [Cadenza for the first movement of Mozart's piano concerto in D minor, K. 466]
[3]p. 26½ x 32 cm.
Werke, vol. 15, p. 105.
Former owner: Jerome Stonborough.
On p. 1 an autograph note by Clara Schumann explaining her use of several passages of this cadenza in a cadenza of her own for the same concerto.
LIBRARY OF CONGRESS, WHITTALL FOUNDATION

Brahms, Johannes—*continued*

346. [Cadenzas for the 1st and 2nd movements of Mozart's piano con-
certo in G major, K. 453]
[2]p. 18½ x 23 cm.
Werke, vol. 15, p. 102.
Former owner: Jerome Stonborough.
LIBRARY OF CONGRESS, WHITTALL FOUNDATION

347. [Concerto, piano, no. 1, op. 15, D minor]
Concert. Joh. Brahms. Op. 15.
24 p. 24½ x 33½ cm.
Composer's reduction for 2 pianos (with the 1st piano part indi-
cated but not completely written out).
This work was originally composed as a sonata for 2 pianos, then as
a symphony, and finally as a concerto.
The full score was published in 1861, the present reduction in 1873,
by J. Rieter-Biedermann in Leipzig and Winterthur.
Former owner: Jerome Stonborough.
LIBRARY OF CONGRESS, WHITTALL FOUNDATION

348. [Concerto, piano, no. 1, op. 15, D minor]
Concert. Johs. Brahms. Op. 15.
60 p. 26 x 33 cm.
Composer's arrangement for piano 4 hands.
Published in 1864 by J. Rieter-Biedermann in Winterthur.
Former owner: Jerome Stonborough.
LIBRARY OF CONGRESS, WHITTALL FOUNDATION

349. [Concerto, piano, no. 2, op. 83, B flat major]
166 p. 26 x 35 cm.
Full score.
Title-page lacking.
Published in 1882 by N. Simrock in Berlin.
Werke, vol. 6, p. 92.
MRS. ETELKA FREUND MILCH

350. [Concerto, violin, op. 77, D major]
Concert.
105 p. 26 x 33 cm.
Full score, with corrections in the hand of Joachim.
Published in 1879 by N. Simrock in Berlin.
Werke, vol. 5, p. 1.
See H. Spivacke, "A recent gift from Mr. Fritz Kreisler," *Library
of Congress Quarterly Journal*, VI, no. 3 (May, 1949), 57-62,
with facsimile of one page.
Former owners: Joseph Joachim, Fritz Kreisler.
LIBRARY OF CONGRESS

351. [Dein blaues Auge]
[2]p. 25 x 31 cm.
Song with piano accpt.

Brahms, Johannes—*continued*

Text by Klaus Groth.
First line: Dein blaues Auge hält so still.
Published as no. 8 of op. 59, *Lieder und Gesänge*, in 1873 by
J. Rieter-Biedermann in Leipzig.
Werke, vol. 24, p. 162.

352. [Deutsche Volkslieder für vierstimmigen Chor gesetzt, nos. 1-14]
14 leaves. 25½ x 32½ cm.
Leaves numbered I, 1-7; II, 1-7; music on recto only of each leaf,
except nos. I, 4-5.
Published in 1864 by J. Rieter-Biedermann in Leipzig.
Werke, vol. 21, p. 127-143.
Former owner: Jerome Stonborough.

353. Ein deutsches Requiem . . . [op. 45]
52 p. 25 x 34 cm.
Composer's reduction of the full score for piano 4 hands.
The text not in Brahms' hand, except for vocal cues.
Published in 1869 by J. Rieter-Biedermann in Leipzig.
Former owner: Jerome Stonborough.

354. [Dem dunkeln Schoss der heilgen Erde]
[2]p. 10½ x 28½ cm.
Score for mixed chorus unaccompanied.
Text from Schiller's *Lied von der Glocke*.
Published in Brahms' Werke, vol. 21, p. 155, in 1927 by Breitkopf
& Härtel in Leipzig.
Previous owner: Jerome Stonborough.

355. 3 geistliche Chöre für Frauenstimmen (ohne Begleitung) von
Johannes Brahms. Op. 34 [!]
[8]p. 26½ x 33 cm.
Published as op. 37 in 1866 by J. Rieter-Biedermann in Leipzig.
Werke, vol. 21, p. 159.
Former owner: Jerome Stonborough.

356. Geistliches Wiegenlied. Em. Geibel nach Lope di Vega.
8 p. 31 x 25 cm.
Song with piano and viola accpt.
First line: Die ihr schwebet um diese Palmen.
In margin: Herrn Professor Bischoff zu frdl. Eri[nner]ung auf
Befehl von Elisabeth v. Herzogenberg v. J. Brahms.
Published as no. 2 of op. 91, *Zwei Gesänge für eine Altstimme mit
Bratsche und Pianoforte*, in 1884 by N. Simrock in Berlin.

Brahms, Johannes—*continued*

Werke, vol. 25, p. 140.
Facsimile of p. 1 in V. A. Heck catalogue 33, p. 36.
Former owner: Helmut von Hase.   GALERIE ST. ETIENNE

357.   [Two gigues and a sarabande]
       [4]p. 27 x 34½ cm.
       For piano: the gigues in D minor and B minor; the sarabande in
          B minor.
       On p. 1: Januar 55; on p. 4 Febr. 55.
       Published in Brahms' Werke, vol. 15, p. 53 and 58, in 1927 by
          Breitkopf & Härtel in Leipzig.
       The *Sarabande* had previously been published, with facsimile, by
          the Deutsche Brahmsgesellschaft in 1917.
       Former owner: Jerome Stonborough.
                              LIBRARY OF CONGRESS, WHITTALL FOUNDATION

358.   Herbstgefühl. von Schack.
       [4]p. 26 x 32½ cm.
       Song with piano accpt.
       First line: Wie wenn im frostgen Windhauch.
       Published as no. 7 of op. 48, *Sieben Lieder,* in 1868 by N. Simrock
          in Berlin.
       Werke, vol. 24, p. 60.
       On p. 4 is the end of his *Serenade* (op. 58, no. 8) with caption-title:
          Serenade v. Schack, S[eite] 5.
       On p. 4: 26ten Mai 67.   LIBRARY OF CONGRESS

359.   In den Beeren. Hans Schmidt.
       [4]p. 25 x 33 cm.
       Song with piano accpt.
       First line: Singe, Mädchen, hell und klar.
       Published as no. 3 of op. 84, *Romanzen und Lieder für eine oder
          zwei Stimmen,* in 1882 by N. Simrock in Berlin.
       Werke, vol. 25, p. 89.
       Former owners: Ottilie von Balassa, Jerome Stonborough.
                              LIBRARY OF CONGRESS, WHITTALL FOUNDATION

360.   In der Gasse v. Fr. Hebbel.
       [2]p. 25½ x 32½ cm.
       Song with piano accpt.
       First line: Ich blikke hinab in die Gasse.
       Original title, *Spuck,* cancelled.
       Published as no. 6 of op. 58, *Lieder und Gesänge,* in 1871 by
          J. Rieter-Biedermann in Leipzig.
       Werke, vol. 24, p. 124.
       Former owners: Ottilie von Balassa, Jerome Stonborough.
                              LIBRARY OF CONGRESS, WHITTALL FOUNDATION

Brahms, Johannes—*continued*

361. [In meiner Nächte Sehnen]
     [3]p. 25½ x 33 cm.
     Song with piano accpt.
     First line as above.
     Published as no. 5 of op. 57, *Lieder und Gesänge von G. F.
     Daumer,* in 1871 by J. Rieter-Biedermann in Leipzig.
     Werke, vol. 24, p. 194.
     Former owners: Ottilie von Balassa, Jerome Stonborough.
                           LIBRARY OF CONGRESS, WHITTALL FOUNDATION

362. [Intermezzo, piano, op. 118, no. 1, A minor]
     [4]p. 12 x 20 cm.
     Published in 1893 by N. Simrock in Berlin.
     Werke, vol. 14, p. 141.   LIBRARY OF CONGRESS

363. [Intermezzo, piano, op. 118, no. 4, F minor]
     [6]p. 25½ x 34 cm.
     On p. 4-6 his *Romanze,* piano, op. 118, no. 5, F major.
     Published as nos. 4 and 5 of *Sechs Klavierstücke* in 1893 by
     N. Simrock in Berlin.
     Werke, vol. 14, p. 152 and 156.   MR. GREGOR PIATIGORSKY

364. [Intermezzo, piano, op. 119, no. 1, B minor]
     5 p. 12 x 19½ cm.
     Published in 1893 by N. Simrock in Berlin.
     Werke, vol. 14, p. 163.   LIBRARY OF CONGRESS

365. Der Kranz. Hans Schmidt.
     [3]p. 25½ x 33 cm.
     Song with piano accpt.
     First line: Mutter hilf mir armen Tochter.
     Published as no. 2 of op. 84, *Romanzen und Lieder für eine oder
     zwei Singstimmen,* in 1882 by N. Simrock in Berlin.
     Werke, vol. 25, p. 85.
     Former owners: Ottilie von Balassa, Jerome Stonborough.
                           LIBRARY OF CONGRESS, WHITTALL FOUNDATION

366. Liebesklage des Mädchens aus Des Knaben Wunderhorn. Joh.
     Brahms. Op. 48, no. 3.
     [1]p. 24½ x 33 cm.
     Song with piano accpt.
     First line: Wer sehen will zween lebendige Brunnen.
     Published as no. 3 of op. 48, *Sieben Lieder,* in 1868 by N. Simrock
     in Berlin.
     Werke, vol. 24, p. 52.   MR. JOHN BASS

367. Das Lied vom Herrn von Falkenstein.
     [8]p. 25 x 34 cm.
     Song with piano accpt.

Brahms, Johannes—*continued*

Text from Uhland's *Volkslieder.*
First line: Es reit der Herr von Falkenstein.
Published as no. 4 of op. 43, *Vier Gesänge,* in 1868 by J. Rieter-
Biedermann in Leipzig.
Werke, vol. 24, p. 12.
Former owner: Jerome Stonborough.

368. Lieder und Gesänge von Platen und Daumer in Musik gesetzt für
eine Singstimme mit Begleitung des Pianoforte von Johannes
Brahms. Op. 32.
1 leaf, [6]p. 24½ x 33½ cm.
Songs with piano accpt., nos. 7-9 only.
Texts by Daumer.
First lines (no separate titles): 7. Bitteres zu sagen denkst du; 8. So
stehn wir, ich und meine Weide; 9. Wie bist du, meine Königin.
Published in 1864 by J. Rieter-Biedermann in Leipzig.
Werke, vol. 23, p. 98-106.
Former owner: Jerome Stonborough.

369. [Lieder und Romanzen für Frauenchor. Op. 44]
12 Lieder für Frauenchor mit willkürlicher Begleitung des
Pianoforte von Johannes Brahms. Op. (Heft, 1,2).
1 leaf, [22]p. 27 x 23 cm.
Vocal score without piano accpt.
Title-page in Brahms hand, omitting opus no.
Published in 1866 by J. Rieter-Biedermann in Leipzig.
Werke, vol. 21, p. 164.
Former owner: Jerome Stonborough.

370. [Lieder und Romanzen für Frauenchor. Op. 44]
Pianoforte zu den Frauenchor-Liedern . . .
8 p. 22 x 18 cm.
The optional accpt. lacking in the preceding ms.
Former owner: Jerome Stonborough.

371. Mädchenlied. Paul Heyse (nach dem Italienischen).
[2]p. 35½ x 26½ cm.
Song with piano accpt.
First line: Am jüngsten Tag.
At end: Joh. Brahms, für Julie.
Published as no. 6 of op. 95, *Sieben Lieder,* in 1884 by N. Simrock
in Berlin.
Werke, vol. 25, p. 176.

372. Magyarisch von Daumer. Joh. Brahms. Op. 46, no. 2.
        [2]p. 25 x 32 cm.
      Song with piano accpt.
      First line: Sah dem edlen Bildnis.
      Published in 1868 by N. Simrock in Berlin.
      Werke, vol. 24, p. 22.   MR. RUDOLF F. KALLIR

373. [Mein wundes Herz]
        [2]p. 25½ x 33 cm.
      Song with piano accpt.
      Text by Klaus Groth.
      First line: Mein wundes Herz verlangt nach milder Ruh.
      Published as no. 7 of op. 59, *Lieder und Gesänge*, in 1873 by
        J. Rieter-Biedermann in Leipzig.
      Werke, vol. 24, p. 159.
      Previous owner: Jerome Stonborough.
                      LIBRARY OF CONGRESS, WHITTALL FOUNDATION

374. [Meine Liebe ist grün]
        Junge Lieder. F. S. No. 1.
        [4]p. 16½ x 17½ cm.
      Song with piano accpt.
      Text by Felix Schumann.
      At end: 24. dec. 73 morgens.
      Published as no. 5 of op. 63, *Lieder und Gesänge*, in 1874 by C. F.
        Peters in Leipzig. Nos. 5 and 6 have the title: *Junge Lieder*
        I and II.
      Werke, vol. 24, p. 188.
      Former owners: Marie Schumann, Edward Speyer.
                                              PRIVATE COLLECTOR

      Nächtens.
        see his *Sehnsucht*

375. [O wüsst' ich doch den Weg zurück]
        [3]p. 25 x 32½ cm.
      Song with piano accpt.
      Text by Klaus Groth.
      At end: Johs. Brahms. Rüschlikon 74.
      Published as no. 8 of op. 63, *Lieder und Gesänge*, in 1874 by C. F.
        Peters in Leipzig.
      Werke, vol. 24, p. 199.
      Former owner: Sir George Henschel.   MR. FRANK BLACK

376. [Prelude and fugue, organ, no. 1, A minor]
        Präludium u. Fuge für die Orgel, meiner lieben Clara zum 7ten
          Mai 1856.
        [4]p. 27 x 23 cm.
      At end, a long note to Clara Schumann signed by Brahms.

Brahms, Johannes—*continued*

Published in 1927 in Brahms' Werke, vol. 16, p. 1, by Breitkopf &
Härtel in Leipzig.
Former owner: Jerome Stonborough.

377. [Prelude and fugue, organ, no. 2, G minor]
Praeludium und Fuge für die Orgel. Johs. Brahms.
[8]p. 27 x 35 cm.
At end: Febr. 57.
Published in 1927 in Brahms' Werke, vol. 16, p. 7, by Breitkopf &
Härtel in Leipzig.
Former owner: Jerome Stonborough.

378. [Psalm 51. Op. 29, no. 2]
Schaffe in mir, Gott, ein rein Herz, für fünfstimmigen Chor a
capella [!]
[11]p. 34 x 26½ cm.
Caption-title: Aus dem 51ten Psalm.
Published as no. 2 of *Zwei Motetten für fünfstimmigen gemischten
Chor a cappella* in 1864 by Breitkopf & Härtel in Leipzig.
Werke, vol. 21, p. 19.

379. [Quartet, piano and strings, no. 2, op. 26, A major]
Quartett für Pianoforte, Violine, Viola u. Violoncello componirt
von Johannes Brahms. Op. 26.
83 p. 34 x 25 cm.
Score.
At end: J. Brahms. Ende Nov. 1861.
Published in 1863 by N. Simrock in Berlin.
Werke, vol. 8, p. 154.
Former owner: Oscar Bondy.

380. [Quintet, piano and strings, op. 34, F minor]
Quintett für Pianoforte, 2 Violinen, Bratsche und Violoncello
componirt . . . von Johs. Brahms. Op. 34.
[72]p. 26 x 34 cm.
Score.
Published in 1865 by J. Rieter-Biedermann in Leipzig.
Werke, vol. 8, p. 1.
Former owner: Jerome Stonborough.

381. Regenlied, von Klaus Groth. J. Brahms.
[6]p. 25 x 33 cm.
Song with piano accpt.
First line: Walle, Regen, walle nieder.
Published as no. 3 of op. 59, *Lieder und Gesänge*, in 1873 by
J. Rieter-Biedermann in Leipzig.
Werke, vol. 24, p. 142.

Brahms, Johannes—*continued*

Romanze, piano, op. 118, no. 5, F major.
See his *Intermezzo*, piano, op. 118, no. 4, F minor

382. [Ruhe, Süssliebchen]
Magelone no. 9 (Schlummerlied).
[5]p. 25 x 32 cm.
Song with piano accpt.
Published as no. 9 of op. 33, *Romanzen aus L. Tieck's Magelone*,
in 1865-69 by J. Rieter-Biedermann in Leipzig.
Title cancelled and number IX substituted.
Werke, vol. 23, p. 158.
Former owner: Jerome Stonborough.
LIBRARY OF CONGRESS, WHITTALL FOUNDATION

383. Schicksalslied. J. Brahms.
36 p. 24 x 32½ cm.
Full score (chorus and orchestra).
At end: Mai 1871.
Published as op. 54 in 1871 by N. Simrock in Berlin.
Werke, vol. 19, p. 23.
Cf. E. N. Waters, "A Brahms manuscript: the *Schicksalslied*,"
Library of Congress Quarterly Journal, III, no. 3 (May, 1946),
14-18.
Former owner: Frau Michael Balling.   LIBRARY OF CONGRESS

384. [Die Schnur, die Perl' an Perle]
[4]p. 25 x 33 cm.
Song with piano accpt.
Published as no. 7 of op. 57, *Lieder und Gesänge von G. F. Daumer*,
in 1871, by J. Rieter-Biedermann in Leipzig.
Werke, vol. 24, p. 100.   MR. HENRY S. DRINKER

385. Schwermuth.
[2]p. 25½ x 32½ cm.
Song with piano accpt.
Text by Carl Candidus.
First line: Mir ist so weh ums Herz.
Published as no. 5 of op. 58, *Lieder und Gesänge*, in 1871 by
J. Rieter-Biedermann in Leipzig.
Werke, vol. 24, p. 122.
Former owners: Ottilie von Balassa, Jerome Stonborough.
LIBRARY OF CONGRESS, WHITTALL FOUNDATION

386. Sehnsucht. Franz Kugler.
8 p. 26 x 34 cm.
Quartet for mixed voices unaccompanied.
First line: Es rinnen die Wasser.
On p. 5-8: *Nächtens*. Franz Kugler.

Brahms, Johannes—*continued*

At end: J. Brahms. Ischl, Frühling 91. An Frau Antonia Speyer-Kufferath auf freundliches Verlangen u. in herzlicher Gesinnung. J. B.
Published as nos. 1 and 2 of *Sechs Quartette*, op. 112, in 1891 by C. F. Peters in Leipzig.
Werke, vol. 20, p. 193 and 198.
Former owner: Edward Speyer. PRIVATE COLLECTOR

Serenade. Song. Op. 58, no. 8
see his *Herbstgefühl*

387. [Sextet, strings, no. 1, op. 18, B flat major]
Sextett für 2 Violinen, 2 Violen u. 2 Violoncelli componirt von Johannes Brahms. Opus 18.
61 [i.e. 65]p. 25½ x 34½ cm.
Score.
At end: Johs. Brahms. 1860.
Published in 1862 by N. Simrock in Berlin.
Werke, vol. 7, p. 1.
Former owner: Oscar Bondy.
LIBRARY OF CONGRESS, WHITTALL FOUNDATION

388. [Sextet, strings, no. 1, op. 18, B flat major]
Thema mit Variationen von Johs. Brahms.
[7]p. 24 x 33 cm.
Composer's arrangement for piano solo of the second movement, made for Clara Schumann.
On cover, in Brahms' hand: zum 13ten September 1860 als freundlicher Gruss. J. B.
Published in 1927 in Brahms' Werke, vol. 15, p. 59, by Breitkopf & Härtel in Leipzig.
Former owner: Jerome Stonborough.
LIBRARY OF CONGRESS, WHITTALL FOUNDATION

389. [Sextet, strings, no. 2, op. 36, G major]
Sextett für 2 Violinen, 2 Bratschen u. 2 Violoncelli von Johannes Brahms. Op. 36.
54 p. 25 x 33 cm.
Score.
Published in 1866 by N. Simrock in Bonn.
Werke, vol. 7, p. 45.
Former owner: Oscar Bondy. MR. ADOLF BUSCH

390. [Sextet, strings, no. 2, op. 36, G major]
Sextett von Johs. Brahms. Op. 36.
42 p. 24½ x 34 cm.
Composer's arrangement for piano 4 hands.
Published in 1866 by N. Simrock in Bonn.
LIBRARY OF CONGRESS, WHITTALL FOUNDATION

Brahms, Johannes—*continued*

So stehn wir, ich und meine Weide.
See his *Lieder und Gesänge von Platen und Daumer*

391. [So willst du des Armen]
[4]p. 25 x 34 cm.
Nr. 5 aus Magelone.
Song with piano accpt.
Published as no. 5 of op. 33, *Romanzen aus L. Tieck's Magelone,*
in 1865-69 by J. Rieter-Biedermann in Leipzig.
Werke, vol. 23, p. 132.
Former owners: Ottilie von Balassa, Jerome Stonborough.
LIBRARY OF CONGRESS, WHITTALL FOUNDATION

392. Sommerabend. Hans Schmidt.
[3]p. 25½ x 33 cm.
Song with piano accpt.
First line: Geh' schlafen, Tochter, schlafen!
Published as no. 1 of op. 84, *Romanzen und Lieder für eine oder
zwei Stimmen,* in 1882 by N. Simrock in Berlin.
Werke, vol. 25, p. 81.
Former owners: Ottilie von Balassa, Jerome Stonborough.
LIBRARY OF CONGRESS, WHITTALL FOUNDATION

393. [Sonata, 2 pianos, op. 34b, F minor]
Sonate. Joh. Brahms.
56 p. 25½ x 32½ cm.
An independent composition, rather than an arrangement of the
Piano Quintet, op. 34a.
Published in 1872 by J. Rieter-Biedermann in Leipzig.
Werke, vol. 11, p. 1.
Former owner: Frau Michael Balling.   PRIVATE COLLECTOR

394. Spannung (Niederrheinisches Volkslied).
[4]p. 25 x 32 cm.
Song with piano accpt.
First line: Gut'n Abend, gut'n Abend, mein tausiger Schatz.
Published as no. 5 of op. 84, *Romanzen und Lieder für eine oder
zwei Stimmen,* in 1882 by N. Simrock in Berlin.
Werke, vol. 25, p. 96.
Former owners: Ottilie von Balassa, Jerome Stonborough.
LIBRARY OF CONGRESS, WHITTALL FOUNDATION

395. [Strahlt zuweilen auch ein mildes Licht]
[2]p. 25½ x 32½ cm.
Song with piano accpt.
Published as no. 6 of op. 57, *Lieder und Gesänge von G. F. Daumer,*
in 1871 by J. Rieter-Biedermann in Leipzig.
Werke, vol. 24, p. 98.
Former owners: Ottilie von Balassa, Jerome Stonborough.
LIBRARY OF CONGRESS, WHITTALL FOUNDATION

Brahms, Johannes—*continued*

396. [Symphony, no. 1, op. 68, C minor]
        . . . Simphonie, C moll, op. 68. Partitur: II, III, IV Satz.
        [94]p. 26 x 33½ cm.
      Full score (first movement lacking).
      At end: J. Brahms, Lichtenthal, Sept. 76.
      Former owner: Mrs. Meyer Davis.
      Published in 1877 by N. Simrock in Berlin.
      Werke, vol. 1, p. 1.   PRIVATE COLLECTOR

397. [Symphony, no. 1, op. 68, C minor]
        Symphonie (C moll) von Johannes Brahms.
        47 p. 26 x 33 cm.
      Composer's reduction for piano 4 hands.
      At end: Frankfurt Mai 77. J. Br.
      Published in 1877 by N. Simrock in Berlin.
                      LIBRARY OF CONGRESS, WHITTALL FOUNDATION

398. [Symphony, no. 3, op. 90, F major]
        Symphonie F dur. Seinem herzlich geliebten Hans v. Bülow in
          treuer Freundschaft. Johs. Brahms. Wien, 8 Januar 1890.
        [103]p. 27 x 36 cm.
      Full score.
      Facsimile of p. 1 in *Library of Congress Quarterly Journal*, V, no. 1
        (Nov. 1947), 44.
      Published in 1884 by N. Simrock in Berlin.
      Werke, vol. 2, p. 3.
      Former owners: Hans von Bülow, Jerome Stonborough.
                      LIBRARY OF CONGRESS, WHITTALL FOUNDATION

399. [Symphony, no. 3, op. 90, F major]
        Dritte Symphonie von Johannes Brahms.
        64 p. 25½ x 32 cm.
      Composer's arrangement for 2 pianos.
      Published in 1884 by N. Simrock in Berlin.
                      LIBRARY OF CONGRESS, WHITTALL FOUNDATION

400. Tragische Ouvertüre. Johannes Brahms. Op. 81.
        56 p. 27 x 35 cm.
      Full score.
      Published in 1881 by N. Simrock in Berlin.
      Werke, vol. 3, p. 37.
      Former owner: George T. Keating.
      Facsimile of p. 1 in Van Patten, *Catalogue*, p. 38.
                      MEMORIAL LIBRARY OF MUSIC, STANFORD UNIVERSITY

401. [Traun! Bogen und Pfeil]
        Magelone. IIte Romanze.
        [2]p. 25 x 34 cm.
      Song with piano accpt.

Brahms, Johannes—*continued*

Published as no. 2 of op. 33, *Romanzen aus L. Tieck's Magelone,* in
    1865-69 by J. Rieter-Biedermann in Leipzig.
Werke, vol. 23, p. 116.
Former owner: Jerome Stonborough.

402.   [Treue Liebe dauert lange]
        Magelone no. 15. J. Brahms.
        [5]p. 24 x 33½ cm.
    Song with piano accpt.
    Published as no. 15 of op. 33, *Romanzen aus L. Tieck's Magelone,*
        in 1865-69 by J. Rieter-Biedermann in Leipzig.
    Werke, vol. 23, p. 189.
    Former owner: Jerome Stonborough.

403.   [Trio, piano and strings, op. 8, B major]
        Trio für Pianoforte, Violine und Cello von Johannes Brahms.
           Werk 8.
        59 p. 25 x 32 cm.
    Score of the first version.
    At end: Hannover. Januar 54. Kreisler jun.
    Published in 1854 by Breitkopf & Härtel in Leipzig.
    Werke, vol. 9, p. 1.
    Former owner: Breitkopf & Härtel.

404.   [Trio, piano and strings, op. 87, C major]
        Trio. Johannes Brahms. Op. 87.
        38 p. 27½ x 35½ cm.
    Score.
    Published in 1883 by N. Simrock in Berlin.
    Werke, vol. 9, p. 121.
    Former owner: Oscar Bondy.

405.   [Trio, violin, horn and piano. Op. 40, F minor]
        Trio für Violine, Horn (oder Violoncello) und Pianoforte von
           Johannes Brahms. Op. 40.
        2 leaves, 24, 10 p. 25 x 34½ cm.
    Score.
    Pp. 9-10 at end of 1st movement in the hand of a copyist.
    Published in 1868 by N. Simrock in Berlin.
    Werke, vol. 9, p. 209.
    Former owner: Oscar Bondy.

406.   Über die Heide. Theodor Storm.
        [2]p. 26 x 33 cm.
    Song with piano accpt.

Brahms, Johannes—*continued*

At end: An Ludwig Rottenberg fröhlicheren Wanderschritt wünschend! J. Brahms.
Published as no. 4 of op. 86, *Sechs Lieder,* in 1882 by N. Simrock in Berlin.
Werke, vol. 25, p. 122.   MR. WERNER JOSTEN

407. [Unbewegte laue Luft]
[4]p. 25 x 32½ cm.
Song with piano accpt.
Published as no. 8 of op. 57, *Lieder und Gesänge von G. F. Daumer,* in 1871 by J. Rieter-Biedermann in Leipzig.
Werke, vol. 24, p. 104.
Former owners: Ottilie von Balassa, Jerome Stonborough.
LIBRARY OF CONGRESS, WHITTALL FOUNDATION

408. Ungarische Tänze. J. Brahms.
32 p. 26 x 32 cm.
Full score of the composer's transcription for full orchestra of nos. 1, 3 and 10 of the set originally written for piano 4 hands.
Published in 1874 by N. Simrock in Berlin.
Werke, vol. 4, p. 143-164.
Former owner: George T. Keating.
MEMORIAL LIBRARY OF MUSIC, STANFORD UNIVERSITY

409. [Variations, piano, op. 24]
Variationen für eine liebe Freundin. Aria di Händel. Johs. Brahms. Sept. 61.
1 leaf, 20 p. 26½ x 34½ cm.
On cover, sketches for his piano quartet in A major, op. 26.
Former owners: Clara Schumann, Jerome Stonborough.
LIBRARY OF CONGRESS, WHITTALL FOUNDATION

410. [Variations, piano 4 hands, op. 23]
Variationen über ein Thema von Robert Schumann für das Pianoforte zu vier Händen componirt und dem Fräulein Julie Schumann gewidmet von Johannes Brahms. Op. 23.
27 p. 25½ x 33 cm.
Published in 1863 by J. Rieter-Biedermann in Leipzig.
Werke, vol. 12, p. 2.
Former owner: Jerome Stonborough.
LIBRARY OF CONGRESS, WHITTALL FOUNDATION

411. Vergebliches Ständchen (Niederrheinisches Volkslied).
[4]p. 25½ x 32½ cm.
Song with piano accpt.
First line: Guten Abend, mein Schatz.
Published as no. 4 of op. 84, *Romanzen und Lieder für eine oder zwei Stimmen,* in 1882 by N. Simrock in Berlin.
Werke, vol. 25, p. 92.   THE NEWBERRY LIBRARY

Brahms, Johannes—*continued*

412. Verzweiflung. Nr. 10. J. Brahms.
    [4]p. 25 x 32 cm.
    Song with piano accpt.
    First line: So tönet denn, schäumende Wellen.
    Published as no. 10 of op. 33, *Romanzen aus L. Tieck's Magelone,*
        in 1865-69 by J. Rieter-Biedermann in Leipzig.
    Werke, vol. 23, p. 165.
    Former owners: Gustav Oberlaender, George R. Siedenburg.

413. Von waldbekränzter Höhe.
    [4]p. 26 x 33 cm.
    Song with piano accpt.
    Published as no. 1 of op. 57, *Lieder und Gesänge von G. F. Daumer,*
        in 1871 by J. Rieter-Biedermann in Leipzig.
    Werke, vol. 24, p. 80.
    Former owners: Ottilie von Balassa, Jerome Stonborough.

414. Vorüber!
    [2]p. 25½ x 32½ cm.
    Song with piano accpt.
    Text by Friedrich Hebbel.
    First line: Ich legte mich unter den Lindenbaum.
    Published as no. 7 of op. 58, *Lieder und Gesänge,* in 1871 by
        J. Rieter-Biedermann in Leipzig.
    Werke, vol. 24, p. 126.
    Former owners: Ottilie von Balassa, Jerome Stonborough.

415. [Waltzes, piano 4 hands, op. 39]
    11 p. 25½ x 33 cm.
    Composer's arrangement for piano 2 hands of the 16 waltzes
        originally composed for 4 hands.
    Published in 1867 by J. Rieter-Biedermann in Leipzig.
    Werke, vol. 14, p. 33.
    Former owner: Jerome Stonborough.

416. [Waltzes, piano 4 hands, op. 39]
    Walzer (erleichterte Ausgabe). J. B. Op. 39.
    10 p. 25½ x 33 cm.
    The composer's simplified version of the 2 hand arrangement in
        the preceding ms.
    Published in 1867 by J. Rieter-Biedermann in Leipzig.
    Werke, vol. 14, p. 37.
    Former owner: Jerome Stonborough.

Brahms, Johannes—*continued*

417. [War es dir, dem diese Lippen bebten]
      [4]p. 24½ x 33½ cm.
      Song with piano accpt.
      Published as no. 7 of op. 33, *Romanzen aus L. Tieck's Magelone*,
      in 1865-69 by J. Rieter-Biedermann in Leipzig.
      Werke, vol. 23, p. 147.
      Former owner: Jerome Stonborough.

418. [War es dir, dem diese Lippen bebten]
      [5]p. 24½ x 34 cm.
      A slightly different version of the preceding song, transposed from
      D major to D flat major.
      At end: Fräulein Ottilie Hauer [Balassa] zu freundlichen Geden-
      ken. Johs. Brahms.
      Former owners: Ottilie von Balassa, Jerome Stonborough.

419. [Wenn du nur zuweilen lächelst]
      [2]p. 25 x 33 cm.
      Song with piano accpt.
      Published as no. 2 of op. 57, *Lieder und Gesänge von G. F. Daumer*,
      in 1871 by J. Rieter-Biedermann in Leipzig.
      Werke, vol. 24, p. 86.
      Former owners: Ottilie von Balassa, Jerome Stonborough.

      Wie bist du, meine Königin
      See his *Lieder und Gesänge von Platen und Daumer*

420. [Wie froh und frisch]
      Magelone no. 14.
      [4]p. 25 x 33½ cm.
      Song with piano accpt.
      Title cancelled and number XIV substituted.
      Published as no. 14 of op. 33, *Romanzen aus L. Tieck's Magelone*,
      in 1865-69 by J. Rieter-Biedermann in Leipzig.
      Werke, vol. 23, p. 183.
      Former owner: Jerome Stonborough.

421. [Wie rafft' ich mich auf]
      [3]p. 25½ x 33 cm.
      Song with piano accpt.
      Text by August von Platen.
      Published as no. 1 of op. 32, *Lieder und Gesänge von Platen und
      Daumer*, in 1864 by J. Rieter-Biedermann in Leipzig.
      Werke, vol. 23, p. 79.
      Former owner: George T. Keating.

Brahms, Johannes—*continued*

422. [Wir müssen uns trennen]
    Magelone No. 8.
    [4]p. 25 x 34 cm.
    Song with piano accpt.
    Published as no. 8 of op. 33, *Romanzen aus L. Tieck's Magelone*,
      in 1865-69 by J. Rieter-Biedermann in Leipzig.
    Werke, vol. 23, p. 152.   MRS. MEYER DAVIS

Brauer, Max, 1855-1918
423. Streichquartett in C dur.
    Parts. 32 x 25 cm.
    Former owners: Jean Becker, K. Koester.   LIBRARY OF CONGRESS

Braun, J. B. M.
424. LaFayette en Amérique. Poëme de Mr. de Béranger, mis en musique
      et dédiée aux Américains des Etats-Unis de l'Amérique septen-
      trionale par J.B.M. Braun.
    1 leaf, 12 p. 35 x 27 cm.
    Full score (men's chorus and orchestra).
    Some parts laid in, with a piano score (3 p.).
                                                   LIBRARY OF CONGRESS

Bretón y Hernández, Tomás, 1850-1923
425. "Tabaré." Drama lírico en tres actos (el tercero tiene dos cuadros).
      Letra y música de T. Bretón . . .
    2 leaves, 154 p. 35 x 25½ cm.
    Piano-vocal score.
    First performed in Madrid, March 26, 1913.
                                                   LIBRARY OF CONGRESS

Bridge, *Sir* Frank, 1879-1941
426. Andante ben moderato e tranquillo.
    1 leaf, [1]p. 28 x 38 cm.
    For organ, in B minor.
                            MEMORIAL LIBRARY OF MUSIC, STANFORD UNIVERSITY

427. . . . Divertimenti for flute, oboe, clarinet & bassoon . . . Frank Bridge.
    1 leaf, 31 p. 35 x 26 cm.
    Score.
    Dedicated to Mrs. E. S. Coolidge, Oct. 30, 1938.
    At end: F. B., Friston 1934-38. Feb. 27th, 1938.
    First performance at Washington, D.C., April 14, 1940.
                            LIBRARY OF CONGRESS, COOLIDGE FOUNDATION

428. "Dweller in my deathless dreams." Rabindranath Tagore ("The
      Gardener"). Frank Bridge.
    1 leaf, [7]p. 36 x 27 cm.
    Song with piano accpt.

Bridge, *Sir* Frank—*continued*

First line: You are the evening cloud.
At end: Finston FB June 1st 1925.
Dedicated to Mrs. E. S. Coolidge.
Published by Augener, Ltd., in London.

429.   "Heart's ease." Frank Bridge.
        [3]p. 36½ x 26½ cm.
    For piano 2 hands.
    At end: April 26th. 1921.
    Published ca. 1922 by Augener, Ltd., in London.

430.   A merry, merry Xmas.
        1 leaf, 9 numbered leaves. 12 x 29½ cm.
    Score (piano, clarinet, oboe and trombone).
    Variations on *Good king Wenceslas.*
    Parts indicated for Sprague, Peggy, John and Santa Claus.

431.   [Quartet, strings, no. 3]
        . . . Quartet no. 3. Frank Bridge.
    Score.
    At end: 1925-27.
    Dedicated to Mrs. E. S. Coolidge.
    Published in 1928 by Augener, Ltd. in London.

432.   [Quartet, strings, no. 4]
        String quartet no. 4. Frank Bridge.
        Score (1 leaf, 53 numbered leaves) and parts. 37 x 26½ cm.
    Music on recto only of score.
    At end: F.B. Nov. 6th, 1937. Friston, Sussex.
    First performed at the Berkshire Festival, Sept. 23, 1938.
    Published in 1939 by Augener, Ltd. in London.

433.   . . . Sonata. Violin and piano. Frank Bridge.
        Score (1 leaf, 39 p.) and violin part. 36 x 26 cm.
    At end: FB. Friston, Nov. 21, 1932.
    Dedicated to Mrs. E. S. Coolidge.
    Published in 1933 by Augener, Ltd. in London.

434.   Trio. Violin, cello & piano. Frank Bridge.
        1 leaf, 73 p. 36 x 26½ cm.
    Score.
    Dedicated to Mrs. E. S. Coolidge, Jan. 31st, 1929.
    Published in 1930 by Augener, Ltd. in London.

Britten, Benjamin, 1913-

435. Peter Grimes.
       3 vols. (266, 198, 142 p.). 44½ x 28½ cm.
       Full score of the opera.
       Text by Montagu Slater.
       At end of vol. 3: London: Feb. 10th 1945.
       First performed June 7, 1945 at Sadler's Wells Theatre in London.
                     LIBRARY OF CONGRESS, KOUSSEVITZKY FOUNDATION

436. [Quartet, strings, no. 1, op. 25, D major]
            . . . Quartet no. 1 in D major. Benjamin Britten. July 1941
            Escondido, California.
            32 numbered leaves, 35 x 27 cm.
       Score.
       Music on recto only.
       Published in 1942 by Boosey & Hawkes in London.
                     LIBRARY OF CONGRESS, COOLIDGE FOUNDATION

Bruch, Max, 1838-1920

437. Altes Lied. Aus den Julius-Liedern von E. Geibel.
            [2]p. 24½ x 32½ cm.
       Song with piano accpt.
       First line: Jede Jahreszeit hat ihr Freud' und Leid.
       At end: Max Bruch. Brüssel, im Juni 1854.
       Published as no. 1 of *Sechs Gesänge* ca. 1856 by Breitkopf & Härtel
       in Leipzig.
       Former owner: Edward Speyer.   LIBRARY OF CONGRESS

438. Heldenfeier.
            [16]p. 33½ x 27 cm.
       Score (chorus and organ).
       Text by Margarete Bruch.
       Published as op. 89 in 1915 by F. E. C. Leuckart in Leipzig.
                     MEMORIAL LIBRARY OF MUSIC, STANFORD UNIVERSITY

439. Lied der Deutschen in Oesterreich. Max Bruch.
            [4]p. 24½ x 32 cm.
       Unison chorus for tenors and basses with piano accpt.
       At end: Liverpool, 2 Mai 1882. Max Bruch.
       Former owner: Hugo Riesenfeld.   LIBRARY OF CONGRESS

440. Romanze für Violine mit Orchester von Max Bruch. Op. 42.
            Partitur . . .
            44 p. 34 x 27 cm.
       Full score.
       At end: Bonn 25 Febr. 1874. M.B. (Max Bruch).
       Published in 1874 by N. Simrock in Berlin.   LIBRARY OF CONGRESS

Bruch, Max—*continued*

441. Schwedische Tänze für Violine mit Orchester bearbeitet von Max
      Bruch. Partitur. (No. 1) Manuscript.
      1 leaf, 9 p. 33½ x 25 cm.
      Full score.
      At head of title: Berlin-Friedenau. 14 Sept. 1897.

                                              LIBRARY OF CONGRESS

Bruckner, Anton, 1824-1896

442. Nachruf. Gedicht von Heinrich v. d. Mattig.
      [4]p. 24½ x 31 cm.
      Full score (4-part men's chorus and organ).
      At end: Wien den 19. Oktober 1877. Anton Bruckner mpria.
      Dedicated to Joseph Seiberl.   MR. RUDOLF F. KALLIR

443. [Symphonies, nos. 8-9]
      [10]p. 36 x 27 cm.
      On cover, in hand of Viktor Christ, the former owner: Autographe
      von Anton Brucker. Skizzen theils aus der 8. theils aus der 9.
      Symphonie, am 31. October von ihm zum Andenken erhalten.

                                              LIBRARY OF CONGRESS

Brüll, Ignaz, 1846-1907

444. Aprilabend. Ged. v. Max Kalbeck, componirt von Ignaz Brüll.
      [2]p. 35 x 26 cm.
      Song with piano accpt.   NEW YORK PUBLIC LIBRARY

Brunetti, Gaetano, 1750-1808

445. [Divertimento, 2 violins, no. 2, D major]
      Divertimento secondo a due violini fatto per uso del exmo. sr.
      duca d'Alba, composto da G. Brunetti.
      [7]p. 22 x 32 cm.
      Score.   LIBRARY OF CONGRESS

446. Minuetes y contradanzas concertadas con vls, oboes, flautos,
      clarinettos, trompas, viola, faggottes y basso, compuestas para el
      exmo. senor duque de Alba por Dn. Gayetano Brunetti. Ano de
      1789.
      [92]p. 21½ x 31 cm.
      Full score.   LIBRARY OF CONGRESS

447. . . . Missa a . . . 8 violines y trompas, de Gaetano Brunetti. 1766.
      118 leaves. 29 x 21 cm.
      Full score, Latin text.   LIBRARY OF CONGRESS

448. [Overtures, nos. 1-6]
      Overtura I[-VI] con violini, oboè, corni, viola e basso de Gno.
      Brunetti.
      99 leaves. 21½ x 30 cm.
      Full score.
      No. 1 in E flat; 2 in D; 3 in F; 4 in C; 5 in B flat; 6 in D.

                                              LIBRARY OF CONGRESS

Brunetti, Gaetano—*continued*

449. [Quartet, strings, no. 51, F major]
  Quartetto. Originale. No. 51.
  [27]p. 22 x 31½ cm.
  Score.   LIBRARY OF CONGRESS

450. [Quintets, oboe, 2 violins, viola and violoncello. Nos. 32-37]
  6 vols. 22 x 32 cm.
  Scores.
  No. 32 in F, 33 in E flat, 34 in D, 35 in G, 36 in B flat, 37 in C.
                                      LIBRARY OF CONGRESS

451. [Quintets, strings, nos. 10-11, 16-19, 21-31]
  17 vols. 22 x 32 cm.
  Scores.
  No. 10 in E flat, 11 in A, 16 in B flat, 17 in G, 18 in F, 19 in A,
  21 in B flat, 22 in E, 23 in D, 24 in B flat, 25 in D, 26 in C,
  27 in E flat, 28 in C, 29 in E, 30 in G, 31 in E.
  Titles, in addition to serial numbers above, give Roman numerals
  from I to VI.   LIBRARY OF CONGRESS

452. [Quintet, strings, no. 38, C major]
  [48]p. 22 x 32 cm.
  Score (some passages in viola part marked for oboe).
                                      LIBRARY OF CONGRESS

453. Sinfonia concertante: violino primo principale, violino 2. principale,
  violini di accompagnamento, oboe, fagotti, corni, viola, violoncello
  e basso . . . Originale . . . [17]87.
  86 p. 31 x 22 cm.
  Full score, in C major.
  Former owner: George B. Weston.   HARVARD UNIVERSITY LIBRARY

454. Sinfonia concertante a più istrumenti obligati . . . No. 5. 1794.
  [101]p. 22 x 31 cm.
  Full score, in C major.   LIBRARY OF CONGRESS

455. [Sonata, violin and figured bass, no. 1, E flat major]
  Sonata I a violino solo e basso, fatta per uso del exmo. sor. ducha
    d'Alba composta di Dn Gaetano Brunetti, anno 1778.
  [7]p. 22 x 31 cm.
  Score.   LIBRARY OF CONGRESS

456. [Sonata, violin and figured bass, no. 4, D major]
  Sonata IV de violin y baso, echa para el exmo. sor. duque de Alba.
    Compuesta por Don Cayetano Brunetti.
  [7]p. 22 x 31½ cm.
  Score.
  At head of title: No. 2.   LIBRARY OF CONGRESS

457. [Sonata, violin and figured bass, no. 5, D major]
  Sonata quinta, di violino e basso. fatta espresamente per l'uso

del seremo. sigr. principe di Asturias (e non altro). Composto
da Gaetano Brunetti.
[11]p. 22 x 32 cm.
Score.
At head of title: No. 13.   LIBRARY OF CONGRESS

458. [Sonata, violin and figured bass, no. 10, F major]
. . . Sonata X, di violino e basso, fatta espressamente per l'uso del
seremo. sigr. principe d'Asturias (e non altro). Composta da
Gaetano Brunetti.
[8]p. 22 x 32 cm.
Score.
At head of title: No. 1.   LIBRARY OF CONGRESS

459. [Sonata, violin and figured bass, no. 11, E major]
Sonata XI, di violino e basso, fatta esspressamente per l'uso del
seremo. sigr. principe d'Asturias (e non altro). Composta da
Gaetano Brunetti.
[13]p. 22 x 32 cm.
Score.
At head of title: No. 2.   LIBRARY OF CONGRESS

460. [Sonata, violin and figured bass, no. 13, D major]
. . . Sonata XIII, di violino e basso, fatta esspresamente per l'uso
del seremo. principe d'Asturias (e non altro). Composta da
Gaetano Brunetti.
[11]p. 22 x 32 cm.
Score.
At head of title: No. 7.   LIBRARY OF CONGRESS

461. [Symphony, no. 10, B flat major]
. . . Sinfonia con violini, oboe, corni, viola, fagotto e basso. No. 10.
[36]p. 22 x 32 cm.
Full score.   LIBRARY OF CONGRESS

462. [Symphony, no. 14, C major]
Sinfonia in C con violini, oboes, corni, trombbe, viola, fagotto e
basso. No. 14.
22 leaves. 22 x 31 cm.
Full score.   LIBRARY OF CONGRESS

463. [Symphony, no. 17, B flat major]
Sinfonia con violini, oboes, viola, corni, fagotto e basso. No. 17.
Originale [17]79.
[47]p. 22 x 31 cm.
Full score.   LIBRARY OF CONGRESS

464. [Symphony, no. 18, D major]
Sinfonia in D con violini, oboe, corni, trombe, viola, fagotto e
basso. No. 18.
[60]p. 22 x 31 cm.
Full score.   LIBRARY OF CONGRESS

Brunetti, Gaetano—*continued*

465. [Symphony, no. 19, B minor]
Sinfonia in bem. con violini, oboe, corni, trombbe, viola, fagotto e basso. No. 19.
[48]p. 22 x 31½ cm.
Full score.   LIBRARY OF CONGRESS

466. [Symphony, no. 22, G minor]
Sinfonia con violini, oboes, corni, viola, fagotto e basso. Originale. No. 22. [17]83.
[39]p. 22 x 31 cm.
Full score.   LIBRARY OF CONGRESS

467. [Symphony, no. 23, F major]
. . . Sinfonia con violini, oboes, corni, viola, fagotto e basso. Originale. No. 23. [17]83.
[44]p. 22 x 31 cm.
Full score.   LIBRARY OF CONGRESS

468. [Symphony, no. 24, C major]
Sinfonia con violini, oboe, corni, fagotto, viola e basso. Originale. No. 24. [17]83.
[59]p. 22 x 31 cm.
Full score.   LIBRARY OF CONGRESS

469. [Symphony, no. 25, D major]
. . . Sinfonia con violini, oboe, corni, viola, fagotto e basso. N. 25. [17]83.
[57]p. 22 x 32 cm.
Full score.   SIBLEY MUSICAL LIBRARY

470. [Symphony, no. 27, B flat major]
. . . Originale. No. 27. [17]87.
[46]p. 22 x 32 cm.
Full score.   LIBRARY OF CONGRESS

471. [Symphony, no. 29, C major]
. . . Sinfonia con violini, oboe, corni, viola, fagotto e basso. No. 29. [17]83.
[65]p. 22 x 32 cm.
Full score.   SIBLEY MUSICAL LIBRARY

472. [Symphony, no. 30, E flat major]
Sinfonia con violini, oboe, corni, fagotto, viola e basso. No. 30. [17]83.
[39]p. 22 x 32 cm.
Full score.   LIBRARY OF CONGRESS

473. [Symphony, no. 31, D minor]
. . . Sinfonia con violini, oboes, corni, viola, fagotto e basso. Originale. No. 31. 1783.
[47]p. 22 x 32 cm.
Full score.   LIBRARY OF CONGRESS

Brunetti, Gaetano—*continued*

474. [Symphony, no. 33, E flat major]
. . . Il Maniatico, sinfonia a violini, oboes, corni, viola, fagotto, violoncello obligato e basso di Gaetano Brunetti. . . .
[52]p. 22 x 31½ cm.
Full score.
On page 1: No. 33 originale. 1780.
Former owner: Werner Wolffheim (catalogue, II, 81)

Bühler, Franz, 1760-1824

475. [Mass, B flat major]
[83]p. 27 x 35 cm.
Full score, Latin text.
Former owner: A. Bottée de Toulmon.

476. [Mass, F major]
[77]p. 26 x 33 cm.
Full score, Latin text.
Former owner: A. Bottée de Toulmon.

477. [Mass, op. 11]
Messe solennelle. Bühler. Op. 11.
[152]p. 27 x 33½ cm.
Full score, Latin text.
Former owner: A. Bottée de Toulmon.

478. Offertorium, op. 15. No. 1. Jubilate Deo omnes terrae. No. 2. Laudate Dominum, glorificate Deum. No. 3. Apprehendite disciplinam. No. 4. Levavi oculos meos.
4 vols. 35 x 27 cm.
Full score, Latin text.
Former owner: A. Bottée de Toulmon.

Bülow, Hans Guido von, 1830-1894

479. [Julius Caesar, incidental music]
Caesar.
[2]p. 34 x 27 cm.
Sketches.
Published in 1867 by B. Schott's Söhne in Mainz.

Bull, Ole Bornemann, 1810-1880

480. Afsted over Hav!
[9]p. 25 x 31½ cm.
Full score (voice and orchestra).
On p. 8-9, a chorus with orchestra accpt., incomplete.

Bull, Ole Bornemann—*continued*

481. Her hvor i alt.
      [3]p. 25 x 31½ cm.
      Full score (voice and orchestra).
      At end: Ole Bull, Dec. 1849.   LIBRARY OF CONGRESS

482. Huldresang.
      [4]p. 25 x 31½ cm.
      Full score (voice and orchestra).   LIBRARY OF CONGRESS

Burgmüller, Norbert, 1810-1836

483. Polonaise für das Pianoforte componirt . . . von Norbert Burgmüller.
      [6]p. 25 x 31 cm.
      At end: Düsseldorf den 23ten November 1832.
      Former owner: Hubert F. Kufferath.   LIBRARY OF CONGRESS

484. No. 2. Scheiden und meiden.
      [4]p. 33 x 20 cm.
      Song with piano accpt.
      First line: So soll ich nun dich meiden.
      At end: 8.7.1834.
      Published as no. 2 of op. 10 by Hofmeister in Leipzig.
      On p. 4, the beginning of *Morgenlied,* no. 4.
      Former owner: Hubert F. Kufferath.   LIBRARY OF CONGRESS

Burian, Hans, 1874-

485. . . . 5 Lieder für 1 Singstimme u. Klavier von Hans Burian.
      1 leaf, [19]p. 33½ x 27 cm.
      Dedicated to Mrs. E. S. Coolidge.
      Each song signed, and dated 1924 or 1925.
              LIBRARY OF CONGRESS, COOLIDGE FOUNDATION

Busoni, Ferruccio Benvenuto, 1866-1924

486. Rondeau harlequinesque (Rondo arlecchinesco). Ferruccio Busoni . . .
      59 numbered leaves. 35 x 27 cm.
      Music on recto only of each leaf.
      Full score.
      At end: New York, 8 Juni, 1915. Ferruccio Busoni.
      Published as op. 46 in 1916 by Breitkopf & Härtel in Leipzig.
      Dedication to Frederick Stock.
      Former owner: Wilhelm Heyer (catalogue, vol. IV, no. 1673,
      p. 870).   LIBRARY OF CONGRESS

Cadou, André

487. [Hamlet, incidental music]
      12 leaves. 35 x 27 and 30 x 23 cm.
      Consists of trumpet calls, voice part of songs, and piano score of
      instrumental numbers.   FOLGER SHAKESPEARE LIBRARY

Caldara, Antonio, 1670-1736

488. La primavera. Cantata basso solo d. Ant. Caldara.
pp. 33-[40]. 16 x 22 cm.
For bass solo and figured bass accpt.
At end: Fine li 4 luglio 1730 in casa maggiore.

Callcott, John Wall, 1766-1821

489. Hence the zephyr's sportive wing. A rondeau by J. W. Callcott.
[2]p. 24 x 27½ cm.
For piano, with some indication of instrumentation.
At head of title: J. W. Callcott (September 4, 1783).

Cambini, Giovanni Giuseppe, 1746-1825

490. Boccherini, Luigi, 1743-1805.
[Sonata, violin and piano, op. 5, no. 4, D major]
Quartetto IV per due violini, viola e violoncello di Luigi
Boccherini.
[26]p. 22 x 30 cm.
Cambini's arrangement for string quartet of Boccherini's sonata.
Former owner: George B. Weston.　

491. Boccherini, Luigi, 1743-1805.
[Sonata, violin and piano, op. 5, no. 5, G minor]
Quartetto V per due violini, viola e violoncello di Luigi
Boccherini.
[21]p. 22 x 30 cm.
Cambini's arrangement for string quartet of Boccherini's sonata.
Former owner: George B. Weston.　

492. [Quintets, 2 violins, viola, 2 violoncellos, nos. 1-6, op. 1]
3 vols. 22½ x 30 cm.
Score (and parts in the hand of a copyist).
Score of nos. 1-3 (E flat, D and F) lacking.
Title of no. 4; *Quintetto IV per due violini, due violoncelli e viola.*
Other titles vary slightly.
No. 4 in C minor, 5 in G, 6 in C.
Opus nos. not given in the mss. until no. 41.　

493. [Quintets, 2 violins, viola, 2 violoncellos, nos. 7-12, op. 2]
6 vols. 22½ x 30 cm.
No. 7 in B flat, 8 in F, 9 in G minor, 10 in A, 11 in D, 12 in E flat.

494. [Quintets, 2 violins, viola, 2 violoncellos, nos. 13-18, op. 3]
6 vols. 22½ x 30 cm.
No. 14 has score of 1st movement only (complete in parts).
No. 13 in D minor, 14 in B flat, 15 in B minor, 16 in C, 17 in D
18 in F.

Cambini, Giovanni Giuseppe—*continued*

495. [Quintets, 2 violins, viola, 2 violoncellos, nos. 19-24, op. 4]
  3 vols. 22½ x 30 cm.
 No. 21 lacks 2nd movement (complete in parts); nos. 22-23 lack score; no. 24 lacks both score and parts.
 No. 19 in E, 20 in A, 21 in C minor, 22 in E minor, 23 in G.

496. [Quintets, 2 violins, viola, 2 violoncellos, nos. 25-30, op. 5]
  6 vols. 22½ x 30 cm.
 Score of no. 26 has first 3 pages of 1st movement only; score of no. 27 has first 16 bars of 1st movement only.
 No. 25 in F, 26 in E flat, 27 in C, 28 in E flat, 29 in B flat, 30 in C.

497. [Quintets, 2 violins, viola, 2 violoncellos, nos. 31-36, op. 6]
  6 vols. 22½ x 30 cm.
 No. 31 in D, 32 in A, 33 in F minor, 34 in A, 35 in B flat, 36 in C minor.

498. [Quintets, 2 violins, viola, 2 violoncellos, nos. 37-42, op. 7]
  6 vols. 22½ x 30 cm.
 No. 41 marked *5e de l'oeuvre* 7; opus no. given thus in following mss.
 No. 37 in F, 38 in A, 39 in E flat, 40 in G, 41 in C, 42 in C minor.

499. [Quintets, 2 violins, viola, 2 violoncellos, nos. 43-48, op. 8]
  5 vols. 22½ x 30 cm.
 No. 45 lacks score and parts.
 No. 43 in C, 44 in D minor, 46 in A, 47 in D, 48 in E flat.

500. [Quintets, 2 violins, viola, 2 violoncellos, nos. 49-54, op. 9]
  5 vols. 22½ x 30 cm.
 No. 52 lacks score.
 No. 49 in G, 50 in E, 51 in F, 52 in E minor, 53 in B flat, 54 in E flat.

501. [Quintets, 2 violins, viola, 2 violoncellos, nos. 55-60 op. 10]
  4 vols. 22½ x 30 cm.
 Nos. 59-60 lack score.
 No. 55 in C, 56 in F, 57 in G minor, 58 in B flat, 59 in E, 60 in F minor.

502. [Quintets, 2 violins, viola, 2 violoncellos, nos. 61-66, op. 11]
  3 vols. 22½ x 30 cm.
 Nos. 61-63 lack score; no. 62 also lacks parts.
 No. 61 in D, 63 in E flat, 64 in A minor, 65 in D, 66 in F.

Cambini, Giovanni Giuseppe—*continued*

503. [Quintets, 2 violins, viola, 2 violoncellos, nos. 67-72, op. 12]
    6 vols. 22½ x 30 cm.
    No. 67 in E flat, 68 in G, 69 in F, 70 in C, 71 in E flat, 72 in B flat.

504. [Quintets, 2 violins, viola, 2 violoncellos, nos. 73-78, op. 13]
    6 vols. 22½ x 30 cm.
    No. 73 in A minor, 74 in G, 75 in F, 76 in D, 77 in F, 78 in C.

505. [Quintets, 2 violins, viola, 2 violoncellos, nos. 79-84, op. 14]
    6 vols. 22½ x 30 cm.
    No. 79 in A, 80 in B flat, 81 in E minor, 82 in G, 83 in E flat, 84 in D.

506. [Quintets, 2 violins, viola, 2 violoncellos, nos. 85-90, op. 15]
    4 vols. 22½ x 30 cm.
    No. 87 lacks score and parts; No. 90 lacks score.
    No. 85 in C minor, 86 in F, 88 in B flat, 89 in A, 90 in C minor.

507. [Quintets, 2 violins, viola, 2 violoncellos, nos. 103-108, op. 18]
    2 vols. 22½ x 30 cm.
    Nos. 103-104 and 107-108 lack score and parts.
    No. 105 in D minor, 106 in B flat.

508. [Quintets, 2 violins, viola, 2 violoncellos, nos. 109-111, op. 19]
    3 vols. 22½ x 30 cm.
    No. 109 in G minor, 110 in C minor, 111 in E flat.

509. Simphonie concertante. Cambini.
    30 p. 30 x 23 cm.
    Full score, in F major.
    Former owner: Hugo Riesenfeld.

Caplet, André, 1878-1923

510. Légende.
    [1]p. 30 p. 36 x 27 cm.
    Full score (saxophone solo and orchestra).
    At end: Rome, Déc. 1903.
    Former owner: Mrs. R. J. Hall.

511. Légende. Réduction pour piano à quatre mains.
    [1], 25 p. 36 x 27 cm.
    At end: André Caplet, Rome, décembre 1903.
    Former owner: Mrs. R. J. Hall.

Capoul, Joseph Victor Amédée, 1839-1924

512. Méha. Chanson hongroise. Paroles et musique de Victor Capoul.
   [3]p. 35 x 27 cm.
   Song with piano accpt.

   MEMORIAL LIBRARY OF MUSIC, STANFORD UNIVERSITY

Carafa, Michele Enrico, 1787-1872

513. Quando in campo il suon di guerra; cavatina del sigr. Michele
   Caraffa[!].
   [10]p. 21½ x 29 cm.
   Song with piano accpt.
   Former owner: Otto E. Albrecht.   LIBRARY OF CONGRESS

Carrera

514. [La desdeñosa]
   Ton[adillas] a 3. La desdeñosa. Sra. Prado. Verano 1782.
   Carerra [!].
   13 numbered leaves. 22½ x 32 cm.
   Full score, Spanish text.   NEW YORK PUBLIC LIBRARY

Cartoni, Nicola

515. La morte di Oloferne. Dramma sacro posto in musica da N.C. . . .
   2 vols. (1 leaf, 287, 258 p.). 16 x 21 cm.
   Full score, Italian text.
   Dedicated to Carrick Moore.   LIBRARY OF CONGRESS

Carvalho, João de Sousa, died 1798

516. . . . Everardo secondo, rè di Lituania.
   2 vols. 24 x 31½ cm.
   Full score, Italian text.
   At head of title Orig[ina]le di Gio. de Sousa Carvalho, 5 luglio 1782.
   LIBRARY OF CONGRESS

517. . . . Testoride Argonauta. Dramma da rappresentarsi . . . li 5 luglio
   [1780].
   2 vols. 23 x 33 cm.
   Full score, Italian text.
   Text by Gaetano Martinelli.   LIBRARY OF CONGRESS

Casamorata, Luigi Ferdinando, 1807-1881

518. Beatrice, cantata pel centenario di Dante, di Napoleone Giotti.
   [91]p. 23 x 30 cm.
   Full score, Italian text.
   Former owner: Natale Gallini (catalogue, no. 44).

   MEMORIAL LIBRARY OF MUSIC, STANFORD UNIVERSITY

519. Vivaldi, Antonio, ca. 1677-1741.
    [Concerto grosso, op. 3, no. 11, D minor]
    . . . Concerto grosso in re minore (n. 11 de "L'estro armonico"
    (1716). Versione pianistica di Alfredo Casella.
    1 leaf, 23 p. 32 x 24 cm.
    At end: Alfredo Casella. Baltimore, S.U.A., febbraio 1936 XIV.
    Dedicated to Mrs. E. S. Coolidge.
    LIBRARY OF CONGRESS, COOLIDGE FOUNDATION

520. [Concerto, violin, A minor]
    Concerto in la minore per violino ed orchestra: a—primo tempo;
    b—adagio; c—rondo—trascrizione per violino e pianoforte dell'
    autore. Alfredo Casella. (A.D. MCMXXVIII).
    49 p. 34 x 27 cm.
    At end: Cominciato il 13/2 MXMXXVII a Roma—terminato il
    2/7 MCMXXVIII a Boston, Mass.
    Dedicated to Joseph Szigeti.
    Published in 1929 by Universal Edition in Vienna.
    MEMORIAL LIBRARY OF MUSIC, STANFORD UNIVERSITY

521. Partita per pianoforte e piccola orchestra. Alfredo Casella (1924-25).
    159 p. 43½ x 29½ cm.
    Full score.
    At end: Cominciato a Roma il 20 giugno MCMXXIV, finito a
    Champoluc Valdostano, il 20 agosto MCMXXV.
    Dedicated to Mrs. E. S. Coolidge.
    Published in 1926 by Universal Edition in Vienna.
    LIBRARY OF CONGRESS, COOLIDGE FOUNDATION

522. Sinfonia per pianoforte, clarinetto, tromba e violoncello. Alfredo
    Casella. (MCMXXXII).
    2 leaves, 15 p. 32½ x 24 cm.
    Score.
    Written for the 10th anniversary of the League of Composers, 1933
    Published ca. 1933 by A. and G. Carisch in Milan.
    LEAGUE OF COMPOSERS

523. Sonata in do maggiore per pianoforte e violoncello. Alfredo Casella
    (MCMXXVII).
    25 p. 44 x 29 cm.
    Score.
    At end: Cominciato il 28 agosto, finito il 8 settembre MCMXXVII
    A.C.
    Dedicated to Mrs. E. S. Coolidge.
    LIBRARY OF CONGRESS, COOLIDGE FOUNDATION

524. Clementi, Muzio, 1752-1832.
    [Trio, piano and strings, op. 27, no. 2. D major]
    . . . Trio in D. Autograph of the transcription by Casella. 1932
    30 p. 35 x 26 cm.

Casella, Alfredo—*continued*

Score.
Dedicated to Mrs. E. S. Coolidge.
Published in 1936 by G. Schirmer in New York.

525. Sammartini, Giovanni Battista, 1701-1775.
  [Trio-sonata, A major]
  . . . Sonata a tre per violino, violoncello e pianoforte di G. B. Sammartini.
  Trascrizione strumentale e realizzazione del basso numerato di Alfredo Casella.
  42 p. 29 x 22 and 32½ x 23½ cm.
  Score.
  Dedicated to Mrs. E. S. Coolidge.

526. Bach, Johann Sebastian, 1685-1750.
  [Musikalisches Opfer, trio-sonata]
  Sonata a tre dalla "Musikalisches Opfer" (1747) di G. S. Bach. Trascrizione per violino, violoncello e pianoforte ed interpretazione del "continuo" originale di Alfredo Casella. (1933 XII).
  1 leaf, 33 [i.e. 34]p. 33 x 24 cm.
  Score.
  4th movement in another hand.
  Dedicated to Mrs. E. S. Coolidge.

Castelnuovo-Tedesco, Mario, 1895-

527. [Quartet, strings, G major]
  Quartetto in sol. Mario Castelnuovo-Tedesco (1929).
  2 leaves, 56 p. 32 x 23 cm.
  Score.
  Dedicated to Mrs. E. S. Coolidge, Firenze, 1930.
  At end: Mario Castelnuovo-Tedesco, Migliano di Lari, 12 giugno 1930.
  Published in 1931 by G. Ricordi in Milan.

Catalani, Alfredo, 1854-1893

528. . . . Serenata andalusa per violino e pianoforte d'Alfredo Catalani.
  1 leaf, 12 p. 35 x 24 cm.
  Score.
  Dedicated to Tivadar Nachez.
  Former owner: Natale Gallini (catalogue, no. 65).
  Facsimile of one page in Abbiati, *Storia della musica*, IV, 232.
  At end: Firenze 10 dicembre 1887.
  Unpublished.

Chaĭkovskiĭ, Petr Il'ich, 1840-1893

529. Aveux passionés. P. Tschaikovsky.
    [3]p. 30 x 22 cm.
    For piano 2 hands.
    Not listed in the thematic catalogue of his works, nor in G. Abraham, *The Music of Tchaikovsky*.
    Facsimile of p. 1 in V. A. Heck catalogue 33, p. 41.

Chaminade, Cécile, 1861-1944

530. L'absente. Poësie de E. Guinand. C. Chaminade.
    [7]p. 35 x 27 cm.
    Song with piano accpt.
    First line: Vois le vent chassant la nue.
    Published as no. 17 of her *Album of 20 Songs* in 1893 by G. Schirmer in New York.
    Former owner: Otto E. Albrecht.

531. L'amour captif. Thérèse Maquet. C. Chaminade.
    [4]p. 35 x 26½ cm.
    Song with piano accpt.
    First line: Mignonne, à l'amour j'ai lié les ailes.
    Former owner: Manuscript Society of New York.
    Published in 1894 by G. Schirmer in New York.

532. [Madrigal]
    Tes baisers. Madrigal no. 1. C. Chaminade. Poésie de Georges van Ormelingen.
    [5]p. 35 x 26½ cm.
    Song with piano accpt.
    The title: *Tes baisers* has been cancelled.
    First line: Tes doux baisers sont des oiseaux.
    Published in 1893 by G. Schirmer in New York.

Chausson, Ernest, 1855-1899

533. Cantique à l'épouse.
    [4]p. 36½ x 27 cm.
    Song with piano accpt.
    Text by Albert Jounet.
    First line: Epouse au front lumineux.
    At end: Bois St. Martin 23 juin 1898. Ernest Chausson.
    Published as no. 7 of op. 36 in 1898 by A. Rouart, Lerolle in Paris.

534. Chanson perpétuelle pour voix de soprano et orchestre. Opus 35 [!]
    [7]p. 35½ x 27 cm.
    Reduction for voice and piano.
    Text by Charles Cros.

Chausson, Ernest—*continued*

First line: Bois frissonnants, ciel étoilé.
Published as op. 37 by A. Durand et fils in Paris.

535. . . . Poème pour violon et orchestre. Ernest Chausson. Op. 25.
    1 leaf, 54 p. 39 x 27½ cm.
    Full score.
    At end: Glion—Bas Bel Air juin-juillet 1896. Ernest Chausson.
    Dedicated to Eugene Ysaÿe.
    Published in 1907 by Breitkopf & Härtel in Leipzig.
    Former owners: Eugène Ysaÿe, Fritz Kreisler.
    See H. Spivacke, "A recent gift from Mr. Fritz Kreisler, *"Library
    of Congress Quarterly Journal,* VI, no. 3 (May, 1949), 57-62,
    with facsimile of one page.

536. Poème de l'amour et de la mer. II. La mort de l'amour.
    1 leaf [5]p. 35½ x 27 cm.
    Composer's reduction of the full score for voice and piano of the
    last part of the second section, beginning: Le temps des lilas.
    Another copy (5 p.) of the same.
    Published ca. 1892 by E. Baudoux in Paris.

Cherubini, Maria Luigi Carlo Zenobio Salvatore, 1780-1842

537. Médée, Opéra en 3 actes d'Hofman [!], Musique de Cherubini.
    Représenté dans le Théâtre de la rue Feydeau . . . 13 mars
    1797 . . .
    1 leaf, 528 p. 29 x 22 cm.
    Full score, with many deletions and corrections.
    Facsimile of p. 1 in Van Patten, *Catalogue,* p. 55.

538. O salutaris.
    1 leaf, 30 x 21 cm.
    Sketch, on verso only, on leaf originally used by Rousseau for bas-
    soon part of an unidentified opera.
    Former owner: Wilhelm Heyer (catalogue, IV, no. 447); George B.
    Weston.

539. Ottava della Gerusalemme Liberata di Torquato Tasso, scelta nel
    canto d'Armida e Rinaldo, posta in musica da L. Cherubini . . .
    Parigi maggio 1834.
    fol. 9v-11v. 18 x 25½ cm.
    In Demidov, Album of autographs.
    For voice, violin and piano (or harp).
    First line: Ella dinanzi al petto.

540. [Quartet, strings, no. 6, A minor]
    Quatuor 6m. pour deux violons, alto et basso par L. Cherubini
    (Paris, 1835).
    [2]p. 22½ x 27½ cm.
    Fragment of score.   THE PIERPONT MORGAN LIBRARY

Chevreuille, Raymond, 1901-

541. . . . 5me quatuor à cordes. Raymond Chevreuille . . .
    37 p. 36 x 27 cm.
    Score.
    At end. Raymond Chevreuille. Février 1943.
    Written in memory of Alphonse Onnou.
                    LIBRARY OF CONGRESS, COOLIDGE FOUNDATION

Chopin, Frydryk Franciszek, 1810-1849

It is well known that Chopin aimed at simultane-
ous publication of his works in France, Germany and
England. Only the French editions are indicated
here. For the others the reader is referred to the
standard biographies.

542. Allegro de concert pour le piano forté dédié à Mlle. F. Müller (de
    Vienne) par F. Chopin. Oeuv. 46 . . .
    1 leaf, [13]p. 21½ x 28 cm.
    Published in 1841 by M. Schlesinger in Paris.
    Werke, vol. X, no. 6.   HEINEMAN FOUNDATION

543. [Ballade, piano, no. 1, op. 23, G minor]
    Ballade pour le piano forte . . . par F. Chopin. Op. 23 . . .
    1 leaf, [15]p. 23 x 30½ cm.
    Dedicated to Baron de Stockhausen.
    Published in 1836 by M. Schlesinger in Paris.
    Werke, vol. I, no. 1.   MR. GREGOR PIATIGORSKY

544. [Ecossaises, piano, nos. 2 and 3, op. 72, no. 3, G major, D flat major]
    On p. 2 of his *Piosnka litewska*.
    Published in 1855 by A. M. Schlesinger in Berlin.
    Werke, vol. XIII, p. 79-80.
    Former owner: George T. Keating.
                    MEMORIAL LIBRARY OF MUSIC, STANFORD UNIVERSITY

545. [Etude, piano, op. 10, no. 7, C major]
    [2]p. 35 x 26 cm.
    Published in 1833 by M. Schlesinger in Paris.
    Werke, vol. II, no. 7.   THE ERNEST SCHELLING COLLECTION

Chopin, Frydryk Franciszek—*continued*

546. [Impromptu, piano, no. 2, op. 36, F sharp major]
   [2]p. 22 x 27 cm.
   Fragment.
   Former owner: Mme. Essipof Leschetizky.

547. [Mazurka, piano, op. 6, no. 3, E major]
   Mazur.
   [4]p. 10½ x 18 cm.
   In an autograph album.
   Published in 1832 by M. Schlesinger in Paris.
   Werke, vol. III, no. 3.

548. [Mazurka, piano, op. 33, no. 4, B minor]
   fol. 7-8. 23½ x 30½ cm.
   On recto of fol. 7 only the indication "no. 4."
   Published in 1838 by M. Schlesinger in Paris.
   Werke, vol. III, no. 25.

549. [Mazurka, piano, op. 41, no. 2, E minor]
   E moll. Palma. 28 9bre. Mazur.
   [5]p. 22 x 28½ cm.
   Published in 1840 by Troupenas in Paris.
   Werke, vol. III, no. 27.
   At foot of p. 1, the first draft of the *Prelude,* piano, op. 28, no. 4,
      E minor.
   On p. 2-5, unidentified sketches.
   Former owner: Pauline Viardot-García.

550. [Nocturne, piano, op. 62, no. 1, B major]
   2 Nocturnes pour le piano dédiés à Mademoiselle R. de Körneritz
      par F. Chopin. Op. 62. Paris Brandus Leipsic Haertel, Londres
      Wessel. Nro. 1.
   4 p. 22 x 28½ cm.
   Published in 1846 by the three firms mentioned in title.
   Werke, vol. IV, no. 17.
   Former owners: Alex. C. Grzymala Turzanski Kahanowicz, Francis
      J. L. Beckman, archbishop of Dubuque.

551. [Piosnka litewska]
   [2]p. 18½ x 22 cm.
   Song with piano accpt.
   Signed in upper right corner of p. 1: F. Chopin.
   Text by Stef. Witwicki.
   First line: Bardzo raniuchno.

Chopin, Frydryk Franciszek—*continued*

Published as no. 16 of his *Siebzehn polnische Lieder,* op. 74, in
1855 by A. M. Schlesinger in Berlin.
Werke, vol. XIV, no. 16.
On p. 2, two *Ecossaises.* See separate entry.
Former owner: George T. Keating.
Facsimile in Van Patten, *Catalogue,* p. 58.

MEMORIAL LIBRARY OF MUSIC, STANFORD UNIVERSITY

552. [Polonaise, piano, op. 53, A flat major]
Polonaise pour le piano, dédiée à monsieur Auguste Léo par
F. Chopin . . . op. 53.
[6]p. 21 x 27 cm.
Facsimile of first page in *Notes,* VII (1949-50), 201.
Published in 1843 by M. Schlesinger in Paris.
Werke, vol. V, no. 6.   HEINEMAN FOUNDATION

[Prelude, piano, op. 48, no. 4. E minor]
See his *Mazurka,* piano, E minor

553. [Waltz, piano, op. 69, no. 1, F minor]
. . . Valse. A Mme. Peruzzi, hommage de F. Chopin. 1837.
[1]p. 23 x 30½ cm.
Published in 1855 by Meissonier fils in Paris.
Werke, vol. XIII, no. 24.
Former owners: Mr. and Mrs. Robert Woods Bliss.

HARVARD UNIVERSITY, DUMBARTON OAKS

Ciccarelli, Angelo, 1806-?

554. Katharina von Guise. Melodrama in zwei Aufzügen von Felix
Romani. Aus dem Italienisch ins Deutsche übersetzt von N. N.
In Musick gesetzt von Angelo Ciccarelli.
2 vols. (449, 393 p.) 23½ x 32 cm.
Full score, Italian and German text.   LIBRARY OF CONGRESS

555. Romance.
[3]p. 12 x 20 cm.
Song with piano accpt.
Text by Princess Natalie Kourakin.
First line: Quand tu m'aimais, je chérissais la vie.
At end: Angelo Ciccarelli, Dresde. 18. 3. 1840.
Former owner: Joseph Muller.   NEW YORK PUBLIC LIBRARY

Cimarosa, Domenico, 1749-1801

556. [Che legge spietava]
Rec'vo con aria Che legge spietava di Domenico Cimarosa, fatta
per uso della sigra. D. Costanza Pallante. 1772.
19 p. 21½ x 29 cm.
Score for voice and strings.
Recitative begins: (Arbace) Che giurai! che promisi!

Cimarosa, Domenico—*continued*

Apparently unpublished.
Facsimile of title-page in Abbiati, *Storia della musica,* III, 101.
Facsimile of p. 1 in Van Patten, *Catalogue,* p. 61.
Former owner: Natale Gallini (catalogue, no. 12).
MEMORIAL LIBRARY OF MUSIC, STANFORD UNIVERSITY

557. [Fragment of an unidentified song or aria]
     [2]p. 22 x 29½ cm.
     Song with piano accpt., last two pages only.
     Fragment begins: Vid'io il vostro affetto. *Ancor per me,* given as
     title by Van Patten (*Catalogue,* no. 219), occurs in middle of
     the fragmentary text.
MEMORIAL LIBRARY OF MUSIC, STANFORD UNIVERSITY

558. [Le magie di Merlino e Zoroastro]
     [8]p. 22 x 29½ cm.
     Full score of a *Preludio* and an aria for Stella, Si la cantante me
     mett' a fare. MR. ARTURO TOSCANINI

559. . . . Messa a 3 voci con vvni, oboè, trombe e basso di Domenico
     Cimarosa.
     15 p. 22 x 28½ cm.
     Full score, Latin text. MR. RUDOLF F. KALLIR

Clapisson, Antonin Louis, 1808-1866

560. [Collection of compositions and fragments, vocal and instrumental]
     [38]p. 25½ x 34 cm. LIBRARY OF CONGRESS

561. . . . Les amoureux de Perrette (Opéra-comique en un acte) . . .
     [313]p. 34½ x 27 cm.
     Full score, French text.
     First performed at Baden-Baden, 1855. LIBRARY OF CONGRESS

562. Le coq . . . Ls. C.
     [536]p. 35 x 26½ cm.
     Full score of the opera in two acts, French text.
     Unpublished. LIBRARY OF CONGRESS

563. Enfants, n'y touchez pas. Paroles de Mr. Hte Guérin. Musique de
     Clapisson.
     [1]p. 27 x 35 cm.
     Song with piano accpt.
     First line: Du nid charmant caché sous la feuillée.
LIBRARY OF CONGRESS

564. [Madame Grégoire, opéra-comique en trois actes]
     2 vols. 35 x 27 cm.
     Full score, French text.
     Libretto by Scribe and Henri Boisseaux.
     First performed at Paris, February 8, 1861. LIBRARY OF CONGRESS

Clapisson, Antonin Louis—*continued*

565. [Les mystères d'Udolphe . . . Ls. C.]
    2 vols. 35 x 27 cm.
    Full score of the opéra-comique in 3 acts, French text.
    Libretto by Scribe and Germain Delavigne.
    First performed at Paris, November 4, 1852.   LIBRARY OF CONGRESS

566. [Trio, piano and strings, B flat minor]
    Finale. Trio pour piano, violon et violoncelle. L C.
    [7]p. 35 x 27 cm.
    Score of the last movement.   LIBRARY OF CONGRESS

567. Les trois Nicolas . . . Ls C . . .
    2 vols. 35 x 27 cm.
    Full score of the opéra-comique in 3 acts, French text.
    Libretto by Scribe, Bernard Lopez and Gabriel de Lurieu.
    First performed at Paris, December 16, 1858.   LIBRARY OF CONGRESS

Clarke, Rebecca, 1886-

568. . . . Rhapsody for 'cello & piano by Rebecca Clarke.
    Score (1 leaf, 62 p.) and violoncello part.
    Dedicated to Mrs. E. S. Coolidge.
    Commissioned for the Berkshire Festival, 1923.
                LIBRARY OF CONGRESS, COOLIDGE FOUNDATION

569. Sonata for viola and piano. Poète, prends ton luth; la vie de la
    jeunesse Fermente cette nuit dans les veines de Dieu. Alfred de
    Musset 'La nuit de mai.'
    52 p. 33 x 26½ cm.
    Score.
    At end: July 1919.
    Published in 1921 By J. & W. Chester in London.
                LIBRARY OF CONGRESS, COOLIDGE FOUNDATION

570. . . . Trio for piano, violin & 'cello.
    56 p. 34½ x 25½ cm.
    Score.
    Honorable mention, Berkshire Festival, 1921.
    Published in 1928 by Winthrop Rogers in London.
                LIBRARY OF CONGRESS, COOLIDGE FOUNDATION

Clay, Frederic, 1838-1889

571. "Lalla Rookh." Cantata, words by W. G. Wills. Music by Frederic
    Clay. Full score.
    [1], 352 p. 36 x 25 cm.
    At end: Frederic Clay. 8 February 1877.   LIBRARY OF CONGRESS

572. [Autographs]
A miscellaneous collection of sketches and fragments in skeleton
and full score.   LIBRARY OF CONGRESS

573. [Autographs]
A miscellaneous collection of sketches and fragments for piano.
                                             LIBRARY OF CONGRESS

574. [Capriccio, piano, F major]
Cappriccio pel pianoforte di Muzio Clementi, composto nel 1800,
riscritto con qualche cambiamento in Roma 1807.
[4]p. 22 x 28 cm.
Incomplete.
A revision of the version in the Breitkopf & Härtel edition of his
Oeuvres, vol. XII.   LIBRARY OF CONGRESS

575. Duettino I [-2]. M. Clementi.
[10]p. 24 x 29 and 29½ x 23 cm.
For piano 4 hands.
No. 1 in C major; no. 2 in G major, begins on p. 8, incomplete.
On p. 6-7, a *Mazurka.* See separate entry.   LIBRARY OF CONGRESS

576. Duetto per 2 pianoforte di Muzio Clementi.
[6]p. 21 x 26 cm.
In B flat major.   LIBRARY OF CONGRESS

577. Mazurka, a Polonaise, in which eight cavaliers, in boots, strike their
heels together at the places marked . . .
On p. 6-7 of his *Duettino* I-[2].   LIBRARY OF CONGRESS

578. [Monferrinas, piano]
[8]p. 20 x 26 cm.
No. 3 in C, 4 in C minor, 8 in E flat, 9 in G, and two others
(unnumbered) in B flat and D, followed by a *Tarantella* and
an *Air russe.*
These compositions do not appear in his *12 Monferrinas,* London,
1812.   LIBRARY OF CONGRESS

579. Motivi per esser trattati da me Muzio Clementi Paris Aug. 2, 1821.
[2]p. 30 x 24 cm.
For piano 2 hands.   LIBRARY OF CONGRESS

580. [Nonet, E flat major]
Nonetta di Muzio Clementi.
[6]p. 24 x 32½ cm.
Incomplete fragment of score (horn, clarinet, oboe, flute, bassoon,
violin, viola, violoncello and double bass). LIBRARY OF CONGRESS

581. [Overture]
All[egr]o per l'overtura di M. Clementi.
[2]p. 26 x 35 cm.
Sketch, scored for violins, viola and bass.   LIBRARY OF CONGRESS

Clementi, Muzio—*continued*

582. [Préludes et cadences pour le pianoforte seul, op. 19]
[20]p. 22 x 30½ cm.
A revision of the version in the Breitkopf & Härtel edition of his *Oeuvres,* vol. XII.
Published in 1788 by Leduc in Paris and other publishers.

LIBRARY OF CONGRESS

583. Rondeau per soprano e cembalo solo, fatto per il Cecarelli, idea di Sacchini, variata da me Clementi.
[6]p. 23½ x 32 cm.
First line: Vieni oh caro amato.
Facsimile in Van Patten, *Catalogue,* p. 64.

MEMORIAL LIBRARY OF MUSIC, STANFORD UNIVERSITY

584. [Rondo, piano, B flat major]
Rondo di Muzio Clementi.
[2]p. 20 x 26 cm.
On p. 2, a *Fuge* in C major, incomplete.   LIBRARY OF CONGRESS

585. [Sonata, piano, op. 2, no. 1. C major]
[2]p. 23½ x 30 cm.
Contains the last 10 bars of 1st movement, followed by a complete *Larghetto cantabile* in F otherwise unknown. Probably designed for a new edition of the sonata, but apparently unpublished.

LIBRARY OF CONGRESS

586. [Sonatas, piano, op. 14]
Three sonatas for pianoforte. Op. 14.
[18]p. 21 x 28 cm.
Published in London in 1784.   LIBRARY OF CONGRESS

587. [Sonata, piano, op. 33, no. 1. F major]
Sonata di Muzio Clementi (Op. I di l'origi.) Rifatta a Roma 1807, con molti cambiamenti, imbellimenti.
[4]p. 21½ x 28½ cm.   LIBRARY OF CONGRESS

588. [Sonata, piano, G major]
Sonata di M. Clementi fatta 1768, mai publicata.
[2]p. 21½ x 27 cm.
Fragment of 19 bars, followed by other unidentified sketches.

LIBRARY OF CONGRESS

589. [Sonata, 2 pianos, op. 12, B flat major]
Duetto per 2 pianoforte di Muzio Clementi.
[6]p. 21 x 26 cm.
The last 30 bars lacking.
Published in London in 1784.   LIBRARY OF CONGRESS

590. Sonata for the piano forte, with an accompaniment for the flute— arranged from a celebrated overture composed by Siber [?].
[16]p. 24 x 30 cm.
Score.   LIBRARY OF CONGRESS

Clementi, Muzio—*continued*

591. [Sonatas, violin and piano, op. 5]
  Tre sonate pel pianoforte con violino di Muzio Clementi Op. 5.
   Rifatti a Roma 1807.
  [18]p. 19 x 29 cm.
 Score of no. 1; piano part only of nos. 2-3.
 Published in 1780 by Bailleux in Paris. LIBRARY OF CONGRESS

592. [Symphony, no. 1, C major]
  [104]p. 34 x 24 cm.
 Full score.
 On the mss. of Clementi's symphonies in the Library of Congress,
  in part completed and published by Alfredo Casella (Milan,
  Ricordi, 1936), cf. Saint-Foix, "Les symphonies de Clementi,"
  Rivista musicale italiana, XXXI (1924), 1-22.
           LIBRARY OF CONGRESS

593. [Symphony, no. 2, D major]
  [69]p. 34 x 24 cm.
 Full score.   LIBRARY OF CONGRESS

594. [Symphony, no. 2, D major]
  Minuetto pastorale. Allegretto vivace.
  [12]p. 30 x 24 cm.
 Full score.
 On p. 1 a cancelled sketch in full score with this note: "N.B.
  Minuetto under this to be shortened for another symphony in D."
           LIBRARY OF CONGRESS

595. [Symphony, no. 3, G major]
  Min[ue]tto All[egre]tto.
  [2]p. 24 x 30 cm.
 Incomplete sketch in full score for the so-called "National"
  symphony.
 On p. 2 a cancelled sketch in full score. LIBRARY OF CONGRESS

596. [Symphony, no. 4, D major]
  [44]p. 24 x 30 cm.
 Full score.   LIBRARY OF CONGRESS

597. [Symphony, B flat major]
  Sinfonia di Muzio Clementi.
  [2]p. 17 x 25½ cm.
 Sketch in full score for the adagio and beginning of the allegro
  vivace movements.   LIBRARY OF CONGRESS

598. [Symphony, C major]
  Sinfonia di Muzio Clementi. MS dell autore.
  [8]p. 24 x 30 cm.
 Sketches for the beginning of an adagio.
 The title-page is covered with sketches for other movements.

Clementi, Muzio—*continued*

> Among them is one for the first 6 bars of the movement in the so-called "National" symphony which begins with the inverted *God save the king;* therefore this score may be the beginning of this 3rd symphony which is lacking in the Library of Congress autograph of that work.　　　LIBRARY OF CONGRESS

599.　[Symphony, G major]
> Per mia sinf[onia] in G col Vive Henri 4, e Char[mante] Gab[rielle].
> [4]p. 26½ x 24 cm.
> Incomplete sketch of an andante movement in D major, scored for violins, viola and bass.　　　LIBRARY OF CONGRESS

Coleridge-Taylor, Samuel
see Taylor, Samuel Coleridge-, 1875-1912

Collingwood, Lawrance (Arthur), 1887-

600.　The cloths of heaven. W. B. Yeats.
> [3]p. 30½ x 24 cm.
> Song with piano accpt.
> First line: Had I the heavens' embroidered cloths.
> Unpublished.　　　MR. ALFRED J. SWAN

601.　Elegy. Words by Ernest Dowson. Music by Lawrance Collingwood.
> [7]p. 30½ x 24 cm.
> Song with piano accpt.
> First line: You could have understood me, had you waited.
> Unpublished.　　　MR. ALFRED J. SWAN

602.　"Exceeding sorrow." Ernest Dowson.
> [3]p. 30½ x 24 cm.
> Song with piano accpt.
> First line: Exceeding sorrow consumeth my sad heart.
> At end: Lawrance A. Collingwood. Jan. 1928.
> Unpublished.　　　MR. ALFRED J. SWAN

603.　June. Robert Bridges.
> [3]p. 30½ x 24 cm.
> Song with piano accpt.
> First line: When June is come, then all the day.
> Unpublished.　　　MR. ALFRED J. SWAN

604.　Mamble, words by J. Drinkwater, music by Lawrance Collingwood.
> [4]p. 30½ x 24 cm.
> Song with piano accpt.
> First line: I never want to Mamble.
> Unpublished.　　　MR. ALFRED J. SWAN

605. Nightingales, words by Robert Bridges . . . music by Lawrance
Collingwood.
[7]p. 30½ x 24 cm.
Song with piano accpt.
First line: Beautiful must be the mountains.
Unpublished.   MR. ALFRED J. SWAN

606. When that I loved a maiden. Words by Robert Bridges. Music by
Lawrance Collingwood.
[5]p. 30½ x 24 cm.
Song with piano accpt.
Unpublished.   MR. ALFRED J. SWAN

607. . . . The wood of flowers, words by James Stephens, music by
Lawrance Collingwood.
[3]p. 30½ x 24 cm.
Song with piano accpt.
First line: I went to the wood of flowers.
Unpublished.   MR. ALFRED J. SWAN

Cooke, Benjamin, 1734-1793

608. [Autographs, miscellaneous]
[187]p. 29 x 22½ cm.
Contents: *Sinfonie; Ode for Christmas Day by Taylor White, Esqr.;
"Wherewithall shall a young man cleanse his way"; "Call to thy
remembrance, O Lord;" "Them that are meek;" Occasional
anthem for . . . William, duke of Cumberland; "The elders of
Israel sit on the ground;" "How are the mighty fallen."*
All the above works in full score.   LIBRARY OF CONGRESS

Cornelius, Peter (Carl August), 1824-1874

609. [Trost in Tränen. Op. 14]
. . . 9t. August 1872. Wie kommt's dass du so traurig bist.
[12]p. 33 x 24½ cm.
Score for baritone solo, mezzosoprano, tenor, bass I-II, with piano
accpt.
Text by Goethe.
Published in 1873 by E. W. Fritzsch in Leipzig.
Werke, vol. II, p. 153.
Former owner: Anton Gloetzner.   LIBRARY OF CONGRESS

Corti, Mario

610. Tartini, Giuseppe, 1692-1770.
[Concerto, violin, A major]
Giuseppe Tartini . . . Concerto in la maggiore per violino,
orchestra d'archi e cembalo rifatto e instrumentato sull' auto-
grafo per uso di Mrs. F. S. Coolidge de Mario Corti (estate
1924) . . .

Corti, Mario—*continued*

    1 leaf, 11, [1]p. 44½ x 29 cm.
    Arranger's reduction of his full score for violin and piano.
    Published in full score and in this version in 1926 by G. Ricordi
    in Milan.   LIBRARY OF CONGRESS, COOLIDGE FOUNDATION

Cowen, Sir Frederic Hymen, 1852-1935

611. The language of flowers. F. H. Cowen.
    [131]p. 23½ x 30 cm.
    Full score of a ballet suite.
    Published by Metzler & Co. in London.   BOSTON PUBLIC LIBRARY

Cramer, Johann Baptist, 1771-1858

612. [Quintet, piano, violin, viola, violoncello & double bass, op. 69,]
    J. B. Cramer's 2. Quintetto for piano forte, violin, alto, violon-
    cello & contra basso, op. 69, as performed at the Philharmonic
    Concert by the author, J. Cramer, A. Moralt, Lindley &
    Dragonetti.
    [48]p. 23½ x 29½ cm.
    Score.
    At end: J. B. Cramer, Oct. 17, 1823.
    Former owner: William H. Cummings (catalogue, no. 530).
        LIBRARY OF CONGRESS

613. The two styles, ancient and modern, a music effusion for the piano
    forte, composed . . . by J. B. Cramer. Op. 96.
    7 p. 22 x 29 cm.
    At foot of p. 1: Paris Feb. 20th, 1842.
    Dedicated to Rev. Edward Goddard.
    Former owner: Joseph W. Drexel.   NEW YORK PUBLIC LIBRARY

Creyghton, Robert, ca. 1639- ca. 1733

614. [Church music]
    63 leaves. 32 x 20 cm.
    Services and (reversing the ms.) anthems; tenor parts only.
    A few leaves in other hands; some works by other composers.
    On fol. lv: Eccliae Wellen. D.D.D. Rob. Creyghton praecentor
    1691.
    Former owner: William H. Cummings (catalogue, no. 550).
        LIBRARY OF CONGRESS

Croft, William, 1678-1727

615. Anthem of 5, 6 and 8 voices. Dr. W. Croft.
    [16]p. 23½ x 30 cm.
    First line: Hear my prayer, O Lord.   LIBRARY OF CONGRESS

Croft, William—*continued*

616. O praise the Lord of heaven. Anthem with organ accompaniment.
24 p. 24 x 30 cm.
Former owner: Thomas W. Taphouse.

617. Te Deum in B by Wm. Croft for 4.5.6. voc. . . .
[23]p. 33 x 20 cm.
On p. 17: *Jubilate* in B minor.
Former owner: William H. Cummings (catalogue, no. 535).

Crotch, William, 1775-1847

618. Anthem "The Lord is king." Psalm XCVII with solos for a treble
or tenor voice composed by Wm. Crotch . . . March & April
1838 . . .
72 p. 30 x 24 cm.
Full score, mixed chorus.
At end: W. Crotch, April 10, 1838.
Former owner: William H. Cummings (catalogue, no. 546).

Cui, César (Antonovich), 1835-1918

619. . . . Kinzhal. Slova Lermontova, muzyka TS. Kiui.
[4]p. 27½ x 35 cm.
Song with piano accpt.
At end: 1892, S. Peterburg.
Dedicated to Aleksandr Andreevich Filonov.
Published as no. 7 of op. 49 in 1895 by Belaieff in Leipzig.
Former owner: Manuscript Society of New York.

620. [Songs, op. 33]
[8]p. 26½ x 38½ cm.
Songs with piano accpt.
Contents.—*Oni liubili drug druga* (Lermontov)—*Solovei* (Pushkin)
—*Metel'shumit* (Lermontov).
Published as nos. 5, 1 and 7 of op. 33 in 1886 by V. Bessel in
St. Petersburg.

Curschmann, Karl Friedrich, 1804-1841

621. [Die Perle auf Lindahaide]
Lindahaide, Romanzen u. Gesänge von Fr. Curschmann. Op. 28.
25 p. 31 x 25 cm.
Text by Fr. Foerster.
Contents.—no. 2. *Der König und seine Ritter* (bass solo and male
chorus)—no. 3. *Huldhilda* (tenor solo and mixed chorus)—no. 5.
Der Ritterdank (soprano solo and mixed chorus).

Curschmann, Karl Friedrich—*continued*

The other numbers composed by Carl Eckert.
Published ca. 1841 by A. M. Schlesinger in Berlin.

622. Ruhe der Liebe, Gedicht von Fr. Rückert, componirt von Fr.
     Curschmann. d. 6ten July 1837.
     [2]p. 26½ x 34 cm.
     Song with piano accpt.
     First line: Du bist die Ruh'.
     Published as no. 3 of his op. 16 by A. M. Schlesinger in Berlin.

Czerny, Carl, 1791-1857

623. Beethoven, Ludwig van, 1770-1826
     [Concertos, op. 37, 61, 73 and 58]
     Clavierbegleitung zu den Concerten in C moll, D dur, Es dur u.
     G dur.
     [99]p. 25 x 32 cm.
     Reduction for piano of the orchestra part of Beethoven's concertos
     no. 3 for piano in C minor, for violin in D minor, no. 5 for piano
     in E flat and no. 4 for piano in G.
     Each concerto signed by Czerny with dates of beginning and ending.
     They extend from Sept. 17, 1817 to May 17, 1818.
     Unpublished?

624. Etude courante composé [!] pour le piano par Charles Czerny.
     Oeuvre 765. Vienne, chez A. Diabelli & Comp. . . .
     [2]p. 32 x 24 cm.
     At head of title: *Nouveautés du jour. Cah. 45.*

625. Für das Mozart-Album. Mélodie sentimentale et Cadence agitée
     pour le piano par Charles Czerny. Oeuvre 688 . . .
     [4]p. 24 x 20½ cm.
     Published in August Pott's *Mozart-Album* ca. 1840 by Joh. Peter
     Spehr in Braunschweig.

Danzi, Franz, 1763-1826

626. [Unidentified fragments]
     [4]p. 23½ x 20 cm.
     Fragments in full score evidently for an unidentified opera.

David, Félicien, 1810-1876

627. Eoline.
     [2]p. 35 x 26½ cm.
     Song with piano accpt.
     Text by Edouard Plouvier.

David, Félicien—*continued*

First line: Bel ange ou femme.
Published as no. 23 of *Cinquante mélodies* by E. Gérard et cie.
in Paris.   MEMORIAL LIBRARY OF MUSIC, STANFORD UNIVERSITY

David, Ferdinand, 1810-1873

628. [Concerto, violin, op. 35. D minor]
Concert no. 5. D moll. Partitur.
99 p. 26½ x 34½ cm.
Published (parts) in 1857 by Breitkopf & Härtel in Leipzig.
BOSTON PUBLIC LIBRARY

Davy, John, 1763-1824

629. The wife and the mistress. A comic burletta, as performed at Sadlers
Wells, composed by John Davy of Exeter.
1 leaf, 88 p. 30 x 23 cm.
Full score.
First performed April 18, 1796.
Former owner: William H. Cummings (catalogue, no. 573).
LIBRARY OF CONGRESS

Debussy, Claude (Achille), 1862-1918

630. . . . Apparition, Poésie de Stéphane Mallarmé, musique de Cl. Ach.
Debussy.
[4]p. 35 x 27 cm.
Song with piano accpt.
First line: La lune s'attristait.
Dedicated to Madame Vasnier, Ville d'Avray. 8.2.84.
Published as no. IV of *Quatre mélodies de Claude Debussy* in the
supplement to the special Debussy number of *La revue musicale*,
May, 1926.   LIBRARY OF CONGRESS

631. Choeur des brises.
1 leaf, [4]p. 35 x 27 cm.
Sketch of an unidentified composition for voices and instruments.
At end: A. Cl. Debussy.
Facsimile of p. 3-4 in Van Patten, *Catalogue*, p. 66.
MEMORIAL LIBRARY OF MUSIC, STANFORD UNIVERSITY

632. Daniel. Cantate. Personnages: le prophète Daniel. Balthazar, roi
d'Assyrie. Adéna sa femme (La scène se passe à Babylone dans
le palais du roi). A. Cl. Debussy.
1 leaf, [20]p. 35 x 27 cm.
First draft, incomplete.
Composed 1880-84.
Text by Emile Cécile.
Unpublished.   MR. GREGOR PIATIGORSKY

Debussy, Claude (Achille)—*continued*

633. En sourdine. Poésie de P. Verlaine. Musique de Cl. Debussy.
    [3]p. 35 x 27 cm.
    Song with piano accpt.
    First line: Calmes dans le demi-jour.
    At end: Vienne. 16 Sep. 82.
    A different setting from that in his *Fêtes galantes,* 1892.
    Published as *Calmes dans le demi-jour (En sourdine)* in 1944 by
    Elkan-Vogel Co. in Philadelphia.   MR. GREGOR PIATIGORSKY

634. [Fantoches]
    . . . Fêtes galantes. Poésies de Verlaine. Musique de A. Claude
        Debussy.
    1 leaf, [4]p. 35 x 27 cm.
    Song with piano accpt.
    First line: Scaramouche et Pulcinella.
    At end: 8 janvier 82. A. Cl. Debussy.
    Dedicated to Mme. Vasnier (the published version to Mme.
        Lucien Fontaine).
    Caption title: *Fantoches.*
    Published as no. 2 of his *Fêtes galantes* (first series) in 1892 by
        Jean Jobert in Paris.   MR. ARTURO TOSCANINI

635. La mer.
    1 leaf, 26 numbered leaves. 40 x 30 cm.
    First draft of the full score.
    Music on recto only.
    At end: Dimanche 5 mars 1905 à 6 h. du soir. Claude Debussy.
    Published as *La mer, trois esquisses symphoniques* in 1905 by
        A. Durand in Paris.   SIBLEY MUSICAL LIBRARY

636. Nocturnes. Nuages, Fêtes, Sirènes. CD. 1897-1899.
    22 leaves. 40 x 30 cm.
    Music on recto only.
    Original sketches in condensed score.
    At end: Vendredi—15 D. 3h du matin.
    Dedicated to Georges Hartmann.
    According to a note this ms. was presented by the composer to his
        first wife as a New Year's gift, Jan. 1, 1901.
    Published (full score) in 1908 by A. Durand in Paris.
                                        LIBRARY OF CONGRESS

637. Noël pour célébrer Pierre Louÿs, pour toutes les voix y compris
        celle du peuple. 24 déc. 1903.
    [2]p. 26 x 20 cm.
    Score (6-part mixed chorus and piano).
    Parts for Petites filles, filles, femmes du monde, le peuple.
    First line: Noël, noël, pour monsieur Pierre Louys.
    At end: Claude Debussy, le 25ème jour de décembre, 1903.
    Unpublished. MEMORIAL LIBRARY OF MUSIC, STANFORD UNIVERSITY

Debussy, Claude (Achille)—*continued*

638. [Nuit d'étoiles]
Song with piano accpt.
Text by Théodore de Banville.
First line: Nuit d'étoiles, sous tes voiles.
Published ca. 1877 by Bulla in Paris.
Former owner: Frank Laforge.   MISS LILY PONS

639. Ode bachique tirée d'Hmnys [!], comédie de Th. de Banville.
Musique de C. Debussy.
11 p. 35½ x 27 cm.
Duet with piano accpt.
First line: À toi, Lyaeos, glorieux Bacchos!
Text is the entire Scene VII between Hymnis and Anacreon of
*Hymnis, comédie lyrique en un acte par Théodore de Banville,
musique de Jules Cressonnois.* Paris, Tresse, 1880.
Unpublished and unmentioned in lists of the composer's works.
                              MR. ARTURO TOSCANINI

640. Pelléas et Mélisande.
128 leaves. 40 x 30 cm.
Music on recto only (except for occasional corrections).
First draft.
Former owner: Eben B. Jordan.
Published in 1902 by A. Durand in Paris.
                    NEW ENGLAND CONSERVATORY OF MUSIC

641. . . . Pierrot. Poésie, Th. de Banville. Musique sur l'air de [Au clair
de la lune], Cl. Ach. Debussy.
[4]p. 27 x 35 cm.
Song with piano accpt.
First line: Le bon Pierrot que la foule contemple.
On p. 4 unidentified pencil sketches.
Dedicated to Mme. Vasnier.
Published as no. III of *Quatre mélodies de Debussy* in the supple-
ment to the special Debussy number of *La revue musicale,* May,
1926.   LIBRARY OF CONGRESS

642. [Préludes, piano, Book I, no. 12. Minstrels]
Minstrels. Transcription pour piano et Hartmann. Claude De-
bussy. 17 janvier 14.
1, 4 numbered leaves. 40 x 29 cm.
Composer's transcription for violin and piano.
Music on recto only.
Former owner: Arthur Hartmann.   SIBLEY MUSICAL LIBRARY

643. [Preludes, piano, Book II, no. 2. Feuilles mortes]
[3]p. 28 x 29 cm.
First draft, in pencil, on p. 1 and 3.
On p. 2, sketches for another piece.   MR. GREGOR PIATIGORSKY

Debussy, Claude (Achille)—*continued*

644. [Rhapsody, saxophone and orchestra]
Esquisse d'une rapsodie mauresque pour orchestre et saxophone principal . . . Claude Debussy, 1901-1908.
1, 14 numbered leaves. 35 x 27 cm.
Music on recto only (except for occasional corrections).
Short score with indication of instrumentation.
Dedicated to Elise Hall.
Published in 1919 by Durand et fils in Paris (orchestration completed by Roger-Ducasse).

NEW ENGLAND CONSERVATORY OF MUSIC

645. . . . Rondel chinois. Musique chinoise (d'après des manuscrits du temps) par Cl. Ach. Debussy.
[3]p. 27 x 35 cm.
Song with piano accpt.
First line: Sur le lac bordé d'azalée.
Unpublished.
At head of title: A Madame Vasnier, la seule qui peut chanter et faire oublier tout ce que cette musique a d'inchantable et de chinois.
Cf. "La jeunesse de Claude Debussy" in the special Debussy number of *La revue musicale,* May, 1926. p. [17], 25.

LIBRARY OF CONGRESS

646. [La Saulaie]
[1]p. 20 x 30 cm.
Sketch for voice and orchestra.
Begins: Mais il touchait son luth. This is line 5 of Pierre Louÿs' translation of Dante Gabriel Rosetti's *Willowwood,* sonnets nos. 24-27 of his *House of Life.* Composition was begun in the fall of 1896 (cf. "Lettres inédites de Claude Debussy à Eugène Ysaÿe," in *Les annales politiques et littéraires,* August 25, 1933, p. 225-26, and *Correspondance de Claude Debussy et Pierre Louÿs,* Paris, 1945, p. 76).
At end: A. Cl. Debussy.
Former owner: George T. Keating.

MEMORIAL LIBRARY OF MUSIC, STANFORD UNIVERSITY

647. . . . Séguidille. Poésie de Th. Gauthier. Musique de A. Cl. Debussy.
[7]p. 35 x 27 cm.
Song with piano accpt.
First line: Un jupon serré sur les hanches.
At end: A. Cl. Debussy.
Dedicated to Mme. Vasnier.
Apparently unpublished.

MR. GREGOR PIATIGORSKY

648. Suite pour violoncelle et orchestre. 4. Intermezzo. Piano et violoncelle.
[5]p. 35 x 27 cm.

Debussy, Claude (Achille)—*continued*

This composition seems otherwise unknown, either in the original form or in the reduction for violoncello and piano.

Published in 1944 by Elkan-Vogel Co. in Philadelphia, as *Intermezzo*.   MR. GREGOR PIATIGORSKY

Dehn, Siegfried Wilhelm, 1799-1858

649. Fughetto a 2.
        [2]p. 27 x 34 cm.
        For piano.
        At end: S. W. Dehn. Berlin, Nov. 1840.
        Former owner: Samuel P. Warren.   LIBRARY OF CONGRESS

Delibes, (Clément Philibert) Léo, 1836-1891

650. Alger. Cantate-opéra. 15 août 1865. Paroles de Méry.
        [38]p. 35 x 27 cm.
        Full score.
        At end: Léo Delibes. 9 août 1865.
        First performed August 15, 1865 at the Opéra, Paris.
                                                        LIBRARY OF CONGRESS

651. Le Boeuf Apis.
        1 vol. 35 x 27 cm.
        Full score of the operetta in 2 acts.
        First performed April 25, 1865 at the Théâtre des Bouffes-Parisiens
          in Paris.   LIBRARY OF CONGRESS

652. Le Boeuf Apis. No. 4. Chant de Fleur de Lotus. Fleur-de-Lotus.
        Les 6 esclaves.
        [19]p. 35 x 27 cm.
        Full score.   LIBRARY OF CONGRESS

653. Méhul, Etienne Nicolas, 1763-1817.
        Le chant du départ.
        [20]p. 35 x 27 cm.
        Full score (mixed chorus and orchestra) of Delibes' arrangement.
                                                        LIBRARY OF CONGRESS

654. [Coppélia. Mazurka]
        Mazurka Coppélia 4 mains.
        [10]p. 27 x 36 cm.
        Composer's arrangement for piano 4 hands.   LIBRARY OF CONGRESS

655. [Le Corsaire. Le Pas des fleurs]
        Le Pas des fleurs. Divertissement pour Le Corsaire.
        1 vol. 35 x 27 cm.
        Full score.
        With this are: *Le Rhin allemand. Ch. Delioux* and *Ier acte. Variation de Mlle. Grantzow,* both in full score.
                                                        LIBRARY OF CONGRESS

Delibes, (Clément Philibert) Léo—*continued*

656. [La cour du roi Pétaud]
     1 vol. 35 x 27 cm.
     Full score of the opéra-bouffe in 3 acts.
     Libretto by Ph. Gille et Jaime fils.
     First performed April 26, 1869 at the Théâtre des Variétés in Paris.

657. [Cynthia]
     16, 5, 4 numbered leaves. 35 x 27 cm.
     Full score of the incidental music for the play by Meilhac.
     At end of Entr'acte: L. D. 30 mai 90.

658. [Cynthia]
     12 numbered leaves. 27 x 35 cm.
     Piano-vocal score.

659. Les deux vieilles gardes.
     1 vol. 27 x 35 cm.
     Full score of the opéra-bouffe in one act.
     Libretto by Villeneuve and Lemonnier.
     First performed August 8, 1856 at the Théâtre des Bouffes-Parisiens
     in Paris.

660. [Les deux vieilles gardes]
     2. Vieilles gardes (opérette bouffe).
     [1]p. 20 x 28 cm.
     Piano-vocal score of no. 2: Viv' la polka, moi j'raffol'.
     At end: Léo Delibes. 12 avril 59.
     Former owner: Hugo Riesenfeld.

661. Les eaux d'Ems.
     1 vol. 27 x 35 cm.
     Full score of the operetta in one act.
     First performed in July, 1862, at the Kursaal in Bad Ems.
     Libretto by Henri Crémieux and Ludovic Halévy.

662. L'Ecossais de Chatour. Musique de L. Delibes. Partition d'orchestre.
     1 vol. 32 x 24½ cm.
     Full score of the opéra-bouffe in one act.
     Libretto by A. Jaime and Ph. Gille.
     First performed January 16, 1869 at the Théâtre des Bouffes-
     Parisiens in Paris.

663. Epithalame, poésie d'Edouard Grenier. . . . Léo Delibes, novre 87.
     8 leaves. 27 x 35 cm.
     Music on recto only.
     Song with piano accpt.
     First line: Quand les bruns matelots.

Delibes, (Clément Philibert) Léo—*continued*

Dedicated to Mlle. Valentine de Menasce.
At end: Léo Delibes. Choisy-au-bac, 11 novbre 87.
Published by Heugel in Paris.

664. Fanfares A, B. Exposition universelle 1889.
     8, 10 numbered leaves. 35 x 27 cm.
     Music on recto only.
     Full score.
     At end: Léo Delibes. Choisy-au-bac. 7bre 89.

665. [Garin]
     Musique composée pour Garin (Théâtre français).
     Consists of 2 compositions in full score numbered 1 and 2, and
     2 compositions in piano-vocal score numbered 1 and 3.

666. Honneur au frère Garnier. Cantate.
     5 numbered leaves. 27 x 35 cm.
     Music on recto only.
     For narrator and chorus with piano accpt.
     At end: L. D. juin 89.
     Written for a ceremony in honor of J. L. C. Garnier, architect
     of the Paris Opéra.

667. Horse-guard's march. Léo Delibes juin 1861.
     [17]p. 27 x 35 cm.
     Full score.

668. Le jardinier et son seigneur.
     1 vol. 35 x 27 cm.
     Full score of the opéra-comique in one act.
     Libretto by Barrière.
     First performed May 1, 1863 at the Théâtre Lyrique in Paris.

669. Jean de Nivelle.
     1 vol. 35 x 27 cm.
     Full score of the opéra-comique in three acts.
     Many numbers signed and dated from 1877 to 1880.
     Includes *fragments supprimés* and *récitatifs et fragments*.
     First performed March 8, 1880 at the Opéra Comique in Paris.
     Libretto by E. Gondinet and Ph. Gille.

670. Jean de Nivelle.
     1 vol. 27 x 35 cm.
     Piano-vocal score.

671. Kassya.
     6 vols. 36 x 27 cm.
     Piano-vocal score of the opera in 4 acts.

Delibes, (Clément Philibert) Léo—*continued*

Libretto by Henri Meilhac and Ph. Gille.
First performed March 24, 1893 at the Opéra-Comique in Paris.

672. Lakmé.
     3 vols. 35 x 27 cm.
     Full score of the opéra-comique in 3 acts.
     Libretto by Edmond Gondinet and Ph. Gille.
     First performed April 14, 1883 at the Opéra-Comique in Paris.
     Contains also: *Fragments de la grande partition supprimée pour
     la gravure.*

673. Lakmé.
     1 vol. 35 x 27 cm.
     Piano-vocal score.
     With numerous added *Récitatifs.*

674. [Marlbrough s'en va-t'en guerre]
     1 vol. 35 x 27 cm.
     Full score of the operetta in 4 acts.
     Libretto by Siraudin and W. Busnach.
     First performed December 12, 1867 at the Théâtre de l'Athénée
     in Paris.

675. [La maschera]
     Airs de ballet intercalés dans La maschera.
     [48]p. 35 x 27 cm.
     Full score.

676. Mon ami Pierrot.
     1 vol. 35 x 27 cm.
     Full score of the operetta in one act.
     At end: Léo Delibes. 3 juillet 62.
     First performed in July, 1862, at the Kursaal in Bad Ems.

677. Monsieur Griffard.
     1 vol. 27 x 35 cm.
     Full score of the opéra comique in one act.
     At end: Léo Delibes. 26 7bre. 57.
     First performed October 3, 1857, at the Théâtre Lyrique in Paris.

678. Monts d'Auvergne. Grande fantaisie pour trompes de chasse en ré.
     17 leaves. 27 x 35 cm.
     Score.
     At head of title: *Concours ouvert par la Saint-Hubert Vichyssoise.*
     Another autograph of the score is signed and dated: (7bre 10).
     L-D. St. Nectaire 31 août 90.

Delibes, (Clément Philibert) Léo—*continued*

679. Les Norvégiennes.
      8 leaves. 35 x 27 cm.
    Duet with piano accpt.
    At end: Léo D. 1867-1868.
    Text by Ph. Gille. LIBRARY OF CONGRESS

680. [Les Norvégiennes]
      Glisse, glisse, traineau rapide.
      21 p. 24 x 31½ cm.
    Full score (soprano and alto solo with orchestra).
    At end: Léo D. mai '70.
UNIVERSITY OF CALIFORNIA AT LOS ANGELES,
WILLIAM ANDREWS CLARK MEMORIAL LIBRARY

681. [Note-books]
      7 vols. 16½ x 26 cm.
    Autograph fragments of musical compositions.
LIBRARY OF CONGRESS

682. Les nymphes des bois: Choeur pour voix de femmes . . .
      [27]p. 35 x 27 cm.
    Full score.
    At end: Léo Delibes mars 1867.
    Published by Heugel et Cie. in Paris. LIBRARY OF CONGRESS

683. Les nymphes des bois. Choeur pour voix de femmes. Poésie de
    Ch. Nuitter.
      11 p. 35 x 27 cm.
    Piano-vocal score.
    Contains separate parts for voice and harp. LIBRARY OF CONGRESS

684. [Oluber]
      Cantate Oluber.
      25 leaves. 27 x 35 cm.
    Piano-vocal score.
    At end: L. D. 6 janvier 81. LIBRARY OF CONGRESS

685. L'omelette à la Follembûche. Opérette-bouffe en un acte. Paroles
    de MM. Marc-Michel et Labiche. Musique de Léo Delibes.
      1 vol. 26½ x 34 cm.
    Full score.
    First performed June 8, 1859 at the Théâtre des Bouffes-Parisiens
    in Paris. LIBRARY OF CONGRESS

686. Rigaudon.
      3 numbered leaves. 27 x 35 cm.
    Music on recto only.
    For piano.
    At end: L. D. Choisy 24 octobre 87.
    Published by Heugel et Cie. in Paris. LIBRARY OF CONGRESS

Delibes, (Clément Philibert) Léo—*continued*

687. Le roi l'a dit.
    1 vol. 27 x 35 cm.
    Piano-vocal score.
    Text by Edmond Gondinet.
    First performed May 24, 1873 at the Opéra Comique in Paris.

688. Le roi s'amuse. Musique de scène . . . L. D. 7bre. 8bre. 82.
    77 leaves. 35 x 27 cm.
    Full score.
    First performed November 22, 1882 in Paris.

689. Romance hongroise sans paroles.
    [5]p. 27 x 35 cm.
    For piano.
    Published by Heugel et Cie. in Paris.

690. Sérénade (A quoi rêvent les jeunes filles).
    4 leaves. 35 x 27 cm.
    For voice and piano.
    First line: Ninon, Ninon, que fais-tu de la vie?
    Text by Alfred de Musset.
    Also mandolin and harp parts, sketches and fragments mostly in Delibes' autograph.
    Published by Heugel et Cie. in Paris.

691. Le serpent à plumes.
    [179]p. 32 x 24½ cm.
    Full score of the opéra-bouffe in one act.
    Text by Ph. Gillet.
    First performed December 16, 1864 at the Théâtre des Bouffes-Parisiens in Paris.

692. Les six demoiselles à marier.
    [70]p. 27 x 35 cm.
    Full score of the opéra-bouffe in one act.
    Text by E. Jaime and Choller.
    First performed November 12, 1856 at the Théâtre des Bouffes-Parisiens in Paris.
    At end: L. D. qui n'est pas fâché d'avoir fini, novembre 56.

693. La source.
    1 vol. 35 x 27 cm.
    Full score of Act II (2nd and 3rd tableaux) of the ballet in 3 acts and 4 tableaux. The music was composed in collaboration with Minkous, Delibes supplying only the 2nd and 3rd tableaux.
    Text by Charles Nuitter and Saint-Léon.
    First performed November 12, 1866 at the Opéra in Paris.
    Produced later at Vienna under the title: *Naïla, die Quellenfee.*

Delibes, (Clément Philibert) Léo—*continued*

694. Souvenir d'Allemagne—Impromptu.
        [3]p. 27 x 35 cm.
      Sketch for piano 2 hands.
      At end: Léo Delibes 10 août 60.
      Unpublished?   LIBRARY OF CONGRESS

695. Souvenir lointain (romance sans paroles).
        [3]p. 27 x 35 cm.
      For piano 2 hands.
      Published by Heugel et Cie. in Paris.   LIBRARY OF CONGRESS

696. Sylvia.
        1 vol. 35 x 27 cm.
      Full score of the ballet in 3 acts and 3 tableaux.
      Text by Jules Barbier and Reynach.
      At end: Fini. Mai 1876.
      First performed June 14, 1876 at the Opéra in Paris.
                                                      LIBRARY OF CONGRESS

697. Sylvia.
        1 vol. 27 x 35 cm.
      Piano-vocal score, with numerous fragments.
      At end: 24 8bre. 75.   LIBRARY OF CONGRESS

                    Delius, Frederick, 1863-1934
698. Over the hills and far away. Fantasia. Frederick Delius (1897).
        38 p. 36 x 27 cm.
      Full score.
      Published in 1950 by G. Schirmer in New York.
                  MEMORIAL LIBRARY OF MUSIC, STANFORD UNIVERSITY

                    Denza, Luigi, 1846-1922
699. . . . Venetia. Song. The words by Ed. Teschemacher. The music
      by L. Denza.
        [11]p. 30 x 23½ cm.
      Song with piano accpt.
      First line: The sounds of day are dying.
      Original title, *The blue Venetian sea,* deleted.
                                           MRS. EUGENE ALLEN NOBLE

                    Dessauer, Joseph, 1798-1876
700. [Sechs Lieder. Op. 46]
        [37]p. 25½ x 33 cm.
      Songs with piano accpt.
      No. 1 lacking.
      Published by V. Kratochwill in Vienna.
      Former owner: Joseph Muller.   NEW YORK PUBLIC LIBRARY

Diabelli, Anton, 1781-1858

701. Der allererste Anfang im Pianofortespiel, bestehend in einer Vorübung von 5 Noten und 12 Übungsstrecken (durchaus im Violinschlüssel für beide Hände) um die nötige Kenntnis des gewöhnlichsten Tactarten und Eintheilung zu erlangen, verfasst von Anton Diabelli. Opus 181.
8 p. 11 x 16 cm.   MR. ARTURO TOSCANINI

Dick, Marcel

702. . . . II string quartet for 2 violins, viola and 'cello (1938) . . . by Marcel Dick.
1 leaf, 104 p. 34 x 26½ cm.
Score.
Dedicated to Mrs. E. S. Coolidge.
LIBRARY OF CONGRESS, COOLIDGE FOUNDATION

Dittersdorf, Karl Ditters von, 1739-1799

703. . . . Sonata per il forte piano di Carlo de Dittersdorf, 1799 . . .
[11]p. 23 x 32 cm.
"N. II in A."
K. Krebs, Dittersdorfiana, 238.
Former owner: Baron Stillfried.   LIBRARY OF CONGRESS

Döhler, Theodor, 1814-1856

704. 12ème nocturne composé par Théodore Doehler. Op. 70. . . .
[4]p. 27 x 34 cm.
For piano.
Published ca. 1852 by Brandus & Cie. in Paris.
MR. CARL TOLLEFSEN

Domange, madame Albert, 1858-

705. Suite pour piano et violin. 1. Jour de fête; 2. Eglogue; 3. Cortège champêtre. Musique de Mel-Bonis (1926).
27 p. 35 x 27 cm.
Score.
Mélanie Bonis, pseud. for Mme. Domange.
LIBRARY OF CONGRESS, COOLIDGE FOUNDATION

Done, the reverend Mr.

706. The perfection of true love.
[2]p. 31 x 19½ cm.
Song with figured bass.
At foot of p. 1: His own ms. By the Revd. Mr. Done of Dulwich College 1730.
On p. 2 is the song, *The Apology*, beginning: Frown not, my dear, nor be severe.   LIBRARY OF CONGRESS

Donizetti, Gaetano, 1797-1848

The numbers following the titles of Donizetti's works are those of the list of his compositions in G. Zavadini, *Donizetti, vita, musiche, epistolario* (Bergamo, 1948), p. 169-218.

707. A Clori [Z. 507]
    [2]p. 21 x 28 cm.
Song with piano accpt.
First line: Trova un sol, mia bella Clori.
Unpublished.
Former owner: Walter Toscanini.   DR. FRANK BLACK

708. [Ah, che il destino. Z. 573]
    Duetto, e terzetto se si vuole. Ah, che il destino mio bel tesoro. Scritto espressamente per le gentilissime signe. Tina, e Tude Betti, e Cr. Pucci dal suo devotissimo servitore Gaetano Donizetti in Bologne l'anno 1817. Li 21 agosto 1817.
    [5]p. 23½ x 29½ cm.
Apparently unpublished.   MR. WALLACE GOODRICH

709. [Betly, ossia La capanna svizzera. Z. 54]
    Duetto aggiunto dal maestro Donizetti pella Betly in due atti per soprano e basso.
    29 p. 28 x 39½ cm.
Full score of a duet beginning "Io so ben," written for the revised version of the opera in 2 acts.
Former owner: Natale Gallini (catalogue, no. 39).
      MEMORIAL LIBRARY OF MUSIC, STANFORD UNIVERSITY

710. [Il campanello. Z. 53]
    [22]p. 27 x 39½ cm.
Fragment of full score, beginning with the duet between Enrico and Annibale: Ho una bella, un' infidele.
      MR. ARTURO TOSCANINI

711. [Come, come estinguere]
    [10]p. 22 x 28 cm.
Full score (of an aria?).
Not listed in Zavadini.   MR. CARL TOLLEFSEN

712. [La favorite. Z. 63]
    [644]p. 26½ x 35 cm.
Full score of the opera in 4 acts.
On p. 1, written across unused staves; *Prélude. La favorite.* Donizetti. 1840. Paris. Alphonse Royer. Gustave Vaez (Each signature an autograph).
Many corrections and deletions.
On p. 23, between *Prelude* and Act I: Drame en 4 actes, original de Donizetti, Paris 8 7bre 1840.
Text by E. Scribe, A. Royer and G. Vaez.
First performed December 2, 1840 at the Opéra in Paris.
      MRS. MARIE SALABERT

Donizetti, Gaetano—*continued*

713. [Otto mese in due ore. Z. 23]
　　　Nel vostro sen più vi ritrovo.
　　　[8]p. 27 x 39 cm.
　　Full score of an aria for soprano, apparently for insertion in the
　　opera, although not found in libretto or full score.

NEW YORK PUBLIC LIBRARY

714. Il pegno. Canzonetta. [Z. 455]
　　　[1]p. 22 x 28 cm.
　　Song with piano accpt.
　　First line: Questi capelli bruni.
　　At end: Dontti 1832.
　　This is presumably Zavadini 455 and perhaps identical with Z. 474,
　　listed under the first line.
　　Published as no. 9 of *Donizetti per camera.*
　　Former owner: Joseph Muller.　　NEW YORK PUBLIC LIBRARY

715. [Quale artir il cor t'accende]
　　　Duetto scritto espressamente per i sigri Clementino Cornesti e
　　　　Nicola Cartoni dell' amico Donizetti. 1822, 19 Xbre.
　　　1 leaf, [18]p. 21½ x 29 cm.
　　Duet with piano accpt.
　　Zavadini 455 is a duet with the same title and date substituting
　　Clementina Carnevali for Clementino Cornesti, but without
　　mention of the first line.　　MR. ARTURO TOSCANINI

716. [Quando verrà sul colle. Z. 472]
　　　Cantabile per tenore.
　　　fol. 43v-44r. 18 x 25½ cm.
　　In Demidov, Album of autographs.
　　Song with piano accpt., first line as above.
　　Published as no. 4 of *Donizetti per camera.*　　LIBRARY OF CONGRESS

717. [Spirito di Dio benefico]
　　　[2]p. 23½ x 33 cm.
　　Aria for bass with cembalo accpt., incomplete.
　　Not in Zavadini.　　LIBRARY OF CONGRESS

718. [Il tuo soave impero]
　　　Cavatina. Donizetti.
　　　[5]p. 22 x 28 cm.
　　Full score of an aria.
　　Not in Zavadini.　　MR. ARTURO TOSCANINI

Doppler, Albert Franz, 1821-1888

719. Liszt, Franz, 1811-1886.
　　　[Hungarian rhapsodies]
　　　6 vols. 33 x 26 cm.
　　Arranged for orchestra by Liszt and Doppler, in Doppler's auto-
　　graph, with changes and corrections in Liszt's hand.

Doppler, Albert Franz—*continued*

Full scores.
Four of the six rhapsodies are dated, from 1857 to 1860.
These correspond to nos. 14, 12, 6, 2, 5, 9 in the original piano series.
Former owner: Rafael Joseffy.   LIBRARY OF CONGRESS

Dowland, John, 1562-1626

720. [Collection of songs and dances for the lute by Dowland and others]
   136 leaves. 29 x 20 cm.
   Some leaves wanting at the beginning; 54 leaves blank.
   One page of the tablature is in Dowland's autograph, signed: Jo.
   Doulande, bacheler of musick. His autograph signature is at the
   end of 4 other compositions.   FOLGER SHAKESPEARE LIBRARY

Dragonetti, Domenico, 1763-1846

721. Duetto for contrabass & violoncello composed by Sig. Domenico
   Dragonetti.
   Parts (3, 3 p.). 30 x 23½ cm.   BOSTON PUBLIC LIBRARY

Dresden, Sem, 1881-

722. [Sonata, violin and piano]
   [29]p. 34 x 27½ cm.
   Score of slow movement (sehr langsam) only.
   At end: Berlin, 9 Juni, 1905.
   Unpublished.   DR. ARNOLD DRESDEN

Dressler, Friedrich August,

723. [Kriemhild]
   . . . Die Meer-Weiber-Scene für Solo, Declamation, und Frauenchor, aus dem Trauerspiel "Kriemhild" von Arnd-Kürenberg,
   componirt von Friedrich August Dressler, Op. 10, no. 2.
   Partitur.
   68 p. 33½ x 27 cm.
   Former owner: George Riddle.   BOSTON PUBLIC LIBRARY

724. [Macbeth]
   Scene Hecate. Hekate Scene, componirt für Tenor und Alt Solo,
   Männerchöre, gemischten Chor und Declamation mit Orches-
   ter Begleitung von Friedrich August Dressler. Partitur. Act
   III, Scene V.
   57 p. 34 x 26 cm.
   Contains also: End of Act II (piano-vocal score), Act IV, scene 1
   (piano-vocal score) and part for alto.
   German and English text.   BOSTON PUBLIC LIBRARY

725. [Macbeth. Overture]
   Shakespeare's Macbeth. Melodrama by Friedrich August Dressler.
   Op. 52. Berlin den 20 Dezember 1899.
   1 leaf, 56 p. 34 x 26 cm.
   Full score.   BOSTON PUBLIC LIBRARY

Drobisch, Karl Ludwig, 1803-1854

726. Ouverture für Orchester von K. L. Drobisch. 1825.
[71]p. 22½ x 17½ cm.
Full score.
At end: Fine. den 17. Nov. 1825.   NEW YORK PUBLIC LIBRARY

Dubois, (François Clément) Théodore, 1837-1924

727. Messe solennelle. Choeurs, soli et grand orchestre, par Th. Dubois.
2 leaves, 145 p. 28 x 37 cm.
Full score.
First title-page reads: *Messe pontificale, 1re version, inédite dans cette forme.*
Former owner: Adolphe Pérégally.
MEMORIAL LIBRARY OF MUSIC, STANFORD UNIVERSITY

Dukas, Paul, 1865-1935

728. [Composition for piano 2 hands]
[2] inside p. 18 x 26½ cm.
At end: Paul Dukas. Juin 1925.
Dedicated to S. Koussewitzky.
LIBRARY OF CONGRESS, KOUSSEVITZKY FOUNDATION

Dulcken, Ferdinand Quentin, 1837-1902

729. . . . Ungarische Fantasie über nationale Melodien für Pianoforte mit
Begleitung des Orchesters componirt von Ferdinand Q. Dulcken.
38 [i.e. 40]p. 34 x 26½ cm.
Arrangement for 2 pianos.
Former owner: Rafael Joseffy.   LIBRARY OF CONGRESS

Duncombe, W. D. V.

730. 'Come away, death.' Clown's song in 'Twelfth Night.' Music by
W. D. V. Duncombe.
[3]p. 35 x 27 cm.
Song with piano accpt.   FOLGER SHAKESPEARE LIBRARY

731. "Pardon, goddess of the night." Dirge from Shakespeare's "Much
ado about nothing." Music by W. D. V. Duncombe, M.A.
[3]p. 26 x 36½ cm.
For 4-part mixed chorus with piano accpt.
Dedicated to W. A. Barrett, April, 1882.
FOLGER SHAKESPEARE LIBRARY

Dupin, Paul, 1865-1949

732. Chant pour saxophone . . . poème de Emile Verhaeren, musique de
Paul Dupin, à ceux qui partent.
28 p. 35 x 26 cm.
Full score (solo saxophone, harps, violas and chorus).
Dedicated to Mrs. Elise Hall.
At end: Bruxelles, octobre 1910. Paul Dupin.
NEW ENGLAND CONSERVATORY OF MUSIC

Durante, Francesco, 1684-1755

733. Dixit [Dominus]
[55]p. 22 x 27 cm.
Full score (4-part chorus, oboe, violins and bass).
At head of title: *Dixit breve. Durante.*
Former owner: George B. Weston. HARVARD UNIVERSITY LIBRARY

734. Stabat Mater a tre voci con ripieni di Francesco Durante.
60 p. 22 x 28 cm.
For 2 sopranos and alto solo and 2-part women's chorus unaccompanied.
The first 8 p. are not in Durante's hand. The ms. lacks 8 p.
Former owner: Natale Gallini (catalogue, no. 7).
MEMORIAL LIBRARY OF MUSIC, STANFORD UNIVERSITY

Eberwein, Karl, 1786-1868

735. Gesang. Pianoforte.
[2]p. 19½ x 16½ cm.
First line: Nur einen Reichthum.
Part of a birthday letter written by Eberwein at Weimar, October 17, 1855. LIBRARY OF CONGRESS

Eckert, Carl (Anton Florian), 1820-1879

736. Des Müllers Abendlied. C. Eckert. Lieder. Op. 10.
[3]p. 13 x 17½ cm.
Song with piano accpt.
First line: Vom Himmel seh' ich blinken.
On title-page: Zum 11ten October 1836 von F. F[oerster] und C. E[ckert].
Published as no. 1 of op. 10 by A. M. Schlesinger in Berlin.
LIBRARY OF CONGRESS

Egidi, Epimaco

737. Redenta, opera in quattro atti di C. Teodorico Ponzani, musica del mro. Ep. Egidi.
[298]p. 21½ x 28 cm.
Piano-vocal score. LIBRARY OF CONGRESS

Eitner, Robert, 1832-1905

738. Judith, biblisches Drama nach dem alten Testament bearbeitet von Carl Schulze, componirt für Chor, Solo und Orchester von Robert Eitner. 1859.
2 vols. (vi, 135, 128 p.) 33½ x 26 cm.
Full score. LIBRARY OF CONGRESS

Elgar, *Sir* Edward (William), 1857-1934

739. [Salut d'amour. Op. 12]
Liebesgruss für Violine mit Begleitung Pianoforte [!]. Edward Elgar. Op. 6 [!] July 1888 . . .
[6]p. 35 x 26½ cm.

Elgar, *Sir* Edward (William)—*continued*

Reduction for violin and piano of the original version for orchestra. Published in 1900 by B. Schott's Söhne in Mainz. Facsimile of p. 1 in Van Patten, *Catalogue*, p. 86.

MEMORIAL LIBRARY OF MUSIC, STANFORD UNIVERSITY

740. [Variations on an original theme (Enigma). Op. 36]
To my friends pictured within. Variations for full orchestra composed by Edward Elgar. Op. 36. (Arranged for pianoforte solo). 47 p. 31 x 23½ cm.
Published (full score) in 1899 by Novello & Co. in London.
Former owner: George T. Keating.

MEMORIAL LIBRARY OF MUSIC, STANFORD UNIVERSITY

Ellerton, John Lodge, 1801-1873

741. The bridal of Triermain. Opera in 5 acts. Composed by J. L. Ellerton. 215 p. 24½ x 32 cm.
Piano-vocal score.   BOSTON PUBLIC LIBRARY

742. Carlo Rosa, opera semiseria in 3 atti, composta e ridotta per voce e cembalo da J. L. Ellerton. 1857.
[197]p. 24 x 31 cm.
Piano-vocal score, German text.
At end: J. L. E. Decr. 20, 1857.   BOSTON PUBLIC LIBRARY

743. Il marito a vista. Opera semiseria, le parole scritte dal sr. Maggioni, la musica di J. Lodge Ellerton.
[174]p. 23 x 28 cm.
Full score.   BOSTON PUBLIC LIBRARY

Enesco, Georges, 1881-

744. [Quartet, piano and strings, no. 2. Op. 30, D minor]
... 2d Quatuor pour piano, violon, alto et violoncelle (ré mineur). Georges Enesco. Op. 30.
Score ([2], 84 p.) and parts. 33½ x 27 cm.
At end: Georges Enesco. Sinaïa-Luminish, ce 4 mai 1944.
Dedicated to Gabriel Fauré.

LIBRARY OF CONGRESS, COOLIDGE FOUNDATION

745. ... Silence! ... Albert Samain (Au jardin de l'infante). Georges Enesco.
[5]p. 35½ x 26½ cm.
Song with piano accpt.
First line: Le silence descend en nous.
At end: Georges Enesco. Paris le 23 avril 1905.
Dedicated to Mlle. Victoire Péridé.
Former owners: Blanche Marchesi, George T. Keating.

MEMORIAL LIBRARY OF MUSIC, STANFORD UNIVERSITY

Erk, Ludwig (Christian), 1807-1883

746. Morgenwanderung. Ged. v. E. Geibel. Ludwig Erk. 27 Mai '79.
    [1]p. 13 x 31 cm.
    Song with piano accpt.
    First line: Wer hier im Fremden wandern will.
    Former owner: Joseph Muller.   NEW YORK PUBLIC LIBRARY

Erlanger, Camille, 1863-1919

747. Le bon gîte.
    [4]p. 40 x 30 cm.
    Song with piano accpt.
    Text by Paul Déroulède.
        MEMORIAL LIBRARY OF MUSIC, STANFORD UNIVERSITY

Ernst August Carl Johannes Leopold Alexander Eduard, Herzog von Sachsen-Coburg-Gotha, 1818-1893

748. [Diana von Solange]
    12, 268 p. 33½ x 26 cm.
    Full score of the opera in 5 acts.
    Text by O. Prechtler.
    First performed December 5, 1858, at Coburg.
        BOSTON PUBLIC LIBRARY

Ernst, Heinrich Wilhelm, 1814-1865

749. Valse non dansante.
    [2]p. 9 x 14 cm.
    For piano.
    On p. 2: . . . Hch. Ernst, Pesth, 31ten August 1845.
    Based almost entirely on the piano introduction to Schubert's song:
    Auf dem Wasser zu singen.   LIBRARY OF CONGRESS

Esser, Heinrich, 1818-1872

750. Abschied, von J. N. Vogl.
    [2]p. 27 x 34 cm.
    Song with piano accpt.
    First line: Ade du lieber Tannenwald.
    At end: Mainz den 24ten August 1842.
    Published ca. 1855 by B. Schott's Söhne in Mainz.
        LIBRARY OF CONGRESS

Fall, Leo, 1873-1925

751. [Brüderlein fein]
    65 p. 34½ x 26½ cm.
    Full score.   MR. ERNST SCHNEIDER

752. "Brüderlein fein." Ein altwiener Singspiel in einem Act von Julius
    Wilhelm. Musik von Leo Fall.
    36 p. 33 x 24 cm.
    Piano-vocal score.   MR. ERNST SCHNEIDER

Fall, Leo—*continued*

753. [Die Dollarprinzessin]
Dollarprinzessin. Clavierauszug mit Text. Leo Fall.
1 vol. 35 x 27 cm.
First performed November 2, 1907, in Vienna.

754. [Der fidele Bauer]
192 p. 34½ x 26½ cm.
Piano-vocal score (first and second drafts).
First performed July 27, 1907, in Mannheim.

755. [Die geschiedene Frau]
203 p. 39½ x 29 cm.
Full score.
Text by V. Leon.
First performed December 23, 1908, in Vienna.

756. [Die geschiedene Frau]
1 vol. 34½ x 26½ cm.
Piano-vocal score.

757. [Der goldene Vogel]
1 vol. 35 x 27 cm.
Sketches.
Text by Paul Frank and Julius Wilhelm.
First performed May 21, 1920, in Dresden.

758. Liebt sie ihn? Musik von Leo Fall.
64 p. 24 x 33 cm.
Sketches for an unfinished operetta.

759. [Lieder]
[35]p. 35 x 27 cm.
Songs with piano accpt.
Contents.—1. *Zigeunermusik* (M. della Gracie).—2. *Liebesge-schichte* (S. A. Weiss).—3. *Rosen* (S. A. Weiss).—4. *Meine Mutter, die braune Zigeunerin* (?).—5. *Sei nur ruhig, lieber Robin* (Robt. Hamerling).—6. *Am Canale Grande* (S. A. Weiss).—7. *Totengraeber Hochzeit* (Robt. Hamerling).—8. *Wal-deszauber* (S. A. Weiss).
Published in 1907 by Harmonie in Berlin.

760. Madame Pompadour. Operette in 3 Acten von Schanzer u. Welisch.
Musik von Leo Fall.
156 p. 32½ x 25 cm.
Piano-vocal score.
First performed September 9, 1922, in Berlin.

Fall, Leo—*continued*

761. [Der Rebell]
     1 vol. 34 x 27 cm.
     Full score.
     Text by Ernst Welisch and Rud. Bernauer.
     First performed November 29, 1905, in Vienna.
                                        MR. ERNST SCHNEIDER

762. [Die Rose von Stamboul]
     236 p. 39½ x 29 cm.
     Full score.
     Text by Jul. Brammer and Alfr. Grünwald.
     First performed December 2, 1916, in Vienna.
                                        MR. ERNST SCHNEIDER

763. [Die Rose von Stamboul]
     188 p. 34½ x 26½ cm.
     Piano-vocal score.   MR. ERNST SCHNEIDER

764. Tangoparodie.
     1 leaf, 12 p. 35 x 27 cm.
     Full score.   MR. ERNST SCHNEIDER

765. Tausend und ein Souper! Operette von Brammer u. Grünwald.
     Musik von Leo Fall.
     1 vol. 35 x 27 cm.
     Full score.   MR. ERNST SCHNEIDER

Faning, (Joseph) Eaton, 1850-1927

766. Daybreak. Eaton Faning.
     [11]p. 35 x 27 cm.
     Full score.   BOSTON PUBLIC LIBRARY

Farjeon, Harry, 1878-1948

767. Two free fugues for piano. Harry Farjeon.
     [10], 12 p. 30½ x 24 cm.
     Published in 1923 by Bosworth & Co. in London.
                                     LIBRARY OF CONGRESS

Farnaby, Giles, 1560-1640

768. The psalmes of David, to fower parts, for viols and voyce, the first
     book Dorick mottoes, the second, divine canzonets, composed by
     Giles Farnaby bachilar of musicke with a prelud, before the
     psalmes, cromaticke.
     [5], 136 p. 13½ x 18½ cm.
     Cantus part (melody) only of an unpublished collection of psalm
     harmonizations.
     Dedicated to Dr. Henry King.
     Former owner: Francis Hopkinson.
     The tunes are taken, with one exception, from Ravenscroft's
     Psalter of 1621.
     Autograph?   UNIVERSITY OF PENNSYLVANIA LIBRARY

Fauche, Mary

769. The Shepherd king, or the Conquest of Sidon. A pastoral and English opera by Mary Fauche. Op. 1. The words by Mrs. B. Wyatt. In the year 1823.
118 leaves. 28 x 33 cm.
Full score. BOSTON PUBLIC LIBRARY

Faulkes, William, 1863-1933

770. Six pieces for the organ composed by William Faulkes. Op. 128.
[3], 47 p. 30 x 24 cm.
Published in 1909 by Arthur P. Schmidt in Boston. LIBRARY OF CONGRESS

Fauré, Gabriel Urbain, 1845-1924

771. [Barcarolle, piano, no. 10. Op. 104, no. 2, A minor]
. . . 10ème Barcarolle op. ? Gabriel Fauré . . . octobre 1913.
1 leaf, 6 numbered leaves. 35½ x 27 cm.
Dedicated to Mme. Léon Blum.
Former owner: René Brancour.
Published in 1913 by A. Durand & fils in Paris. MR. GREGOR PIATIGORSKY

772. [Donc ce sera par un clair jour d'été]
[7]p. 35 x 27 cm.
Song with piano accpt.
Text by Paul Verlaine.
Published in 1892 as no. 7 of *La bonne chanson*, op. 61, by J. Hamelle in Paris. SIBLEY MUSICAL LIBRARY

773. [La lune blanche luit dans les bois]
[7]p. 35 x 27 cm.
Song with piano accpt.
Text by Paul Verlaine.
Published in 1891 as no. 3 of *La bonne chanson*, op. 61, by J. Hamelle in Paris. SIBLEY MUSICAL LIBRARY

774. [Nocturne, piano, no. 12. Op. 107, E minor]
12e Nocturne. Gabriel Fauré. (1916).
11 leaves. 35 x 27 cm.
Verso of leaves usually blank.
Published in 1916 by A. Durand & fils in Paris. MR. GREGOR PIATIGORSKY

775. Nocturne, poésie de Villiers de l'Isle Adam. Gabriel Fauré.
[7]p. 35 x 27 cm.
Song with piano accpt.
At end: 4 février 1892. Gabriel Fauré.
Published in 1886 [?] as no. 2 of op. 43 by J. Hamelle in Paris. LIBRARY OF CONGRESS

Fauré, Gabriel Urbain—*continued*

776. Préludes, no. 4. Gabriel Fauré, 1912 [F major]
6 leaves. 35 x 27 cm.
Music on recto only.
Published as no. 4 of op. 103, *Neuf préludes,* in 1910 by Heugel &
Cie. in Paris.   ISABELLA STEWART GARDNER MUSEUM

777. Prison, poésie de Paul Verlaine.
[8]p. 35 x 27 cm.
Song with piano accpt.
At end: 4 décembre 1894. Gabriel Fauré.
Published in 1900 as no. 1 of op. 83 by J. Hamelle in Paris.
                     LIBRARY OF CONGRESS

778. [Quintet, piano and strings, op. 115, C minor]
2ème quintette. Gabriel Fauré. Mars 1921.
[136]p. 34½ x 27 cm.
Score.
Published in 1921 by A. Durand & fils in Paris.
                     HARVARD UNIVERSITY LIBRARY

Fémy, [Ambroise ?], fl. 18th century

779. Scène à l'honneur de son altesse monseigneur le prince héréditaire
d'Orange . . . par Mr. Fémy. A Liège ce 25 février 1794.
1 leaf, [30]p. 29½ x 24 cm.
Full score (voice and orchestra).
At end: Finis ce 22 févr. 1794.   LIBRARY OF CONGRESS

Fenaroli, Fedele, 1730-1818

780. [Qui tollis]
17 p. 22½ x 30 cm.
Score for soprano, orchestra and organ.
Former owner: Natale Gallini (catalogue, no. 8).
                 MEMORIAL LIBRARY OF MUSIC, STANFORD UNIVERSITY

Fesca, Friedrich Ernst, 1789-1826

781. [Ha, nun ist mein Werk gelungen]
No. 14 Aria Atto III.
1 leaf, 16 p. 26 x 32 cm.
Full score of an aria from an unidentified opera.
Former owner: Joseph Muller.   NEW YORK PUBLIC LIBRARY

782. [Süss war die Liebe mir]
6, [2]p. 19 x 23½ cm.
Full score of a soprano aria from an unidentified opera.
                     YALE UNIVERSITY SCHOOL OF MUSIC

Fétis, François Joseph, 1784-1871

783. Concours de violin (1859).
[6]p. 36½ x 27½ cm.
Full score (violin and string orchestra).
Written for the Brussels Conservatory. 　　LIBRARY OF CONGRESS

Field, John, 1782-1837

784. Andante pour le pianoforte à quatre mains par John Field. Tiré de
la Gazette Musicale.
[3]p. 24 x 31½ cm.
Former owner: William H. Cummings (catalogue, no. 670).
　　　　　　　　　　　　　　　　　　　　　LIBRARY OF CONGRESS

785. Compositions for piano by John Field, written by his own hand.
[61]p. 26 x 34 cm.
Contents: p. 1. *Preludio,* C minor (unidentified). p. 2. *Rondeau,*
E flat major. (This is the solo part of the 3rd movement of his
Concerto no. 4 in E flat major). p. 13. [*Air écossais*], B flat major
(The 2nd movement of his Concerto no. 1 in E flat major.) p. 18.
Concerto (The 1st movement, allegro, of his Concerto no. 1).
p. 24. *Rondo* (The 3rd movement, allegro vivace, of his Concerto
no. 1). p. 31. *Poco adagio,* E flat major. (The 2nd movement of
his Concerto no. 2 in A flat major). p. 34. *Rondo.* (The 2nd
movement, moderato innocente, of his Concerto no. 2). p. 48.
Adagio (the 2nd movement of his Concerto no. 5 in C major),
followed on same page by *Allegro* [*Rondo*] (the 3rd movement
of the same concerto). p. 59. *Serenade,* B flat major. (This is
the first draft, with corrections and numerous variations from the
published version, of his famous Nocturne no. 5).
　　　　　　　　　　　　　　　　　　　　　LIBRARY OF CONGRESS

786. Duets.
[71]p. 31 x 23 cm.
A collection of arrangements of contemporary songs and instrumental music for piano 4 hands; also melodies with text but
without accpt., in other hands. It may include some original
4-hand compositions by the very young composer.
On fly-leaf, probably in the autograph of the father, John Field,
junr. 1789.
Former owner: Joseph Muller. 　　NEW YORK PUBLIC LIBRARY

787. [Nocturne, piano, no. 5, B flat major]
Nocturne.
[3]p. 21 x 28½ cm.
Van Patten, *Catalogue,* no. 323, incorrectly gives the sub-title:
Incendie par l'orage, which belongs to his Concerto no. 5 for
piano.
Former owners: Robert Muller, Prince Dolgorouki, Arthur F. Hill.
　　　　　MEMORIAL LIBRARY OF MUSIC, STANFORD UNIVERSITY

Field, John—*continued*

788. [Nocturne, piano, no. 5, B flat major]
      [13]p. 34 x 25 cm.
      Arrangement for piano and orchestra, the orchestral accpt., incomplete, in Field's hand, the original piano composition in another hand.
      Former owner: Hugo Riesenfeld.   NEW YORK PUBLIC LIBRARY

Fischer, Anton Joseph, fl. 18th century

789. Duettini di camera. Soprano e basso . . . Antonio Giuseppe Fischer.
      1 leaf, [52]p. 25 x 22 cm.
      Duets for soprano and bass with piano accpt.   LIBRARY OF CONGRESS

Fitelberg, Jerzy, 1903-1951

790. [Quartet, strings, no. 4]
      . . . Tema con variazioni.
      Score (1 leaf, 62 p.) and parts. 35 x 27 cm.
      Awarded the Elizabeth Sprague Coolidge prize, 1936.
                            LIBRARY OF CONGRESS, COOLIDGE FOUNDATION

Fitzwilliam, Edward Francis, 1824-1857

791. [The Queen of a day]
      [188]p. 23 x 29 cm.
      Full score of the opera.
      Caption title: *Our young queen.*
      First performed August 13, 1851, at the Haymarket Theatre,
      London.   BOSTON PUBLIC LIBRARY

Flies, Bernhard, 1768-1840

792. Wiegenlied von Gotter in Musik gesetzt von Flies.
      [1]p. 23½ x 33 cm.
      Song with piano accpt.
      First line: Schlafe mein Prinzchen, es ruhn.
      Published ca. 1795 by Böheim in Berlin.
      Long attributed to Mozart (K. 350) and published in his Werke, series VII, no. 12.
      Former owner: Max Friedländer.
                            MEMORIAL LIBRARY OF MUSIC, STANFORD UNIVERSITY

Florimo, Francesco, 1800-1888

793. [Notte amica]
      [4]p. 39 x 28 cm.
      Song with piano accpt., first line as above.
      Former owner: Natale Gallini (catalogue, no. 41).
                            MEMORIAL LIBRARY OF MUSIC, STANFORD UNIVERSITY

Flotow, Friedrich, Freiherr von, 1812-1883

794. Martha. Text nach St. G. von W. Friedrich, componirt im Jahre 1847 in Wien, Teuchendorf u. Wutzig, gegeben in Wien zum ersten Male 27 Nov. 1847 . . . F. von Flotow.
   4 vols. (258, 140, 119, 118 p.) 33 x 26 cm.
   Full score.
   First performed Nov. 25, 1847 in Vienna.
   Facsimile of p. 1 in Van Patten, *Catalogue,* p. 79.
   MEMORIAL LIBRARY OF MUSIC, STANFORD UNIVERSITY

795. Naïda (auf französisch Le vannier), Oper in drei Akten, Text von H. de St. Georges et Léon Halévy, deutsch von Franz Dingelstedt, Musik von Friedrich von Flotow . . .
   1 leaf, 621 p. 32 x 25 cm.
   Full score, German and Italian text.
   On title-page: Deutsche Original-Partitur von mir selbst geschrieben, beendet im Jahre 1864 in Wien. Fr. von Flotow.
   Unpublished.
   First performed December 11, 1865 in St. Petersburg.
   LIBRARY OF CONGRESS

Franck, César (Auguste), 1822-1890

796. L'ange gardien.
   [3]p. 35½ x 27 cm.
   2-part chorus with piano accpt.
   Author of text unknown.
   First line: Veillez sur moi quand je m'éveille.
   Published ca. 1886 by Enoch frères et Costallat in Paris.
   MEMORIAL LIBRARY OF MUSIC, STANFORD UNIVERSITY

797. Fugues vocales.
   309 p. 34½ x 26 cm.
   Fugues in 2 to 8 parts (without text).
   Many fugues are dated, and the source of the subject is given.
   Apparently written during his studies at the Paris Conservatory.
   BOSTON PUBLIC LIBRARY

798. Bizet, Georges, 1838-1875.
   [L'Arlésienne]
   Intermezzo (entr'acte); transcription pour piano et orgue. Transcription de l'Arlésienne de G. Bizet par C. F.
   [4]p. 35 x 26 cm.
   UNIVERSITY OF CALIFORNIA AT LOS ANGELES,
   WILLIAM ANDREWS CLARK MEMORIAL LIBRARY

799. Nocturne. Poésie de L. de Fourcaud.
   [2]p. 35 x 27 cm.
   Song with piano accpt.
   First line: O fraîche nuit, nuit transparente.
   Published in 1885 in the *Album du Gaulois.*   MR. ALEXANDER GINN

Franck, César (Auguste)—*continued*

800. Panis angélicus, solo de ténor ou soprano avec accompagnement
d'orgue, de harpe, violon ou violoncello. Musique de César
Franck. . . .
Score (4 p.) and parts. 35½ x 27½ cm.
First performance noted on cover: March 30, 1879.
Former owners: Eugénie Chauvot, Alexandre Georges.

801. Le sylphe. Paroles d'Alexandre Dumas, musique de C. Franck.
[2]p. 35½ x 26½ cm.
Song with piano and violoncello accpt.
First line: Je suis un sylphe, une ombre, un rien.
Published ca. 1843 by Richault in Paris.
Former owner: George T. Keating.

Franco, Johan, 1908-

802. Serenade concertante per pianoforte e orch. (da camera). Johan
Franco (1938).
49 p. 34½ x 26 cm.
Full score.
At end: A' Veen, 27 Juli 1938.
Dedicated to Mrs. E. S. Coolidge.

Franz, Robert, 1815-1892

803. [Am Strom]
No. 3. Am Strome. Robert Franz.
[4]p. 27 x 32 cm.
Song with piano accpt.
Text by Eichendorff.
First line: Der Strom glitt einsam hin.
Published 1857 as no. 3 of op. 30, *Sechs Gesänge,* by Fr. Kistner
in Leipzig.
Former owner: George T. Keating.

804. Auf dem Meere v. H. Heine.
p. 4 of his *O säh ich auf das Heide dort.*
Song with piano accpt.
First line: Aus der Himmelsaugen droben.
Published ca. 1845 as no. 3 of op. 5, *Zwölf Gesänge,* by C. F. W.
Siegel in Leipzig.
Former owners: Frau Lisbeth Bethge; Pauline Woltmann.

Franz, Robert—*continued*

805. Es klingt in der Luft.
     [3]p. 26½ x 33½ cm.
     Song with piano accpt.
     Text by Max Waldau, first line as above.
     Published ca. 1850 as no. 2 of op. 13, *Sechs Dichtungen von Max Waldau,* by F. Whistling in Leipzig.   LIBRARY OF CONGRESS

806. Sechs Gesänge für eine Singstimme mit Begleitung des Pianoforte componirt von Robert Franz. Op. 44.
     [24]p. 27 x 34 cm.
     Published ca. 1868 by Fr. Kistner in Leipzig.
     Former owner: Joseph Muller.   NEW YORK PUBLIC LIBRARY

807. Liebchen ist da . . .
     [2]p. 24 x 31 cm.
     Song with piano accpt.
     Text by J. Schröer.
     First line: Blümlein im Garten, schaut euch doch um.
     Published ca. 1845 as no. 2 of op. 5, *Zwölf Gesänge,* by C. F. W. Siegel in Leipzig.   NEW ENGLAND CONSERVATORY OF MUSIC

808. [O säh ich auf das Heide dort]
     [4]p. 24½ x 31 cm.
     Song with piano accpt.
     Text by Robert Burns (O wert thou in the cauld blast).
     Published ca. 1845 as no. 5 of op. 1, *Zwölf Gesänge,* by F. Whistling in Leipzig.
     On p. 4: *Auf dem Meere v. H. Heine.*
     Former owners: Frau Lisbeth Bethge, Pauline Woltmann.
                        NEW ENGLAND CONSERVATORY OF MUSIC

809. So weit von hier! . . . Rob. Franz. 28 Aug. 54.
     [4]p. 27 x 34 cm.
     Song with piano accpt.
     Text by Robert Burns.
     Published 1855 as no. 6 of op. 22, *Sechs Gesänge,* by B. Senff in Leipzig.   HARVARD UNIVERSITY, ISHAM MEMORIAL LIBRARY

810. [Umsonst]
     [2]p. 17½ x 26 cm.
     Song with piano accpt.
     Text by W. Osterwald.
     First line: Des Waldes Sänger singen.
     Published ca. 1848 as no. 6 of op. 10, *Sechs Gesänge,* by F. Whistling in Leipzig.
     Former owner: Mrs. Benjamin Harrison.   LIBRARY OF CONGRESS

Franz, Robert—*continued*

811. [Verwittert und geborsten]
       [3]p. 26½ x 34 cm.
     Song with piano accpt.
     Apparently unpublished.
                        HARVARD UNIVERSITY, ISHAM MEMORIAL LIBRARY

812. Wenn ich auf dem Lager liege. Robert Franz.
       [3]p. 27 x 34½ cm.
     Song with piano accpt.
     Text by Heine.
     Published in the *Album für Musik* in 1857 by Payne in Leipzig,
         then as no. 6 of op. 37, *Sechs Gesänge,* in 1866 by Fr. Kistner
         in Leipzig.
     Former owner: Joseph Muller.   NEW YORK PUBLIC LIBRARY

813. [Widmung]
       [2]p. 27 x 34 cm.
     Song with piano accpt.
     Text by Wolfgang Müller.
     First line: O danke nicht für diese Lieder.
     Published ca. 1850 as no. 1 of op. 14, *Sechs Gesänge,* by Fr. Kistner
         in Leipzig.
     Former owner: Max Friedländer.   MR. FRANZ ROEHN

814. Will über Nacht wohl durch das Thal, v. W. Osterwald.
       [3]p. 23½ x 32 cm.
     Song with piano accpt., first line as above.
     At end: 15/6/45.
     Published ca. 1845 as no. 4 of op. 5, *Zwölf Gesänge,* by C. F. W.
         Siegel in Leipzig.   LIBRARY OF CONGRESS

     Frederick II (the great), king of Prussia, 1712-1786
815. [Sonata, flute and harpsichord, no. 4. B flat major]
       Solo per il flauto di Federico.
       [4]p. 36 x 22 cm.
     Score of incomplete *Cantabile* and of complete *Allegro* and *Presto.*
     Werke, vol. I, no. 4.
     Former owners: Alois Fuchs, Wilhelm Heyer (catalogue, vol. IV,
         p. 110-113), Dayton C. Miller.   LIBRARY OF CONGRESS

     Frischenschlager, Friedrich Friedwig, 1885-
816. . . . Konzertante Musik für Klavier und Kammerorchester von Fried-
         rich Frischenschlager. Op. 51. Graz, am 20. Oktober 1931.
       1 leaf, 61 p. 33 x 25½ cm.
     Full score.
     Dedicated to Mrs. E. S. Coolidge.
                        LIBRARY OF CONGRESS, COOLIDGE FOUNDATION

Fromm, Carl Joseph, 1873-1923

817. Die Praterfee; Wiener Lebensbild mit Gesang u. Tanz von Aug.
Neidhardt. Musik von Carl. Jos. Fromm. Partitur.
86 p. 35 x 27 cm.
Full score.
At end: Carl Jos. Fromm . . . 20/7/1904.   LIBRARY OF CONGRESS

Fuchs, Robert, 1847-1927

818. Serenade (nr. 5, D dur). Robert Fuchs, op. 53.
[95]p. 34 x 26 cm.
Full score.
At end: Wien, den 21. September, 94. Rob. Fuchs.
Published in 1894 by C. Hofbauer in Leipzig.
Former owner: George Fischer.   LIBRARY OF CONGRESS

Gade, Niels Wilhelm, 1817-1890

819. Allegro grazioso. Niels W. Gade.
[1]p. 25 x 33½ cm.
For piano 2 hands.
At end: Novbr. 49.   LIBRARY OF CONGRESS

Galliard, Johann Ernst, 1678-1749

820. The four chorus's in the tragedy of Julius Caesar. Written by his
grace John Sheffield, late duke of Buckinghamshire &c, set to
musick by J. E. Galliard.
310 p. 29½ x 22½ cm.
Full score.
Note on fly-leaf by Katherine, duchess of Buckingham, signed K.B.
August 1723.   BOSTON PUBLIC LIBRARY

Galuppi, Baldassare, 1706-1785

821. Salmo "Qui habitare" a voce sola, e coro a 4 con stromenti.
[24]p. 23½ x 32½ cm.
Full score.
First voice (alto) is designated "Serafina" and 2nd voice (tenor)
"Orsosa."
Presumably performed at the Ospedale dei Mendicanti in Venice,
where the composer was maestro di musica and Serafina Meller
a soloist.
Former owners: Domenico Dragonetti, Vincent Novello.

LIBRARY OF CONGRESS

Garcin, Jules Auguste, 1830-1896

822. Concertino pour alto. Op. 19. Partition.
74 p. 35½ x 26 cm.
Full score (viola and orchestra).
Published ca. 1870 by Lemoine & Cie. in Paris (viola and piano).

BOSTON PUBLIC LIBRARY

823. Fantaisie pour violon et clarinette sur les motifs de La somnabule.
 Op. 12.
 [52]p. 35 x 26 cm.
 Full score (violin, clarinet and orchestra).   BOSTON PUBLIC LIBRARY

824. Fantaisie sur le Freischütz. Op. 15.
 [56]p. 35 x 26 cm.
 Full score (violin and orchestra).   BOSTON PUBLIC LIBRARY

825. Les noces de Prométhée (Cantate).
 [68]p. 35½ x 26 cm.
 Full score.
 At end: 4 juin 67.   BOSTON PUBLIC LIBRARY

826. Valse brillante pour violon. Op. 13.
 [55]p. 35½ x 26 cm.
 Full score (violin and orchestra).   BOSTON PUBLIC LIBRARY

Generali, Pietro, 1782-1832

827. Lo sposo in bersaglio, burletta in due atti.
 42 p. 21 x 28 cm.
 Full score of the overture.
 At end: Originale di Pietro Generali, Firenze nell' autunno del 1808.
 Former owner: Natale Gallini (catalogue, no. 28).
 MEMORIAL LIBRARY OF MUSIC, STANFORD UNIVERSITY

Gericke, Wilhelm, 1845-1925

828. . . . Romanza for violin and piano accompaniment by Wilhelm
 Gericke (1866) orchestrated by request for a privat [!] concert
 in Beacon Street 152.
 1, 8 numbered leaves. 37½ x 28 cm.
 Full score.   ISABELLA STEWART GARDNER MUSEUM

829. Brahms, Johannes, 1833-1897.
 [Walzer, op. 39]
 . . . Waltzes by Johannes Brahms, orchestrated by request for a
 privat [!] concert in Beacon Street 152 (by Wilhelm Gericke).
 1, 16 numbered leaves. 37½ x 28 cm.
 Full score.   ISABELLA STEWART GARDNER MUSEUM

Ghys, Joseph, 1801-1848

830. Variations brillantes et concertantes pour violon et violoncelle (sur
 l'air de God save the King) . . . par J. Ghys et Servais . . . Op. 38.
 [14]p. 29½ x 23½ cm.
 Caption title: *Duo concertant* . . .
 At head of title: Londres 1835, Petersburg 1842.
 Violin part in the autograph of Ghys; violoncello part in autograph
 of A. F. Servais.
 Former owner: Joseph Muller.   NEW YORK PUBLIC LIBRARY

Giardini, Felice di, 1716-1796

831. Sei duetti . . .
    20 p. 29 x 22 cm.
    Contains 5 vocal duets with bass and 6 unaccompanied terzetts, the latter unknown to Eitner.
    Dedicated to the marchioness of Rockingham.
    Former owner: Joseph Muller.   NEW YORK PUBLIC LIBRARY

Gibbs, Cecil Armstrong, 1889-

832. Cradle song.
    [2]p. 30 x 24 cm.
    For 4-part male chorus unaccompanied [?]
    Text by William Blake.
    First line: Sleep, sleep, beauty bright.
    Published in 1935 by Boosey and Hawkes in London.
    MEMORIAL LIBRARY OF MUSIC, STANFORD UNIVERSITY

Glazunov, Aleksandr Konstantinovich, 1865-1936

833. [Concerto, violin, op. 82, A minor]
    Concerto.
    45 p. 26½ x 38 cm.
    Composer's reduction for violin and piano.
    Published in this version in 1905 by M. P. Belaieff in Leipzig.
    Former owner: Serge Korgaeff.   DARTMOUTH COLLEGE LIBRARY

834. Preludio e fuga. Alexandre Glazounow . . .
    23 p. 33 x 26½ cm.
    For piano 2 hands.
    Dedicated to Leonid Nicolaiev.
    At end: 31 iiulia 1926, Gatchina. Okonchatel'no pererabotano 17 avgusta 1929g., Antib, A. Glazunov.
    Published in 1930 by G. Schirmer in New York.
    LIBRARY OF CONGRESS

835. [Symphony, no. 7, op. 77, F major]
    7-aia simfoniia—F dur—podrobnyu eskiz.
    1 leaf, [52]p. 26 x 34 cm.
    Reduction for piano solo (incomplete).
    Published (full score) in 1902 by M. Belaieff in Leipzig.
    Former owner: A. S. Taneiev.   WALTER R. BENJAMIN

Glinka, Mikhail Ivanovich, 1804-1857

836. [Chao-kang. Ballet]
    7 p. 22½ x 32 cm.
    Piano reduction of two variations.
    MEMORIAL LIBRARY OF MUSIC, STANFORD UNIVERSITY

Gluck, Christoph Willibald, Ritter von, 1714-1787

837. [Aristeo]
Primo coro nel Aristeo che ancora si balla.
fol. 27-30. 22 x 30 cm.
Full score of the 1st chorus of the one-act opera written as part of *Le feste d'Apollo,* for the wedding of the Infante Don Ferdinando to Maria Amalia at the court of Parma in 1769.
Text by C. I. Frugoni.
Former owner: Alois Fuchs.　　　THE ROSENBACH COMPANY

838. [Orphée et Euridice]
[2]p. 29 x 21½ cm.
Fragment of full score of no. 43, Orphée's aria: J'ai perdu mon Euridice.
Fragment begins: [ton époux fi]dèle, entends ma voix.
Facsimile in Van Patten, *Catalogue,* p. 92.
Former owner: George T. Keating.
　　　MEMORIAL LIBRARY OF MUSIC, STANFORD UNIVERSITY

Godard, Benjamin, 1849-1895

839. . . . Chant et baiser. Karl Simrock, traduit par N. Martin. Voix et piano. Benjamin Godard. 1871.
[4]p. 34½ x 26½ cm.
First line: Si pour te prouver ma tendresse.
Former owner: Arthur Hartmann.　　　SIBLEY MUSICAL LIBRARY

840. Trois fragments poétiques pour piano par Benjamin Godard . . .
[7]p. 35 x 27½ cm.
Contents: No. 1, *Depuis l'heure charmante* (Lamartine). No. 3, *Elle est jeune et rieuse* (Victor Hugo).
These pieces also exist for orchestra.
Published in 1906 by Heugel & Cie. in Paris.
　　　MEMORIAL LIBRARY OF MUSIC, STANFORD UNIVERSITY

Goldmark, Karl, 1830-1915

841. Die beiden Gemperlein. Meiner lieben Minna zu ihrem Geburtstag von Grossi. Gmunden 2ten Juli 1899.
7 leaves. 21½ x 29 cm.
Song with piano accpt.
First line: Dieses Bildnis wunderschön.　　　MR. RUDOLF F. KALLIR

842. [Die Königin von Saba. Op. 27]
[91]p. 33½ x 26½ cm. and [41]p. 25½ x 33 cm.
Sketches for the opera, both in score and piano reduction.
　　　MEMORIAL LIBRARY OF MUSIC, STANFORD UNIVERSITY

843. [Quintet, piano and strings, op. 54, C major]
Clavier-Quintett von Carl Goldmark. Op. 54.
1 leaf, [81]p. 33 x 26 cm.
Score.

Goldmark, Karl—*continued*

Signed and dated at the end of each movement, as follows: I. Gmunden 22/9/914 Carl Goldmark. II. 26/7/914 Gmunden C. Goldmark. III. Gmunden 8/10/914 C. Goldmark. IV. Wien 16/11/914 C. Goldmark.

Unpublished and unknown to most reference works.

GALERIE ST. ETIENNE

844. [Suite, violin and piano, no. 2, op. 43, E flat major]
8 numbered leaves. 33 x 25½ cm.
Score of 4th movement and excerpt from 2nd movement.
On fol. 7: 28 November 1892, Gmunden.
Published in 1893 by N. Simrock in Berlin. LIBRARY OF CONGRESS

Goossens, Eugene, 1893-

845. The Constant nymph. MS of some incidental music to "The Constant nymph." Written on "S. S. Carmania" in July 1926.
[19]p. 32 x 24 cm.
Songs with piano accpt.
For a dramatization of the novel by Margaret Kennedy.

SIBLEY MUSICAL LIBRARY

846. Judith, an opera in one act. Music by Eugene Goossens. Libretto by Arnold Bennett. Founded on the Apocryphal book of Judith. Original manuscript.
1 leaf, 131, 5 p. 36 x 23 cm.
Piano-vocal score.
First performed June 25, 1929 at Covent Garden Theatre in London.

SIBLEY MUSICAL LIBRARY

847. Quartet, no. 2 for strings, op. 59.
37 leaves. 35 x 27 cm.
Score.
Dedicated to Mrs. E. S. Coolidge.

LIBRARY OF CONGRESS, COOLIDGE FOUNDATION

848. Phantasy sextet (in one movement) for 3 violins, 1 viola, 2 celli . . . composed by Eugene Goossens in 1923.
1 leaf, 30 p. 36½ x 26½ cm.
Score.
At end: Eugène Goossens. Re-written, re-vised, and finished. Le Chateau Antibes. Alpes Maritimes August 1923.
Commissioned by Mrs. E. S. Coolidge for the Berkshire Music Festival in 1923. LIBRARY OF CONGRESS, COOLIDGE FOUNDATION

Gounod, Charles François, 1818-1893

849. "Adam could find no solid peace," a part song by Charles Gounod.
[1], 14 p. 27 x 20 cm.
At end: Ch. Gounod, London, 15 9ber 72.
Published by A. Weekes and Co. in London.

850. [Domine salvum fac. C major]
[3]p. 13 x 22½ cm.
For tenor and bass with organ accpt.

851. D'un coeur qui l'aime, mon Dieu! Fragment d'Athalie. (Double
choeur à 8 voix, sans accomp.'ts . . . 15 janvier 1851.
16 p. 24 x 30½ cm.
Text by Jean Racine.

852. Faust (opéra en cinq actes). Ch. Gounod. Choeur des soldats
(arrangé à 4 voix d'hommes par l'auteur).
[6]p. 18½ x 26½ cm.
Facsimile of p. 1 in Van Patten, *Catalogue*, p. 100.

853. Jésus de Nazareth. Chant évangélique pour baryton solo et choeurs.
1 leaf, [22]p. 35½ x 26 cm.
Full score (solo, chorus and orchestra, 1864) of the solo song written in Rome, 1840-43.
Text by A. Porte.

854. Magnificat for soprano solo, chorus & organ. Composed for his friend
E. Silas by Ch. Gounod May 1874.
3 leaves. 23½ x 30½ cm.
Parts for soprano, tenor and bass.

855. [Mass, no. 2, G major]
. . . Deuxième messe pour les sociétés chorales à 4 voix d'hommes,
avec accompagnement d'orgue (ad libitum). Ch. Gounod . . .
8 août 1862.
93 p. 15 x 22½ cm.

856. O that we two [were maying].
[7]p. 17½ x 27 cm.
Pencil sketch of a song with piano accpt.
Text by Charles Kingsley.
Former owner: Hans D. Gaebler.

857. Près du fleuve étranger &c . . . (Paroles de A. Quètelart). Para-
phrase du psaume "Super flumina Babylonis, &c." Choeur avec
orchestre, composé par Charles Gounod.
32 p. 35 x 26 cm.
Full score.
Published by Le Beau in Paris.

Gounod, Charles François—*continued*

858. [Sérénade de Marie Tudor]
    Sérénade avec accompagnement d'orchestre par Charles Gounod.
    [16]p. 35 x 26 cm.
    Full score.
    Text by Victor Hugo.
    First line: Quand tu chantes bercée le soir.
                                    THE PIERPONT MORGAN LIBRARY

859. La Toussaint.
    [3]p. 30 x 22½ cm.
    Song with piano accpt.
                    MEMORIAL LIBRARY OF MUSIC, STANFORD UNIVERSITY

Granados y Campina, Enrique, 1868-1916

860. Goyesca [!], literas y calesas ò Los majos enamorados, drama lirico
    en 1 acto y 3 cuadros. Letra, F. Periquet. Musica, E. Granados.
    Reduccion piano y canto. E.G.
    2 leaves, [159]p. 34½ x 25 cm.
    Piano-vocal score.
    Dated: Barcelona, May 28, 1914.
    First performed January 28, 1916 at the Metropolitan Opera House
    in New York.   HISPANIC SOCIETY OF AMERICA

861. [Goyescas. Intermezzo]
    20 p. 34 x 27 cm.
    Full score, with composer's corrections.
                            THE ERNEST SCHELLING COLLECTION

Grazioli, Filippo, 1773-1840

862. Maria Stuarda, opera inedita in due atti (divisa in 3 parti) del
    maestro Filippo Grazioli fatta l'anno 1828. Partitura originale.
    3 vols. (176, 198, 278 p.). 33 x 39½ cm.   LIBRARY OF CONGRESS

863. Il pellegrino bianco. Opera semiseria in due atti (divisa in tre parti)
    del maestro Filippo Grazioli, rappresentata in Firenze nel Teatro
    del Cocomero nel Carnevale del anno 1821 . . . Partitura
    originale.
    3 vols. 33 x 39½ cm.   LIBRARY OF CONGRESS

Grechanīnov, Aleksandr Tīkhonovich, 1864-

864. Dva puti. Hymne.
    [4]p. 35 x 27 cm.
    For 4-part mixed chorus and piano.
    Published as *The Lord is my light* (words adapted from Psalm
    XXVII) by G. Schirmer in New York.   G. SCHIRMER

Grechanīnov, Aleksandr Tīkhonovich—*continued*

865. [The Lord's Prayer. No. 2 in A flat. Op. 107, no. 3]
The Lord's Prayer. For soprano and mixed choir.
[3]p. 35 x 26½ cm.
Score, title and text in English and Russian.
Published in 1932 by G. Schirmer in New York.   G. SCHIRMER

866. . . . Op. 142. Missa oecumenica pour 4 voix soli, choeur, orchestre
et orgue . . .
[1], 148 p. 40 x 28½ cm.
Full score.
Dedicated to Natalie K. Koussevitzky.
LIBRARY OF CONGRESS, KOUSSEVITZKY FOUNDATION

867. . . . Op. 142. Missa oecumenica pour 4 voix soli, choeur, orchestre
et orgue.
[1], 75 p. 34 x 25 cm.
Piano-vocal score.
At end: Paris 1935.
LIBRARY OF CONGRESS, KOUSSEVITZKY FOUNDATION

868. Op. 114. 5 piesen na slova M. Lermontova.
[20]p. 35 x 27 cm.
Songs with piano accpt.
Published in 1931 by G. Schirmer in New York.   G. SCHIRMER

869. Na nivy zheltye. Slova gr. A. Tolstogo. Muzyka A. Grechaninova.
1 leaf, [4]p. 38½ x 25½ cm.
Song with piano accpt.
Published as no. 11 of his *Romanzen* by A. Gutheil in Moscow.
Text by A. Tolstoi.
MEMORIAL LIBRARY OF MUSIC, STANFORD UNIVERSITY

Greene, Maurice, 1696-1755
870. Te Deum in D composed for voices and orchestra by Dr. Maurice
Greene.
[144]p. 24½ x 18½ cm.
Full score.
Composed in 1745.
Former owner: William H. Cummings (catalogue, no. 757).
LIBRARY OF CONGRESS

Grell, Eduard August, 1800-1886
871. Chorāle vierstimmig ausgesetzt von E. A. Grell. Berlin am 13ten
September 1808.
[65]p. 23 x 30 cm.
Former owner: Joseph Muller.   NEW YORK PUBLIC LIBRARY

872. Den blonde Pige (Björnson). Edvard Grieg.
[4]p. 33 x 25 cm.
Song with piano accpt.
First line: Jeg elsker dig, du blonde Pige.
Published as no. 1 of his *Fünf [nachgelassene] Lieder* by C. F.
Peters in Leipzig.   MR. STORM BULL

873. . . . Zwei elegische Melodien nach Gedichten v. A. O. Vinje für
Streichorchester componirt von Edvard Grieg. Op. 34. Klavier-
auszug zu 2 Händen vom Componisten.
1 leaf, 6 p. 34 x 26 cm.
At end: 9/3/87.
The songs are *Herzewunden* and *Letzter Frühling*, nos. 3 and 2
of his op. 33.
Published ca. 1887 by C. F. Peters in Leipzig.
MEMORIAL LIBRARY OF MUSIC, STANFORD UNIVERSITY

874. I liden højt deroppe. (Jonas Lie). Edvard Grieg.
[2]p. 34½ x 26 cm.
Song with piano accpt.
Published as no. 3 of op. 39, *Fünf Lieder*, by C. F. Peters in Leipzig.
LIBRARY OF CONGRESS

875. Vandring i Skoven.
[2]p. 26½ x 20½ cm.
Song with piano accpt.
Text by Hans Christian Andersen.
First line: Min søde Brud, min unge Viv.
Published as no. 1 of op. 18, *Acht Lieder*, by C. F. Peters in Leipzig.
Former owner: H. Oskar Arnoldsen.
At end: Edvard Grieg 13/2/73.
UNIVERSITY OF CALIFORNIA AT LOS ANGELES,
WILLIAM ANDREWS CLARK MEMORIAL LIBRARY

Gruber, Josef, 1855-1933

876. Immakulata-Messe. Jos. Gruber. Op. 173.
[17]p. 25½ x 32 cm.
For 4-part male chorus and organ.
Published ca. 1905 by J. Fischer & Bro. in New York.
LIBRARY OF CONGRESS

877. XX Offertoria Commune Sanctorum für vier Männerstimmen componirt von Josef Gruber. Op. 161.
[22]p. 32 x 25 cm.
Published in 1905 by J. Fischer & Bro. in New York.
LIBRARY OF CONGRESS

Gruber, Josef—*continued*

378. Vier Tantum ergo für vier Frauenstimmen oder Knabenstimmen componirt von Josef Gruber, op. 183a.
[5]p. 25 x 32 cm.
Published in 1906 by J. Fischer & Bro. in New York.

379. Vier Tantum ergo für vier Männerstimmen componirt von Josef Gruber, op. 183b.
[5]p. 24 x 32 cm.
Published in 1906 by J. Fischer & Bro. in New York.

Grüters, August, 1841-1911

380. "Feenmärchen." Concertstück für Orchester von Aug. Gruters.
55 p. 35½ x 26 cm.
Full score.
At head of title: *Une*[!] *conte de fée, grand morceau d'orchestre* . . .
At end: Croyes, le 2 mai 1867.

Guhr, Karl Wilhelm Ferdinand, 1787-1848

381. [Concerto, violin, F minor]
[81]p. 23 x 31 cm.
Full score.

Guilmant, Félix Alexandre, 1837-1911

382. Deux pièces pour orgue par Alexandre Guilmant. (Op. 82).
7 p. 35 x 27 cm.
At end: Alex. Guilmant. Octobre 1893.

Gumbert, Ferdinand, 1818-1896

383. Das theure Vaterhaus. Lied componirt von Ferd. Gumbert.
[3]p. 24 x 32½ cm.
Song with piano accpt.
First line: Ich weiss mir etwas Liebes.
Former owner: The Royal Collection, Lisbon.
Published as op. 9 ca. 1845 by A. M. Schlesinger in Berlin.

Gyrowetz, Adalbert, 1763-1850

384. [Mass, C major]
[48]p. 25 x 33 cm.
Score (4-part male chorus and figured bass).
At end: Gyrowetz, den 21ten May, 1841.

Habert, Fanny

885. La fille de Jaïre.
   125 p. 35½ x 26½ cm.
   Full score of the scène lyrique (solo voices, chorus and orchestra),
   with piano reduction underneath.
   Submitted in the Concours Rossini, 1878-79.

Hahn, Reynaldo, 1875-1947

886. . . . Les muses pleurant la mort de Ruskin. R. H. 1902.
   17 p. 33 x 28 cm.
   Score (9 solo "muses," 4-part women's chorus of "springs and foun-
   tains" and accompaniment of "lyres.").
   Published in 1925 by Heugel & Cie. in Paris.

887. [Portraits de peintres; pièces pour piano d'après les poésies de Marcel
   Proust]
   13 leaves. 35½ x 27 cm.
   Music on recto only of each leaf.
   Titles of parts (each in a separate folder): *Albert Cuyp; Paulus
   Potter; Anton van Dyck; Antoine Watteau.*
   Published in 1896 by Heugel & Cie. in Paris.

888. Le ruban dénoué. Suite de valses. Souvenirs d'Albi et ailleurs.
   Nos. 1-8, 10-12.
   138 p. 36½ x 27 cm.
   For 2 pianos.
   Published in 1917 by Heugel & Cie. in Paris.

Halévy, Jacques François Fromental Elie, 1799-1862

889. Blanche. Mélodie. Paroles de M. de St. Georges, musique de
   F. Halévy.
   [2]p. 35 x 27 cm.
   Song with piano accpt.
   First line: L'ai-je rêvé, ou l'ai-je vue?
   Published by Léon Escudier in Paris.

890. L'éclair, opéra-comique en trois actes, paroles de MM. de Planard
   et de Snt. Georges. Musique de F. Halévy.
   [634]p. 34 x 26 cm.
   Full score.
   First performed December 30, 1835, in Paris.
   Former owners: M. Osiris, C. W. Salabert.

Halévy, Jacques François Fromental Elie—*continued*

891. Poësie du seizième siècle (de Mlle. du Rocher). Mise en musique
F. Halévy. Paris 27 décembre 1848.
1 leaf, 6 p. 15½ x 24 cm.
Song with piano accpt.
First line: Quand je suis de vous absente.
Dedicated to the Duchess of Orléans.
Former owner: Le comte de Paris.
MEMORIAL LIBRARY OF MUSIC, STANFORD UNIVERSITY

Handel, George Frederic, 1685-1759

892. [The choice of Hercules]
Symphony, before, and during the entry of Alcides.
[3]p. 24½ x 28½ cm.
Full score of the beginning of the cantata, lacking in the British
Museum autograph score.   MISS DAISY WOOD HILDRETH

893. [Languia di bocca lusinghiera]
Cantata.
[10]p. 17½ x 24 cm.
Full score (soprano, violin, oboe and continuo).
Published in 1869 by Schott frères in Paris.
Werke, vol. 52b, no. 28.
Former owners: George E. J. Powell, Frederick Locker-Lampson,
Dr. Christian A. Herter.   NEW YORK PUBLIC LIBRARY

894. [Messiah. No. 6. But who may abide]
[2]p. 22 x 29½ cm.
Tenor solo with figured bass.
At head of title: For Mr. Low. Messiah, part the first. G. F. Handel.
Former owner: George T. Keating.
This ms. is declared by Dr. J. M. Coopersmith to be a forgery by
Tobia Nicotra.
MEMORIAL LIBRARY OF MUSIC, STANFORD UNIVERSITY

895. [Theodora. Lost in anguish quite despairing]
4p. 22½ x 29 cm.
Full score of an aria interpolated in the opera.
Not in the score in Werke, vol. 8.
Former owner: William H. Cummings (catalogue, no. 134).
LIBRARY OF CONGRESS

896. [Và, và, speme infida pur]
Duetto.
[3]p. 30 x 24 cm.
Duet for 2 sopranos with harpsichord accpt.
Published as no. 5 of his *Thirteen celebrated Italian duets* ca. 1775
by W. Randall in London.
Werke, vol. 32, no. 5.
Former owners: Philip Hayes, G. Malchair.
MEMORIAL LIBRARY OF MUSIC, STANFORD UNIVERSITY

Hanslick, Eduard, 1825-1904

897. "Ich sah ein Sternlein fallen" . . . Gedicht von Ad. Wolf, componirt v. Eduard Hanslick . . .
[4]p. 27½ x 21 cm.
Song with piano accpt.
Published by C. Hofbauer in Leipzig. LIBRARY OF CONGRESS

Harrison, Julius Allen Greenway, 1885-

898. The bonnie harvest moon, two part-song for treble voices. Words by John Barr, music by Julius Harrison.
[7]p. 30 x 23 cm.
Piano accpt.
First line: Of all the seasons in the year.
Published in 1919 [?] by J. Fischer & Bro. in New York.
LIBRARY OF CONGRESS

899. Cleopatra.
62 p. 36½ x 27 cm.
Sketches for the cantata.
Dated: June 20, 1907.
Former owner: Gerald Cumberland.
MEMORIAL LIBRARY OF MUSIC, STANFORD UNIVERSITY

900. "Under the greenwood tree" (William Shakespeare) . . . Part-song for S.S.A. Julius Harrison.
[6]p. 31 x 24 cm.
Vocal score with piano reduction (for rehearsal).
At end: J. H. 1911. LIBRARY OF CONGRESS

Harsányi, Tibor, 1898-

901. . . . Aria—Cadence—Rondo pour violoncelle et orchestre (ou piano).
Partition de piano.
18 p. 35 x 27 cm.
Dedicated to Mrs. E. S. Coolidge.
At end: Paris, mai-juin 1930.
LIBRARY OF CONGRESS, COOLIDGE FOUNDATION

Hartmann, Paul, von An der Lan-Hochbrunn, 1863-1914

902. . . . Drei eucharistische Gesänge (1 & 2. O salutaris, 3. Panis angelicus) für eine Singstimme mit Orgel oder Harmonium-Begleitung von Dr. P. Hartmann von An der Lan-Hochbrunn, O.F.M.
9 p. 34 x 27 cm.
At foot of title-page: München . . . 16 September 1908.
Published in 1910 by J. Fischer & Bro. in New York.
LIBRARY OF CONGRESS

903. . . . 3 Kirchen-Motetten (1. Regina coeli, 2. Si quaeris und 3. Sponsabo te) für 2 Singstimmen und Orgel oder Harmonium . . .
9 p. 34 x 27 cm.
At foot of title-page: München 16. September 1908.
Published in 1910 by J. Fischer & Bro. in New York.

LIBRARY OF CONGRESS

904. La morte del Signore. Oratorio sacro in due parti per soli, cori, grande orchestra ed organo . . .
112 p. 33 x 23½ cm.
Piano-vocal score, Latin text.
At end: Bozen (Tirolo) 16 Feb. 1906. Dr. P. Hrt.
Published in 1910 by J. Fischer & Bro. in New York.

LIBRARY OF CONGRESS

905. [The seven last words of Christ on the Cross]
[59]p. 34 x 27 cm.
Sketches for the oratorio.
At beginning: New York 20 April 1907; at end: 31 August 1907.
Published in 1908 by J. Fischer & Bro. in New York.

LIBRARY OF CONGRESS

906. [The seven last words of Christ on the Cross]
[70]p. 34 x 27 cm.
Full score (without vocal parts). LIBRARY OF CONGRESS

Hasse, Johann Adolf, 1699-1783

907. Credo pieno di Giov. Adolfo Hasse.
[64]p. 22 x 30½ cm.
Full score (chorus and orchestra), in F major.

LIBRARY OF CONGRESS

Hassenhut, Ignaz,

908. Zriny. Tragische Oper in drey Acten nach Theodor Körner's Trauer-spiel, bearbeitet von Joh. Bapt. Edler von Rettich. Zu Musik gesetzt von Ig. Hassenhut.
2 vols. (396, 269 p.) 26 x 33½ cm.
Full score.
Dated: Paris den 28 November 1840. BOSTON PUBLIC LIBRARY

Hatton, John Liptrot, 1809-1886

909. [Henry VIII. Incidental music]
149 p. 35 x 26½ cm.
Full score of the music to Shakespeare's play.
Performed in 1855 at the Princess Theatre in London.

FOLGER SHAKESPEARE LIBRARY

Hatton, John Liptrot—*continued*

910. [Incidental music to plays for the Princess Theatre, London]
192 p. 35 x 25½ cm.
Full score.
Contents.—*Overture, entr'actes & incidental music in The First Printer.—Tartar march. Janu*ʳʸ *1856.—March for Hamlet.—[Incidental music] to Shakespeare's play of The Winter's Tale.*

911. [Macbeth. Incidental music]
120 p. 27 x 37 cm.
Full score of the music to Shakespeare's play.
On p. 1: J. L. Hatton Oct: 1858.
On p. 77-118: *Overture to King John.* J. L. Hatton, Sept. 1858.

912. Ode for St. Bartholomew's Hospital, written by W. H. Bellamy. The music composed . . . by John L. Hatton. London, 1855.
[7]p. 28½ x 22 cm.
Piano-vocal score.

913. [Richard II. Incidental music]
114 p. 36 x 27 cm.
Full score of the music to Shakespeare's play.
Title-page reads: *Overture to Richard 2d. J.L.H. March 1857.*

914. Serenade "Stars of the summer night," poetry by Longfellow set to music for four voices—counter-tenor, 2 tenors and bass by J. L. Hatton.
[3]p. 30½ x 24½ cm.
On title-page: This copy for Jonas Chickering Esq. London October 1857.

Hauptmann, Moritz, 1792-1868
915. Gute Nacht (Sie an ihn).
[1]p. 20 x 25 cm.
Song with piano accpt.
First line: Die gute Nacht die ich dir sage.
At end: M. Hauptmann, Dresden 12 Juli '38.
Former owner: Joseph Muller.

Hauser, Miska, 1792-1868
916. Du bist wie eine Blume, von Heine.
[3]p. 14 x 22 cm.
Song with piano accpt.
Published by V. Kratochwill in Vienna.
Former owner: Joseph Muller.

917. [Ah, tu non senti amico]
      2 leaves. 22½ x 30 cm.
      Sketches for the aria.
      Presented to Mme. Wartel by August Artaria, Feb. 7, 1843.
                                                    THE PIERPONT MORGAN LIBRARY

918. [Als ich einst mit Weibesschönheit]
      [4]p. 22½ x 30 cm.
      Song with piano accpt.
      Published in his Werke, series XX, no. 45.
                                                    NEW YORK PUBLIC LIBRARY

919. Armida.
      [48]p. 22 x 30 cm.
      Fragment of full score, beginning with Adagio: Lasciarla oh dio.
      The opera was first performed at Esterhazy, February 26, 1784.
      Former owner: Charles Sumner.   HARVARD UNIVERSITY LIBRARY

920. Cantata.
      [28]p. 16½ x 22 cm.
      Fragment of full score (soprano and orchestra).
      Recitative begins: Miseri noi. Aria begins: Funesto orror di morte.
      According to Dr. A. van Hoboken, only the text and a few correc-
        tions in the score are autograph.
      Former owner: William H. Cummings (catalogue, no. 860).
                                                    LIBRARY OF CONGRESS

921. [Cantata for the birthday of Prince Esterhazy]
      In nomine Domini. Giuseppe Haydn 764.
      37 p. 34 x 23 cm.
      Full score.
      Recitative begins: Qual dubbio. Aria begins: Se ogni giorno.
      On p. 38 is the recitative, with continuo: *Saggio il pensier.*
      Unpublished.
      Former owner: Hermine Wittgenstein.
                                         LIBRARY OF CONGRESS, WHITTALL FOUNDATION

922. [Divertimento, baritone, viola and bass, no. 24, D major]
      Divertimento 24do per il pariton. In nomine Domini di me
        Giuseppe Haydn 1766 mpria.
      [2]p. 35½ x 22 cm.
      Score.
      At end: seg. trio, but the trio is lacking.
      Facsimile of p. 1 in Van Patten, *Catalogue,* p. 117.
      Unpublished.
      Former owner: Johann Nepomuk Kaffka.
                                    MEMORIAL LIBRARY OF MUSIC, STANFORD UNIVERSITY

Haydn, Franz Joseph—*continued*

923. [Divertimento, baritone, viola and bass, no. 105, G major]
    Divert. 106to [!] in nomine Domini di Giuseppe Haydn mpria.
    1772.
    [3]p. 23 x 32½ cm.
    Score.
    Published as supplement to *Neue Zeitschrift für Musik,* vol.
    LXXXIII, no. 4 (January 27, 1916).
    Facsimile of p. 1 in Parke-Bernet sale catalogue 318, p. 61.
    Former owners: Joseph Liebeskind, Hugo Riesenfeld.
                                                    WALTER J. JOHNSON

924. [Philemon und Baucis]
    Canzonetta.
    [4]p. 22 x 31 cm.
    Song with piano accpt.
    First line: Ein Tag der allen Freude bringt.
    The only autograph fragment extant of this marionette opera.
    Unpublished.
    Former owner: Max Friedländer.   SIBLEY MUSICAL LIBRARY

925. [Quartet, strings, op. 64, no. 2, B minor]
    Quartetto 2do in H minore di me Giuseppe Haydn. 790.
    29 [i.e. 30]p. 21½ x 28½ and 21½ x 31½ cm.
    Score.
    Published ca. 1792 as no. 2 of Set II of *Three Quartets,* op. 65, by
    J. Bland in London.   MR. GREGOR PIATIGORSKY

926. [Quartet, strings, op. 64, no. 6, E flat major]
    Quartetto 5do in Es di me Giuseppe Haydn mpria 1790.
    31 p. 21½ x 32½ cm.
    Score.
    Published ca. 1792 as no. 2 of Set I of *Three Quartets,* op. 65, by
    J. Bland in London.
    Former owners: Dannie N. Heineman, Oscar Bondy.
                        LIBRARY OF CONGRESS, WHITTALL FOUNDATION

927. [Quartet, strings, op. 103, B flat major]
    In nomine Domini di me Giuseppe Haydn m.p. 803.
    [6]p. 23 x 31 cm.
    Score.
    This unfinished quartet, Haydn's last work, consists of an *Andante
    grazioso* and a *Menuet.*
    Published in 1806 by Breitkopf & Härtel in Leipzig.
    Former owner: Breitkopf & Härtel.   BROUDE BROTHERS

928. [Die Schöpfung]
    [1]p. 22½ x 31 cm.
    First sketch for the *Vorstellung des Chaos.*
    Former owners: Alexander Posonyi, Anton Schmid.
                                          NEW YORK PUBLIC LIBRARY

Haydn, Franz Joseph—*continued*

929. [Sonata, piano, no. 52, E flat major]
> Sonata composta per la celebre signora Terese di Janson. In nomine Domini, di me Giuseppe Haydn, Londra, 794.
> [19]p. 23½ x 30 cm.

Published as op. 82 by Artaria in Vienna and as op. 78 by Longman, Clementi & Cy. in London, both in 1798.

Werke, series XIV, no. 52.

930. [Symphony, no. 90, C major]
> Sinfonia in C di me Giuseppe Haydn mpria 1788.
> [1], 67 p. 23 x 31 cm.

Full score.

Published as op. 51, no. 7 by Imbault in Paris.

Former owners: Count d'Ogny, Wittgenstein family.

931. [Symphony, no. 94, G major]
> [14]p. 25 x 31½ cm.

Full score of the 2nd movement, marked Andante.

"This version of the movement, a theme with variations, does not have the well-known 'surprise,' which was a fortissimo chord with a sharp drum stroke midway through the theme (cf. *Musical Times,* May 1909, p. 300); the instrumentation of the theme also differs from the version usually heard.

On p. 1 are the final 6 measures of the first movement." (E. N. Waters.)

Facsimile of first page of 2nd movement in *Library of Congress Quarterly Journal* IX, no. 1 (November 1951), opp. p. 35.

Former owner: Hermine Wittgenstein.

932. [Symphony, no. 96, D major]
> Sinfonia in D für das Klavier arrangirt . . .
> [9]p. 24 x 29½ cm.

Composer's reduction for piano 2 hands, omitting the 2nd movement.

This arrangement unpublished.

Former owners: Ferdinand Ries, William Ayrton, Edward Speyer.

933. [Trachten will ich nicht auf Erden]
> [3]p. 21 x 31 cm.

Song with piano accpt.

At end: Joseph Haydn mpria, den 14ten 10bris 790.

On p. 3, in another hand, marches and *Integer vitae.*

Published as no. 33 of his *Canzonetten und Lieder* in 1931 by C. F. Peters in Leipzig.

Werke, series XX, no. 43.

Former owners: S. Tauber, Johannes Brahms, Franz Amerling.

Haydn, Franz Joseph—*continued*

934.   [Trio, piano and strings, E flat major]
          [2]p. 23 x 32 cm.
          Score of a fragment of the last movement (presto), bars 82-131.
          Peters edition, no. 8; Breitkopf & Härtel ed. no. 12.

935.   [Variations, piano, F minor]
          Sonata.
          [12]p. 23 x 30½ cm.
          At head of title: Andante. In nomine Domini di me Giuseppe
          Haydn mpria. 1793.
          Known also as *Andante con variazioni,* op. 83.
          Published ca. 1799 by Artaria & Co. in Vienna.
          Former owners: Frederick Locker-Lampson, Dr. Christian A. Herter.

Haydn, (Johann) Michael, 1737-1806

936.   Graduale pro festo sti. Michaëlis archangeli et ssrum angelorum, di
          Giov. Mich. Haydn mpria. 3 Novbr. 1793.
          p. 9-12. 23 x 31½ cm.
          For solo voice with piano or organ accpt.
          Former owner: Jerome Stonborough.

937.   [Kommt her, ihr Menschen]
          [4]p. 22 x 30½ cm.
          Full score of a church aria for soprano and orchestra.
          At end: 13 Jan. 772.

Hayes, Philip, 1738-1797

938.   The Judgement of Hermes.
          210 p. 24 x 29½ cm.
          Full score of the oratorio.
          At end: Finish'd March 1, 1783, begun about the middle of January—Phil. Hayes.
          Former owner: William H. Cummings (catalogue, no. 865).

Heller, Stephen, 1813-1888

939.   . . . Capriccietto. Op. 156. Stephen Heller.
          [4]p. 26½ x 35 cm.
          For piano 2 hands.
          Dedicated to Mme. Hélène Balli, née Clado.

940.   La chasse. Etude composée pour la "Méthode des méthodes" pa
          Stephen Heller.
          [1], 7 p. 32 x 24 cm.
          For piano 2 hands.
          Published as op. 29 by Schlesinger in Paris.

Heller, Stephen—*continued*

941. ... Deutsche Tänze. St. Heller.
     [4]p. 25 x 32½ cm.
     For piano 2 hands.
     On p. 4 a *Funeral song* (4 part men's chorus, unaccompanied).

942. [Nocturne, piano, op. 103, G major]
     Nocturne pour piano ... par Stephen Heller. Op. 103.
     1 leaf, 8 p. 27 x 35 cm.
     Former owner: Joseph Muller.

Hellmesberger, Georg, junior, 1830-1852
943. The American songs by Mr. George Hellmesberger.
     Score (7 p.) and violin part. 25½ x 33 cm.
     For violin and piano.
     Former owner: Joseph Muller.

Hellwig, Karl Friedrich Ludwig, 1773-1838
944. Der 91te Psalm. Componirt von Ludwig Hellwig. Berlin, 1803 ...
     [46]p. 20½ x 22 cm.
     For solo voices and 4-part mixed chorus.
     An autograph note by Karl Fr. Zelter indicates the composer revised
     the score in 1813.

Hennessy, Swan, 1866-1929
945. "Nur wer die Sehnsucht kennt." Lied von Goethe in Musik gesetzt
     ... von Swan Hennessy. Op. 14 (1894).
     4 leaves. 30 x 24 cm.
     Music on recto only.
     Song with piano accpt.
     Dedicated to David Bispham.

Henry, Leigh (Vaughan), 1889-
946. ... Mistress Coolidge's coronal; a consort (chamber pieces for
     strings). LH. Leigh Henry (1930) ...
     Score (12 p.) and parts. 37 x 27½ cm.
     Dedicated to Mrs. E. S. Coolidge.
     At end: LH. New York, October 5th, 1930.

Henschel, *Sir* George, 1850-1934
947. The Clown's song from Shakespeare's "Twelfth Night."
     [2]p. 26½ x 34 cm.
     Song with piano accpt.
     First line: Come away, come away, death.
     Published in 1883 by Arthur P. Schmidt in Boston.

Henschel, *Sir* George—*continued*

948. [Mass, D major]
    1 leaf, [18]p. 31 x 23½ cm.
    For 4-part chorus with organ accpt.
    Former owner: Arthur Foote.   SIBLEY MUSICAL LIBRARY

949. Salomo, Ballade von Heine.
    [4]p. 26 x 33 cm.
    Song for solo voice, unaccompanied except for introduction and interludes.
    Dated: December 29, 1898.
    Published as op. 54 by A. M. Schlesinger in Berlin.
    Former owner: David Bispham.   NEW YORK PUBLIC LIBRARY

Henselt, Adolf von, 1814-1889

950. Die Fontaine von Ad. Henselt. Op. 6.
    [3]p. 25 x 22½ cm.
    For piano 2 hands, in F major.
    Published ca. 1865 as no. 1 of *Deux Nocturnes* by A. M. Schlesinger in Berlin.   LIBRARY OF CONGRESS

Hentschel, Theodor, 1830-1892

951. Des Königs Schwert. Oper in 3 Acten von Franz Bittong. Musik von T. Hentschel.
    3 vols. (174, 150, 185 p.) 32 x 26 cm.
    Full score.   LIBRARY OF CONGRESS

Hepworth, George, 1825-1918

952. Ouverture no. 2.
    [33]p. 26½ x 16½ cm.
    Full score.
    At end: August 1858.   BOSTON PUBLIC LIBRARY

Hermann, E. Hans G., 1870-1931

953. Über den Bergen. Gedicht von Carl Busse. Musik von Hans Hermann.
    [3]p. 33 x 26½ cm.
    Song with piano accpt.
    Published as op. 8 by Eisoldt und Rohkrämer in Berlin.
    NEW YORK PUBLIC LIBRARY

Hérold, Louis Joseph Ferdinand, 1791-1833

954. [Air de ballet]
    [2]p. 32 x 22 cm.
    For piano 2 hands.
    Former owners: Alfred de Beauchêne, Edward Speyer.
    LIBRARY OF CONGRESS

Hervé, [i.e.] Florimond Ronger, 1825-1892

955. [L'oeil crevé]
Couplets des cabaretières chantés dans l'Oeil crevé, d'Hervé.
[3]p. 28 x 22½ cm.
Piano-vocal score.
First line: Qu'ils sont gentils.   LIBRARY OF CONGRESS

Hillemacher, Paul Joseph Guillaume, 1852-1933

956. [Ici-bas tous les lilas meurent]
[2]p. 35 x 27 cm.
Song with piano accpt.
Text by Sully-Prudhomme.
Published by Leduc in Paris.   LIBRARY OF CONGRESS

Hiller, Ferdinand von, 1811-1885

957. Trois caprices pour le pianoforte . . . par Ferdinand Hiller. Op. 12.
1 leaf, 15 p. 31 x 24 cm.
Dedicated to Frédéric Chopin.
                   MEMORIAL LIBRARY OF MUSIC, STANFORD UNIVERSITY

958. [Concerto, piano, op. 69, F sharp minor]
Concert für das Pianoforte mit Begleitung des Orchesters componirt von Ferdinand Hiller. Op. 69. Partitur . . .
1 leaf, 71 p. 26½ x 33½ cm.
Published in 1861 by A. Cranz in Hamburg.
                                        BOSTON PUBLIC LIBRARY

959. "Wanderers Nachtlied," für eine Singstimme mit Pianoforte . . .
[3]p. 29½ x 23 cm.
Song with piano accpt.
First line: Über allen Gipfeln ist Ruh.
Text by Goethe.
Dedicated to Frau Willemer.   LIBRARY OF CONGRESS

Himmel, Friedrich Heinrich, 1765-1814

960. An die Natur.
[3]p. 25 x 31 cm.
Song with piano accpt.
First line: Nein, es ging uns nicht verloren.
Followed by: *Liebe*. First line: Engelselig ist das Leben.
                                        LIBRARY OF CONGRESS

Hindemith, Paul, 1895-

961. . . . Konzertmusik für Klavier, Blechbläser und Harfen. Partitur.
Berlin, Juli 1930.
1 leaf, [33]p. 42 x 32 cm.
At head of title: Paul Hindemith. 1930.
At end: San Bernardino, 13 August 1930.

Hindemith, Paul—*continued*

Dedicated to Mrs. E. S. Coolidge.
Published in 1931 by B. Schott's Söhne in Mainz.

962. . . . Konzertmusik für Streichorchester und Blechbläser. Partitur
Geschrieben für das Bostoner Symphonie-Orchester.
71 p. 33 x 26 cm.
At head of title: Paul Hindemith. 1930.
At end: Andermatt 27 Dez. 30.
Published in 1931 by B. Schott's Söhne in Mainz.

Hoffmann, Johann Lorentzius, fl. 1720

963. [Songs for one or two voices with figured bass]
292 p. 16 x 20 cm.
On inside front cover: Johann Lorentzius Hoffmann 1720.
The only known ms. of this composer.
Former owners: Philipp Spitta, Janos Scholz.

Holbrooke, Josef, 1878-

964. The Bathers.
6 leaves. 32 x 27 cm.
Song with piano and flute accpt.
Text by Gerald Cumberland.

965. [Quartet, piano, violin, viola and violoncello, no. 2. Op. 31, D minor
Symphonic quartet, opus 31, no. 2 [!]
1 leaf, 63 p. 20½ x 10 cm.
Score.
Published with title: *Byron,* in 1915 by J. and W. Chester i
London.
Former owner: William Wallace.

966. [Sextet, piano, clarinet and strings, no. 1, op. 20]
Slavonic dance.
1 leaf, 18 p. 30 x 24 cm.
Composer's reduction of one of 4 dance movements, for piano
hands.
Published in its original form as a sextet in 1904 by Ricordi i
London.

967. [Suite, orchestra, no. 3, op. 40]
Les hommages. Grande suite no. III. Arranged for string orche
tra. Opus 37[!]
54 p. 29½ x 23 cm.
Composer's arrangement from the original for full orchestra.

Holbrooke, Josef—*continued*

The movements are designated: *Wagner, Grieg, Dvorak* and *Tchaikovsky.*

Published in this version in 1909 by J. and W. Chester in London.

Former owner: William Saunders.

Hollaender, Victor, 1866-1940

968. . . . Gretchen's Hochzeitsabend. Ballade von Ernst von Wildenbruch. Musik von Victor Hollaender. Manuscript. London, June, 1896. 1 leaf, [13]p. 35 x 27½ cm.

Song with piano accpt.

First line: Schön Gretchen am Tag.

Published by C. F. Kahnt in Leipzig.

969. Die Prinzessin vom Nil. Musik von Victor Hollaender, Text von Arthur Landsberger und Franz Cornelius. [54]p. 35 x 27 cm.

Piano-vocal score.

First performed September 18, 1915 in Berlin.

Holmès, Augusta (Mary Anne), 1847-1903

970. Les sept ivresses. II. Le vin. [3]p. 44½ x 31 cm.

Song with piano accpt.

First line: Vins d'Espagne et vins de Hongrie.

Former owner: Joseph Muller.

Published by A. Durand et fils in Paris.

Holmes, George

[Vocal compositions]
    See Smith, John Stafford, ca. 1750-1836.
        [Anthems, motets, songs . . .]

Holst, Gustave Theodor, 1874-1934

971. Between us now. Song, words by Thomas Hardy. Gustav von Holst. [4]p. 31 x 24 cm.

Song with piano accpt.

No. 5 of op. 15, *Six baritone songs;* composed 1902-03; unpublished.

Former owner: David Bispham.

972. Calm is the morn. Words by Tennyson, music by Gustav von Holst. [4]p. 30 x 24 cm.

Song with piano accpt.

No. 1 of op. 16; composed 1902-03; unpublished.

Former owner: David Bispham.

Holst, Gustave Theodor—*continued*

973.   . . . A Fugal concerto for flute and oboe (or two violins) with accompaniment for string orchestra. Gustav Holst. Op. 40, no. 2 . . .
1 leaf, 13 p. 37 x 27½ cm.
Full score.
At end: May 11, 1923. 11 a.m. Michigan University Library, Ann Arbor, Carrell 722.
Note on title-page: First performed May 17 at President Burton's house [by] members of Chicago Symphony Orchestra, Frederick A. Stock, conductor.
Published in 1923 by Novello & Co. in London.

UNIVERSITY OF MICHIGAN, GENERAL LIBRARY

974.   The Golden goose.
113 p. 36 x 25½ cm.
Full score of the ballet, partly in the hand of the composer.
Published in 1928 by Oxford University Press in London.

LIBRARY OF CONGRESS

975.   In a wood. Words by Thomas Hardy, music by Gustav von Holst.
[4]p. 30 x 23½ cm.
Song with piano accpt.
First line: Pale beech and pine tree blue.
No. 4 of op. 15, *Six baritone songs;* composed 1902-03; unpublished.
Former owner: David Bispham.   NEW YORK PUBLIC LIBRARY

Honegger, Arthur, 1892-

976.   . . . Concerto da camera pour flûte, cor anglais, et orchestre à cordes. A. Honegger 1948.
22 p. 33 x 27 cm.
Full score.
At end: Paris 28 octobre 48.
Dedicated to Mrs. E. S. Coolidge.

LIBRARY OF CONGRESS, COOLIDGE FOUNDATION

977.   . . . Concerto da camera pour flûte, cor anglais, et orchestre à cordes. A. Honegger 1948.
19 [i.e. 20]p. 35 x 27 cm.
Reduction for flute, English horn and piano.
At end: Paris 24 octobre 1948.

LIBRARY OF CONGRESS, COOLIDGE FOUNDATION

978.   La danse des morts. Paul Claudel.
[1]p. 35 x 24½ cm.
For 4-part mixed chorus and piano.
First line: Je prendrai les enfants d'Israël.   MR. RUDOLF F. KALLIR

◄{ 150 }►

979. [Duo for trombone and piano]
    [1]p. 35 x 27 cm.
    Dedicated to Serge Koussevitzky.
    At end: Hommage du trombone exprimant la tristesse de l'auteur
       absent.   LIBRARY OF CONGRESS, KOUSSEVITZKY FOUNDATION

980. Les mille et une nuits.
    [4]p. 33 x 27 cm.
    Sketches.   MEMORIAL LIBRARY OF MUSIC, STANFORD UNIVERSITY

981. [Quartet, strings, no. 3]
    3eme quatuor pour 2 violons, alto, violoncelle. A. Honegger.
       1936-1937.
    22 p. 36½ x 27 cm.
    Score.
    At end: Paris. Septembre 1936.
    Dedicated to Mrs. E. S. Coolidge.
    Published in 1938 by Maurice Sénart in Paris.
                LIBRARY OF CONGRESS, COOLIDGE FOUNDATION

982. [Symphony, no. 1]
    Symphonie pour orchestre. A. Honegger.
    1 leaf, 135 p. 34½ x 26½ cm.
    Full score.
    At end: Composé à Paris décembre 1929 à avril 1930. Orchestré à
       Mougins avril-mai 1930.
    On verso of preliminary leaf: Au Boston Symphony Orchestra et à
       son chef Serge Koussevitzky je dédie cette symphonie avec l'ex-
       pression de mon entière admiration. A. Honegger 1930.
    Published in 1931 by Maurice Sénart in Paris.
                BOSTON SYMPHONY ORCHESTRA

983. [Symphony, no. 5]
    Symphonie no. V (di tre re). A. Honegger.
    56 p. 35 x 27 cm.
    Full score.
    At head of title: For the Koussewitzky Music Foundation. Dedi-
       cated to the memory of Natalia Koussewitzky.
    At end: Paris 10 novembre 50; orchestré 3 décembre 50.
           LIBRARY OF CONGRESS, KOUSSEVITZKY FOUNDATION

Hook, James, 1746-1827

984. [The Ascension, a sacred oratorio]
    408 p. 23 x 29 cm.
    Piano-vocal score, composed 1776.
    Former owners: W. J. Brown, William H. Cummings (catalogue,
       no. 902).   LIBRARY OF CONGRESS

Hook, James—*continued*

985. [Concerto, organ, F major]
  Concerto per il organo o cembalo. Originale. J. Hook. 1797 . . .
  43 p. 30 x 24 cm.
 Full score.
 Former owner: William H. Cummings (catalogue, no. 903).

986. [Manuscript sketch book]
  [82]p. 16 x 20 cm.
 Contains numerous "subjects" for various dances, such as hornpipe,
  waltz, schottisch, contredance, some of which have names; also
  themes for canons, fugues, songs, etc.
 Dated on p. 1: Nov. 27, 1816; on p. 3: Dec. 7, 1816.
 Together with this book are 42 p. of loose sketches.
 Former owner: William H. Cummings.

987. [O whither fair maid]
  [10]p. 16 x 20 cm.
 Full score (voice and orchestra).
 At head of title: Ah well aday. Mrs. Bland. J. Hook. May 8th 1815.
 Former owner: William H. Cummings.

Horn, Charles Edward, 1786-1849

988. Oh my heart is sad for Araby. The words by Mrs. Crawford, au-
  thoress of Kathleen Mavourneen . . .
  [3]p. 34½ x 25 cm.
 Song with piano accpt.

989. What shall be my theme, words by T. H. Bayly, composed by
  Charles E. Horn.
  [2]p. 23½ x 30½ cm.
 Song with piano accpt.
 At end: June 1831.
 Former owner: Miss Lillian Shattuck.

Huë, Georges (Adolphe), 1858-1948

990. Dévouement à la patrie! Choeur à 3 voix (Corneille). Musique de
  Georges Huë.
  2 leaves. 35 x 27 cm.
 Trio for women's voices, unaccompanied.
 Music on recto only.
 First line: Mourir pour son pays.

Hüttel, Joseph, 1893-

991. Divertissement grotesque pour flûte, hautbois, clarinette, basson, cor
  et piano, en 2 parties. 1. Prélude. 2. Marche. 3. Pavane. I. Partie.
  4. Menuet espagnol. 5. Sarabande. 6. Finale. II. Partie. . . .
  Score (38 leaves) and parts. 34 x 27 cm.

Hüttel, Joseph—*continued*

At end: Fin. (23.II.1929).
Awarded the Coolidge Foundation Prize, 1929.

Hullah, John Pyke, 1812-1884
992. [The barbers of Barsora, comic opera in 2 acts. Words by J. Maddi-
son Morton, music by John Hullah]
[542]p. 35 x 26 cm.
Full score.   BOSTON PUBLIC LIBRARY

Hummel, Johann Nepomuk, 1778-1837
993. [Concerto, piano, op. 113, A flat major]
Grand concerto in A♭ pour le pianoforte avec accompagnement
de grand orchestre composé . . . par J. N. Hummel . . . Oeuvre
113.
[70]p. 12½ x 20½ cm.
Piano part only.
Followed by 147 p. of orchestra parts.
Published in 1883 (for 2 pianos) by Breitkopf & Härtel in Leipzig.
Former owners: J. Beale, G. Manwell.   LIBRARY OF CONGRESS

994. [Rondo villageois]
The Scotsh [!] contradance-rondo, for the pianoforte; composed
by J. N. Hummel. Op. 122 . . .
1 leaf, [2]p. 23 x 30 cm.
Published by J. André in Offenbach.   LIBRARY OF CONGRESS

Huybrechts, Albert, 1899-1938
995. . . . Trois poèmes d'Edgar Poe; traduction de Stéphane Mallarmé
pour chant et piano . . .
2 leaves, 16 p. 36 x 27 cm.
Dedicated to Mrs. E. S. Coolidge.
At end: Bruxelles, avril, 1928.

996. Sonate pour violon et piano.
Score (1 leaf, 39 p.) and part. 31 x 23 cm.
Coolidge Foundation Prize, 1926.

Indy, (Paul Marie Théodore) Vincent d', 1851-1931
997. O gai soleil (Canon in epidiapente).
[1]p. 15 x 27 cm.
Duet for soprano and alto, unaccompanied.
Published in 1909 in the *Supplément* to the *Revue Musicale*.

Indy, (Paul Marie Théodore) Vincent d'—*continued*

998. Sur la mer. Choeur pour voix de femmes. Opus 32.
      1 leaf, 9 p. 35½ x 27 cm.
      Text by the composer.
      Published by J. Hamelle in Paris.
                          MEMORIAL LIBRARY OF MUSIC, STANFORD UNIVERSITY

Ippolitov-Ivanov, Mikhail Mikhailovich, 1859-1935
999. . . . Kartinka epizod iz zhizni Shuberta. Op. 61. M. Ippolitov-Ivanov.
      [1], 65 p. 35½ x 26 cm.
      Full score.
      On p. 2 another title (in Russian): *In memory of the great Schu-
      bert. Episodes from the life of Schubert, symphonic picture for
      full orchestra* . . .
      Unpublished.
                          FREE LIBRARY OF PHILADELPHIA, FLEISHER COLLECTION

Jackson, William, 1815-1866
1000. The Mariner's toast, a national song as sung by Mr. Bridgewater
       at the Canterbury Catch Club &c, the words by I. R. Stevens, the
       music by Wm. Jackson . . .
       1 leaf, 5p. 30 x 24½ cm.
                          MEMORIAL LIBRARY OF MUSIC, STANFORD UNIVERSITY

Jacob, Maxime, 1906-
1001. . . . Trois romances sans paroles. Maxime Jacob.
       [8]p. 36 x 27 cm.
       For piano 2 hands.
       Dedicated to Jane Mortier.
       At end: décembre-janvier 25-26. Maxime Jacob.   PIERRE BÉRÈS

Jadassohn, Salomon, 1831-1902
1002. Etude für piano . . . von S. Jadassohn.
       [2]p. 29 x 22 cm.
       Dedicated to Alexander Lambert, the former owner.
                          NEW YORK PUBLIC LIBRARY

Joachim, Joseph, 1831-1907
1003. Variationen für Violine mit Orchesterbegleitung von Joseph
       Joachim.
       1 leaf, 86 p. 32½ x 25 cm.
       Full score.
       Published ca. 1882 by Bote und Bock in Berlin.   WALTER SCHATZKI

Joly, Alfred

1004. . . . Le panier de Jeanne, opérette en un acte, paroles de Mr.
Delteil . . .
[194]p. 26 x 34 cm.
Full score.
At end: Laus Deo. Alfred Joly. Fécit anno 1884.

Jommelli, Niccolò, 1714-1774

1005. Te Deum a 5 voci con V.V. ed stromenti di fiato non obligati di
Niccolò Jommelli.
40 p. 21 x 28 cm.
Full score.
Former owners: John Robinson, William H. Cummings (catalogue,
no. 935).

Jones, Robert, fl. 1597-1617

1006. [The love of change]
[1]p. 32 x 21½ cm.
Song with figured bass.
First line: The love of change hath changed the world throughout.
At end: R. Jones.
Cf. J. Q. Adams, "A new song by Robert Jones," *Modern Language
Quarterly*, I (1940), 45-48.

Kabalevskiĭ, Dimitriĭ, 1904-

1007. Improvisation. Op. 23, no. 1. D. Kabalevskii.
[5]p. 26½ x 35 cm.
For violin and piano.
At end: D. Kabalevskiĭ 9 IV. 1923. Moskva.

Kalliwoda, Johannes Wenzeslaus, 1801-1866

1008. [Polka, piano, F major]
[2]p. 23½ x 27½ cm.

Kalomiris, Manolis, 1883-

1009. [L'anneau de la mère]
Le réveillon de Noël, (prélude au 3me acte de l'opéra "L'anneau
de la mère) par Manolis Kalomiris . . .
1 leaf, [1], 15 p. 34½ x 27 cm.
Full score.
Title-page in Greek and French.

Kéler-Béla, 1820-1882

1010. Am schönen Rhein gedenk' ich Dein! Walzer v. Kéler Béla opus 83.
[2]p. 25 x 34 cm.
For piano 2 hands.
At end: Herrn Kapellmeister Schlösser . . . Wiesbaden 19 Aug.
1869.
Real name: Albert von Kéler.
Published by Bote und Bock in Berlin. LIBRARY OF CONGRESS

Ketten, Henri, 1848-1883

1011. . . . Never! 4eme feuille d'album pour le piano par Henry Ketten.
Op. 59.
1 leaf, [6]p. 35 x 27 cm.
Dedicated to Mrs. George Chickering. NEW YORK PUBLIC LIBRARY

Kienlen, Johann Christoph, 1784-1830

1012. Lieder aus Goethe's Faust in Musik gesetzt . . . von Kienlen.
[16]p. 24 x 34½ cm.
YALE UNIVERSITY LIBRARY, SPECK COLLECTION

King, Oliver A., 1855-1923

1013. Alla marcia (concluding voluntary) composed by Oliver King. Op.
92, no. 2.
[1], 5 p. 35 x 27 cm.
For organ. BOSTON PUBLIC LIBRARY

1014. Andante religioso. Op. 92, no. 1.
[3]p. 31 x 23½ cm.
For organ. BOSTON PUBLIC LIBRARY

Kistler, Cyrill, 1848-1907

1015. Arm Elselein. Ein Bühnenfestspiel in einem Aufzuge. Handlung
frei nach Andersen. Musik von Cyrill Kistler, op. 117.
2 leaves, 234 p. 34 x 27 cm.
Full score.
Dated: den 9. February 1901.
First performed in 1902 in Schwerin. LIBRARY OF CONGRES

1016. [Baldurs Tod. Musikdrama in 3 Akten. Dichtung v. Frhrr. v
Sohlen. Musik v. Cyrill Kistler.
3 vols. (143, 101, 131p.) 35 x 26 cm.
Full score.
Dated at end of each act: Act I, den 14 Jänner 1892; Act II, den 2
Februar 1892; Act III, den 10 Juni 1892.
First performed October 25, 1905 at Düsseldorf.
LIBRARY OF CONGRES

Kistler, Cyrill—*continued*

1017. [Faust, erster Teil. Musikdrama in vier Akten nach Wolfgang von
     Goethe]
     4 vols. (116, 111, 87, 98 p.) 35 x 27 cm.
     Full score.
     At end: Vollendet den 13. August 1905. Bad Kissingen.
                                                        LIBRARY OF CONGRESS

1018. Kunihild und der Brautritt auf Kynast. Oper in drei Acten von
     Cyrill Kistler.
     3 vols. (152, 178, 209 p.) 33 x 25½ cm.
     Full score.
     At end: Vollendet den 17 November 1882. Bad Köchel.
     First performed March 20, 1884 at Sondershausen.
                                                        LIBRARY OF CONGRESS

Knecht, Justin Heinrich, 1752-1817

1019. Postludium für die Orgel oder das Clavier enthaltend vier Fugen-
     Sätze worunter der erste Satz aus dem Hauptthema der letzten
     Bachischen Fuge à tre Soggetti entlehnt, aber mit neuen Gegen-
     sätzen begleitet ist, die drei andern Sätze hingegen ganz neu
     erfunden, und anfangs einzeln ausgeführt, am Ende aber alle
     mit einander vereinigt sind von [Knecht (name partly in musical
     notes)].
     [28]p. 35 x 21½ cm.
     Former owners: J. C. H. Rinck, Lowell Mason, Samuel P. Warren.
                                                        LIBRARY OF CONGRESS

Kodály, Zoltán, 1882-

1020. [Concerto, orchestra]
     . . . Concerto dedicated to the Chicago Symphony Orchestra.
     1 leaf, 89 p. 34 x 26½ cm.
     Full score.   CHICAGO SYMPHONY ORCHESTRA

1021. . . . Theater Ouverture. Manuskript Partitur.
     83 p. 35 x 27 cm.
     Full score.
     Former owner: Arturo Toscanini.
     Published in 1932 by Universal Edition in Vienna. MR. HANS LANGE

Köhler, Johann Heinrich Robert, 1807-1872

1022. Juchhe. Gedicht von Reinicke. Musik v. R. Köhler.
     [4]p. 35 x 22 cm.
     Song with piano accpt.
     First line: Wie ist doch die Erde so schön.   LIBRARY OF CONGRESS

Kontski, Antoine de, 1817-1899

1023. . . . Romance "Priez pour moi!" Paroles de Millevoye, musique de
Antoine de Kontski.
[4]p. 24 x 31 cm.
Song with piano accpt.
Former owner: The Royal Collection, Lisbon. LIBRARY OF CONGRESS

Korbay, Francis Alexander, 1846-1913

1024. . . . The ordeal. Words by T. Campbell. Music by Francis Korbay.
1 leaf, [4]p. 35 x 27 cm.
Song with piano accpt.
First line: The ordeal's fatal trumpet sounded.
Dedicated to David Bispham.   NEW YORK PUBLIC LIBRARY

1025. . . . Where shall the lover rest. Words by Walter Scott. Music by
Francis Korbay.
[8]p. 35 x 27 cm.
Song with piano accpt.   NEW YORK PUBLIC LIBRARY

Krebs, Johann Ludwig, 1713-1780

1026. Sonata a 2 trav. e cembalo di J. L. Krebs.
[2]p. 33½ x 21 cm.
Score of parts of 2 sonatas for 2 flutes and bass. On p. 1, the end of
1st movement, complete largo and allegro of sonata in A minor;
on p. 2 first movement (vivace) complete of a sonata in C major.
Former owner: George B. Weston.   HARVARD UNIVERSITY LIBRARY

1027. Toccata per l'organo pieno col pedale di Joh: Lud: Krebs. No. 288.
[11]p. 36½ x 21½ cm.
Former owner: Eduard August Grell.   ESTATE OF FRANK A. TAFT

Křenek, Ernst, 1900-

1028. . . . Die Jahreszeiten, vier kleine a cappella Chöre nach Gedichten
von Hölderlin. Ernst Krenek. Op. 35. 1925.
12 p. 33½ x 26½ cm.
Dated on cover: Cassel, 6 Oktober 1925.
Published in 1925 by Universal Edition in Vienna.

LIBRARY OF CONGRESS

1029. . . . Vier kleine a-cappella-Chöre nach Texten von Goethe. Op. 47.
[11]p. 34 x 26½ cm.
At end: Evian-les-Bains 31ten Juli 1926.
Dedicated to Paul Bekker.
Published in 1927 by Universal Edition in Vienna.

MR. RUDOLF F. KALLIR

1030. Der Triumph der Empfindsamkeit (Goethe). Ernst Krenek. Op.
43.
102 p. 35 x 27 cm.
Full score.

Křenek, Ernst—*continued*

At end: Cassel, 7 April 1926.
Former owner: Paul Bekker.
Published in 1932 by Universal Edition in Vienna.

Kreutzer, Conradin, 1780-1849

1031. [Das Nachtlager in Granada]
Nro. 3. Romanze "Ein Schütz bin ich" aus der Oper Das Nachtlager in Granada von Conr. Kreutzer . . .
[4]p. 32½ x 25 cm.
Piano-vocal score.

1032. 2 Romanze aus dem Trauerspiel Enzio von Raupach componirt von
Conradin Kreutzer. Oeuvre 40.
1 leaf, [10]p. 32 x 25 cm.
Songs with piano accpt.
First lines: Sie haben den König gefangen; Ich habe sie einmal
gesehen.

Krüger, Wilhelm, 1820-1883

1033. Brillante Polonaise für das Pianoforte componirt . . . von Wilhelm
Krüger. Berlin, den 28 April 1842.
[7]p. 34 x 27 cm.
Former owner: Joseph Muller.

Kücken, Friedrich Wilhelm, 1810-1882

1034. Deutscher Marsch. Gedicht von Fr. Rastige. Musik von Fr. Kücken.
[1]p. 31 x 28 cm.
Song with piano accpt.
At end: Fr. Kücken. Stuttgart, den 10 September 1859.
Former owner: Joseph Muller.

1035. Hymne zur Confirmationsfeier . . . des Kronprinzen von Hannover, Gedicht von Ed. Hobein, componirt für gemischten Chor
von Fr. Kücken.
[3]p. 34½ x 26½ cm.

1036. Lied im Volkston "O weine nicht." Gedicht von Theobald Kerner,
componirt von Fr. Kücken.
[3]p. 25 x 33 cm.
Song with piano accpt.
Former owner: Joseph Muller.

037. Motette für die kirchliche Confirmationsfeier . . . des Kronprinzen
von Hannover componirt nach Worten der heiligen Schrift für
Sopran, Alt, Tenor, Bass (Chor) von Fr. Kücken. [Op. 73]
[4]p. 34½ x 26½ cm.

Küffner, Joseph, 1776-1856

1038. Ouverture par Joseph Küffner, opus 172. Den 10ten November 1824.
41p. 23 x 31 cm.
Full score, in D minor. LIBRARY OF CONGRESS

Kummer, Friedrich August, 1797-1879

1039. Elegia.
[2]p. 20 x 25 cm.
For violoncello and piano.
At end: Dresden Aug. 1841. F. A. Kummer.
Former owner: Joseph Muller. NEW YORK PUBLIC LIBRARY

Lachner, Franz, 1803-1890

1040. Das Mädchen aus der Fremde von Friedrich von Schiller in Musik gesetzt von Franz Lachner.
[3]p. 21 x 32 cm.
Song with piano accpt.
First line: In einem Thal bei armen Hirten. LIBRARY OF CONGRESS

1041. Sturmesmythe, von Lenau. Männerchor mit Orchesterbegleitung ... componirt von Franz Lachner. Op. 112. Partitur.
36 p. 28½ x 21 cm.
At end: Trier, d. 3. 10. 62. F. Lachner. BOSTON PUBLIC LIBRARY

Ladmirault, Paul Emile, 1877-1944

1042. Revoici le printemps, choeur à 3 voix égales. P. Ladmirault (Poésie de Baïf—xvie siècle). Voix d'hommes seules.
[3]p. 35 x 27 cm. MR. ALFRED J. SWAN

Lafont, Charles Philippe, 1781-1839

1043. Rondo villageois pour violon par Ch. Lafont. Partitura.
18 p. 35 x 27 cm.
Full score (violin and string orchestra).
Former owner: Joseph Muller. NEW YORK PUBLIC LIBRARY

Lajtha, László, 1891-

1044. [Quartet, strings, no. 3, op. 11]
... László Lajtha. Op. 11. III String quartet.
1 leaf, 31p. 34 x 26½ cm.
Score.
Dedicated to Mrs. E. S. Coolidge.
Published in 1932 by Universal Edition in Vienna.
LIBRARY OF CONGRESS, COOLIDGE FOUNDATION

Lalo, Edouard (Victor Antoine), 1823-1892

1045. L'aube naît.
   [4]p. 35½ x 27 cm.
   Song with piano accpt.
   Text by Victor Hugo.
   Published as no. 3 of *Mélodies pour chant et piano* by J. Hamelle
   in Paris.   MEMORIAL LIBRARY OF MUSIC, STANFORD UNIVERSITY

Lamberg, Joseph, 1852-?

1046. Capricietto. Pianoforte.
   [5]p. 34½ x 26 cm.
   Former owner: Ossip Gabrilowitsch.   NEW YORK PUBLIC LIBRARY

1047. Romance pour piano.
   [3]p. 34½ x 26 cm.
   Former owner: Ossip Gabrilowitsch.   NEW YORK PUBLIC LIBRARY

1048. Scherzo pour pianoforte.
   7 p. 34½ x 26 cm.
   Former owner: Ossip Gabrilowitsch.   NEW YORK PUBLIC LIBRARY

Lanner, Joseph (Franz Carl), 1801-1843

1049. Alpen Ländler. Original Partitur . . . comp. v. J. Lanner.
   1 leaf, 18 p. 25 x 32 cm.
   Full score (including 4 voices, wind and rain machines).
   Caption title: *Steyerische Alpen Ländler v. J. Lanner. Mit Gott.*
   Unpublished.
   Former owners: Alexander Posonyi; Wilhelm Heyer (catalogue,
   vol. IV, no. 1554).   LIBRARY OF CONGRESS

1050. Terpsichoren-Walzer: mit Gott v: J: Lanner.
   14 p. 25 x 32 cm.
   Full score of his op. 12.
   Published in piano reduction ca. 1825 by A. Diabelli in Vienna.
   Werke, vol. I, no. 3.
   Former owners: Alexander Posonyi, Wilhelm Heyer (catalogue,
   vol. IV, no. 1552).
            MEMORIAL LIBRARY OF MUSIC, STANFORD UNIVERSITY

Lassen, Eduard, 1830-1904

1051. [Über allen Zauber Liebe. Op. 73]
   Symphonisches Zwischenspiel (Intermezzo) zu Calderon's
   Schauspiel "Über allen Zauber Liebe" von Lassen.
   1 leaf, 45 [i.e. 49]p. 33½ x 26 cm.
   Full score, with corrections and additions in the hand of Liszt.
   Former owner: Aloys Obrist.   SIBLEY MUSICAL LIBRARY

Lehmann, Liza, 1862-1918

1052. "Love, if you knew the light." A fragment. The words by Robert Browning (from "A Lover's quarrel"). The music by Liza Lehmann.

[3]p. 35 x 27 cm.

Song with piano accpt.

Published in 1922 by G. Schirmer in New York.

Lekeu, Guillaume, 1870-1894

1053. Fantaisie pour orchestre sur deux airs populaires angevins. G. Lekeu. Réduction pour piano à quatre mains.

17 p. 35 x 27 cm.

At end: Réduction pour piano à 4 mains terminée le 10 juin 1892.

Original version for orchestra published in 1909 by A. Rouart-Lerolle in Paris.

Leo, Leonardo (Oronzo Salvatore de), 1695-1744

1054. [Introits, graduals, offertories, etc., a Miserere and a Te Deum]

[283]p. 21½ x 27 cm.

Contains 13 numbers, mostly for soprano, alto, tenor and bass with figured organ bass. Each number is signed and dated, the dates running from February to April 1744. Nearly every number has the note: per la Real Cappella [Naples].

Former owners: Carlo Broschi Farinelli, Samuel P. Warren. The contents are inaccurately described in G. Leo's *Leonardo Leo*, 1905, p. 78-79 and in the catalogue of the Warren library.

Leoncavallo, Ruggiero, 1858-1919

1055. . . . La chanson des yeux de A. Chénier. Fragment, musique de R. Léoncavallo.

[3]p. 34 x 26 cm.

Song with piano accpt.

First line: Ne me regarde point.

1056. . . . Déclaration. Paroles d'A. Silvestre. Musique de R. Léoncavallo.

[3]p. 34 x 26 cm.

Song with piano accpt.

First line: Quel charme est donc en vous.

1057. Pagliacci; dramma in un atto, parole e musica di R. Leoncavallo . . .

[1], 304 p. 35 x 27 cm.

Full score.

At end: R. Leoncavallo.

First performed May 21, 1892 at the Teatro del Verme in Milan, in two acts. The introduction to Act 2 is in this ms. marked *Intermezzo*. See *Report of the Librarian of Congress*, 1938-39, p. 180-81.

Leschetizky, Theodor, 1830-1915

1058. Contes de jeunesse. Suite de morceaux pour piano, hommage à Chopin par Théodore Leschetizky. Op. 46, no. IX . . .
[1], 10 p. 33 x 26 cm.   ISABELLA STEWART GARDNER MUSEUM

1059. Die erste Falte: Un coup de hasard; frei nach dem Französischen von Mosenthal. Oper in einem Aufzug von Theodor Leschetitzky. Partitur.
vii, 208 p. 26½ x 38½ cm.
First performed October 9, 1867 at the Deutsches Landestheater in Prag.   LIBRARY OF CONGRESS

Lesueur, Jean François, 1760-1837

1060. [La mort d'Adam]
[1]p. 22 x 20½ cm.
Fragment of full score.
Former owner: Joseph Muller.   NEW YORK PUBLIC LIBRARY

Levey, William Charles, 1837-1894

1061. Beda. Ballet composed by William Charles Levey. Orchestra score.
172 p. 29½ x 24 cm.
First performed in October 1868 in London. BOSTON PUBLIC LIBRARY

Liadov, Anatol Konstantinovich, 1855-1914

1062. . . . Bagatelle.
[2]p. 25½ x 38 cm.
For piano 2 hands.
At end: An. Liadov, 18go oktiabria 89g.
At head of title: V al'bom Antonu Grigor'evichnu Rubinshteinu.
LIBRARY OF CONGRESS

Lindpaintner, Peter Joseph von, 1791-1856

1063. Die Fahnenwacht. P. Lindpaintner.
[2]p. 36 x 28 cm.
Song with piano accpt.
First line: Der Sänger hält im Feld.
Published as op. 114 by J. Schuberth & Co. in Leipzig.
LIBRARY OF CONGRESS

1064. Wehmuthsthräne.
[2]p. 22 x 32 cm.
For 4-part male chorus unaccompanied.
First line: Thräne die dem Aug' entquillt.
At end: Stuttgart im April 1834. P. J. Lindpaintner.
Former owner: Joseph Muller.   NEW YORK PUBLIC LIBRARY

Liszt, Franz, 1811-1886

Reference is given to the detailed lists of the composer's works in Peter Raabe's *Franz Liszt*, vol. 2 (Stuttgart, 1931) and in the supplementary volume to the 3rd edition of Grove's *Dictionary* (London, 1940), p. 368-402.

1065. Schubert, Franz Peter, 1797-1828.
[Die Allmacht]
14 p. 35 x 27 cm.
Liszt's arrangement for tenor solo, male chorus and orchestra.
Full score.
At end: 21. Februar, 71.
Published in 1872 by J. Schuberth & Co. in Leipzig.
Raabe 652; Grove 668.
Former owner: Rafael Joseffy.   LIBRARY OF CONGRESS

1066. An den heiligen Franziskus (von Paula); Gebet, für Männer Stimmen (Soli und Chor) mit Begleitung des Harmoniums (oder Orgel) und 3 Posaunen und Pauken, ad libitum, von Franz Liszt.
7 p. 34 x 25½ cm.
Score, German and Hungarian text.
Published in 1875 by Táborszky & Parsch in Budapest.
Werke, series V, no. 5.
Raabe 494; Grove 511.
Former owner: Rafael Joseffy.   LIBRARY OF CONGRESS

1067. [Canzone napolitana]
2 leaves. 28 x 40 cm.
For piano 2 hands.
Caption title deleted; title and signature at end.
Published in 1843 by Meser in Dresden.
Raabe 92; Grove 161.   MRS. MEYER DAVIS

1068. [Christus. No. 5]
"Die heiligen drei Könige"; Marsch.
15 p. 27 x 35 cm.
Reduction of full score for piano 4 hands.
Published in 1873 by J. Schuberth & Co. in Leipzig.
Raabe 335, 2; Grove 411, 2.   LIBRARY OF CONGRESS

1069. Beethoven, Ludwig van, 1770-1827.
[Concerto, piano, no. 4, op. 58, G major]
Beethoven. 4tes Concert.
[40]p. 37½ x 23½ cm.
Score for 2 pianos, the orchestra accpt. arr. by Liszt for 2nd piano
Published in 1879 by J. G. Cotta in Stuttgart.
Former owner: Rafael Joseffy.   LIBRARY OF CONGRES

1070. Beethoven, Ludwig van, 1770-1827.
[Concerto, piano, no. 5, op. 73, E flat major]
Beethoven. 5tes Concert.
[47]p. 34 x 24 cm.

Score for 2 pianos, the orchestra accpt. arr. by Liszt for 2nd piano.
Published in 1879 by J. G. Cotta in Stuttgart.
Former owner: Rafael Joseffy.   LIBRARY OF CONGRESS

1071.   [Das deutsche Vaterland]
    Arndt. Das deutsche Vaterland! (Neue Version) den Berliner,—
    Wiener,—Königsberger,—Breslauer,—Hallenser und Jenenser
    Studenten sympatisch gewidmet von Dr. Franz Liszt.
    1 leaf, 5 p. 25 x 33 cm.
For 4-part male chorus.
At end: 10 April F. Liszt.
The second version, apparently unpublished.
Facsimile of p. 1 in Henrici auction catalogue no. LXXX.
Raabe 545, Grove 567.
Former owner: Mrs. Marie Louise Zimbalist.
                                                       CURTIS INSTITUTE OF MUSIC

1072.   [Elegy, violin and piano, no. 2]
    2te Elegie.
    [6]p. 32 x 23½ cm.
For piano 2 hands (the first version); incomplete.
Dedicated to L. Ramann.
Published in 1878 by C. F. Kahnt in Leipzig.
Werke, series II, vol. 9.
Raabe 77, Grove 109.
Former owners: Wilhelm Heyer (catalogue, vol. IV, no. 1590a),
    Joseph Muller.   NEW YORK PUBLIC LIBRARY

1073.   [Elegy, violin and piano, no. 2]
    2te Elegie.
    [6]p. 32 x 23½ cm.
For violin and piano.
Published in 1878 by C. F. Kahnt in Leipzig.
Raabe 472, Grove 483.
Former owners: Wilhelm Heyer (catalogue, vol. IV, no. 1590b),
    Joseph Muller.   NEW YORK PUBLIC LIBRARY

1074.   [Fantaisie über Motive aus Beethoven's Ruinen von Athen]
    [2]p. 33 x 24½ cm.
Version for piano solo of Liszt's arrangement for piano and orchestra. At head of title: Version für Pianoforte allein. N.B. Bis zum
letzten Takt der Seite 44 bleibt die Version für Pianoforte allein
dieselbe wie in der Partitur (mit Hinzufügung der kleinen Noten
für die Orchester-Eintritte). The piano solo part is written out
only where it differs from the solo part in the version for piano
and orchestra.
Published in 1865 by C. F. W. Siegel in Leipzig.
Raabe 126, Grove 174.   LIBRARY OF CONGRESS

Liszt, Franz—*continued*

1075. [Eine Faust-Symphonie]
2ter Satz der Faust Symphonie. Gretchen.
[31]p. 35 x 27 cm.
Score for brass and timpani (material for rehearsals).

MR. GREGOR PIATIGORSKY

1076. Meyerbeer, Giacomo, 1791-1864.
[Festmarsch zu Schiller's 100-jähriger Geburtsfeier]
[2]p. 33 x 27 cm.
Fragment of full score.
Raabe 226, Grove 334.

NEWBERRY LIBRARY

1077. Wagner, Richard, 1813-1883.
[Der fliegende Holländer. Senta's ballad]
Ballade, aus der Oper "Der fliegende Holländer" von Richard
Wagner. Transcription für Pianoforte von F. Liszt.
[6]p. 27 x 35 cm.
At end: 2ten Januar 72.
Published in 1873 by Meser in Dresden.
Raabe 274, Grove 226.
Former owner: Rafael Joseffy.

LIBRARY OF CONGRESS

1078. Weber, Carl Maria (Friedrich Ernst), Freiherr von, 1786-1826.
Freyschütz Ouverture von C. M. von Weber. Clavier Partitur
von F. Liszt.
[31]p. 33 x 25½ cm.
Published in 1847 by A. M. Schlesinger in Berlin.
Raabe, 289, Grove 360.

SIBLEY MUSICAL LIBRARY

1079. [Grande valse de bravura]
Valse di bravura à 4 ms.
[3]p. 25 x 34 cm.
Arrangement for piano 4 hands of the 1st version for piano 2 hands.
Published in 1836 by Latte.
Raabe 298, Grove 389.
Former owner: George R. Siedenburg.

DR. LUDWIG LOEWENSTEIN

1080. [Hungarian rhapsody, no. 15, A minor]
Rákóczy.
[4]p. 33 x 25½ cm.
For piano 2 hands, simplified version.
At end: F. Liszt à son ami Szerdahelyi mai 1851. Weimar.
Published as *Comorn, marche de Rakoczy* in 1852 by Wessel,
Ashdown in London.
Raabe 106, 15; Grove 157, 15.

MRS. WALTER T. ROSEN

1081. [Hungarian rhapsody, piano, no. 16, A minor]
Zu den Munkácsy Festlichkeiten in Budapest. A Budapesti
Munkácsy-ünnepèlyhez. Ungarische Rhapsodie von F. L.
[9]p. 33 x 25½ cm.

Incomplete.
Published in 1882 by Táborsky & Parsch in Budapest.
Werke, series II, vol. 12.
Raabe 106, 16; Grove 157, 16.
Former owner: Rafael Joseffy.   LIBRARY OF CONGRESS

1082. Weber, Carl Maria, Freiherr von, 1786-1826.
    Jubel-Ouverture von C. M. von Weber. Clavier Partitur von
       Franz Liszt.
    31 p. 33 x 25½ cm.
Published in 1847 by A. M. Schlesinger in Berlin.
Raabe 290, Grove 361.   SIBLEY MUSICAL LIBRARY

1083. Die Legende der heiligen Elisabeth. Clavier Auszug . . . F. Liszt.
    4 leaves, 14, 11 p. 27 x 34 and 27 x 37 cm.
Piano-vocal score, incomplete.
At end: Septembre. Rome! 62.
Published in 1867 by C. F. Kahnt in Leipzig.
Raabe 477, Grove 495.   PAUL GOTTSCHALK

1084. Weber, Carl Maria, Freiherr von, 1786-1826.
    Leyer und Schwerdt, nach Kö[r]ner-Weber's Leyer und Schwerdt,
       Héroïde für das Pianoforte von Franz Liszt.
    1 leaf, 14 p. 25 x 33 cm.
At end: Krzizanowitz, 10 April, 1848.
Published in 1848 by A. M. Schlesinger in Berlin.
Raabe 285, Grove 237.   LIBRARY OF CONGRESS

1085. [Das Lied der Begeisterung]
    [2]p. 33½ x 25½ cm.
For 4-part male chorus unaccompanied.
At end: F. Liszt, in Raiding geboren! Mai, 74, Pest.
Published in 1871 by Táborsky & Parsch in Budapest, with Hun-
    garian title: *A lelkesed és dala.*
Raabe 561, Grove 584.
Former owner: Franz Joseffy.   LIBRARY OF CONGRESS

1086. Schubert, Franz Peter, 1797-1828.
    Lied der Mignon.
    [3]p. 26½ x 17 cm.
Liszt's arrangement for voice and piano of Schubert's song *So lasst*
    mich scheinen (op. 62, no. 3; Schubert's Werke, series XX, no.
    490). Liszt transposes the song from B to B flat major and changes
    both vocal part and accompaniment, by turns simplifying and
    enriching, and adding measures. This version is unknown to
    Raabe and Grove. Liszt orchestrated this song in 1860 (Raabe
    651, 3; Grove 667, 3).   LIBRARY OF CONGRESS

1087. Bülow, Hans Guido von, 1830-1894.
[Mazurka-Fantaisie. Op. 13]
15 p. 33 x 24 cm.
Full score of Liszt's transcription for orchestra of the original composition for piano.
Published in 1868 by F. E. C. Leuckart in Leipzig.
Raabe 446, Grove 26.
Former owners: Hans von Bülow, Martin Krause, George T. Keating.
Facsimile of p. 1 in Van Patten, *Catalogue,* p. 124.
MEMORIAL LIBRARY OF MUSIC, STANFORD UNIVERSITY

1088. [Mignon's Lied]
[6]p. 34 x 27 cm.
Original draft, for voice and piano, of the 3rd version (voice and orchestra) of the song composed in 1842.
Text by Goethe.
First line: Kennst du das Land.
Published (full score) in 1861 by C. F. Kahnt in Leipzig.
Werke, series VII, vol. 2.
Raabe 592c, Grove 594.
Former owners: Hans von Bülow, Martin Krause.
YALE UNIVERSITY LIBRARY, SPECK COLLECTION

1089. Weber, Carl Maria, Freiherr von, 1786-1826.
Oberon. Ouverture von C. M. von Weber. Clavier Partitur von F. Liszt . . .
[25]p. 33 x 25½ cm.
Published in 1847 by A. M. Schlesinger in Berlin.
Raabe 288, Grove 359.   SIBLEY MUSICAL LIBRARY

1090. [Der Papst-Hymnus]
[6]p. 35 x 27 cm.
For piano 4 hands.
Liszt made an organ version (Raabe 391, Grove 449) and also incorporated the *Papst-hymnus* as no. 8 in his oratorio *Christus* (Raabe 478, Grove 496).
Published in 1865 by Ed. Bote und G. Bock in Berlin.
Raabe 336, Grove 407.   NEW YORK PUBLIC LIBRARY

1091. Polnisch (Polonais).
8 p. 33 x 26 cm.
For piano 2 hands.
Published as no. 12 of his *Weihnachtsbaum, Arbre de Noël* in 1882 by Adolph Fürstner in Berlin.
Werke, series II, vol. 9.
Raabe 71, 12; Grove 99, 12.
Former owner: Rafael Joseffy.   LIBRARY OF CONGRESS

1092.   Les préludes. Symphonische Dichtung von F. Liszt.
      1 leaf, 28 p. 25 x 33½ cm.
    Composer's arrangement for 2 pianos.
    Published in 1856 by Breitkopf & Härtel in Leipzig.
    Raabe 359, Grove 426.   THE ROSENBACH COMPANY

1093.   [Psalm 129. De profundis]
      Der 129. Psalm.
      [2]p. 25 x 17 cm.
    Sketches (melody with German text), differing considerably from
      the version published in 1883 by C. F. Kahnt in Leipzig.
    Raabe 492b, Grove 509, 2.   LIBRARY OF CONGRESS

1094.   [Rákóczy-Marsch für grosses Orchester von Franz Liszt]
      22 p. 33 x 24½ cm.
    Full score.
    At end: 23 décembre 67.
    Published in 1871 by J. Schuberth in Leipzig.
    Raabe 439, Grove 23.   HENRY E. HUNTINGTON LIBRARY

1095.   Réminiscences de Don Juan.
      37 p. 31 x 23½ and 24 x 29 cm.
    For piano 2 hands.
    Published ca. 1843 by A. M. Schlesinger in Berlin.
    Raabe 228, Grove 203.   MISS YRSA HEIN

1096.   [Réminiscences de Don Juan]
      Cadenz. Don Juan Fantasia. Seite 15, Zeile 3.
      [6]p. 26 x 17 cm.
    Followed on p. 1 by *Varianten zu den 6ten Heft der Soirées de
    Vienne,* and on p. 3-6 by *Veränderungen in der Tarantelle aus
    der "Stumme von Portici."*
    Inscribed to Sophie Menter, Rom, September 69.
                          LIBRARY OF CONGRESS

1097.   Salve Polonia! . . . (pour grand orchestre) par Franz Liszt.
      [14]p. 36½ x 27 cm.
    Full score; incomplete.
    Partly in another hand.
    Published in 1883 by C. F. Kahnt in Leipzig.
    Later used in his unfinished oratorio *Die Legende vom heiligen
    Stanislaus.*
    Raabe 430, Grove 19.
    Former owner: Rafael Joseffy.   LIBRARY OF CONGRESS

1098.   Schubert, Franz Peter, 1797-1828.
      Soirées de Vienne. Valses-Caprices d'après F. Schubert, . . . par
      F. Liszt, en neuf livraisons. Vienne, Spina.
      1 leaf, [57]p. 27½ x 34½ cm.
    For piano 2 hands.

Liszt, Franz—*continued*

Dedicated to S. Löwy.
Published in 1852-53 by C. A. Spina in Vienna.
Raabe 252, Grove 212.
Former owners: Marie Breidenstein, Alfred Stern, George Darm-
stadt.
Cf. E. N. Waters, "Liszt's *Soirées de Vienne*," in *Library of Con-
gress Quarterly Journal*, VI, no. 2 (Feb. 1949), 10-19, with fac-
simile of 2 pages.   LIBRARY OF CONGRESS

[Soirées de Vienne]
see also no. 1096.

1099.   Mendelssohn-Bartholdy, (Jacob Ludwig) Felix, 1809-1847.
        [Ein Sommernachtstraum. Hochzeitsmarsch]
        1 leaf, [9]p. 33 x 27 cm.
        Arrangement for piano 2 hands.
        Published in 1851 by Breitkopf & Härtel in Leipzig (together with
        Elfenreigen from the same work).
        Raabe 219, Grove 195.
        Former owners: Al. Winterberger, Johann Sikemeier, Karl Hey-
        mann, Mr. and Mrs. Robert Woods Bliss.
                            HARVARD UNIVERSITY, DUMBARTON OAKS

1100.   Eine Symphonie zu Dante's Divina Commedia.
        [71]p. 40 x 33 and 34½ x 27 cm.
        Full score.
        Published in 1859 by Breitkopf & Härtel in Leipzig.
        Werke, series I, vol. 7.
        Raabe 426, Grove 15.
        Former owner: Artur Nikisch.   WALTER SCHATZKI

1101.   Egressy, Béni, 1814-1851.
        Szózat und ungarischer Hymnus. Gedichte von Vörösmarty und
            Kölcsey, componirt von Erressy [!] Béni und F. Erkel. Für
            Clavier gesetzt von F. Liszt . . .
        1 leaf, [12]p. 33 x 26 cm.
        At end: Maÿ 73, Pest.
        Dedicated to Count Julius Andrassy.
        Published in 1873 by Rózsavölgyi & Co. in Budapest.
        Raabe 158, Grove 271.
        Former owner: Rafael Joseffy.   LIBRARY OF CONGRESS

        Auber, Daniel François Esprit, 1782-1871.
        [La muette de Portici. Tarantelle]
        [Tarantelle de bravura d'après la Tarantelle de La Muette de
            Portici]
        see no. 1096.

Liszt, Franz—*continued*

1102. [Te Deum laudamus, no. 1]
Te Deum.
[6]p. 35 x 26½ cm.
For 8-part mixed chorus with accpt. of organ and 2 horns, 2 trumpets, tenor and bass trombone and timpani (ad lib.)
At end: Mai 67 F. Liszt.
The first 2 pages contain the composition entire on 3 staves, the upper staff for the voice parts, mainly in unison. However, the voice part at the passage beginning "Te ergo quaesimus" is cancelled and appears on p. 4 in 8-part harmony. The wind and timpani parts are given on p. 5-6 with the words of the text for cues.
First published in 1936 in his Werke, series V, vol. 7, p. 161, where date of composition is given as 1853.
Raabe 533, Grove 557 (date of composition suggested as 1859).
CURTIS INSTITUTE OF MUSIC

1103. "Todten Tanz," für Pianoforte allein.
[7]p. 33½ x 24½ cm.
Transcription for piano 2 hands of his work for piano and orchestra.
Published in 1865 by C. F. W. Siegel in Leipzig.
Raabe 188, Grove 297. LIBRARY OF CONGRESS

1104. Széchényi, Imre *gróf*, 1825-1898.
Ungarischer Marsch v. Fr. Liszt.
[9]p. 34½ x 27½ cm.
For piano 2 hands.
Note on p. 1: Motiv vom Grafen Imre Széchényi.
Published in 1878 by Rózsavölgyi & Co. in Budapest.
Raabe 261, Grove 358. LIBRARY OF CONGRESS

1105. Ungarisches Königs-Lied nach einer alten ungarischen Weise.
F. Liszt.
10 p. 33 x 25 cm.
For mixed chorus with piano accpt.
Text by Kornél Ábrányi.
First line: Sei gesegnet, König der Magyaren.
Published in 1884 by Táborsky & Parsch in Budapest.
Raabe 563, Grove 586. WALTER R. BENJAMIN

1106. Ungarischer Marsch, zur Krönungsfeier in Ofen-Pest]
12 p. 35 x 27 cm.
Full score.
Published in 1871 by J. Schuberth & Co. in Leipzig.
Raabe, 438, Grove 24.
Former owner: Rafael Joseffy. LIBRARY OF CONGRESS

1107. [Unidentified fragment of an oratorio]
p. 13-16. 35 x 26½ cm.
Full score (soprano solo, chorus, orchestra and organ).
At end: terminé 21 août 74.
Text: elle dicte par chants pieux et sa voix répond au génie du haut des cieux.
Former owners: Carl Göpfart, Adolf Ruthardt, Carl F. Tollefsen.
MR. SAMUEL R. ROSENBAUM

1108. [Unidentified fragment of an oratorio]
[4]p. STANFORD UNIVERSITY LIBRARY

1109. [Unidentified work for piano 2 hands]
[5]p. 34 x 27 cm.
Former owner: Rafael Joseffy. LIBRARY OF CONGRESS

1110. [Valse oubliée, piano, no. 2]
Seconde valse oubliée.
2 leaves. 35 x 27 cm.
Incomplete.
Dedicated to Baronne [Olga] de Meyendorff.
Published in 1884 by Ed. Bote & G. Bock in Berlin.
Werke, series II, vol. 10.
Raabe 37, 2; Grove 128, 2.
Former owner: Frédéric de Scennis. NEW YORK PUBLIC LIBRARY

1111. Le vieux vagabond.
[4]p. 24 x 32 cm.
Song with piano accpt.
Text by Béranger.
First line: Dans ce fossé cessons de vivre.
Published in 1917 in his Werke, series VIII, no. 1.
Raabe 565, Grove 623. NEW YORK PUBLIC LIBRARY

1112. "Vom Fels zum Meer." Marsch für grosses Orchester von F. Liszt (Partitur).
7 leaves. 36 x 26½ cm.
Raabe 435, Grove 33.
This ms., the property of Mrs. Henry C. Stokes of Paoli, Penna., was destroyed by fire in 1948.

Litolff, Henry Charles, 1818-1891

1113. Grand caprice sur des motifs de l'opéra Lucrezia Borgia transcrite pour le piano . . . par Henri Litolff, op. 20.
[12]p. 32 x 23½ cm. LIBRARY OF CONGRESS

1114. [Opuscules, piano, op. 25]
[6]p. 27 x 34 cm.
No. 1 lacking.
Contents.—*Vagabond polkas* (no. 1 & 2).—*Tempo di mazurka.—Valse styrienne.—La polonaise.* LIBRARY OF CONGRESS

Llobet, Miguel, 1875-1938

1115. Falla, Manuel de, 1876-1946.
Sept chansons populaires espagnoles, par Manuel de Falla. Transcription pour chant et guitare par Miguel Llobet.
[38]p. 30 x 21½ cm.
Each song paged separately, signed and dated: M. Llobet. Barcelona, marzo 1931.
Performed April 24, 1931 at the Coolidge Festival in Washington.
LIBRARY OF CONGRESS, COOLIDGE FOUNDATION

Loder, Edward James, 1813-1865

1116. [The Night dancers, a grand romantic opera in 2 acts]
2 vols. 37½ x 24 cm.
Full score.
Text by George Soane.
First performed as *The Wiles of the night dancers* October 28, 1846 at the Princess Theatre in London.
Former owners: Charles Jefferys, Harry Wall, William H. Cummings (catalogue, no. 1005).   LIBRARY OF CONGRESS

1117. [Raymond and Agnes, a new grand opera in three acts]
4 vols. 38½ x 24½ cm.
Full score.
Text by Edward Fitzball.
First performed August 13, 1855 at Manchester.
Former owners: Charles Jeffreys, Harry Wall, William H. Cummings (catalogue, no. 1005).   LIBRARY OF CONGRESS

Löhr, Hermann Frederic, 1872-1943

1118. Little grey home in the west.
1 leaf, [3]p. 30½ x 24½ cm.
Song with piano accpt.
Text by D. Eardley-Wilmot.
Published in 1911 by Chappell & Co. in London.
MEMORIAL LIBRARY OF MUSIC, STANFORD UNIVERSITY

Loewe, Johann Carl Gottfried, 1796-1869

1119. Der barmherzige Bruder, eine Tondichtung von Loewe.
[4]p. 39½ x 25 cm.
For piano 2 hands.
Published in 1831 by H. Wagenführ in Berlin.
LIBRARY OF CONGRESS

1120. Frühzeitiger Frühling.
[2]p. 16½ x 22½ cm.
For 4-part mixed chorus unaccompanied.
Text by Goethe.

Loewe, Johann Carl Gottfried—*continued*

First line: Tage der Wonne, kommt ihr so bald?
Published as no. 1 of op. 79, *Vierstimmige Gesänge,* in 1841 by
Wilhelm Paul in Dresden.

1121. [Gesang der Geister über den Wassern. Op. 88]
[2]p. 32 x 21 cm.
Fragment of his part-song for 4 voices and piano.
Published in 1842 by A. M. Schlesinger in Berlin.

1122. Die Heilung des Blindgeborenen. Vokal-Oratorium in 4 Abtheil-
ungen mit Orgel oder Pianoforte comp. von Carl Lowe. Op. 131.
[34]p. 34 x 27 cm.
Published ca. 1860 by Heinrichshofen in Magdeburg.
Facsimile of p. 1 in Van Patten, *Catalogue,* p. 141.
Former owners: Gustav Oberlaender, George T. Keating.

1123. Die Hochzeit der Thetis, Gedicht von Schiller, (Übersetzung der
Iphigenie in Aulis des Euripides, Ende des 4ten Actes) als grosse
Festcantate für Solo- und Chorgesang mit Orchesterbegleitung zu
Concert-Aufführungen componirt von Dr. C. Loewe. Op. 120.
[33]p. 27½ x 39 cm.
Full score.
Published in 1851 by A. M. Schlesinger in Berlin.

1124. Das Hohelied Salomonis. Oratorium von Loewe. Klavierauszug
vom Komponisten.
[6], 136 p. 34 x 27 cm.
The text of this unpublished oratorio, composed in 1855, was
written by Wilhelm Telschow and not by L. Giesebrecht, as
stated by Espagne. The autograph full score was in the Preus-
sische Staatsbibliothek, Berlin.

1125. Acht Lieder mit Begleitung des Pianoforte von J. C. G. Loewe.
1 leaf, [8]p. 35 x 20½ cm.
Published in 1891 as *Acht Jugendlieder* by Breitkopf & Härtel
in Leipzig.
Former owner: Hugo Riesenfeld.

1126. Prinz Eugen der edle Ritter, für eine Singstimme mit Begleitung
des Pianoforte. Ballade von Freiligrath componirt von C. Loewe.
Op. 92.
[4]p. 23 x 36 cm.
On p. 4 are 9 bars of his song *Der Mohrenfürst,* op. 97, no. 1.
Published in 1844 by Ed. Bote & G. Bock in Berlin.
Former owner: Max Friedländer.

Lombard, Emile

1127. Le mariage impromptu. Opéra comique en un acte, paroles de
       Pigault Lebrun, musique d'Emile Lombard.
       1 leaf, 248 p. 30 x 23½ cm.
       Full score of version with small orchestra.
       First performed July 29, 1860.   LIBRARY OF CONGRESS

1128. Le mariage impromptu. Opéra comique en un acte, paroles de
       Pigault Lebrun, musique d'Emile Lombard. Partition d'orchestre.
       1 leaf, 277 p. 34½ x 26½ cm.
       Full score of the "grande partition."
       Dated: Marseille, 1872.   BOSTON PUBLIC LIBRARY

Lopatnikov, Nikolai, 1903-

1129. [Quartet, strings, no. 2, op. 6]
       . . . Deuxième quatuor pour 2 violons, alto et violoncelle . . .
       [1], 72 p. 33 x 26 cm.
       Score.
       Dedicated to Mrs. E. S. Coolidge.
       Awarded the Belaieff prize, 1929.
       Published in 1933 by M. P. Belaieff in Leipzig.
                LIBRARY OF CONGRESS, COOLIDGE FOUNDATION

Lortzing, (Gustav) Albert, 1801-1851

1130. Hiller, Johann Adam, 1728-1804.
       Lied aus "Die Jagd" von Joh. Aug. [!] Hiller, neubearbeitet von
       Albert Lortzing.
       [5]p. 27 x 35 cm.
       At head of title: No. 25 Polacca.
       Full score.
       Former owner: Joseph Muller.   NEW YORK PUBLIC LIBRARY

Lotti, Antonio, ca. 1667-1740

1131. Madrigale a 4 voci di Antonio Lotti quale cantavasi il giorno dell'
       Ascenzione in Venezia dentro il Bucintoro alla presenza del
       serenissimo principe.
       [15]p. 18 x 24 cm.
       Latin text, but another hand has added an English text, beginning:
       All hail Britannia in song triumphant.
       Bound in with his *Messa a 4º*.
       Former owner: William H. Cummings (catalogue, no. 1007).
                                        LIBRARY OF CONGRESS

1132. Messa a 4º sopra il quinto tono di Antonio Lotti.
       [54]p. 18 x 23½ cm.
       For 4-part chorus unaccompanied.
       Bound with this are his *Miserere, Regina coeli* and *Madrigale*.
       Former owner: William H. Cummings (catalogue, no. 1007).
                                        LIBRARY OF CONGRESS

1133. Miserere a 4° di Antonio Lotti.
  [32]p. 18 x 24 cm.
  For 4-part chorus unaccompanied.
  Bound in with his *Messa a 4°*.
  Former owner: William H. Cummings (catalogue, no. 1007).

1134. Regina coeli a 4° di Antonio Lotti.
  [5]p. 18 x 22 cm.
  For 4-part chorus unaccompanied.
  Bound in with his *Messa a 4°*.
  Former owner: William H. Cummings (catalogue, no. 1007).

Lührss, Carl, 1824-1882

1135. [Quartet, strings, op. 38, no. 3, A minor]
  Quartett (A moll) für II Violinen, Viola & Violoncello componirt von Carl Lührss. Partitur.
  72 p. 28½ x 23 cm.

L'vov, Aleksiei (Feodorovich), 1798-1870

1136. Les adieux. Hymne composé à l'occasion de la sortie des élèves de l'Institut Patriotique à St. Petersbourg, par A. Lvoff.
  11 p. 24½ x 29½ cm.
  Score for 4-part chorus, harp or piano, clarinet, bassoon and double bass.

1137. [Russian national anthem]
  12 p. 31 x 24½ cm.
  Full score (4-part mixed chorus and orchestra).
  Signed and dated: 1833.
  Former owner: C. Lipinski.

Mackenzie, *Sir* Alexander Campbell, 1847-1935

1138. "La belle dame sans merci" (after Keats). Ballad for orchestra. A. C. Mackenzie. Op. 29.
  69 p. 31½ x 38 cm.
  Full score.
  At end: May 4th 1883. Westwood House, Sydenham. A. C. M.
  Published in 1884 by Novello & Co. in London.

Mahler, Gustav, 1860-1911

1139. [Das irdische Leben]
  1 leaf, 19 p. 35 x 27 cm.
  Full score (voice and orchestra).

Mahler, Gustav—*continued*

First line: Mutter, ach, Mutter, es hungert mich.
Published as no. 5 of *Des Knaben Wunderhorn* in 1900 by Josef
  Weinberger in Leipzig.   MRS. ALMA MAHLER WERFEL

1140. Das klagende Lied.
      [119]p. 35 x 26½ cm.
      Full score.
      Published in 1914 by Universal Edition in Vienna.
                              MRS. ALMA MAHLER WERFEL

1141. [Das klagende Lied]
      3 leaves. 33 x 26 and 35 x 27 cm.
      Sketches.   MRS. ALMA MAHLER WERFEL

1142. [Liebst du um Schönheit]
      1 leaf. 27 x 22½ cm.
      Song with piano accpt.
      Text by Rückert.
      Published as no. 2 of *Sieben Lieder aus letzter Zeit* in 1905 by
        C. F. Kahnt in Leipzig.   MRS. ALMA MAHLER WERFEL

1143. [Das Lied von der Erde]
      1 leaf, [218]p. 34 x 26½ cm.
      Full score.
      Published in 1912 by Universal Edition in Vienna.
                              MRS. ALMA MAHLER WERFEL

1144. [Das Lied von der Erde]
      42 leaves. 34½ x 26½ cm.
      First draft, for voice and piano, without orchestral interludes, and
        lacking the definitive title.
      Titles of movements 3-5 in this ms. (*Der Pavillon aus Porzellan,
        Am Ufer,* and *Der Trinker im Frühling*) were changed in final
        version.
      At end of 2nd movement: Toblach, Juli 1908.
      At end of 4th movement: Toblach 21 August 1908.
                              MRS. ALMA MAHLER WERFEL

1145. [Quartet, piano and strings, A minor]
      Clavier-Quartett von Gustav Mahler. 1876.
      1 leaf, 19 p. 33 x 26 cm.
      Score of first movement; unpublished.   MRS. ALMA MAHLER WERFEL

1146. [Der Schildwache Nachtlied]
      [3]p. 26 x 35 cm.
      Sketch for song with piano accpt.
      First line: Ich kann und mag nicht fröhlich sein.
      Published as no. 1 of *Des Knaben Wunderhorn* in 1900 by Josef
        Weinberger in Leipzig.   LIBRARY OF CONGRESS

Mahler, Gustav—*continued*

1147. [Sketches]
A large group of sketches, partly analyzed by Alban Berg, mostly instrumental, and of various sizes.   MRS. ALMA MAHLER WERFEL

1148. [Symphony, no. 3, D minor]
[7]p. 35½ x 27 cm.
Sketch for the 4th movement, entitled: *Was das Kind erzählt.*
Former owner: Natalie Bauer-Lechner.
MEMORIAL LIBRARY OF MUSIC, STANFORD UNIVERSITY

1149. [Symphony, no. 3, D minor]
[4]p. 35½ x 27 cm.
Sketches, dated 1893, Steinbach.
Former owner: Natalie Bauer-Lechner.
MEMORIAL LIBRARY OF MUSIC, STANFORD UNIVERSITY

1150. [Symphony, no. 4, G major]
[1]p. 26½ x 34½ cm.
Sketches   MEMORIAL LIBRARY OF MUSIC, STANFORD UNIVERSITY

1151. [Symphony, no. 4, G major]
73 leaves. 27 x 34½ cm.
Sketches.   MRS. ALMA MAHLER WERFEL

1152. [Symphony, no. 5, C sharp minor]
. . . V. Symphonie für grosses Orchester von Gustav Mahler . . .
1 leaf, [304]p. 34½ x 26 cm.
Full score.
Dedicated to Alma Mahler, Wien, Oktober, 1903.
Published in 1904 by C. F. Peters in Leipzig.
MRS. ALMA MAHLER WERFEL

1153. [Symphony, no. 8, E flat major]
1 leaf, [237]p. 40 x 30 cm.
Full score.
Each of the two parts of the work has a separate title-page, as follows: 8. *Symphonie. I. Theil (1. Satz) Hymnus "Veni, creator spiritus."* 8. *Symphonie II. Theil. Schlussscene aus Faust.*
Published in 1910 by Universal Edition in Vienna.
MRS. ALMA MAHLER WERFEL

1154. [Symphony, no. 9, C major]
IX. Symphonie. I-[4] Satz. Gustav Mahler.
138 leaves. 34½ x 27 cm.
Full score.
Published in 1912 by Universal Edition in Vienna.
MRS. ALMA MAHLER WERFEL

1155. [Symphony, no. 10]
58 leaves. 26½ x 34½ cm.
Sketches.
Published in facsimile in 1924 by Zsolnay in Berlin.
Published (2 movements) in 1926 by Universal Edition in Vienna.
MRS. ALMA MAHLER WERFEL

Mahler, Gustav—*continued*

1156. Tanzlegendchen.
1 leaf, 12 p. 35 x 27 cm.
Full score (voice and orchestra).   <small>MRS. ALMA MAHLER WERFEL</small>

Malibran, Maria Felicità, 1808-1836

1157. Aria eingelegt in der Oper "Der Liebestrank" von Donizetti, componirt von Mad. Malibran.
20 p. 21 x 33 cm.
Full score.
First line: Bleibe, bleibe, und nimm die Freiheit.
UNIVERSITY OF CALIFORNIA AT LOS ANGELES,
WILLIAM ANDREWS CLARK MEMORIAL LIBRARY

1158. Have I not seen the frowning oak?
[4]p. 15 x 19½ cm.
Song with piano accpt.   <small>LIBRARY OF CONGRESS</small>

Malipiero, Gian Francesco, 1882-

1159. [Cantàri alla madrigalesca per quartetto ad archi]
23 leaves. 25½ x 34 cm.
Sketches, dated 7-V-1931.
With his *Concerti per orchestra.*
Published in 1932 by Heinrichshofen's Verlag in Magdeburg.
Dedicated to Mrs. E. S. Coolidge.
LIBRARY OF CONGRESS, COOLIDGE FOUNDATION

1160. . . . Concerti per orchestra. Esordio—Concerto di flauti—Concerto di oboi—Concerto di clarinetti—Concerto di fagotti—Concerto di trombe—Concerto di tamburi—Concerto di contrabbassi—Commiato.
22 leaves. 25½ x 34 cm.
Sketches, dated: Asolo, 14 aprile 1931. The individual movements are specially dated, the first: 26 III 1931.
Followed by sketches of his *Cantàri alla madrigalesca.*
Dedicated to Mrs. E. S. Coolidge.
Published in 1932 by G. Ricordi & Co. in Milan.
LIBRARY OF CONGRESS, COOLIDGE FOUNDATION

1161. . . . Epodi e giambi, per violino, oboe, viola, fagotto. Partitura.
Score (1 leaf, 16 p.) 40 x 30 cm. and 4 parts. 32 x 28½ cm.
At end: Asolo, 5 giugno MCMXXII.
Dedicated to Mrs. E. S. Coolidge.
Published in 1933 by Wilhelm Hansen in Copenhagen.
LIBRARY OF CONGRESS, COOLIDGE FOUNDATION

1162. Cinque favole per una voce e piccola orchestra. G. Francesco Malipiero (1950).
40 numbered leaves. 36 x 27 cm.
Tissues, music on recto only.

Malipiero, Gian Francesco—*continued*

Full score.
Dedicated to Mrs. E. S. Coolidge.
At end: Asolo 31 luglio 1950.

1163.   Cinque favole per una voce e piccola orchestra.
    1 leaf, [24]p. 33 x 25 cm.
Sketches.
At end: Asolo 25 VII. 1950.

1164.   ... La nave della vittoria. Ricercari II per 11 istrumenti.
    1 leaf, 80 p. 40 x 28½ cm.
Score.
At end: Asolo, 6 dicembre MCMXXVI.
Dedicated to Mrs. E. S. Coolidge.
Published in 1927 by Universal Edition in Vienna.

1165.   La principessa Ulalia. G. Francesco Malipiero (1924).
    50 p. 40 x 29 cm.
Piano-vocal score, Italian and English text (by the composer).
At end: Asolo, 4 febbraio MCMXXIV.
Published in 1925 by C. C. Birchard & Co. in Boston.

1166.   [Quartet, strings, no. 4]
    ... Quarto quartetto.
    27 numbered leaves. 33 x 25½ cm.
Score.
At end: Asolo, 21 V 1934.
Dedicated to Mrs. E. S. Coolidge.
Published in 1936 by Wilhelm Hansen in Copenhagen.

1167.   Rispetti e strambotti.
    Score (41 p.) 40 x 29 cm. and 4 parts. 33 x 24 cm.
For string quartet.
Dedicated to Mrs. E. S. Coolidge.
Berkshire Music Festival Prize, 1920.
Published in 1921 by J. and W. Chester in London.

1168.   . . . Sonata a cinque; flauto, violino, viola, violoncello e arpa.
    Partitura.
    [111]p. 33½ x 24 cm.
At end: Asolo, 7 luglio MCMXXXIV.
Dedicated to Mrs. E. S. Coolidge.
Published in 1936 by G. Ricordi & Co. in Milan.

Malipiero, Gian Francesco—*continued*

1169. Sonata a tre. Primo tempo per violoncello e pianoforte. Secondo tempo per violino e pianoforte. Ultimo tempo per violino, violoncello e pianoforte.
p. 1-18, 27-58. 40 x 28½ cm.
Score.
Each movement dated, as follows: Asolo, 22 gennaio MCMXXVI; Asolo, 21 giugno MCMXXVII; Asolo 14 luglio MCMXXVII.
Dedicated to Mrs. E. S. Coolidge.
Published in 1928 by Universal Edition in Vienna.

1170. ... Stornelli e ballate per quartetto d'archi.
Score (1 leaf, [42]p.) and 4 parts. 33 x 24 cm.
At end: Parma 22.2.1923.
Dedicated to Mrs. E. S. Coolidge.
Published in 1923 by G. Ricordi & Co. in Milan.

1171. ... I trionfi d'Amore; tre commedie in una. I. Castel smeraldo. II. Mascherata. III. Giochi olimpici.
2 leaves, 99 p. 42½ x 30 cm.
Piano-vocal score.
At end: Asolo, 25 giugno MCMXXXI.
Dedicated to Mrs. E. S. Coolidge.

1172. ... Quattro vecchie canzoni, per una voce e sette instrumenti. Partitura ...
1 leaf, 24 p. 39½ x 30 cm.
Score.
At end: Venezia 10.II.1940. XVIII.
Dedication to Mrs. E. S. Coolidge.
Published in 1941 by Edizioni Suvini Zerboni in Milan.

Manuel, Roland, 1891-

1173. [Quartet, harps]
[4]p. 24 x 32½ cm.
Real name: Roland Alexis Manuel Lévy.
At end: Roland-Manuel 16 juin 1925.

Marschner, Franz, 1855-?

1174. Praeludium.
[4]p. 33 x 25½ cm.
For organ.
Former owner: Joseph Muller.

Marschner, Heinrich August, 1795-1861

1175. [Der Bäbu]
No. 8. Recit. und Lied.
[4]p. 34½ x 24½ cm.
Piano-vocal score of recitative: *Komm an mein Herz* and aria: *Grüsst du mir.*
At end: d. 1ten November 1836.
Sketches on p. 1 and 4.
Former owner: Hugo Riesenfeld.   LIBRARY OF CONGRESS

1176. Sangkönig Hiarne, oder das Tyrsingschwert; grosse Oper in 4 Aufzügen von W. Grothe u. F. Rodenberg. Musik von Heinrich Marschner. Clavierauszug vom Componisten.
[247]p. 32 x 24 cm.
Piano-vocal score.
At end: . . . den 27 Oct. 1857.
First performed at Frankfurt am Main in 1863.
                            LIBRARY OF CONGRESS

1177. No. 2. Zum Tanzabend von O. H. Graf von Loeben.
[2]p. 24 x 30 cm.
Song with piano accpt.
At end: H. Marschner, d. 28 Aug. 1828.
On p. 2. No. 3. *Das Bad v. W. Müller.*
                    NEW ENGLAND CONSERVATORY OF MUSIC

1178. . . . Zweÿ Vigilien von F. D., für eine Sopran- oder Tenorstimme, mit Begleitung des Pianoforte, componirt . . . von Heinrich Marschner . . . 120tes Werk.
8 p. 34 x 24 cm.
First lines: Die Lüfte weh'n so schaurig; Spät nach dem Tag.
Published by Breitkopf & Härtel in Leipzig.
                        NEW YORK PUBLIC LIBRARY

Martini, Giambattista, 1706-1784

1179. Canoni.
[136]p. 22 x 30½ cm.
A collection of 302 canons in 2 to 8 parts, in Italian, Latin and French.
Former owner: Natale Gallini (catalogue, no. 4, with facsimile of one page).
        MEMORIAL LIBRARY OF MUSIC, STANFORD UNIVERSIT'

Martinů, Bohuslav, 1890-

1180. [Quintet, strings]
Quintett. 1.2. violini. 1.2. altos. 1 v.cello. B. Martinů . . . Paris.
1 leaf, 25 p. 34 x 27 cm.
Score.
Dedicated to Mrs. E. S. Coolidge.
Published in 1930 by La Sirène Musicale in Paris.
            LIBRARY OF CONGRESS, COOLIDGE FOUNDATION

Martinů, Bohuslav—*continued*

1181. [Sextet, strings]
. . . Sextuor pour cordes (2 violons, 2 altos, 2 violoncelli).
B. Martinu . . .
Score ([1], 33 p.) and parts. 35 x 27 cm.
At end: Paris, mai 20-27, 1932.
Dedicated to Mrs. E. S. Coolidge.
Coolidge prize, 1932.
Published in 1948 by Associated Music Publishers in New York.
LIBRARY OF CONGRESS, COOLIDGE FOUNDATION

1182. [Sextet, strings]
Sketches to string sextet (dedicated to Mrs. E. Sprague Coolidge)
. . . B. Martinu.
[14]p. 35 x 27 cm.
MEMORIAL LIBRARY OF MUSIC, STANFORD UNIVERSITY

Martucci, Giuseppe, 1856-1909
1183. Due romanze per violoncello con accomp. di pianoforte di
G. Martucci. No. 2.
[4]p. 23½ x 33 cm.
MR. ARTURO TOSCANINI

Mascagni, Pietro, 1863-1945
1184. L'amico Fritz.
8 p. 31 x 22½ cm. 48, 35, 43 p. 38½ x 26½ cm.
Piano-vocal score.
Incomplete; lacks 48 p. of published piano-vocal score.
Each number signed and dated. The dates indicate the various
numbers were not composed in the order of the score. They run
from *Cerignola, 4 febbraio '91* (Act II, p. 14) to *Firenze, 6
ottobre '91* (Prelude). Full list in Gallini sale catalogue.
Former owner: Natale Gallini (catalogue, no. 32, with facsimile
of p. 2 of Act I).
Facsimile of p. 8 of *Prelude* in Van Patten, *Catalogue*, p. 166.
First performed October 31, 1891 at the Teatro Costanzi in Rome.
MEMORIAL LIBRARY OF MUSIC, STANFORD UNIVERSITY

1185. Cavalleria rusticana.
277 p. 39 x 27½ cm.
Full score.
First performed May 17, 1890 at Rome.
Facsimile of p. 1 of *Intermezzo* in Van Patten, *Catalogue*, p. 154.
MEMORIAL LIBRARY OF MUSIC, STANFORD UNIVERSITY

1186. . . . Pater noster, volgarizzato da D. Capellina, posto in musica per
canto in chiave di sol, con accompagnamento di quintetto a
corda, da Pietro Mascagni. Premiato con menzione onorevole all'
esposizione musicale di Milano nel 1881. Partitura.
2 leaves, 19 p. 31 x 23 cm.
Dated Oct. 10, 1880.
MEMORIAL LIBRARY OF MUSIC, STANFORD UNIVERSITY

Massarani, Renzo, 1898-

1187. Quartetto pastorale per oboe, fagotto, viola e violoncello. (1923).
4 parts. 33 x 27 cm.   LEAGUE OF COMPOSERS

Massenet, Jules (Emile Frédéric), 1842-1912

1188. Beaux yeux que j'aime.
[5]p. 35 x 27 cm.
Song with piano accpt.
Text by Th. Maquet.
Published ca. 1891 by Heugel et Cie. in Paris.
Former owner: Sybil Sanderson.   MRS. MARION SANDERSON NALL

1189. (Canon à 2 voix) Immortalité. (Poésie de J. Combarieu).
2 p. 35 x 27 cm.
First line: Pour le juste, la vie n'est point ici-bas.
At end: J. Massenet, Sept. 1909.
Published in 1909 in the *Supplément* to the *Revue musicale*.
LIBRARY OF CONGRESS

1190. Esclarmonde.
279 leaves. 35 x 27 cm.
Music on recto only of irregularly numbered leaves.
First draft of the opera.
Dated at beginning: Paris, jeudi 29 avril 88, and at end: 6 juillet 88,
. . . à Paris. Many dates throughout.
First performance May 14, 1889 in Paris.
Former owner: Sybil Sanderson.   MRS. MARION SANDERSON NALL

1191. . . . Noël de fleurs. Poësie de Louis Schneider. Musique de
J. Massenet.
[4]p. 35½ x 27 cm.
Song with piano accpt.
First line: Il pleut des iris, des jasmins.
Dedicated to Mme. Charlotte Lormont.
Published in 1912 by Heugel et Cie. in Paris.
MEMORIAL LIBRARY OF MUSIC, STANFORD UNIVERSITY

1192. . . . Pensée d'automne. Poésie d'Armand Silvestre.
7 leaves. 35 x 27 cm.
Music on recto only of numbered leaves.
Song with piano accpt.
First line: L'an fuit vers son déclin.
At beginning: Paris samedi 24 sept. 87. At end: Paris . . . 25 sept. 87.
Dedicated to Sybil Sanderson.
Published as no. 17 of *20 Mélodies,* vol. 3 by Heugel et Cie. in Paris.
MRS. MARION SANDERSON NALL

1193. La terre promise, oratorio en 3 parties (d'après la Vulgate), musique
de J. Massenet. Part^n pi^o et ch^t (réduction de l'orchestre) . . .
107 leaves. 34½ x 27 cm.
Music on recto only of irregularly numbered leaves.

Massenet, Jules (Emile Frédéric)—*continued*

At end: Massenet, Paris 1900.
Dedicated to Nellie Chapman.
First performed March 15, 1900 in Paris.
Former owners: Nellie Chapman, George T. Keating.

1194.   Thaïs, poème lyrique en 3 actes et 6 tableaux (d'après le roman
de M. Anatole France), poème de Louis Gallet, musique de
J. Massenet.
266 leaves. 35 x 26½ cm.
Music on recto only of irregularly numbered leaves.
First draft (voice and piano) of the opera.
Dated at beginning: Paris . . . 1 avril 1892. At end: Neufchâtel
15 juillet 92. J. Massenet.
First performed March 16, 1894 in Paris.
Former owner: Sybil Sanderson.

1195.   Werther, drame lyrique en 3 actes et 4 tableaux. J. Massenet.
186 leaves. 35½ x 25½ cm.
Music on recto only of irregularly numbered leaves.
First draft (voice and piano) of the opera.
At end: Paris, lundi 14 mars 1887. J. Massenet. Many dates
throughout.
First performed: February 16, 1892 in Vienna.
Former owner: Sybil Sanderson.

Mauke, Wilhelm, 1867-1930
1196.   . . . Der Tugendprinz (Operette). Von Max Neal. (Teilweise
nach einer fremden Idee). Musik von Wilhelm Mauke.
[139]p. 35 x 27 cm.
Piano-vocal score.

Mayr, Johann Simon, 1763-1845
1197.   Arietta per canto e piano.
8 p. 14 x 18½ cm.
First line: Luci mie belle scese dal cielo.
Facsimile of a page in Abbiati, *Storia della musica*, vol. IV, p. 135.
Former owner: Natale Gallini (catalogue, no. 20).

Mayseder, Joseph, 1789-1863
1198.   [Quintet, violins, viola, and violoncellos, no. 3, D major]
3. Quintetto.
[45]p. 37 x 27 cm.
Score.
Another autograph score, [33]p.

Mayseder, Joseph—*continued*

1199.   [Quintet, violins, viola and violoncellos, no. 4, A minor]
        4. Quintetto.
        [25]p. 26 x 35 cm.
        Score.   BOSTON PUBLIC LIBRARY

1200.   [Quintet, violins, viola and violoncellos, no. 5, B flat major]
        5. Quintetto.
        [39]p. 26½ x 35½ cm.
        Score.   BOSTON PUBLIC LIBRARY

1201.   [Quintet, violins, viola and violoncellos, no. 6, A major]
        6. Quintetto.
        [34]p. 26½ x 35½ cm.
        Score.   BOSTON PUBLIC LIBRARY

1202.   [Symphony, E flat major]
        Symphonie.
        [98]p. 26½ x 35 cm.
        p. 1-2 wanting.   BOSTON PUBLIC LIBRARY

Mazzinghi, Joseph, 1765-1839

1203.   Pastoral for three voices.
        2 leaves. 28½ x 27 cm.
        First line: Sublime were the blushes of morn.
        At end: J. Mazzinghi, 28th May 1833.   LIBRARY OF CONGRESS

Méhul, Etienne Nicolas, 1763-1818

1204.   [Sketches for an opera]
        [2]p. 27 x 35 cm.   MR. CARL H. TOLLEFSEN

Mendelssohn-Bartholdy, Felix (Jakob Ludwig), 1809-1847

1205.   Abschiedstafel.
        [2]p. 30½ x 23 cm.
        For 4-part men's chorus, unaccompanied.
        Text by Eichendorff.
        First line: So rückt denn in die Runde.
        Published as no. 4 of op. 75, *Vier Lieder,* by Fr. Kistner in Leipzig.
        Werke, series XVII, no. 131, p. 17.   WALTER R. BENJAMIN

1206.   [Altdeutsches Lied]
        In dem Wald. Altdeutsches Lied.
        [1]p. 30 x 23 cm.
        Song with piano accpt.
        Text by Heinrich Schreiber.
        First line: Es ist in den Wald gesungen.
        Dated January 4, 1841.
        Published as no. 1 of op. 57, *Sechs Lieder,* by Breitkopf & Härtel
            in Leipzig.
        Former owner: L. Mühlenfeld.
                           MEMORIAL LIBRARY OF MUSIC, STANFORD UNIVERSITY

1207. Bach, Johann Sebastian, 1685-1750.
    [Cantata no. 106. Gottes Zeit ist die allerbeste Zeit. S. 106]
    Anhang zu no. 6. Gottes Zeit. Clarinetti & fagotti.
    [4]p. 30½ x 22 cm.
    Parts for clarinets and bassoons to be added to Bach's score.
                                   LIBRARY OF CONGRESS, WHITTALL FOUNDATION

1208. [Sieben Characterstücke, piano, op. 7]
    [2]p. 23 x 19 cm.
    No. 1, *Andante espressivo,* E minor, only.
    At end: d. 18ten Oct. 1828. Felix Mendelssohn-Bartholdy.
    Former owner: Frank Ginn.   MRS. WILLIAM POWELL JONES

1209. [Concerto, violin, op. 64, E minor]
    5 p. 33½ x 28 cm.
    Alterations in the orchestral accpt., comprising both text and music,
    for the Novello edition.
                                     LIBRARY OF CONGRESS, WHITTALL FOUNDATION

1210. [Concertstück, no. 1, op. 113, F minor]
    Die Schlacht bei Prag. Ein grosses Duett für Dampfnudel oder
    Rahmstrudel, Clarinett u. Bassethorn, componirt u. demütig
    dedicirt an Bärman sen. und Bärman jun. von ihrem ganz
    ergebenen Felix Mendelssohn-Bartholdy. Berlin 30 Dec. 1832
    (Ende gut, alles gut). Zum erstenmal gespielt bei Heinrich Bär
    in der Bärenstrasse von den Bärleuten am 1sten Jan. 33.
    [11]p. 31½ x 23 cm.
    Score (clarinet, bassethorn and piano).
    Published in 1869 by J. André in Offenbach.
    Werke, series VII, no. 2.   LIBRARY OF CONGRESS

1211. [Heimkehr aus der Fremde, op. 89]
    Aus der Fremde. Ein Liederspiel gedichtet von C. Klingemann,
    componirt von Felix Mendelssohn-Bartholdy zur Feyer des 26
    December 1829. Clavierauszug.
    [56]p. 31½ x 22½ cm.
    Piano-vocal score (overture and no. 11 for piano 4 hands).
    Note in another hand gives title: *Heimkehr aus der Fremde* and
    indicates the work was written for the silver wedding anniversary
    of the composer's parents, this copy being made for Frau Therese
    Devrient.
    Published in 1851 by Breitkopf & Härtel in Leipzig.
    Werke, series XV, no. 122.
    Facsimile of first 2 pages in *Mendelssohn's Letters,* ed. G. Selden-
    Goth, New York, 1945, p. 66-67.   HEINEMAN FOUNDATION

1212. [Ich hör' ein Vöglein locken]
    Im Frühling.
    [2]p. 21½ x 15½ cm.
    Song with piano accpt.

Mendelssohn-Bartholdy, Felix (Jakob Ludwig)—*continued*

Text by A. Böttger, first line as above.
At end: . . . Felix Mendelssohn-Bartholdy, Leipzig, d. 21sten April 1841.
Published as no. 1 of *Zwei Gesänge* by C. A. Klemm in Leipzig.
Werke, series XIX, no. 153.
Former owner: H. V. Jones.

1213. [Lieder ohne Worte, piano, op. 19b]
       Melodies for the pianoforte composed by Felix Mendelssohn-Bartholdy . . .
       10 p. 23 x 29½ cm.
       Dated: 20 July 1832.
       Published in 1832 by Novello and Co. in London.
       Werke, series XI, no. 75.

1214. [Lieder ohne Worte, piano, op. 19, no. 2, A minor]
       Lied.
       [4]p. 13½ x 18 cm.
       At end: Rom, d. 11 Dec. 1830.

1215. [Lieder ohne Worte, piano, op. 62, nos. 3 and 2]
       Zwei Lieder ohne Worte . . .
       [3]p. 30 x 23 cm.
       Dedicated to Mme. Clara Schumann, den 13ten September 1843.

1216. [Lieder ohne Worte, piano, op. 85]
       Sechs Lieder ohne Worte, opus 85.
       1 leaf, 14 p. 25½ x 32½ cm.
       Inscribed to Frau von Lüttichau, Leipzig, April 4, 1846.
       Published by N. Simrock in Berlin.
       Werke, series XI, no. 81.
       Former owner: George T. Keating.

1217. [Lieder ohne Worte, piano, op. 85, no. 3, E flat major]
       Zwei Lieder ohne Worte . . .
       [5]p. 30½ x 22½ cm.
       Presented to Fraülein Henriette Grabau, den 29sten März 1836.
       F.M.B.
       Followed by *Lieder ohne Worte,* op. 38, no. 2, C minor.

1218. [Octet, strings, op. 20, E flat major].
       Ottetto.
       70 p. 33 x 24 cm.
       Score.
       At end: Berlin d. 15 Oct. 1825.

Mendelssohn-Bartholdy, Felix (Jakob Ludwig)—*continued*

Published in 1832 (parts) and 1848 (score) by Breitkopf & Härtel in Leipzig.
Werke, series V, no. 1.
Former owners: Eduard Rietz, Musikbibliothek Peters.

1219. [Drei Phantasien oder Capricen, piano, op. 16, no. 1, A major]
Andante con moto.
p. 82-84. 18½ x 24 cm.
In the autograph album of Anne Taylor.
At end: Felix Mendelssohn-Bartholdy, Coed Du, d. 4 Sept. 1829.
Published ca. 1830 by Fr. Schreiber in Vienna.
Werke, series XI, no. 55.   MR. LOUIS KRASNER

1220. [Drei Phantasien oder Capricen, piano, op. 16, no. 2, E major]
Scherzo.
[2]p. 31 x 23 cm.
At end: Berlin, den 22ten Febr. 1835. F.M.B.
Werke, series XI, no. 55.   MR. JOHN BASS

1221. [Psalm 95, op. 46]
[4]p. 31½ x 24 cm.
A fragment of the 2nd movement for chorus and orchestra.

1222. [Psalm 95, op. 46]
O come let us worship. No. 2 chorus.
[4]p. 30½ x 24 cm.
Piano-vocal score, beginning: "Kommet herzu."
At foot of p. 1: Leipzig, 5 Dec. 1844. Felix Mendelssohn-Bartholdy.
MRS. EUGENE ALLEN NOBLE

1223. [Ruy Blas]
Chor der Wäscherinnen (aus Victor Hugo's Ruy Blas) . . .
[3]p. 30½ x 24 cm.
Score for 2-part women's chorus and string orchestra.
At end: Felix Mendelssohn-Bartholdy.
First line: Wozu der Vöglein Chöre.
Composed Leipzig, Feb. 14, 1839.
Unpublished in this original version. Published as duet with piano accpt., Op. 77, no. 3, by August Cranz in Hamburg.
Werke, series XVIII, no. 140a.
Facsimile of first page in *Mendelssohn's Letters*, ed. G. Selden-Goth, New York, 1945, p. 282.
Former owner: F. W. Jähns.   HEINEMAN FOUNDATION

1224. [Die schöne Melusine. Overture, op. 32]
Ouvertüre zum Märchen von der schönen Melusine, op. 32.
45 p. 32 x 24 cm.
Full score of the revised version.

At end: Leipzig den 17ten Nov. 1835.

Composed in 1833 and first performed in London, April 7, 1834. The revised version first performed in Leipzig November 23, 1835.

Published in 1836 by Breitkopf & Härtel in Leipzig.

Werke, series II, no. 5.

Former owner: Breitkopf & Härtel.   BROUDE BROTHERS

1225. [Ein Sommernachtstraum, op. 21. Overture]
    Op. 21. Ouverture to Shakespeare's Midsummernightsdream arranged as a duet for two performers by Felix Mendelssohn-Bartholdy.
    1 leaf, [13]p. 23½ x 30 cm.
For piano 4 hands.
Dated on cover: 10th July.   FOLGER SHAKESPEARE LIBRARY

1226. Suleika.
    [2]p. 29 x 22 cm.
Song with piano accpt.
First line: Was bedeutet die Bewegung?
Text by Marianne von Willemer.
At end: Leipzig, 7t Juni 1841. Felix Mendelssohn-Bartholdy.
Published as no. 3 of *Sechs Lieder,* op. 57, in 1843 by Breitkopf & Härtel in Leipzig.
Werke, series XIX, no. 146.
          YALE UNIVERSITY LIBRARY, SPECK COLLECTION

1227. [Symphony, string orchestra, no. 9, C minor]
    Sinfonia IX.
    30 p. 33 x 24½ cm.
Score.
Dedicated to E[duard] R[ietz].
At end: d. 26 Dec. 1823. Felix Mendelssohn-Bartholdy.
Unpublished.
Facsimile of p. 1 in Van Patten, *Catalogue,* p. 176.
      MEMORIAL LIBRARY OF MUSIC, STANFORD UNIVERSITY

1248. [Symphony, no. 1, op. 11, C minor]
    Sinfonia.
    Piano part, 22 p., string parts (in score), 8 p., 25½ x 31 cm.
Arranged for violin, violoncello and piano 4 hands.
      LIBRARY OF CONGRESS, WHITTALL FOUNDATION

1229. [Tutto è silenzio]
    [4]p. 35½ x 26 cm.
Fragment of score of a recitative and aria written in 1829 for Mme. Milder-Hauptmann.
At head of title: Berlin am 23ten Febr. 1829 . . . componirt . . . Felix Mendelssohn-Bartholdy.
      LIBRARY OF CONGRESS, WHITTALL FOUNDATION

Mercadante, Giuseppe Saverio Raffaele, 1797-1870

1230. Rivedersi, . . . Mercadante. Novara, 24 febrajo 1843.
[27]p. 24 x 31 cm.
Score for physharmonica and piano.
The three parts are entitled: *Napoli, Torino, Novara.*
Dedicated to Luigi Paduli.   LIBRARY OF CONGRESS

1231. [Se mai tento dir che t'amo]
[7]p. 22 x 31 cm.
Song with piano accpt.
Followed on p. 6-7 by *Bolero* (First line: Tu que non ignoras lo que
es amor).   WESTERN RESERVE UNIVERSITY LIBRARY

1232. Sei sinfonie a grand' orchestra di Saverio Mercadante.
[369]p. 46½ x 32 cm.
Full score of six overtures.
Contents.—1. *Il campo di crociati.*—2. *L'aurora.*—3. *Il lamento dell'
arabo.*—4. *La religione.*—5. *Ricordi di Donizetti.*—6. *Seconda sin-
fonia caratteristica napolitana.*
Former owner: Natale Gallini (catalogue, no. 33).
Presumably unpublished.
Facsimile of one page in Van Patten, Catalogue, p. 181.
                MEMORIAL LIBRARY OF MUSIC, STANFORD UNIVERSITY

Messiaen, Olivier, 1908-

1233. Turangalîla-Symphonie. Oeuvre commandée à l'auteur par Serge
Koussevitzky et la Fondation Koussevitzky, écrite et orchestrée
du 17 juillet 1946 au 29 novembre 1948. En mémoire de Nathalie
Koussevitzky.
1 leaf, [432]p. 35 x 27 cm.
Full score.
Introductory note and 10 movements paged separately.
                LIBRARY OF CONGRESS, KOUSSEVITZKY FOUNDATION

Meyerbeer, Giacomo, 1791-1864

1234. Canzonetta composta . . . da Giacomo Meyerbeer. Spa, estate 1855.
1 leaf, [3]p. 27 x 38 cm.
Song with piano accpt.
First line: Se per tutte ordisse amore.
Dedicated to Princess Vittoria Augusta di Borbone Capoa.
Published in 1866 by Oreste Morandi in Florence.
                LIBRARY OF CONGRESS

1235. [L'étoile du nord]
10 p. 27 x 37½ cm.
Full score of a scene added to replace the trio bouffe in Act 3, German text.   MR. RUDOLF F. KALLIR

Meyerbeer, Giacomo—*continued*

1236. Hallelujah. Eine Cantatine für 4 Männerstimmen mit Begleitung einer obligaten Orgel und des Chores ad libitum von J. Meyerbeer. [8]p. 25 x 34 cm.
Apparently unpublished.
Former owner: William H. Cummings (catalogue, no. 159).

1237. Le jardin du coeur. Paroles d'Henri Blaze, musique de Giacomo Meyerbeer.
1 leaf, [2]p. 27½ x 35 cm.
Song with piano accpt.
First line: Dans mon coeur vient l'oeillet.
At end: Giacomo Meyerbeer. 16 Xb 47.
Published as no. 15 of *24 Romances et ballades* by M. Schlesinger in Paris. MEMORIAL LIBRARY OF MUSIC, STANFORD UNIVERSITY

1238. [Unidentified composition for piano]
2 leaves. 24 x 33 cm.
Music on recto only.
At end: Paris 8. 1. 46. Giacomo Meyerbeer. THE NEWBERRY LIBRARY

1239. Zur Feier des 15ten Juni 1810 ihrem theuersten Lehrer gewidmet von seinen Schülern Meyerbeer, I. Gaensbacher, C. M. v. Weber. [18]p. 25 x 35 cm.
The ms. was presented to their teacher, Abt Vogler, on his birthday by his three pupils. The compositions, with the exception of no. 2, are by Meyerbeer; Weber did not actually contribute.
Contents (all in Meyerbeer's hand).—*Chor* (Willkommen! Willkommen!)—2. *Solo* (Gebannt von deinem Namen).—3. *Terzetto* (O möchte Gott es doch nur leise).—4. *Duetto* (Die Dankbarkeit nur schüttet hin).—5. *Chor* (Willkommen, theueres Wörtersinn).
Former owner: George T. Keating.

MEMORIAL LIBRARY OF MUSIC, STANFORD UNIVERSITY

Miáskovskiĭ, Nikolai I͡Akovlevich, 1881-1950

1240. . . . Symphonie-Fantaisie composée pour le 50me aniversaire [!] de l'orchestre symphonique de Chicago . . . Partition d'orchestre. Juillet 1940. Moscou. N. Miaskowsky.
[2], 43 p. 35 x 26 cm.
At end: N. Miaskowsky VI-VII 1940. Moscou.

CHICAGO SYMPHONY ORCHESTRA

Migot, Georges, 1891-

1241. . . . Le premier livre de divertissements français à deux & à trois. flûte, clarinette (en la) & harpe par Georges Migot, avril-mai 1925. Comprenant 1) prélude 2) estampie fl. et h. 3) prélude 4) estampie cl. et h. 5) conclusion fl., cl. et h. . . . .
Score (2 leaves, 31 [i.e. 37]p.) and flute part. 35 x 27 cm.

Migot, Georges—*continued*

Note in composer's hand: La flûte, la clarinette et la harpe peuvent être remplacées séparément ou à deux, ou à trois, par un violon, un alto, un piano.
Dedicated to Mrs. E. S. Coolidge.
Published in 1928 by A. Leduc in Paris.

LIBRARY OF CONGRESS, COOLIDGE FOUNDATION

Milhaud, Darius, 1892-

Numbers in brackets refer to the catalogue of Milhaud's works by G. Beck.

1242.   Chant de la mort.
     2 leaves. 34 x 27 cm.
   For 4-part chorus unaccompanied.   THE LEAGUE OF COMPOSERS

1243.   La danse des animaux.
     3 leaves. 34 x 27 cm.
   For 4-part mixed chorus unaccompanied.

THE LEAGUE OF COMPOSERS

1244.   . . . Jacob's dreams. Rêves [!] de Jacob, suite choréographique en cinq parties pour hautbois, violon, alto, violoncelle, contrebasse. Darius Milhaud 1949 . . . [Beck 294]
     1, 20 numbered leaves. 38 x 28 cm.
   Full score.
   At end: Mills 14-29 avril 1949. Milhaud.
   Dedicated to Mrs. E. S. Coolidge.
   Unpublished.   LIBRARY OF CONGRESS, COOLIDGE FOUNDATION

1245.   Jeux de printemps. Darius Milhaud. [Beck 243]
     41 leaves. 38 x 28 cm.
   Tissues, music on recto only.
   Dedicated to Mrs. E. S. Coolidge.
   Full score, for chamber orchestra, of the ballet.
   At end: Milhaud. Mills 19-23 juin 1944.
   Published in 1950 by Salabert in Paris.
   Performed under the title *Imagined wing*.
   First performed October 3, 1944 at the Coolidge Auditorium in the Library of Congress.

LIBRARY OF CONGRESS, COOLIDGE FOUNDATION

1246.   March (for three trumpets, two trombones, 1 bass tuba and 1 percussion. Darius Milhaud [Beck 212]
     [6]p. 32 x 24½ cm.
   Score.
   Note in composer's hand: This march written at the request of the French government was played at the National French Radio from January to June 1940 to accompany the propaganda for the "Armement Bonds."
   Unpublished.   LIBRARY OF CONGRESS

Milhaud, Darius—*continued*

1247. Pastorale. [Beck 229]
        [3]p. 31 x 24½ cm.
        For organ.
        Published in 1942 by H. W. Gray Co. in New York.

1248. [Quartet, strings, no. 8, Beck 121]
        . . . Huitième quatuor à cordes . . . Darius Milhaud . . . 1932.
        1 leaf, 22 p. 35 x 27 cm.
        Score.
        Dedicated to Mrs. E. S. Coolidge, "en souvenir de la 1. audition
        chez Malipiero par le quatuor Pro Arte à Asolo le 13 mai 1933."
        Published in 1936 by Editions sociales internationales in Paris.

1249. [Quartet, strings, no. 9, Beck 140]
        . . . Neuvième quatuor à cordes, 1935.
        1 leaf, 23 p. 33 x 26 cm.
        Score.
        Dedicated to Mrs. E. S. Coolidge.
        Published in 1937 by Editions sociales internationales in Paris.

1250. [Symphony, no. 1, Beck 210]
        . . . Symphonie. I. Pastoral. II. Très vif. III. Très modéré. IV.
        Final. Darius Milhaud. Partition d'orchestre. Aix en Provence
        1939.
        1 leaf, 124 p. 34½ x 26½ cm.
        Dedicated to the Chicago Symphony Orchestra on its 50th anni-
        versary.
        At end: Milhaud, l'Enclos 19 décembre 1939.
        Published in 1949 by Heugel et Cie. in Paris.

1251. [Symphony, no. 2, Beck 247]
        2e symphonie.
        152 [i.e. 153]p. 38 x 28 cm.
        Full score.
        At foot of p. 1: Mills 30 octobre 1944.
        At end: Mills 7 novembre 1944.
        Published in 1950 by Heugel et Cie. in Paris.

Millöcker, Karl, 1842-1899

1252. Quadrille nach Motiven der Volksoper, "Die sieben Schwaben,"
        von C. Millöcker.
        1 leaf, 7p. 32½ x 25 cm.
        For piano 2 hands.

Mojsisovics, Roderich von, 1877-

1253. . . . "Es wird Frühling!" (Chr. Oeser—Tobias Gottfried Schröer 1791-1850) für eine hohe Stimme und Klavier, komponiert von Roderich von Mojsisovics. Op. XVIII/3.
1 leaf, [3]p. 34 x 27 cm.
At end: Beg. 3. Mai 1906, beend. 3. 7ber 1918. R. 11/X 1931.
Dedicated to Mrs. E. S. Coolidge.
First line: Veilchen unter'm Schnee.

LIBRARY OF CONGRESS, COOLIDGE FOUNDATION

Moór, Emanuel, 1863-1931

1254. Mondnacht.
[2]p. 36 x 25 cm.
Song with piano accpt.
Text by Eichendorff.
First line: Es war als hätt' der Himmel.
Published as no. 1 of op. 43 ca. 1895 by Rózsavölgyi in Budapest.
Former owner: David Bispham.   NEW YORK PUBLIC LIBRARY

Moreau, Léon, 1870-1946

1255. Pastorale.
50 p. 35 x 26 cm.
Full score (saxophone and orchestra).
At end: Léon Moreau, mars 1910.
Former owner: Mrs. R. J. Hall.

NEW ENGLAND CONSERVATORY OF MUSIC

Mori, Frank, 1820-1873

1256. Take, oh take those lips away. The words by Shakespeare. The music by Frank Mori.
[4]p. 22 x 29½ cm.
Song with piano accpt.

THE FOLGER SHAKESPEARE LIBRARY

Morlacchi, Francesco, 1784-1841

1257. Kaiser Nicolaus.
6 p. 23 x 31½ cm.
Cantata for solo voice, men's chorus and piano.
Signed: Morlacchi K[öniglich] S[ächischer] Kapellmeister in Teplitz, 26. Oct. 1833.
Former owners: Princess Helbig, Giuseppe Radiciotti, Natale Gallini (catalogue, no. 29).

MEMORIAL LIBRARY OF MUSIC, STANFORD UNIVERSITY

Moscheles, Ignaz, 1794-1870

1258. Französisches Rondo concertant für Pianoforte und Violine in Partitur von I. Moscheles.
[99]p. 24 x 30 cm.

Moscheles, Ignaz—*continued*

On p. 1: Angefangen den 22 July, geendet den 12 August 1819 in Carlsbad. I. Moscheles.
Published as op. 48 by Haslinger in Vienna.
Former owner: Robert Heckmann.   LIBRARY OF CONGRESS

1259.   Gruss und Abschied.
[1]p. 22½ x 27½ cm.
Song with piano accpt.
First line: Sey mir freundlich, Thal, gegrüsst.
At end: . . . Wien den 5ten December 1844. I. Moscheles.
Former owner: Hugo Riesenfeld.   THE HOUSE OF BOOKS

1260.   [Notebook]
76 p. 28 x 23 cm.
"The contents include 19 of Moscheles' songs, 3 of his piano compositions, and 5 songs by other composers (3 by Mendelssohn, one by Cherubini and one by Rosenhain). The piano compositions are the *Romance* in E flat major, the *Nocturne* in F sharp minor, and a *Waltz* in A flat major."
MEMORIAL LIBRARY OF MUSIC, STANFORD UNIVERSITY

1261.   Die Zigeunerin. Lied aus dem Persischen der Hafis, von G. F. Daumer mit Pianoforte-Begleitung komponirt von I. Moscheles.
6 p. 36½ x 26 cm.
First line: Ich schlage dich, mein Tambourin.
Published as no. 2 of op. 119 by Fr. Kistner in Leipzig.
Another version of the song in the following item, and a third in his Notebook, above.
MEMORIAL LIBRARY OF MUSIC, STANFORD UNIVERSITY

1262.   [Die Zigeunerin]
5 p. 23½ x 30 cm.
At end: Leipzig, den 25 Mai 1850.
MEMORIAL LIBRARY OF MUSIC, STANFORD UNIVERSITY

Motta, José Vianna da, 1868-
1263.   Zwei Lieder für eine Singstimme mit Pianofortebegleitung componirt von José Vianna da Motta. Berlin 1886.
[8]p. 35 x 27 cm.
Contents.—*Das Bächlein, Gedicht von Göthe* [by Rudolphi, not by Goethe].—*Wiegenlied aus: "Die Kinder von Finkenrode" von W. Raabe.*
Former owner: The Royal Collection, Lisbon.
First lines: Du Bächlein silberhell und klar; Schaukeln und Gaukeln.   LIBRARY OF CONGRESS

Mouquet, Jules, 1867-

1264. Rapsodie pour saxophone alto mi♭ avec accompagnement d'orchestre. Op. 26. Partition d'orchestre . . .
[3], 46 [i.e. 47]p. 35 x 26 cm.
At end: Jules Mouquet. 1907.
Dedicated to Mrs. Elise (Mrs. R. J.) Hall.

NEW ENGLAND CONSERVATORY OF MUSIC

Mozart, Wolfgang Amadeus, 1756-1791

1265. [Ah! spiegarti, o Dio. K. 178]
[2]p. 14 x 27 cm.
Voice part only of an aria for soprano and piano.
Text from Anfossi's *Il curioso indiscreto*.
On p. 2 sketches for tenor and soprano arias, without text (K. 420,
419). Köchel-Einstein recatalogues as K. 125i, but in revised ed.
(Ann Arbor, 1947) Einstein accepts St. Foix's recataloguing as
K. 417e.
Werke, series XXIV, no. 41.
Former owners: Major von Franck, Miss Ellen A. Willmott, George
T. Keating. MEMORIAL LIBRARY OF MUSIC, STANFORD UNIVERSITY

1266. [Cadenzas. K. 624 A-B]
Cadenza per il clavicembalo.
[2]p. 17 x 23 cm.
Two cadenzas for the 1st and 2nd movements of no. 1 of Mozart's
transcription of 3 piano sonatas of Joh. Christian Bach (op. 5) as
concertos for piano, 2 violins and bass (K. 107).

ERNEST E. GOTTLIEB

1267. [Cadenzas, K. 624, 35-36]
Cadenz im rondeau. 1er Eingang im Rondeau.
[2]p. 23 x 33 cm.
Cadenzas for Mozart's piano concerto, K. 595, B flat major.

MISS YRSA HEIN

1268. [Concerto, piano, K. 238, B flat major]
N. 8. Concerto di cembalo del sgr. cav. Amadeo Wolfg. Mozart
mp nel giannaro 1776 a Salisburgo.
[80]p. 17 x 22 cm.
Full score.
Published in parts as op. 35 in 1793 by J. André in Offenbach.
Werke, series XVI, no. 6.
Facsimile of first page of rondo in R. M. Haas, *Mozart*, p. 64.
Former owners: Wittgenstein family.

LIBRARY OF CONGRESS, WHITTALL FOUNDATION

1269. [Concerto, piano, K. 467, C major]
Concerto di Wolfgango Amadeo Mozart nel febraio 1785.
[87]p. 22½ x 32 cm.
Full score.

Mozart, Wolfgang Amadeus—*continued*

> Published in his *Oeuvres (Konzert 1)* in 1800 by Breitkopf & Härtel in Leipzig.
> Werke, series XVI, no. 21.
> Facsimile of p. 1 in I. C. G. Boerner auction catalogue, no. 87.
> Former owners: Johann André, Wilhelm Taubert, Siegfried Ochs, Wittgenstein family.　　　　　PRIVATE COLLECTOR

1270.　[Concerto, piano, K. 537, D major]
> 108 p. 23½ x 32 cm.
> Full score.
> Published in 1794 as op. 46 by J. André in Offenbach.
> Werke, series XVI, no. 26.
> Facsimile of pp. 3 and 108 in Liepmannssohn auction catalogue, no. 55.
> Facsimile of p. 108 in *Notes*, VII (1949-50), 204.
> Former owner: August André.　　　　　HEINEMAN FOUNDATION

1271.　[Concerto, three pianos, K. 242, F major]
> 74 leaves. 23 x 31½, 26 x 33½ and 27½ x 39 cm.
> Parts in the autograph of Leopold Mozart, with corrections in the composer's hand in the parts for 1st violin, bass and 3rd piano.
> Facsimile of one page in Van Patten, *Catalogue*, p. 188.
> Former owner: Eduard Speyer.
>　　　　　MEMORIAL LIBRARY OF MUSIC, STANFORD UNIVERSITY

1272.　[Concerto, violin, K. 219, A major]
> Concerto di violino di Wolfgango Amadeo Mozart. Salisburgo li 20 di dicembre 1775.
> [92]p. 17 x 23 cm.
> Full score.
> Published by Breitkopf & Härtel in Leipzig.
> Werke, series XII, no. 5.
> Facsimile of p. 1 in *Library of Congress Quarterly Journal*, VI, no. 1 (Nov. 1948), 28; of the violin entrance in 1st movement in R. Haas, *Mozart*, p. 66.
> Former owners: J. B. André, F. A. Grassnick, Joseph Joachim, Wittgenstein family.
>　　　　　LIBRARY OF CONGRESS, WHITTALL FOUNDATION

1273.　[Contra-tanz. Les filles malicieuses. K. 610]
> Les filles malicieuses.
> [2]p. 23½ x 33 cm.
> Score (2 violins, bass, 2 flutes, 2 horns).
> The same dance as K. 609, no. 5, with different scoring.
> Published by Breitkopf & Härtel in Leipzig.
> Werke, series XI, no. 24.
> Former owners: August André, Musikbibliothek Peters, Mrs. Charles H. Swift.　　　　　THE NEWBERRY LIBRARY

Mozart, Wolfgang Amadeus—*continued*

1274. [Contra-tänze. K. 462]
6 Contredanse [!] für 2 Violinen und Bass.
[3]p. 23½ x 33 cm.
Score (no indication of horn and oboe parts, which are found on another leaf, without title).
Published (in parts) by J. André in Offenbach.
Werke, series XI, no. 17.
Former owners: August André, Musikbibliothek Peters, Mrs. Charles H. Swift.   THE NEWBERRY LIBRARY

1275. [Counterpoint exercises. K. Anh. 109d]
[1]p. 16½ x 20½ cm.
Eleven bars of a 4-part movement.
Former owner: Franz J. Schaffer.   THE NEWBERRY LIBRARY

1276. Mozart, (Johann Georg) Leopold, 1719-1787.
Cum sancto spiritu.
[2]p. 23 x 31½ cm.
Fragment of score (4 voices, 2 violins, viola and continuo) in W. A. Mozart's hand of his father's composition. (K. Anh. 109 IX).
          MEMORIAL LIBRARY OF MUSIC, STANFORD UNIVERSITY

1277. [Dances, orchestra, K. 509]
[4]p.
Arrangement for piano of the so-called *Prague Dances*.
Composed 1789-90 rather than 1787. Cf. A. Einstein, "On certain mss. of Mozart's," *Journal of the American Musicological Society*, I (1948), 13-16.
Published in 1790 by Artaria & Co. in Vienna (this arrangement ?).
          PRIVATE COLLECTOR

1278. [Die Entführung aus dem Serail. K. 384]
[1]p. 22½ x 32 cm.
Fragment (first 27 bars) of piano-vocal score of aria no. 12, "Welche Wonne, welche Lust."
Former owners: C. A. André, George T. Keating.
          MEMORIAL LIBRARY OF MUSIC, STANFORD UNIVERSITY

1279. [Ergo interest. K. 143]
[7]p. 22½ x 30 cm.
Recitative and aria for soprano, strings and organ.
Aria begins: Quaere superna.
Werke, series III, no. 21.
Former owners: Otto Jahn, Gustav Schirmer, Samuel P. Warren.
          LIBRARY OF CONGRESS

1280. [Fugue, piano, B minor]
[2]p. 22½ x 30 cm.
Beginning of a hitherto unknown fugue, ca. 1782.
Other sketches on p. 1, and on p. 2, beginning of a 4-part fugue

with continuo. Cf. A. Einstein, "On certain mss. of Mozart's," *Journal of the American Musicological Society,* I (1948), 13-16, (with facsimile).   MR. RUDOLF F. KALLIR

1281. [Fugue, K. 443, G major]
       [2]p. 22½ x 31 cm.
       Score of a 3-part fugue for instruments. The first 37 bars are in Mozart's hand; the rest in the hand of Maximilian Stadler.
       Composed ca. 1782; unpublished.
       Former owner: Julius André.   BOSTON PUBLIC LIBRARY

1282. [Fugues, piano, K. 154a]
       [Zwei kleine Fugen (Versetten) für Klavier (oder Orgel)]
       1 leaf, 21 x 29 cm.
       Rejected in Köchel-Einstein (Anh. 109 VIII) as not Mozart's compositions.
       Former owner: Gustav A. Petter.   E. WEYHE

1283. [In te spero, o sposo amato. K. 440]
       [2]p. 23 x 30 cm.
       Aria for soprano and continuo.
       Text from Metastasio's *Demofoonte,* Act I, scene 2.
       Werke, series XXIV, no. 47.
       Former owners: Natalia Frassini Eschborn, C. V. Werschinger.
                          LIBRARY OF CONGRESS, WHITTALL FOUNDATION

1284. [Marche d'amistà]
       [1]p. 18½ x 28 cm.
       Fragment of 11 bars in full score of an unidentified composition.
       Complete text: Marche d'amistà, a voi le mostro, vi do marche d'amistà.
       Former owners: Alois Fuchs, A. Bottée de Toulmon, Baron Taylor, Nicolai Bagannhevoff, George T. Keating.
                          MEMORIAL LIBRARY OF MUSIC, STANFORD UNIVERSITY

1285. [Mass, C major]
       [1]p. 22½ x 31 cm.
       Beginning of an 8-part fugue, ca. 1782, for the *Quoniam* of the *Mass,* published by A. Einstein, "On certain mss. of Mozart's," *Journal of the American Musicological Society,* I (1948), 13-16.
       Contains also the subject of the *Rondo* from the *Piano concerto,* K. 450.   DR. HERMANN VOLLMER

1286. [Minuets, piano, K. 315a]
       [1]p. 22 x 31½ cm.
       The trio to the last of *Acht Minuette mit Trios,* first identified in Köchel-Einstein, p. 398, 983.
       At end: Finis coronat opus.
       Former owner: Dr. Christian A. Herter.
                                                NEW YORK PUBLIC LIBRARY

1287. [Minuets, orchestra, K. 461]
    [2]p. 22½ x 30½ cm.
    Full score of nos. 5 and 6 of a series of 6 composed in 1784.
    Published (in parts) by J. André in Offenbach.
    Werke, series XI, no. 16.   LIBRARY OF CONGRESS

1288. [Miserere, K. 85]
    Miserere à 3. Del sgr. cavaliere Wolfgango Amadeo Mozart in
    Bologna 1770.
    10 p. 17 x 22½ cm.
    For 3-part chorus (alto, tenor & bass) and continuo.
    pp. 9-10 not in Mozart's hand.
    Werke, series III, no. 8.
    Facsimile of p. 1 in Liepmannssohn auction catalogue, no. 55.
                  CURTIS INSTITUTE OF MUSIC

1289. [Le nozze di Figaro, K. 492, no. 6]
    Atto Imo. Aria di Cherubino, scena V.
    [4]p. 22 x 31 cm.
    Arrangement of the aria: *Non so più*, for soprano, violin and piano.
    Former owner: Julius André.   HEINEMAN FOUNDATION

1290. [Le nozze di Figaro, K. 492, no. 14]
    Atto 2do. Scena III (invece del duetto di Susanna e Cherubino).
    [2]p. 22½ x 31 cm.
    The beginning (4½ bars) of another version of the duet: *Aprite
    presto*. On p. 2 a sketch for no. 27, *Deh vieni, non tardar*.
    Former owner: C. A. André.
    Incorrectly listed in Köchel-Einstein, p. 622, as at University of
    Rochester (Sibley Musical Library).   PAUL GOTTSCHALK

1291. [Le nozze di Figaro, K. 492, no. 26]
    Atto 4to. Scena VI. Figaro solo.
    [3]p. 23 x 31½ cm.
    Full score of recitative: *Tutto è disposto*, lacking in the autograph
    in the Öffentliche Wissenschaftliche Bibliothek in Berlin.
    Former owner: C. A. André.
    Facsimile of p. 1 in Van Patten, *Catalogue*, p. 193.
        MEMORIAL LIBRARY OF MUSIC, STANFORD UNIVERSITY

1292. [Le nozze di Figaro, K. 492, no. 28]
    (Gente, gente, à l'armi, à l'armi) 4to atto—finale.
    1 leaf, [10]p. 22 x 31 cm.
    Score (winds and tympani only).
    This part of the full score is lacking in the autograph in the Öffent-
    liche Wissenschaftliche Bibliothek in Berlin. GALERIE ST. ETIENNE

1293. [Quintet, violins, violas and violoncello K. 515, C major]
    Quintetto.
    [47]p. 23½ x 31½ cm.
    Score.

Mozart, Wolfgang Amadeus—*continued*

Published in 1789 by Artaria & Co. in Vienna.
Werke, series XIII, no. 4.
Former owners: Jenny Lind, J. B. Streicher, Jerome Stonborough.
LIBRARY OF CONGRESS, WHITTALL FOUNDATION

1294.   [Rondo, piano, K. 485, D major]
   [4]p. 23 x 30½ cm.
   At end: Mozart mpria. le 10 de janvier 1786 a Vienne.
   Dedication partly erased: Pour Madselle: Charlotte de Wü . . .
   Published ca. 1787 as *Sonate (Rondo)* by Hoffmeister in Vienna.
   Werke, series XXII, no. 7.
   Facsimile published in 1923 by Universal Edition in Vienna, ed.
      H. Gál, together with *Rondo,* K. 511 in A minor. For other fac-
      similes, cf. Köchel-Einstein, p. 607, and *Notes,* VII (1949-50),
      205.
   Former owners: Franz Nemeczek, Wilhelm Heyer (catalogue, vol.
      IV, no. 187).   HEINEMAN FOUNDATION

1295.   [Rondo, piano and orchestra, K. 386, A major]
   [2]p. 23 x 27 cm.
   Fragment (bars 136-154) of full score.
   Published (as *Konzert-Rondo*), ed. A. Einstein, in 1936 by Uni-
      versal Edition in Vienna.   SIBLEY MUSICAL LIBRARY

1296.   [Der Schauspieldirektor, K. 486, no. 1]
   [2]p. 24 x 31 cm.
   Fragment of 18 bars of the arietta: *Da schlägt die Abschiedsstunde,*
      with 10-line score prepared but only voice and continuo filled in.
   Former owner: Joseph W. Drexel.   NEW YORK PUBLIC LIBRARY

1297.   [Serenade, orchestra, K. 361, B flat major]
   91 [i.e. 97]p. 22½ x 31 cm.
   Full score.
   Caption title: *Gran partitta*[!].
   Published ca. 1803 by the Bureau d'Arts et d'Industrie in Vienna.
   Werke, series IX, no. 12.
   Former owners: Ludwig I of Hessen-Darmstadt, Appold, Schmitt,
      Philipp Ritter, Philipp Schmitt, Princess Marie Schönburg-Erbach
      von Battenberg, Jerome Stonborough.
LIBRARY OF CONGRESS, WHITTALL FOUNDATION

1298.   [Sonata, piano, K. 331, A major]
   Schluss der Rondo turque.
   [1]p. 23 x 31 cm.
   The only extant fragment of this sonata, containing the last 38 bars
      of the last movement *(alla turca).*
   Facsimile in Liepmannssohn auction catalogue, no. 55, and in
      Musical Quarterly, XXXI (1945), opp. p. 493.
PAUL GOTTSCHALK

Mozart, Wolfgang Amadeus—*continued*

1299.　[Sonata, piano 4 hands, K. 381, D major]
　　　　Fragment d'une sonate olographe de W. A. Mozart donnée par
　　　　　sa soeur à la bar^ne de Sonnenbourg au b.^on de Tremont à St.
　　　　　Gilgen, en 1801.
　　　　fol. 6. 22 x 28½ cm.
　　　　Consists of p. 11 and 12 of 13 pages.　　　　　　　E. WEYHE

1300.　[Sonata, violin and piano, K. 296, C major]
　　　　Sonata di Wolfgango Amadeo Mozart mpria li 11 di marzo 1778
　　　　　a Manheim pour mademoiselle Therese [Pierron].
　　　　[10]p. 25 x 35½ cm.
　　　　Score.
　　　　Published (parts) in 1781 by Artaria & Co. in Vienna.
　　　　Werke, series XVIII, no. 24.
　　　　Former owners: Frederick Locker-Lampson, Dr. Christian A. Herter.
　　　　　　　　　　　　　　　　　　　　　　NEW YORK PUBLIC LIBRARY

1301.　[Sonata, violin and piano, K. 379, G major]
　　　　Sonata.
　　　　[10]p. 24½ x 33½ cm.
　　　　Score.
　　　　Published (parts) as no. 5 of op. II, *Six sonates,* ca. 1781 by Artaria
　　　　　& Co. in Vienna.
　　　　Werke, series XVIII, no. 35.
　　　　Former owner: Oscar Bondy.
　　　　　　　　　　　　　　LIBRARY OF CONGRESS, WHITTALL FOUNDATION

1302.　[Symphony, K. 112, F major]
　　　　Sinfonia del sigre cavaliere Amadeo Wolfgango Mozart à Milano.
　　　　　2 di novembre 1771.
　　　　[29]p. 23½ x 30½ cm.
　　　　Full score.
　　　　Werke, series VIII, no. 13.
　　　　Former owners: Otto Jahn, Heinrich Seligmann, G. Fuchs-Selig-
　　　　　mann.
　　　　Facsimile of p. 1 in Lengfeld auction catalogue, no. 42.
　　　　　　　　　　　　　　　　　　　　　　HEINEMAN FOUNDATION

1303.　[Symphony, K. 318, G major]
　　　　Sinfonia di Wolfgango Amadeo Mozart mpr. d. 26 April 79.
　　　　[44]p. 16½ x 23 cm.
　　　　Full score.
　　　　Two separate trumpet parts (23 x 28 cm.) laid in.
　　　　Published before 1792 by Imbault in Paris.
　　　　Werke, series VIII, no. 32.
　　　　Former owner: Carl Liebig.　　　　　NEW YORK PUBLIC LIBRARY

Mozart, Wolfgang Amadeus—*continued*

1304. [Symphony, K. 385, D major (Haffner)]
Synfonia di Amadeo Wolfgango Mozart a Vienna nel mese di luglio 1782 und seine Handschrift.
57 p. 23 x 31 cm.
Full score.
Title in the hand of Leopold Mozart.
Published (parts) as op. VII, no. 1 in 1785 by Artaria & Co. in Vienna.
Werke, series VIII, no. 35.
Facsimile of p. 1 in Scribner Book Store catalogue no. 111, opp. p. 32.
Former owners: Johann André, Julius André, Ludwig II of Bavaria.

1305. Bach, Johann Sebastian, 1685-1750.
[Das wohltemperirte Klavier. Book II, fugues nos. 2, 5, 7, 9]
Bach's Klavier Fugen von Mozart übersetzt für 2 Violinen, Viola e Basso.
[10]p. 23 x 32 cm.
Score of Mozart's arrangement of the fugues (K. 405).
Unpublished.
Above the C minor fugue is a contrapuntal study of 11 bars.
Former owners: August André, Mme. Robert Calmann-Lévy.

1306. [Die Zauberflöte, K. 620, no. 9]
Atto II. Marcia.
[2]p. 14½ x 31 cm.
Fragment of score (12 bars) of an earlier version of the *Priests March*.
Published in Köchel-Einstein (revised ed., Ann Arbor, 1947), p 1040.

Müller, Wenzel, 1767-1835

1307. La rimembranza. Pièce romantique pour le violon avec accompagnement de piano. Wenzel Müller . . .
[2]p. 25½ x 31½ cm.

Musorgskiĭ, Modest Petrovich, 1839-1881

1308. . . . "Kinder-scherzo" dlia fortepiano soch. Modesta Musorgskago
[5]p. 26 x 38 cm.
For piano 2 hands.
At end: Fine. Solo Toshkovo, maia 28go, 1860g.
The second version of the piece first composed in 1859.
Published as no. 4 of *Frühlingsblüten, Album für piano*, in 187 by A. Büttner in St. Petersburg.
Werke, vol. 8, no. 7.

Nachèz, Tivadar, 1859-1930

1309. . . . Concerto, no. 2, in B minor for violin and orchestra by Tivadar
        Nachèz. Violino principale.
    26 [i.e. 28]p. 37 x 27 cm.
Solo violin part only.
Published as op. 36 in 1908 by Fr. Hofmeister in Leipzig.
Former owner: Arthur Hartmann.   SIBLEY MUSICAL LIBRARY

Naumann, Johann Gottlieb, 1741-1801

1310. "Alla luna." Naumann.
    [4]p. 24 x 32 cm.
For voice, violoncello and piano.
Horn part added at the end.
On p. 4: *Ode à mon clavecin,* for same combination.
      LIBRARY OF CONGRESS

1311. [Dieses Pläzchen weih' ich dir]
    [2]p. 24 x 32½ cm.
Song with piano accpt.
At head of title: An einen Freund, bei einem schönen Pläzchen im
    Thal.
On p. 2 another song: *Avant que le soleil.*   LIBRARY OF CONGRESS

Navrátil, Karl, 1867-1936

1312. Béla hora (Blanche montagne). Poëm symphonique for great
        orchestr . . . Partition de clavier.
    [6]p. 33 x 25 cm.
Dedicated to Mrs. Mary Louise Curtis Bok.
      CURTIS INSTITUTE OF MUSIC

1313. Frühlingslied.
    [3]p. 34 x 25½ cm.
Song with piano accpt.
First line: Frühling, Frühling ist es wieder.
      CURTIS INSTITUTE OF MUSIC

1314. [Hermann]
    204 p. 33 x 25 cm.
Full score of the opera.   CURTIS INSTITUTE OF MUSIC

1315. [Hermann]
    54 p. 32 x 25½ cm.
Piano-vocal score.   CURTIS INSTITUTE OF MUSIC

1316. Im Traum.
    [2]p. 34 x 25½ cm.
Song with piano accpt.
First line: Kennst du das Lied.   CURTIS INSTITUTE OF MUSIC

1317. Indianerlegende.
    [4]p. 33 x 25 cm.
Score (strings and harp).
Dedicated to Mrs. Mary Louise Curtis Bok.
      CURTIS INSTITUTE OF MUSIC

1318. Kein Licht, kein Haus.
       5 p. 34 x 25½ cm.
       Song with piano accpt.
       First line: Muss wieder weiter wandern.

CURTIS INSTITUTE OF MUSIC

1319. [Symphony, op. 4, G minor]
       Karl Navrátil. Simfonie. G moll. Op. 4.
       66 p. 31 x 24½ cm.
       Full score.
       At end: Vollendet den 21. November 1902. Karl Navrátil.
       Another copy of the full score.   CURTIS INSTITUTE OF MUSIC

1320. Vorabend (Ludwig Uhland).
       [2]p. 34 x 25½ cm.
       Song with piano accpt.
       First line: Was streift vorher im Dämmerlicht?

CURTIS INSTITUTE OF MUSIC

Neukomm, Sigismund, Ritter von, 1778-1858

1321. [David, an oratorio in 2 parts. The words by John Webb. The
       music by Neukomm. Accomp. for organ]
       203 p. 35 x 26 cm.
       On title-page: S. Neukomm. London July 1834.

BOSTON PUBLIC LIBRARY

1322. Der teutsche Rhein von Bekker, in Musik gesetzt für grosse Chöre
       von 4 Männerstimmen (mit oder ohne Begleitung) vom Ritter
       Sigmund Neukomm.
       [4]p. 30 x 24 cm.
       Dated: Bern 8 Nov. 1840.   LIBRARY OF CONGRESS

1323. Wine! The words by Barry Cornwall, Esq. The music by the
       Chevalier Sigismond Neukomm.
       13 p. 22 x 14 cm.
       Full score.
       At end: London July the 18th 1831. S. N.   BOSTON PUBLIC LIBRARY

Nicolai, (Carl) Otto (Ehrenfried), 1810-1849

1324. . . . Il duolo d'amore. Op. 24, no. 1 für Mezzo-Sopran oder
       Bariton mit Pf. allein.
       [3]p. 25 x 31½ cm.
       First line: Quando da te lontano.
       Published as no. 1 of *Drei Romanzen* in 1838 by A. Diabelli & Co.
       in Vienna.
       Another ms. of this song, with horn obbligato, was in the Wilhelm
       Heyer Collection (catalogue, no. 628).

MEMORIAL LIBRARY OF MUSIC, STANFORD UNIVERSITY

Nicolai, (Carl) Otto (Ehrenfried)—*continued*

1325. [Die lustige Weiber von Windsor. Overture]
        Ouvertüre zu der Oper Die lustigen Weiber von Windsor, für
        das Pianoforte von Otto Nicolai.
        35 p. 23½ x 32½ cm.
    Reduction of the full score for piano 4 hands.
    At end: Berlin d. 29 Decb. 47.
    Published in 1849 by Ed. Bote und G. Bock in Berlin.
                                    THE FOLGER SHAKESPEARE LIBRARY

1326. [Sagt was soll denn das bedeuten]
        [1]p. 23 x 30½ cm.
    For 3-part men's chorus without accompaniment.
    At end: F honni soit qui mal y pense, c'est a dire a ces quintes
        du 24 Sept. 1825. Otto Nicolai.   LIBRARY OF CONGRESS

1327. Salve Regina. Hymne an die heilige Jungfrau für eine Mezzo-
        Sopran-Stimme mit Begleitung von 1 Oboe (oder Violine oder
        Phÿsharmonica) und Pianoforte componirt von Otto Nicolai . . .
        Score [10]p. 25½ x 33½ cm. and parts.   LIBRARY OF CONGRESS

1328. Die Verwandlung. An Lili. Otto Nicolai.
        1 leaf, [5]p. 34 x 23 cm.
    Song with piano accpt.
    First line: Verborgen wuchs ein Veilchen.   LIBRARY OF CONGRESS

1329. Zelters Geburstag. 11 Dec. 33 An der Liedertafel.
        [1]p. 23½ x 16 cm.
    For men's voices unaccompanied.
    First line: Auf, zum Sitz der Geister.
    Text by Ribbeck.   LIBRARY OF CONGRESS

Nowowiejski, Felix, 1877-1946

1330. [Three Latin motets, op. 5]
        [4]p. 33 x 27 cm.
    For mixed chorus without accompaniment.
    Contents.—1. *Adoremus.*—2. *O salutaris.*—3. *Invocation au sacré
        coeur.*
    Published in 1919 by J. Fischer & Bro. in New York.
                                            LIBRARY OF CONGRESS

Offenbach, Jacques, 1819-1880

1331. [Un mari à la porte]
        114 p. 26½ x 34½ cm.
    Full score of the operetta in one act.
    Text by Delacour and Morand.
    First performed June 22, 1859 in Paris.
    Facsimile of p. 1 in Van Patten, *Catalogue*, p. 199.
                MEMORIAL LIBRARY OF MUSIC, STANFORD UNIVERSITY

Offenbach, Jacques—*continued*

1332. [Sketch-book]
      [138]p. 25½ x 34 cm.
      On p. 1-31, sketches for *La belle Hélène;* other titles indicated are
      *Piramus; Palemon; Pourceaugnac; Alchimist; Kiss, kiss; Trauer
      marsch, Vienne 17 mars 65.*   GALERIE ST. ETIENNE

Onslow, George, 1784-1852

1333. Andantino quasi allegretto.
      [2]p. 15½ x 23½ cm.
      Album leaf for piano 2 hands.
      At end: George Onslow, le 25 avril 1843.   LIBRARY OF CONGRESS

Orlamünder

1334. [Concerto, bassoon, B flat major]
      [32]p. 25½ x 32 cm.
      Full score.
      Presumably the concerto published by Schmidt in Heilbronn.
                                                    LIBRARY OF CONGRESS

1335. Ouverture No. 1 par Orlamünder.
      [31]p. 26½ x 31 cm.
      Full score, in B flat major.   LIBRARY OF CONGRESS

Pacini, Giovanni, 1796-1867

1336. Giuditta, oratorio per musica; poesia del sig. Raffaelo Abate, com
      posto espressamente in occasione della centennale festa d
      S. Agata l'anno 1852, consacrata alla sua diletta terra natale d
      Giovanni Pacini Catanese.
      363 p. 25 x 37½ cm.
      Full score.
      Unpublished.
      Former owner: Natale Gallini (catalogue, no. 35).
                                                    H. BITTNER & CO

1337. [Irene o l'assedio di Messina]
      68 p. 23½ x 30 cm.
      Full score of a duet for Gualterio and Eugenio from Act 2 of
      the opera.
      Former owner: Natale Gallini (catalogue, no. 36).
                     MEMORIAL LIBRARY OF MUSIC, STANFORD UNIVERSITY

Paderewski, Ignacy Jan, 1860-1941

1338. Menuet, op. 14. I. J. Paderewski.
      2 leaves, [5]p. 36½ x 25 cm.
      For piano 2 hands.
      Published as no. 1 of op. 14, *Humoresques de concert,* in 1887 by
      Ed. Bote & G. Bock in Berlin.
      Former owner: Christian Zabriskie.   LIBRARY OF CONGRESS

Paër, Ferdinando, 1771-1839

1339. [Numa Pompilio]
Sinfonia dell' opera Numa Pompilio.
43 p. 22 x 29½ cm.
Full score of the overture.
Former owner: Natale Gallini (catalogue, no. 26).
MEMORIAL LIBRARY OF MUSIC, STANFORD UNIVERSITY

1340. [Olinde et Sophronie]
[289]p. 29½ x 43 cm. and [18]p. 34 x 26½ cm.
Full score of the unfinished opera, 1824.   LIBRARY OF CONGRESS

1341. Le refus. Romance . . .
[3]p. 20 x 27 cm.
Song with piano accpt.
First line: Eh! quoi, tu veux aimer encore.
At end: . . . Fd. Paër 1835.
Former owner: Hugo Riesenfeld.   NEW YORK PUBLIC LIBRARY

Paganini, Nicolò, 1782-1840

1342. [Moto perpetuo, op. 11, no. 6]
Allo. vivace a movimento perpetuo per violino con accompto.
di chitarra.
[3]p. 21½ x 29 cm.
Violin part only.
At end: Genova li 6 aprile 1835, N. Paganini.
NEW YORK PUBLIC LIBRARY

1343. [Rondo, violin and violoncello, A major]
[1]p. 26 x 20 cm.
An otherwise unknown occasional composition for a friend, perhaps Sir George Smart.
At end: Nicolò Paganini. Londra li 25 agosto 1831.
MEMORIAL LIBRARY OF MUSIC, STANFORD UNIVERSITY

Paisiello, Giovanni, 1740-1816

1344. [Cantatas]
[91]p. 23 x 29 cm.
Skeleton full score; apparently autograph.
The cantatas have no titles but the first lines are as follows: Ah! frenate il pianto in belle.—Son lungi e non mi brami.—Senza tema in suo camino.—Guerrier che i colpi affretta.—Care luci che regnate.—Al furor d'avversa sorte.—Dimmi che vaga sei.—Ombra sei tu non io.
Former owner: William H. Cummings (catalogue, no. 1216).
LIBRARY OF CONGRESS

345. . . . Missa breve a 4 voci con più stromenti per la cappella del primo console a S. Cloud. An XI. Musica di Giovanni Paisiello.
[45]p. 35 x 27 cm.
Score.   LIBRARY OF CONGRESS

Paisiello, Giovanni—*continued*

1346. [Il Socrate immaginario]
  [19]p. 21 x 27½ cm.
  Full score of the aria: *Se mai vedi.*
  Former owner: Natale Gallini (catalogue, no. 9).

Paladilhe, Emile, 1844-1926

1347. Psyché, offert au journal "l'Hérault" pour son numéro spécial des fêtes de Molière.
  [1]p. 23 x 31½ cm.
  Song with piano accpt.
  First line: Je suis jaloux, Psyché.
  Former owner: Joseph Muller.

Panseron, Auguste Mathieu, 1795-1859

1348. La bague, romance. Paroles de Mr. Henry Leducq; musique d'Auguste Panseron . . .
  [3]p. 35 x 27 cm.
  Song with piano accpt.
  First line: Allez, bague jolie.
  Unpublished.
  Former owner: Joseph Muller.

Paradies, Pietro Domenico, 1707-1792

1349. [Two arias]
  [13]p. 21 x 29½ cm.
  Score for soprano and strings.
  Contents.—*Vorrei dai lacci scogliere.*—*Volga il ciel, felici amanti.*

Parry, *Sir* Charles Hubert Hastings, 1848-1918

1350. Good night. C. H. H. Parry . . .
  1 leaf, [5]p. 30 x 23½ cm.
  Song with piano accpt. (transposed version in G).
  At end: C. P. 29.4.96.
  Text by Shelley.
  First line: Good night. Ah no, the hour is ill.
  Published as no. 2 of his *English Lyrics* (first set) in 1885 by Stanley, Lucas, Weber & Co. in London.

1351. Job.
  300 p. 35 x 27 cm.
  Full score of the oratorio.
  Published as op. 116 in 1897 by Novello, Ewer & Co. in London.

1352. Proud Maisie. Words by Sir Walter Scott, set by C. Hubert H. Parry.
   [3]p. 29½ x 23½ cm.
   Song with piano accpt.
   First line: Proud Maisie is in the wood.
   Published as no. 2 of his *English Lyrics* (fifth set) in 1902 by Novello & Co. in London.   MR. CARL H. TOLLEFSEN

Pepusch, John Christopher, 1667-1752
1353. [Concerto, string orchestra, A minor]
   [18]p. 20 x 25 cm.
   Score.
   On p. 18, a setting for 3 voices unaccompanied of *Te aeternum patrem.*
   Former owners: John Alcott, George Pigott, Thomas W. Taphouse, William H. Cummings (catalogue, no. 1234).   LIBRARY OF CONGRESS

Pergolesi, Giovanni Battista, 1710-1736
1354. Non mi negar, signora.
   [2]p.
   For voice and continuo.
   At end: A Fra Bernardo Feo. Gio: Basta Pergolesi a d. 1731.
   Not in his *Opera omnia.*
   Apparently a forgery by Tobia Nicotra.   LIBRARY OF CONGRESS

Perotti, Giovanni Agostino, 1769-1855
1355. Te Deum laudamus a quattro voci con strumenti del sigr. G. A. Perotti l'anno 1833.
   27 p. 22½ x 32½ cm.
   Full score.   BOSTON PUBLIC LIBRARY

Peterkin, Norman, 1888-
1356. . . . Autumn song for voices and string quartet. Poem by D. G. Rossetti. Music by Norman Peterkin.
   1 leaf, 14 p. 35 x 27 cm.
   Dedication to Carl Engel.
   First line: Know'st thou not at the fall of the leaf.
   At end: Norman Peterkin. May & June 1923 . . .
   Former owner: Carl Engel.   LIBRARY OF CONGRESS

Petit, Raymond, 1893-
1357. Hymne. Raymond Petit. Texte tiré des Upanishads . . .
   1 leaf, 8 p. 33½ x 26½ cm.
   For voice and flute.
   First line: O feu divin, conduis-nous par le droit chemin.
       THE LEAGUE OF COMPOSERS

Petit, Raymond—*continued*

1358. [Trois récits des Evangiles pour ténor et quatuor à cordes]
    5, 18, 12 p. 36½ x 27 cm.
    Score, French text (typewritten English text laid in).
    Dated: 27 sept. 30; octobre 1930; novembre 1930.
                    LIBRARY OF CONGRESS, COOLIDGE FOUNDATION

Piatti, Alfredo Carlo, 1822-1901

1359. Canzonetta.
    4 p. 24 x 30½ cm.
    For violoncello and piano.
    Former owners: Marguerite Jacobson, Natale Gallini (catalogue,
    no. 50).   MEMORIAL LIBRARY OF MUSIC, STANFORD UNIVERSITY

1360. La Suédoise. Caprice sur deux airs nationaux par Alfredo Piatti.
    Op. 11.
    [12]p. 23 x 32 cm.
    For violoncello and piano.
    Former owner: Mrs. G. N. Carozzi.   LIBRARY OF CONGRESS

Piccinni, Niccolò, 1726-1800

1361. [Accanto a un fiumicello]
    [4]p. 20½ x 29½ cm.
    Aria for voice and piano accpt.
    On title-page: Ecrit de sa propre main du célèbre Piccini pour son
    ami J. B. Viotti, à Paris 1783.   LIBRARY OF CONGRESS

Pierné, Henri Constant Gabriel, 1863-1937

1362. Entrée dans le style classique pour grand orgue de Gabriel
    Pierné . . .
    [1], 5 p. 35 x 27 cm.
    At end: Gabriel Pierné. Paris octobre 95.
    Published by Millet & Co. in Boston.   BOSTON PUBLIC LIBRARY

1363. Mathématiques. Canon à l'unisson. (Mouvt. de marche) Gabriel
    Pierné.
    [2]p. 17 x 11 cm.
    For women's chorus unaccompanied.   LIBRARY OF CONGRESS

1364. Sonate da camera pour trois instruments: flûte, violoncelle et piano
    (Prélude, sarabande et final). Gabriel Pierné, op. 48.
    Score (33 p.) and parts. 35 x 27 cm.
    At end: Gabriel Pierné, château de la Peype. Chatte (Isère) 24
    sept. 26.
    Published in 1928 by A. Durand et Cie. in Paris.
                    LIBRARY OF CONGRESS, COOLIDGE FOUNDATION

Pierson, Heinrich Hugo, 1816-1873

1365.　Einleitung . . . Faust II. Theil Sc. 1 Ariel.
　　　[1]p. 33 x 26 cm.
　　　Full score of an addition for the Norwich Festival, 1857.

Pinsuti, Ciro, 1829-1888

1366.　. . . Otto melodie con parole italiane, e accompagnamento di piano
　　　forte composte da Ciro Pinsuti . . .
　　　1 leaf, [73]p. 30 x 24 cm.
　　　Dedication to King Fernando of Portugal.
　　　Not all the songs are in the composer's autograph.
　　　Former owner: The Royal Collection, Lisbon.

Pitoni, Giuseppe Ottavio, 1657-1743

1367.　Hymnus a 8 voci.
　　　[3]p. 27 x 21 cm.
　　　For 8-part mixed chorus, unaccompanied.
　　　First line: Beata es, virgo Maria.
　　　At head of title: die 26 augusto 1724. Roma.
　　　Former owners: R. G. Kiesewetter, Alois Fuchs (?).

Pizzetti, Ildebrando, 1880-

1368.　Tre canzoni per una voce e quartetto d'archi (1926) (I. Donna
　　　lombarda. II. La prigioniera. III. La pesca dell' anello.)
　　　1 leaf, 52 p. 33 x 24 cm.
　　　Score.
　　　At end: Ildebrando Pizzetti gennaro-febraio 1926.
　　　Published in 1927 by G. Ricordi in Milan.
　　　Dedicated to Mrs. E. S. Coolidge.

1369.　Epithalamium; cantata per soli, coro e piccola orchestra, di Ilde-
　　　brando Pizzetti (1939). Testo dai Carmi di Gaio Valerio Catullo.
　　　81 p. 32½ x 23½ cm.
　　　Full score.　

1370.　[Quartet, strings, D major]
　　　. . . Quartetto in re per due violini—viola—e violoncello . . .
　　　Ildebrando Pizzetti.
　　　3 leaves, 48 numbered leaves. 40 x 27 cm.
　　　Score, music on recto only.
　　　Dedicated to Mrs. E. S. Coolidge.
　　　At end: Ildebrando. Milano—27 febraio—1933.
　　　Published in 1933 by G. Ricordi in Milan.

Pizzetti, Ildebrando—*continued*

1371. ... Trio in la per violino, violoncello, e pianoforte.
1 leaf, 70 p. 33 x 24 cm.
Score.
Dedicated to Mrs. E. S. Coolidge, "remembering the two first per-
formances of this Trio—Paris 23, London May 28th [1925]."
Published in 1925 by G. Ricordi in Milan.

LIBRARY OF CONGRESS, COOLIDGE FOUNDATION

Pizzi, Emilio, 1862-1940

1372. Ave Maria. Hear us, o Saviour. For soprano or tenor. Emilio Pizzi.
English words by A. Farman.
6 p. 37 x 28 cm.
Song with piano accpt.
Published in 1902 by J. Fischer & Bro. in New York.

LIBRARY OF CONGRESS

1373. Ave Maria. Sacred song. With violin (or violoncello) and organ
accompaniment ad libitum. Composed by Emilio Pizzi.
[1], 14 p. 37 x 28 cm.
Published in 1902 by J. Fischer & Bro. in New York.

LIBRARY OF CONGRESS

1374. En Espagne. Caprice pour violon et piano par Emilio Pizzi.
15 p. 36 x 27 cm.
Published in 1904 by J. Fischer & Bro. in New York.

LIBRARY OF CONGRESS

1375. O salutaris for quartett. Emilio Pizzi.
6 p. 36 x 25½ cm.
For 4 mixed voices with organ accpt.
Published in 1909 by J. Fischer & Bro. in New York.

LIBRARY OF CONGRESS

1376. O salutaris. For soprano or tenor. Emilio Pizzi.
[4]p. 33 x 25 cm.
Song with organ accpt.
Published in 1903 by J. Fischer & Bro. in New York.

LIBRARY OF CONGRESS

1377. Offertory "Domine Jesu Christe."
8 p. 36 x 27½ cm.
For alto solo and organ.
Published in 1902 by J. Fischer & Bro. in New York.

LIBRARY OF CONGRES

1378. Requiem mass for 4 voices and chorus ad libitum with organ by
Emilio Pizzi.
1 leaf, 44 p. 34½ x 26½ cm.
Published in 1902 by J. Fischer & Bro. in New York.

LIBRARY OF CONGRES

Platania, Pietro, 1828-1907

1379. [Tota pulchra es, Maria]
    [10]p. 29 x 23 cm.
Full score of the composer's orchestration of the 2nd section of
the motet.
The motet in its original form (solo voices, chorus and organ) was
  published in 1898 by Breitkopf & Härtel in Leipzig.
Former owner: Natale Gallini (catalogue, no. 55).
MEMORIAL LIBRARY OF MUSIC, STANFORD UNIVERSITY

Plüddemann, Martin, 1854-1897

1380. [Herr Walter von der Vogelweid']
    . . . Berlt der junge, Herrn Walters von der Vogelweide Singer-
    knabe. I. "Der Waldrast." Dichtung von Joseph Victor Scheffel.
    Componirt für Tenor mit Pianoforte von Martin Plüddemann.
    München, 10. Juli 1879.
    10 p. 34 x 27 cm.
Published as no. 7 of his *Lieder und Gesänge, Altdeutsche Lieder,*
  ca. 1893 by Wilhelm Schmid in Nürnberg.
LIBRARY OF CONGRESS

1381. Ritter Kurt's Brautfahrt (Goethe). M. Plüddemann 1883.
    [9]p. 34 x 27 cm.
Song with piano accpt.
First line: Mit des Bräutigams Behagen.
Published as no. 3 of Band 4 of his *Balladen und Gesänge* in 1893
  by Wilhelm Schmid in Nürnberg.
YALE UNIVERSITY LIBRARY, SPECK COLLECTION

Ponchielli, Amilcare, 1834-1886

1382. Le due gemelle.
    358 p. 25 x 33 cm.
Full score of the ballet.
First performed February 4, 1873 in Milan.
Former owner: Natale Gallini (catalogue, no. 59).
Facsimile of p. 1 in Van Patten, *Catalogue,* p. 211.
MEMORIAL LIBRARY OF MUSIC, STANFORD UNIVERSITY

1383. Scena ed aria per contralto. A. Ponchielli.
    9 p. 23 x 32 cm.
Duet with piano accpt.
First line: Accorge al tempio.
Performed in 1854 at the "finale accademico" of the Milan Con-
servatory.   MEMORIAL LIBRARY OF MUSIC, STANFORD UNIVERSITY

Poniatowski, *Prince* **Josef (Michal Xawery Franciszek Jan), 1816-1873**
1384. All' amante lontano. Melodia composta . . . dal principe Giuseppe
    Poniatowski.
    1 leaf, [9]p. 16½ x 22 cm.

Poniatowski, *Prince* Josef—*continued*

Song with piano accpt.
First line: Mentre solinga al tacito.
At end: Milano. 19 settembre 1842. G. Poniatowski.

1385. [Maria di grazie tante perenne]
[4]p. 33 x 24 cm.
For solo and chorus with piano accpt.
On p. 3-4 are choral settings in another hand. LIBRARY OF CONGRESS

Porpora, Nicola Antonio, 1685-1767?

1386. Motetto a voce sola di Nicolo Porpora. 1712. 27 giugno.
[18]p. 21½ x 28 cm.
For voice and continuo.
First line: Nocte die suspirando ploro.
At end: Finis 28 giugno 1712. N. Porpora.
Former owner: G. W. Teschner. NEW YORK PUBLIC LIBRARY

Portugal, Marco Antonio, 1762-1830

1387. . . . Demofoonte. Drama seria da rappresentarsi nel real teatro di
S. Carlo in Lisbona. Musica di Marco Portogallo.
1 vol. 23 x 32 cm.
Full score of the revised version.
Performed August 15, 1808.
Text by Metastasio, altered by Giuseppe Caravita.
Former owner: Joachim de Vasconcellos, who believed this to be
the autograph. (This is questioned by Carvalhaes in his biog-
raphy of the composer.) LIBRARY OF CONGRESS

Preyer, Gottfried von, 1807-1901

1388. Mignon, Dichtung v. Göthe. Musik v. Gfd. Preyer.
[3]p. 20½ x 28 cm.
Song with piano accpt.
First line: Kennst du das Land.
Apparently unpublished.

YALE UNIVERSITY LIBRARY, SPECK COLLECTION

Prokof'ev, Sergeĭ Sergeevich, 1891-

1389. [Quartet, strings, op. 50, B minor]
Quartet . . . Serge Prokofieff, op. 50, 1930.
33 p. 27 x 35 cm.
Score.
At end: Zakonchenie eskizy 26 Iiun' 1930 partitura 14 dek. 1930.
Paris.
Published in 1932 by Russischer Musikverlag in Berlin and Paris.

LIBRARY OF CONGRESS, COOLIDGE FOUNDATION

Prokof'ev, Sergeï Sergeevich—*continued*

1390. [Symphony, no. 4, op. 47, C major]
        [64]p. 27 x 34 cm.
        Full score.
        At end: June 23rd 1930. 1.15 p.m. Paris. S.P.
                                        BOSTON SYMPHONY ORCHESTRA

Prout, Ebenezer, 1835-1909

1391. Constancy.
        [6]p. 30 x 24 cm.
        Song with piano accpt.
        First line: When the tempest's at the loudest.
        Former owner: William H. Cummings (catalogue, no. 96).
                                        LIBRARY OF CONGRESS

1392. Oh bird, that through the livelong day. Words by W. Reynolds.
        Music by Ebenezer Prout.
        [4]p. 30 x 24 cm.
        Song with piano accpt.
        Former owner: William H. Cummings (catalogue, no. 96).
                                        LIBRARY OF CONGRESS

Puccini, Giacomo, 1858-1924

1393. [Manon Lescaut]
        [4]p. 33½ x 24 cm.
        Sketches for the finale of Act I.
        Facsimile of one page in Van Patten, *Catalogue*, p. 214.
                        MEMORIAL LIBRARY OF MUSIC, STANFORD UNIVERSITY

1394. Vexilla, a 2 voci. G. Puccini.
        [7]p. 28½ x 22 cm.
        For 2-part men's chorus and organ.
        Text by Venantius Fortunatus.
        First line: Vexilla regis prodeunt.
        Composed ca. 1878; unpublished. See *Report of the Librarian of
        Congress*, 1935-36, p. 140.
        Former owner: Adelson Betti.   LIBRARY OF CONGRESS

Püttlingen, Johann Vesque von, 1803-1883

1395. Der Doktor und der Patient, komisches Duett für 2 Bässe mit
        Begleitung des Pianof. in Musik gesetzt . . . von Joh. Vesque
        von Püttlingen. 1845.
        [14]p. 24 x 31½ cm.
        At head of title: Oeuv. 13.
        Pencil sketch of title characters pasted on cover.
                                UNIVERSITY OF PENNSYLVANIA LIBRARY

Purcell, Henry, 1658 (or 1659)-1695

1396. The epicure by Mr. Cowley.
[4]p. 32 x 20 cm.
Song for two voices with harpsichord accpt.
First line: Underneath this mirtle shade.
Works, vol. XXII, no. 27.
Former owner: William H. Cummings (catalogue, no. 169).

1397. Te Deum and Jubilate for voices and instruments made for St.
Cecilias day, 1694.
43 p. 33½ x 20½ cm.
Full score.
Published in 1697 by Henry Playford in London.
Works, vol. XIII.
On last page a setting of a song: *When first Dorinda's piercing eyes*
(not in Complete Works).
Former owner: Arthur F. Hill.

1398. [Trio sonatas]
The score to sonata's of three parts, to two viollins and basse: to
the organ or harpsichord, composed by Henry Purcell.
2 leaves, [56]p. 33½ x 21 cm.
Published in 1683 by J. Playford and J. Carr in London.
Works, vol. V.
Former owner: William H. Cummings (catalogue, no. 1362).

Rachmaninov, Sergei, 1873-1943

Additional autographs in the Rachmaninoff Archives in
the Library of Congress, received too late for inclusion here,
are listed in *Library of Congress Quarterly Journal*, IX, no. 1
(Nov. 1951), 41.

1399. [Concerto, piano, no. 4, op. 40, G minor]
Concert pour piano (no. 4) op. 40. S. Rachmaninoff.
1 leaf, 171 p. 43 x 34 cm.
Full score, with added reduction of orchestra score for a 2nd piano
beneath.
At end: I͡Anuar'—25 Avgusta, New York . . .
Published in 1928 by Edition Tair, in Paris.

1400. Bizet, Georges, 1838-1875.
[L'Arlésienne. Suite no. 1]
Minuet (from L'Arlésienne Suite No. I) by Georges Bizet,
arranged for piano by Sergei Rachmaninoff.
[8]p. 35 x 27 cm.
Published in 1923 by Carl Fischer in New York.

1401. [Monna Vanna]
      100 p. 36 x 27 cm.
    Piano-vocal score of Act I of the unfinished opera (1907).
LIBRARY OF CONGRESS

1402. [Monna Vanna]
      [19]p. 31 x 23 cm.
    Sketches.   LIBRARY OF CONGRESS

1403. Rapsodie sur un thème de Paganini. Op. 43.
      176 p. 34 x 24 cm.
    Full score.
    At end: 18° Avgusta 1934. Senar. Slava Bogu!
    Published in 1934 by Edition Tair in Paris.
    Facsimile of one page in *Library of Congress Quarterly Journal*, IX,
        no. 1 (November, 1951), opp. p. 40.   LIBRARY OF CONGRESS

1404. Symphonic dances. S. R.
      177 p. 37½ x 26 and 39 x 33½ cm.
    Full score.
    Dated at end of each movement: first, 22-IX—8-X 1940; second,
        27-IX-40; third, 29 Octobre 1940.
    Published in 1942 by Charles Foley in New York.
LIBRARY OF CONGRESS

1405. [Symphony, no. 3, op. 44, A minor]
      [194]p. 33½ x 27 cm.
    Full score.
    At end: Konchil. Blagodariu boga! 6-30 IŪnia. Senar.
    Published in 1937 by Edition Tair in Paris.   LIBRARY OF CONGRESS

Raff, Joachim, 1822-1882

1406. [Aus Thüringen. Suite]
      147 p. 33 x 26 cm.
    Full score.
    Published in 1893 by Ries and Erler in Berlin.
    Former owner: Emil Sulzbach.   LIBRARY OF CONGRESS

1407. Liszt, Franz, 1811-1886.
    [Huldigungsmarsch]
    Marsch.
    23 p. 34 x 26 cm.
    Score of Raff's arrangement for military band of Liszt's march,
        originally composed for piano in 1853 (Raabe 49, Grove 141).
LIBRARY OF CONGRESS

1408. [Symphony, no. 10, op. 213, F minor]
      Zur Herbstzeit. Symphonie no. 10, F moll, von Joachim Raff.
      104 p. 32 x 25½ cm.
    Full score.

Raff, Joachim—*continued*

Published in 1882 by C. F. W. Siegel in Leipzig.
This forms the 3rd part of his symphonic cycle *Die Jahreszeiten*.

WALTER R. BENJAMIN

Raimondi, Pietro, 1786-1853

1409. Duetto. "Tutto in petto" di Pietro Raimondi.
    fol. 79-96. 23 x 30 cm.
Full score of a duet for tenor (Fernando) and bass (Filippo).
Former owner: Natale Gallini (catalogue, no. 30).

NEW YORK PUBLIC LIBRARY

1410. Gonzalvo e Zilia.
    89 p. 23 x 30 cm.
Full score of the pantomime.
Former owner: Natale Gallini (catalogue, no. 31).

MEMORIAL LIBRARY OF MUSIC, STANFORD UNIVERSITY

Ravanello, Oreste, 1871-1938

1411. Messa solennelle (XVIIa) in onore di S. Oreste martire di Tyana
a 3 voci pari con accto. d'organo di Oreste Ravanello (op. 83) . . .
    40 p. 31½ x 25 cm.
At end: Padova 19 giugno 1906.
Published in 1906 by J. Fischer & Bro. in New York.

LIBRARY OF CONGRESS

1412. Psalmodia vespertina in festis B.M.V. per annum cum quatuor
antiphonis B.M.V. tribus vocibus aequalibus organo vel harmonio
ad libitum ab Oreste Ravanello composita op. 84.
    29 p. 33½ x 24 cm.
At end: Padova 29 luglio 1906 Oreste Ravanello.
Published in 1907 by J. Fischer & Bro. in New York.

LIBRARY OF CONGRESS

Ravel, Maurice (Joseph), 1875-1937

1413. . . . Chansons madécasses. Texte d'Evariste Parny.
    Score (15 p.) and parts. 34½ x 26½ cm.
For voice and flute, violoncello and piano.
An additional score of no. 2.
At end of no. 2: Maurice Ravel, mai 1925.
Dedicated to Mrs. E. S. Coolidge.
Published in 1926 by A. Durand & Cie. in Paris.

LIBRARY OF CONGRESS, COOLIDGE FOUNDATION

1414. [Tout gai!]
    [3]p. 35 x 26½ cm.
Song with piano accpt.
Text by M. D. Calvocoressi.
Published as no. 5 of *Cinq mélodies populaires grecques* in 1907 by
A. Durand & Cie. in Paris.

MEMORIAL LIBRARY OF MUSIC, STANFORD UNIVERSITY

Reckzeh, Adolph

1415. Oratorien. Das Leben, Sterben, die Auferstehung und Himmel-
fahrt Jesu, in 4 Theile, componirt von Adolph Reckzeh. Op. 123.
Dichtung von Carl Göring.
1 leaf, [116]p. 34 x 24½ cm.
Piano-vocal score.
At end: Adolph Reckzeh. 29.10.77.

Redern, Friedrich Wilhelm, Graf von, 1802-1883

1416. Ballabile. November 1856.
1 leaf, 28 p. 32 x 24½ cm.
Full score.

1417. [Concertouvertüre. E flat major]
37 p. 33 x 26½ cm.
Full score.

1418. Opernscene.
[35]p. 33 x 25½ cm.
Full score.

1419. Ouverture.
[30]p. 28½ x 36 cm.
Full score, in D major.

1420. Ouverture.
[37]p. 28½ x 36 cm.
Full score, in E flat major.

1421. Ouverture à grand orchester, par G. de Redern. Berlin den 10ten
janvier 1818.
39 p. 23½ x 33½ cm.
Full score.

1422. Ouverture pour orchestre.
1 leaf, [34]p. 28 x 36 cm.
Full score, in E flat major.

1423. Der Sturm. December 1856.
1 leaf, [22]p. 33 x 25½ cm.
Full score.

1424. [Thema mit Variationen]
[32]p. 29 x 36 cm.
Full score.

Refice, Licinio, 1885-

1425. Missa choralis tribus vocibus aequalibus concinenda, organo comi-
tante, et alternante cantu populari a Rev. Dom. Licinio Refice
... composita.
38 p. 33 x 24 cm.
Published in 1916 by J. Fischer & Bro. in New York.

1426. Aeolsharfe. Für mittlere Stimme . . . Max Reger, op. 75, no. 11.
[2]p. 35 x 27 cm.
Song with piano accpt.
Text by Hermann Lingg.
First line: Geheimnisvoller Klang, für Geister der Luft besaitet.
Dedicated to Frau Dr. A. Gimkiewicz.
Published in 1905 by Lauterbach & Kuhn in Leipzig.
LIBRARY OF CONGRESS

1427. Einsamkeit. Für tiefe Stimme . . . Max Reger, op. 75, no. 18.
[2]p. 35 x 27 cm.
Song with piano accpt.
Text by Goethe.
First line: Dir ihr Felsen und Bäume bewohnt.
Dedicated to Frau Dr. A. Gimkiewicz.
Published in 1905 by Lauterbach & Kuhn in Leipzig.
LIBRARY OF CONGRESS

1428. [Sonata, clarinet and piano, op. 49, no. 1, A flat major]
9 p. 31 x 27 cm.
Score.
Published in 1901 by Jos. Aibl in Munich.
MEMORIAL LIBRARY OF MUSIC, STANFORD UNIVERSITY

1429. [Sonata, clarinet and piano, op. 49, no. 2, F sharp minor]
1 leaf, 10 p. 31 x 27 cm.
Score.
Published in 1901 by Jos. Aibl in Munich.
MEMORIAL LIBRARY OF MUSIC, STANFORD UNIVERSITY

1430. Zwölf Stücke für die Orgel. Max Reger, Op. 65.
32 leaves. 35 x 28 cm.
The pieces are not arranged in the order as published in 1902 by
C. F. Peters in Leipzig.
No. 2, *Capriccio*, is omitted. Heft II further contains a *Gigue* and
an *Intermezzo*, published as nos. 4 and 6 of Op. 80 in 1904 by
C. F. Peters.   LIBRARY OF CONGRESS, WHITTALL FOUNDATION

1431. Valse d'amour. Max Reger, op. 130, no. 5.
4 p. 34½ x 27 cm.
Composer's reduction for piano 2 hands from the orchestra score
of his *Balletsuite*.
Published in this version in 1913 by C. F. Peters in Leipzig.
LIBRARY OF CONGRESS

Rehfeld, Fabian, 1842-1920

1432. Gavotte für Violine und Pianoforte von Fabian Rehfeld. Op. 59,
no. 3.
Score (4 p.) and part. 33 x 26 cm.
Dedicated to Carl Engel.   LIBRARY OF CONGRESS

Reichardt, Gustav, 1797-1884

1433. Music for ever!
    [1]p. 12 x 20 cm.
    For 4-part men's chorus a cappella.
    First line: Musik durchwebt das ganze Menschenleben.
    Former owner: Joseph Muller.   NEW YORK PUBLIC LIBRARY

Reichardt, Johann Friedrich, 1751-1814

1434. "Gesund an Leib und Seele sein." J. F. Reichardt.
    1 leaf. 18½ x 22 cm.
    For mixed chorus unaccompanied.
    HISTORICAL SOCIETY OF PENNSYLVANIA

1435. [Symphony, no. 2, D minor]
    Simphonia 2. con 2 violini 2 oboe 2 flauti 4 corni viola e basso di
    Giov. Feder. Reichardt.
    [9]p. 20 x 24½ cm.
    Full score.   LIBRARY OF CONGRESS

Reimann, Heinrich, 1850-1906

1436. Phantasie über den Choral: Wie schön leuchtet der Morgenstern,
    für Orgel von Heinrich Reimann, op. 25.
    [25]p. 34 x 27 cm.
    Published in 1895 by Anton J. Benjamin in Leipzig.
    LIBRARY OF CONGRESS

Reinecke, Carl (Heinrich Carsten), 1824-1910

1437. [Ein Abenteuer Händels oder die Macht des Liedes, op. 104]
    [2]p. 30 x 22 cm.
    Fragment of full score.
    Former owner: Joseph Muller.   NEW YORK PUBLIC LIBRARY

1438. Drei Sonatinen für Pianoforte und Violine von Carl Reinecke.
    Op. 108.
    [1], 33 p. 27 x 33 cm.
    Score.
    Published in 1871 by N. Simrock in Berlin.   LIBRARY OF CONGRESS

Reissiger, Karl Gottlieb, 1798-1859

1439. Adèle de Foix.
    1 vol. 24 x 32 cm.
    Full score of the opera.
    Text by Robert Blum.
    Dated on p. 1 of Introduction: d. 12ten May, 1840; at end of Act I:
    finito d. 3 Juni 1840; at end of Act II: finito d. 17 Juni; at end of
    Act IV: finito d. 4 July 1840.
    Performed November 26, 1841 at the Hoftheater in Dresden.
    LIBRARY OF CONGRESS

Reissiger, Karl Gottlieb—*continued*

1440. An Victoire—am Rhein von C. K.
[4]p. 24 x 32 cm.
Song with piano accpt.
First line: Am Rhein! Am Rhein! da wachsen unsere Reben!

1441. Canzonetta di Petrarca.
[1]p. 26½ x 33 cm.
Song with piano accpt.
First line: O dolci sguardi.
Former owner: Joseph Muller.

Rensburg, Jacques E., 1846-1910

1442. . . . Am Meeresstrande. Drei Characterstucke [!] für Violoncell
(Violine od. Viola) mit Orchesterbegleitung von Jacques E.
Rensburg. Op. 4 . . .
56 p. 33½ x 25 cm.
Full score.
Published (for violoncello and piano) by Breitkopf & Härtel in
Leipzig.

1443. . . . Ballade für Violoncel [!] und Orchester von Jacques E.
Rensburg. Op. 5.
34 p. 34 x 25½ cm.
Full score.
Published (for violoncello and piano) by Breitkopf & Härtel in
Leipzig.

1444. Concertstück (Recit. Adagio. All° moderato) für Violoncello Solo
mit Begleitung des Orchesters von Jacques Rensburg. Op. 1.
Cöln August 1869.
71, [2]p. 32 x 24 cm.
Full score.
At end: Cöln 6 Jan. 1869.
Published by Breitkopf & Härtel in Leipzig.

Renzi, Remigio, 1857-

1445. . . . Maria stella maris. Chants poètiques [!] pour grand orgue par
Remigio Renzi . . . Nov. 1904.
23 p. 22 x 29 cm.
Dedicated to Monsignor Giuseppe Beccaria.
Published in 1905 by J. Fischer & Bro. in New York.

1446.   . . . Concerto a cinque per oboe, tromba, violino, contrabbasso, pianoforte e orchestra d'archi. Roma—1933.
     43 p. 48½ x 35 cm.
Full score.
Dated: Roma 25 marzo 1933 'Ai Pini.'
Dedicated to Mrs. E. S. Coolidge.
Published in 1934 by G. Ricordi in Milan.
LIBRARY OF CONGRESS, COOLIDGE FOUNDATION

1447.   [Le fontane di Roma]
     21 numbered leaves. 32 x 25 cm.
Original pencil draft of the symphonic poem, on recto of each leaf.
On the verso of each leaf are sketches for the 3rd act of his *Marie Victoire*, a four-act opera which the composer never allowed to be performed.
Published in 1919 by G. Ricordi in Milan.
LIBRARY OF CONGRESS, COOLIDGE FOUNDATION

1448.   [Metamorphoseon modi XII] (Tema e variazioni) per orchestra. Ottorino Respighi (1930).
     96 p. 39½ x 29 cm.
Full score.
Dedicated to the Boston Symphony Orchestra on its 50th anniversary.
At end: Roma 10 agosto 1930.
Published in 1931 by G. Ricordi in Milan.
BOSTON SYMPHONY ORCHESTRA

1449.   Preludio in si ♭ magg. sopra un corale di Bach per organo. Ottorino Respighi. giugno 1912 . . . Roma 15 novembre 1914.
     [7]p. 34 x 25 cm.
Dedicated to Vittorio Scotti.
Facsimile of p. 1 in International Autographs catalogue 2, p. 28.
MR. RUDOLF F. KALLIR

1450.   Trittico botticelliano per orchestra da camera. I. La primavera. II. L'adorazione dei magi. III. La nascita di Venere. (1927).
     81 p. 40 x 26½ cm.
Full score.
Dedicated to Mrs. E. S. Coolidge.
At end: Abetone. 3 agosto 1927.
Published in 1928 by G. Ricordi in Milan.
LIBRARY OF CONGRESS, COOLIDGE FOUNDATION

Reyer, (Louis Etienne) Ernest, 1823-1909

1451.   Le chant des paysans. E. Reyer.
     [10]p. 35 x 26½ cm.
Full score (chorus and orchestra).
Published by Heugel et Cie. in Paris.   LIBRARY OF CONGRESS

Rheinberger, Josef (Gabriel), 1839-1901

1452. Ouverture zu Shakspeare's 'Zähmung der Widerspenstigen.' Josef
       Rheinberger. Op. 18.
       39 p. 37 x 28½ cm.
       Full score.
       Published in 1874 by Kistner & Siegel in Leipzig.
                                     THE FOLGER SHAKESPEARE LIBRARY

Rhené-Baton (i.e. René Baton), 1879-1940

1453. En Bretagne. Suite pour le piano. Rhené-Baton. Opus 13.
       32 p. 35 x 27 cm.
       Published in 1909 by A. Durand et Cie. in Paris.
                          MEMORIAL LIBRARY OF MUSIC, STANFORD UNIVERSITY

Ricci, Federico, 1809-1877

1454. Frammento di poesia tratto del poema drammatico di Alfredo de
       Musset, "La coupe et les lèvres." Federico Ricci. Pietroburgo.
       24 Xbre. 1856.
       [4]p. 37 x 27 cm.
       Song with piano accpt.
       First line: Parlons sincèrement (from Act 2, scene 3).
       Former owners: Victor Déséglise, Hugo Riesenfeld.   PIERRE BÉRÈS

1455. Romanza.
       [6]p. 35 x 26½ cm.
       Song with piano accpt.
       First line: Pietà, pietà, ti chiede e non rispondi.
       Dedicated to Baron d'Andrian Werburg.
       Former owner: The Royal Collection, Lisbon.
                                            LIBRARY OF CONGRESS

Ricci, Luigi, 1805-1859

1456. Taci mio ben.
       57 p. 23 x 29½ cm.
       Sketch for a soprano and tenor duet with orchestra; only the voice
       parts are completely written in.
       Former owner: Natale Gallini (catalogue, no. 46).
                          MEMORIAL LIBRARY OF MUSIC, STANFORD UNIVERSITY

Richter, Ernest Friedrich (Eduard), 1808-1879

1457. [Quartet, strings, no. 1, op. 25, B minor]
       Streichquartett von Ernst Friedrich Richter.
       [35]p. 34 x 26 cm.
       Reduction for piano 2 hands.
       At end: Den 3ten Mai 1864. Fertig componirt im Nov. 1857.
       Published (in original form) in 1860 by Breitkopf & Härtel in
       Leipzig.   NEW YORK PUBLIC LIBRARY

Ries, Ferdinand, 1784-1838

1458. Rondo polacca for the pianoforte with accomp. of the full orchestra. Composed by Ferd. Ries, Bonn, 1833.

[64]p. 24 x 34 cm.

Full score.

Cover label has title: *Introduction et polonaise pour le [piano] forte et grand orchestre, par Ferd. Ries, op. 174.*

Ries, Hubert, 1802-1886

1459. Ries, Ferdinand, 1784-1838.

[Symphony, no. 5, op. 112, D minor]

Ferd. Ries Op. 112, cinquième symphonie, arrangée pour pianoforte, deux violons et violoncelle par Hub. Ries. Berlin, Juni 1845.

38 p. 27 x 35 cm.

At end: Fine. 13-26 juin 1845.

Former owner: Joseph Muller.

Ritter, Peter, 1763-1846

1460. 1 Adagio u. 2 Menuets für Orchester von Peter Ritter. Autograph.

[18]p. 21 x 34 cm.

Full score.

1461. Alfred. Oper in 3 Aufzügen. Text von Kotzebue. Musik von P. Ritter.

1 vol. 31 x 22½ cm.

Full score of Act I, largely in autograph.

Performed December 26, 1820 at the Hoftheater in Mannheim.

1462. [Allah gibt Licht in Nächten]

[4]p. 26 x 34 cm.

Score for soprano and orchestra.

Text by Mahlmann.

Dedication at head of title: *An Herz! Sei meine Freundin, sanftes Mädchen!*

1463. [Die beiden Eremiten]

[64]p. 31 x 23 cm.

Piano-vocal score of the opera.

At head of title: von Peter Ritter. Klavierauszug. Autograph.

1464. Bianka. Oper in 2 Aufzügen. Text von Professor Grimm. Musik von P. Ritter.

2 vols. 29½ x 22 cm.

Full score.

Text by Albert Ludwig Grimm.

Performed April 22, 1825, at the Hoftheater in Mannheim.

Ritter, Peter—*continued*

1465. [Concerto, bassoon, G major]
Concert pur [!] le fagotto di J. P. Ritter. 1778.
[28]p. 23 x 32 cm.
Full score.

1466. [Concerto, flute, D major]
Concerto I. P. Ritter.
[53]p. 20 x 33 cm.
Full score.

1467. [Concerto, flute, D major]
Concerto per la [!] flauto. Di Piere [!] Ritter.
[16], 18 p. 23 x 32 and 22 x 27 cm.
Full score.

1468. [Concerto, horn and violoncello, E major]
Concertante für Horn u. Violonclle [!] v. P. Ritter.
[42]p. 22 x 35 cm.
Full score.

1469. [Concerto, piano, D major]
Concerto. Di Piere [!] Ritter 1781.
[32]p. 24 x 35 cm.
Full score.

1470. [Concerto, piano, E minor]
Concerto per il cembalo. Peter Ritter.
[165]p. 35½ x 22 cm.
Full score.

1471. [Concerto, violin, C major]
. . . Violin-Concert v. P. Ritter.
[86]p. 21½ x 36 cm.
Full score.

1472. [Concerto, violin, F major]
Violin Concert v. P. Ritter.
[32]p. 23 x 32 cm.
Full score.

1473. [Concerto, 2 violins, D major]
Concertant für 2 Violinen von P. Ritter. Vor dem Jahre 1787
componirt.
[36]p. 36 x 22 cm.
Full score.
Cover title in a modern hand.

1474. [Concerto, violoncello]
. . . Violoncello-Konzert von Peter Ritter. Autograph.
[20]p. 36 x 22 cm.
Full score, incomplete.

Ritter, Peter—*continued*

1475. [Concerto, violoncello, A major]
      Concerto per il violoncello di Pietro Ritter.
      [76]p. 20½ x 33½ and 21 x 35 cm.
      Full score.   LIBRARY OF CONGRESS

1476. [Concerto, violoncello, A major]
      Concerto per il violoncello. Peter Ritter. Autograph.
      [35]p. 31 x 22½ cm.
      Full score.   LIBRARY OF CONGRESS

1477. [Concerto, violoncello, A minor]
      ... Concerto per violoncello von Peter Ritter.
      [54]p. 27 x 35 cm.
      Full score.   LIBRARY OF CONGRESS

1478. [Concerto, violoncello, B flat major]
      Concerto von Peter Ritter.
      [63]p. 26 x 34 cm.
      Full score.   LIBRARY OF CONGRESS

1479. [Concerto, violoncello, B flat major]
      [9]p. 24½ x 33 cm.
      Solo violoncello part only.   LIBRARY OF CONGRESS

1480. [Concerto, violoncello, D minor]
      Concert pour le violoncell [!], composé par P. Ritter.
      1 leaf, 81 p. 21½ x 27½ cm.
      Full score.   LIBRARY OF CONGRESS

1481. [Concerto, violoncello, E major]
      Cello-Concert von Peter Ritter. Autograph.
      79 p. 24 x 31 cm.
      Full score.   LIBRARY OF CONGRESS

1482. [Concerto, violoncello, E flat major]
      Concertino für Violoncello . . . in Es dur. Peter Ritter . . .
         Autograph.
      p. 17-38. 31 x 23 cm.
      Full score, incomplete.   LIBRARY OF CONGRESS

1483. [Concerto, violoncello, G major]
      Concerto. Peter Ritter. Autograph.
      [84]p. 21 x 27½ cm.
      Full score.   LIBRARY OF CONGRESS

1484. Dilara, ein Sing-Spiel in zwey Aufzügen. Text nach Gozzi. Musik
      von P. Ritter.
      2 vols. 24½ x 35 cm.
      Full score.
      Text by Wolfgang Heribert, Freiherr von Dalberg.
      First performed January 14, 1798 at the Hoftheater in Mannheim.
                    LIBRARY OF CONGRESS

1485. Duetto IV pur [!] deux violoncell [!] di Piere [!] Ritter. Autograph.
    Parts. 26 x 21½ cm.   LIBRARY OF CONGRESS

1486. Duetto VI pur [!] deux violoncell [!] di Piere [!] Ritter. Autograph.
    Parts. 28 x 21½ cm.   LIBRARY OF CONGRESS

1487. Entre actes.
    [32]p. 31 x 22½ cm.
    Full score.   LIBRARY OF CONGRESS

1488. Feodora von Kotzebue. Musik von Peter Ritter. (Original-
    Handschrift).
    1 vol. 22 x 29 cm.
    Full score.
    First performed October 11, 1811 at the Hoftheater in Mannheim.
                                                           LIBRARY OF CONGRESS

1489. Das Fest am Rheine. Festspiel zu Ehren der Ankunft des Erb-
    grossherzogs Karl und der Erbgrossherzogin Stephanie aufgeführt
    10 Juli 1806. Musik von P. Ritter.
    1 vol. 31 x 22½ cm.
    Full score.
    Text by S. A. Mahlmann.   LIBRARY OF CONGRESS

1490. Das Gebet des Herrn von P. Ritter. 1832. Autograph.
    [36]p. 35 x 23 cm.
    Full score (mixed chorus, solo voices and orchestra).
                                                           LIBRARY OF CONGRESS

1491. Die Geburt Jesu. Kantate von Peter Ritter. 1832. . . . Autograph.
    2 vols. (66, 50 p.) 35 x 23 cm.
    Full score (mixed chorus, solo voices and orchestra).
                                                           LIBRARY OF CONGRESS

1492. Gloria. Von P. Ritter. Partitur. Autograph.
    [13]p. 31 x 23 cm.
    Full score.   LIBRARY OF CONGRESS

1493. Huldigungsfeier für Stephanie. Peter Ritter. Autograph.
    [110]p. 31 x 23½ cm.
    Full score (mixed chorus and orchestra).   LIBRARY OF CONGRESS

1494. [Johann von Paris]
    Aria zu Johann von Paris von Peter Ritter. Autograph.
    [13]p. 31 x 23 cm.
    Full score (tenor and orchestra).   LIBRARY OF CONGRESS

1495. Die lustigen Weiber. Oper in 4 Aufzügen von Peter Ritter.
    4 vols. 24 x 33 cm.
    Full score, autograph?
    Text by Georg Christian Römer, based on Shakespeare.
    First performed November 4, 1794 at the Hoftheater in Mannheim.
                                                           LIBRARY OF CONGRESS

Ritter, Peter—*continued*

1496. [Die Männer taugen all nicht viel]
    [15]p. 34½ x 21 cm.
Full score of an aria for insertion in a play or opera.

1497. [Mass, A minor]
    Messe von P. Ritter. Autograph.
    [46]p. 23½ x 35½ cm.
Full score (for mixed chorus, orchestra, and organ).

1498. [Mass, B flat major]
    No. 2 der Messen (deutsch). Peter Ritter. Autograph.
    [24]p. 31½ x 23 cm.
Full score (for mixed chorus and organ).

1499. Messgesänge ... von P. Ritter. Mannheim 1822.
    Parts. 20½ x 30 and 20½ x 14½ cm.
For mixed chorus with organ accpt.

1500. ... Das neue Jahr in Famagusta. Oper in 2 Aufzügen. Musik von
    P. Ritter, zum ersten Mal in Mannheim aufgeführt am 1 Januar
    1804.
    167 p. 24½ x 35 cm.
Full score of Act 1 only.
At head of title: Die lustigen Musikanten. Singspiel von Clemens
    Brentano Frankfurt a/M 1803 bei Bernhard Körner unter dem
    Titel: ...

1501. Notturno. Peter Ritter. Autogr.
    [4]p. 24 x 30 cm.
For violin, violoncello and piano, in F major.

1502. O Allah! welch ein Kleinod dank' ich Dir. Peter Ritter. Autograph.
    [2]p. 26 x 34 cm.
Aria for soprano and orchestra.
First line: Die Quelle rauscht, die Mücke schwirrt.

1503. Das Orakel.
    2 vols. 35 x 21 cm.
Full score of the opera in 2 acts.

1504. [Per pietà non ricercate]
    Sopran-Arie für Katharina Breyer componirt von P. Ritter. 1812.
    [8]p. 26 x 33 cm.
Aria with piano accpt.

1505. [Quartet, strings, B flat Major]
    Quinttetto [!]
    28 p. 23 x 37 cm.
Score.

Ritter, Peter—*continued*

1506. [Quartet, strings, C major]
Quarttetto [!] ex C. Violoncello obligato, violino primo obligato,
violino secondo obligato, viola. J. P. Ritter. 1780. St. Urban.
[18]p. 24 x 32 cm.
Score.   LIBRARY OF CONGRESS

1507. [Quartet, strings, D major]
Quartetto. Di Piere [!] Ritter. 1778. Autograph.
[16]p. 22 x 31 cm.
Score.   LIBRARY OF CONGRESS

1508. [Quartet, strings, D major]
Quarttetto [!] di J. P. Ritter.
[8]p. 36 x 21 cm.
Score.   LIBRARY OF CONGRESS

1509. [Quartet, strings, D major]
Quinttetto [!] von P. Ritter.
24 p. 22 x 36 cm.
Score.   LIBRARY OF CONGRESS

1510. [Quartet, strings, F minor]
Quartetto. Di Piere [!] Ritter. 1781.
[7]p. 36 x 21 cm.
Score.   LIBRARY OF CONGRESS

1511. [Quartet, strings, G major]
Quartetto di Piere [!] Ritter.
[13]p. 36 x 21 cm.
Score.   LIBRARY OF CONGRESS

1512. [Quartets, flute, violin, viola and violoncello]
. . . 3 Quartette für Flöte, Violine, Bratsche und V.cello von
P. Ritter.
[40]p. 23 x 35½ cm.
Score.
No. 1 in C major; No. 2 in E flat major; no. 3 in G major.
                                                          LIBRARY OF CONGRESS

1513. [Quartets, strings]
Quartetto [1][-5]. Di Piere [!] Ritter. 1782.
[83]p. 21 x 27 cm.
Score.
No. 1 in G major; no. 2 in C minor; no. 3 in D major; no. 4 in G
minor; no. 5 in C major.   LIBRARY OF CONGRESS

1514. [Quartets, strings]
[80]p. 22 x 35 cm.
Score.
No. 1 in B flat major; no. 2 in A major; no. 3 in C major.
                                                          LIBRARY OF CONGRESS

1515. Recit.-Andante. V. P. Ritter. Für die Altistin Schönberger geschrieben, Autograph.
    [23]p. 31 x 23 cm.
Full score (for alto and orchestra).   LIBRARY OF CONGRESS

1516. [Répète, Echo, les sons touchants]
    [2]p. 23 x 32 cm.
Song with piano and guitar accpt.   LIBRARY OF CONGRESS

1517. Salomons Urtheil. Oper in 3 Aufzügen. Text v. G. Römer n. d. Fr[anzösischen]. Musik v. P. Ritter. Original Partitur.
    2 vols. 31 x 23 cm.
Full score of Acts 1 and 2 only.
First performed at the Hoftheater in Mannheim January 28, 1808.
      LIBRARY OF CONGRESS

1518. [Salomons Urtheil]
    Bass-Arie eingelegt in Salomos Urteil. Peter Ritter. Autograph.
    [17]p. 31 x 23 cm.
Full score of an aria for bass and orchestra.
First line: Ich danke Gott dir für die Krone.   LIBRARY OF CONGRESS

1519. [Septet, viola d'amore, clarinet, flute, viola, bass and 2 horns, E flat major]
    12 p. 31 x 23½ cm.
Score, incomplete.   LIBRARY OF CONGRESS

1520. [Sextet, 2 horns, 2 violas, violoncello and piano, E flat major]
    Sextett von P. Ritter . . .
    [55]p. 31 x 23 cm.
Score.   LIBRARY OF CONGRESS

1521. [Sonata, violoncello and piano, F major]
    Sonate pour piano-forte accompagné[!] de violoncelle.
    [16]p. 31 x 23 cm.   LIBRARY OF CONGRESS

1522. [Sonatas, violin and piano]
    3 sonate per il clavicembalo. Peter Ritter.
    15, 17, 16 p. 22 x 35 cm.
No. 1 in D major, no. 2 in E flat major, no. 3 in G major.
      LIBRARY OF CONGRESS

1523. [Die Spanier in Peru] Autograph.
    [6]p. 22 x 35 cm.
Full score of music to the play.   LIBRARY OF CONGRESS

1524. [Symphony, D major]
    Sinphonia di J. P. Ritter. 1778.
    [11]p. 35 x 22 cm.
Full score.   LIBRARY OF CONGRESS

Ritter, Peter—*continued*

1525. [Symphony, E flat major]
    Sinfonia. Da J. P. Ritter. 1779.
    [23]p. 35½ x 21½ cm.
    Full score.   LIBRARY OF CONGRESS

1526. Der Talisman. Oper von Peter Ritter. Autograph.
    1 vol. 30 x 22 cm.
    Full score.   LIBRARY OF CONGRESS

1527. [Trio, flute, violin and violoncello, C major]
    Trio für Flöte, Violin [!] u. Violoncello von P. Ritter zur Reise in
      die Schweiz componirt für Apold. Eisenmenger. Autograph.
    1 leaf, [12]p. 31 x 22 cm.
    Score.   LIBRARY OF CONGRESS

1528. [Trios, flute, viola and double bass]
    . . . 10 Stücke für Flöte, Bratsche und Bass von Peter Ritter.
    Autograph.
    [24]p. 22 x 27 cm.
    Score.   LIBRARY OF CONGRESS

1529. [Trios, flute, viola da gamba and horn]
    Drei Stücke für Flöte, Viola da gamba und Horn. Componirt
      v. P. Ritter. Autograph.
    [12]p. 22 x 27 cm.
    Score.   LIBRARY OF CONGRESS

1530. [Trios, flute (violin), violoncello and piano]
    3 Klavier-Trios von Peter Ritter. Autograph.
    49 p. 22 x 35½ cm.
    Score.
    No. 1 in F major, no. 2 in A major, no. 3 in C major.
    Title of no. 1: Sonata, d. 11 Sept. 1797.   LIBRARY OF CONGRESS

1531. [Trios, piano and strings]
    Klavier-Trios (Sonaten). Peter Ritter. Autograph.
    [20]p. 31 x 23 cm.
    Score of 5 short pieces.   LIBRARY OF CONGRESS

1532. [Trios, piano and strings]
    2 Klavier-Trios . . . Autograph.
    [28]p. 31 x 24 cm.
    Score.
    No. 1 in B flat major; no. 2 in C major.   LIBRARY OF CONGRESS

1533. Türkisch. Peter Ritter. Autograph.
    [5]p. 33 x 25 cm.
    Full score.   LIBRARY OF CONGRESS

Ritter, Peter—*continued*

1534. Das verlorene Paradies. Oratorium von Peter Ritter. Autograph.
    [256], 328 p. 35 x 21 cm.
    Full score, lacking the overture.
    First performed in 1819 at Mannheim.   LIBRARY OF CONGRESS

1535. Das verlorene Paradies. Klavierauszug mit englischem Text
    (Milton).
    1 vol. 24½ x 31 cm.
    Piano-vocal score (introduction for piano 4 hands).
                                                LIBRARY OF CONGRESS

1536. [Das Wunderglöckchen]
    1 vol. 35 x 22 cm.
    Full score of Act I of the unfinished opera.   LIBRARY OF CONGRESS

1537. Der Zitterschläger v. Peter Ritter. Klavierauszug (ohne Singstim-
    men). Autograph.
    [23]p. 31 x 23 cm.
    Piano score of the opera.   LIBRARY OF CONGRESS

Rodwell, George Herbert Bonaparte, 1800-1852

1538. Yes! I ask you to deceive me. Composed by G. Herbert Rodwell . . .
    4[p.] 42 x 33 cm.
    Song with piano accpt.
    First line: Let no parting word be spoken.
    Dedicated to T. Mackinlay.   MRS. EUGENE ALLEN NOBLE

Röntgen, Julius, 1855-1932

1539. Quartet. "Heer Halewyn song een liedekÿn."
    26 p. 34 x 27 cm.
    Score (string quartet).
    Honorable mention at Berkshire Music Festival, 1922.
                        LIBRARY OF CONGRESS, COOLIDGE FOUNDATION

Rogister, Jean, 1879-

1540. . . . Quatuor No. 4 en ré pour 2 violons, alto et violoncelle. Jean
    Rogister.
    1 leaf, 59 p. 31 x 23 cm.
    Score.
    Dedicated to Mrs. E. S. Coolidge.
    Published in 1929 by Maurice Sénart in Paris.
                        LIBRARY OF CONGRESS, COOLIDGE FOUNDATION

1541. . . . Quintette pour clavecin, deux quintons, viole d'amour et viole
    da gambe. Jean Rogister.
    63 p. 31½ x 22½ cm.
    Score.
    Dedicated to Mrs. E. S. Coolidge.
    At end: Liège, 1934.   LIBRARY OF CONGRESS, COOLIDGE FOUNDATION

Roland-Manuel
see Manuel, Roland

Rolla, Alessandro, 1757-1841

1542. Divertimento ossia sestetto per flauto, violino, due viole, violoncello
e piano-forte composto . . . da Alessandro Rolla.
1 leaf, 21 p. 22½ x 31 cm.
Score.
Apparently unpublished.
Former owner: Natalie Gallini (catalogue, no. 15).
MEMORIAL LIBRARY OF MUSIC, STANFORD UNIVERSITY

Rootham, Cyril Bradley, 1875-1938

1543. Septet for viola, flute, hautboy, clarinet, bassoon, horn, harp by
Cyril Bradley Rootham.
32 p. 37 x 27½ cm.
Score.
Dedicated to Mrs. E. S. Coolidge.
LIBRARY OF CONGRESS, COOLIDGE FOUNDATION

Ropartz, (Joseph) Guy (Marie), 1864-

1544. Le Blé. J. Guy Ropartz.
2 p. 35 x 27 cm.
Song with piano accpt.
First line: Blés d'or, blés ondulés.   LIBRARY OF CONGRESS

Rosé, Alfred, 1902-

1545. . . . Quartett für 2 Violinen, Bratsche und Violoncello von Alfred
Rosé. Wien 1927.
1 leaf, [36]p. 34 x 27 cm.
Score.
Dedicated to Mrs. E. S. Coolidge.
At end: 20 März 1927.
LIBRARY OF CONGRESS, COOLIDGE FOUNDATION

Rosenhain, Jakob, 1813-1894

1546. Mahnung.
p. 9-10. 28 x 23 cm.
In the notebook of Ignaz Moscheles (no. 1260).
Song with piano accpt.
First line: Und willst du dich des Lebens.
Dated at end: July 1838.
Published as no. 6 of op. 21 by Breitkopf & Härtel in Leipzig.
MEMORIAL LIBRARY OF MUSIC, STANFORD UNIVERSITY

Rossini, Gioacchino Antonio, 1792-1868

1547. Il barbier di Siviglia: o sia il conte D'Alma Viva del sigr. Gioacchino
       Rossini . . .
       2 vols. (245, 282 p.) 22 x 35 cm.
       Full score, partly in the composer's autograph.
       At head of title: In Roma nel Carnevale, nel Teatro Argentina.
       Facsimile of the overture published ca. 1946 by Broude Bros. in
       New York in their edition of the score.
       First performed December 26, 1816 at the Teatro Argentina in
       Rome.
       Former owner: C. Lonsdale.   NEW YORK PUBLIC LIBRARY

1548. [Chi m'ascolta il canto usato]
       [3]p. 27 x 35 cm.
       Song with piano accpt.
       At head of title: Rossini al suo amico Luigi Dupré. L'anno 1818.
                                  LIBRARY OF CONGRESS

1549. Chirie a tre voci per contrapunto corale II. Rossini.
       [3]p. 23 x 32 cm.   THE PIERPONT MORGAN LIBRARY

1550. [Mi lagnerò tacendo]
       [3]p. 33½ x 26½ cm.
       Song with piano accpt.
       Text by Metastasio.
       At head of title: . . . Gioacchino Rossini. Paris 8 maggio 1858.
       Dedicated to Carlo Scitivani.
       Former owner: George T. Keating.
          MEMORIAL LIBRARY OF MUSIC, STANFORD UNIVERSITY

1551. [Mi lagnerò tacendo]
       fol. 1v-3r. 18 x 25½ cm.
       In Demidov, Album of autographs.
       Song with piano accpt.
       At end: Aria di camera, composta . . . da G. Rossini. Parigi 26
       marzo 1834.   LIBRARY OF CONGRESS

1552. [Mi lagnerò tacendo]
       [1], 5 p. 21 x 28½ cm.
       Song with piano accpt.
       At end: Firenze 29 febbr. 1852. Gioachino [!] Rossini.
       Former owner: George B. Weston.   HARVARD UNIVERSITY LIBRARY

1553. [Moïse. Moment fatal, que faire, hélas?]
       Duetto.
       [8]p. 25½ x 34 cm.

Rossini, Gioacchino Antonio—*continued*

Vocal parts only (marked Amenophis and Pharaon) of the duet, no. 9.

Facsimile of last page in Van Patten, *Catalogue,* p. 227.

1554.   [Quartets, violins, violoncello and double bass]

Opere di sei sonate, composte dal sigr. Gioacchino Rossini in età d'anni XII in Ravenna l'anno 1804 . . .

Parts. 22 x 30 cm.

Composer's note: Parti di violini primo, violino secondo, violoncello, contrabasso e queste di sei sonate *orrende* da me composte alla villegiatura (presso Ravenna) del mio amico mecenate Agostino Triossi alla età la più infantile non avendo preso neppure una lezione di accompagnamento, il tutto composto e copiato in trè giorni ed eseguito cognoscamente da Triossi contrabasso, Morini (di lui cugino) primo violino, il fratello di questo il violoncello, ed il secondo violino da me stesso, che ero per dir vero, il meno cane. G. Rossini.

In the cover title the word *Sonate* has been substituted for *Quartetti,* and XII for XVI, 1804 for 1809.

Published as *Cinque quartetti* ca. 1829 by G. Ricordi in Milan. No. 3 of this ms. was omitted from the published edition.

Former owners: Signor Mazzoni, William H. Cummings (catalogue, no. 1465).   LIBRARY OF CONGRESS

1555.   Zelmira, dramma per musica di sigr. Gioacchino Rossini. Atto secondo.

184 leaves. 23 x 31 cm.

Full score.

fol. 1-45 in another hand.

Note on fly-leaf says the English edition of the opera was published from this ms.   THE HENRY E. HUNTINGTON LIBRARY

Roth, Feri, 1899-

1556.   Stringquartet (in D) by Feri Roth (1931-1932) . . .

28 p. 33 x 26½ cm.

Score.

Dedicated to Mrs. E. S. Coolidge.

At end: 5.III.1932. New York.   LIBRARY OF CONGRESS

Rousseau, Jean Jacques, 1712-1778

1557.   Air par J. J. Rousseau écrit et copié de sa main. Paroles de Desportes.

[3]p. 21½ x 30½ cm.

Song with string quartet accpt.

First line: O bien heureux qui peut passer sa vie.   E. WEYHE

Rousseau, Jean Jacques—*continued*

1558. Las! mon pauvre coeur.
    5 leaves. 21½ x 28 cm.
    Song with piano accpt.
    Followed by songs, also with words and music by Rousseau: *Ce n'est point en offrant des fleurs,* and *Vous dont le coeur jusqu'alors insensible.*
    Published in his *Les consolations des misères de ma vie* in 1781 by de Roullède de la Chevardière in Paris.
        THE PIERPONT MORGAN LIBRARY

Rousseau, Samuel Alexandre, 1853-1904

1559. Mélodie et canon.
    [7]p. 35 x 26 cm.
    For organ.
    At end: Paris le 20 février 1896. Samuel Rousseau.
        BOSTON PUBLIC LIBRARY

Roussel, Albert (Charles Paul Marie), 1869-1937

1560. Duo pour basson et contrebasse (sur un thème de la "Naissance de la Lyre"). Albert Roussel, en hommage à Serge Koussevitszky.
    1 leaf, 6 p. 35 x 27 cm.
    Score.
    At end: Paris 12 juin, 1925.
    Published by A. Durand & Cie. in Paris.
        LIBRARY OF CONGRESS, KOUSSEVITZKY FOUNDATION

1561. [Symphony, no. 3, op. 42, G minor]
    Symphonie en sol (Op. 42) pour le cinquantième anniversaire du Boston Symphony Orchestra. Albert Roussel.
    1 leaf, 142 p. 39 x 29 cm.
    Full score.
    At end: Albert Roussel. Paris 29 mars 1930.
    Published in 1932 by A. Durand et Cie. in Paris.
        BOSTON SYMPHONY ORCHESTRA

1562. . . . Trio pr. flûte, alto et violoncelle. Albert Roussel, op. 40.
    1 leaf, 18 p. 35 x 27 cm.
    Score.
    Dedicated to Mrs. E. S. Coolidge.
    At end: Vastnival—22 septembre 1929.
    Published in 1930 by A. Durand et Cie. in Paris.
        LIBRARY OF CONGRESS, COOLIDGE FOUNDATION

Rowley, Alec, 1892-

1563. . . . North Sea fantasies for the pianoforte by Alec Rowley. Op. 15.
    1. The bell buoy. 2. Sea-spray. 3. Moonlight. 4. Into the icy blast.
    1 leaf, [9]p. 27 x 36 cm.

Rowley, Alec—*continued*

Dedicated to Herbert Lake.
Published in 1916 by G. Schirmer, Ltd. in London.

1564. . . . Rhapsody (No. 2) in D minor for the organ by Alec Rowley.
1 leaf, [14]p. 30½ x 24½ cm.
Dedicated to Aidan Clarke.
Published in 1921 by Edwin Ashdown, Ltd. in London.

Rubinstein, Anton Gregorievich, 1829-1894

1565. . . . Ballade (Leonore de Bürger) pour le piano composées par Ant. Rubinstein.
7 p. 34 x 26½ cm.
Dedicated to [Ernst Ferdinand] Wenzel.
Published as cahier 1 of his op. 93, *Miscellanées pour piano,* ca. 1884 by B. Senff in Leipzig.
Bound with his *Deux études pour piano.*

1566. . . . Doumka et Polonaise pour le piano composées par Ant. Rubinstein . . .
[4], 4 p. 34 x 26½ cm.
Dedicated to Mlle. Monica Terminsky.
Published as cahier 3 of his op. 93, *Miscellanées pour piano,* ca. 1884 by B. Senff in Leipzig.
Bound with his *Deux études pour piano.*

1567. Die drei Zigeuner, Gedicht von Lenau in Musik gesetzt von Ant. Rubinstein.
[1]p. 32½ x 27 cm.
Song with piano accpt.
First line: Drei Zigeuner fand ich einmal.
Published as no. 5 of his *Sechs Lieder* in 1875 by B. Senff in Leipzig.
Former owner: Frank H. Ginn.

1568. . . . Deux études pour le piano composées par Ant. Rubinstein.
8 p. 34 x 26½ cm.
Dedicated to M. Kross.
Published as cahier 2 of his op. 93, *Miscellanées pour piano,* ca. 1884 by B. Senff in Leipzig.
Bound within same cover are his *Doumka et Polonaise, Ballade, Deux sérénades* and *Scherzo.*

1569. . . . Fantaisie pour le pianoforte composée par Anton Rubinstein, op. 77.
1 leaf, 27 p. 35 x 26 cm.
Published in 1867 by B. Senff in Leipzig.
Former owner: Wilhelm Heyer (catalogue, vol. IV, no. 1436).

1570. Zwölf Lieder des Mirza-Schaffy aus dem Persischen von F. Boden-
stedt in Musik gesetzt für eine Stimme von Ant. Rubinstein.
Op. 34.
31 p. 37 x 25 cm.
Songs with piano accpt.
Published by Fr. Kistner in Leipzig.
Former owner: George T. Keating.
MEMORIAL LIBRARY OF MUSIC, STANFORD UNIVERSITY

1571. Deux marches funèbres, composés par Ant. Rubinstein. No. 2.
Pour le convoi d'un héros.
[1], 4 p. 37½ x 27 cm.
For piano 2 hands.
Published as no. 2 of op. 29 ca. 1855 by Fr. Kistner in Leipzig.
LIBRARY OF CONGRESS

1572. . . . Miniatures, 12 morceaux pour piano par Ant. Rubinstein.
13 leaves. 33 x 24 cm.
Music on recto only, except for fol. 9v.
Published as cahier 9 of his op. 93, *Miscellanées pour piano,* ca.
1884 by B. Senff in Leipzig.
ISABELLA STEWART GARDNER MUSEUM

1573. Ouverture de la tragédie "Antonius et Cléopatre" de Schakspeare
pour orchestre composée par Ant. Rubinstein. Op. 116.
40 p. 34 x 26½ cm.
Full score.
Published in 1890 by B. Senff in Leipzig.
THE FOLGER SHAKESPEARE LIBRARY

1574. Polonaise. Ant. Rubinstein. Op. 14.
[8]p. 34 x 26 cm.
Published as no. 2 of *Le Bal, fantaisie en 10 numéros pour piano,*
ca. 1865 by Ed. Bote & G. Bock in Berlin.
Former owner: Evert J. Wendell.   HARVARD UNIVERSITY LIBRARY

1575. . . . Scherzo pour le piano composé par Ant. Rubinstein.
[4]p. 34 x 26½ cm.
Dedicated to M. Pierre de Tschaikofsky.
Published as cahier 5 of his op. 93, *Miscellanées pour piano,* ca. 1884
by B. Senff in Leipzig.
Bound with his *Deux études pour piano.*   LIBRARY OF CONGRESS

1576. . . . Deux sérénades pour piano composées par Ant. Rubinstein.
6 p. 34 x 26½ cm.
Dedicated to Mlle. Sophie Smiriaguine.
Published as cahier 6 (*Deux sérénades russes*) of his op. 93, *Mis-
cellanées pour piano,* in 1884, by B. Senff in Leipzig.
Bound with his *Deux études pour piano.*   LIBRARY OF CONGRESS

Rubinstein, Anton Gregorievich—*continued*

1577. [Soirées musicales, op. 109]
    23, 4 p. 34 x 25 cm.
Each piece has a separate title and dedication.
Published as *Soirées musicales, neuf morceaux pour piano,* ca. 1884 by B. Senff in Leipzig.
Former owner: Wilhelm Heyer (catalogue, vol. IV, no. 1478).

SIBLEY MUSICAL LIBRARY

Rungenhagen, Karl Friedrich, 1778-1851
1578. Frohe Erinnerungen von Bornemann und Rungenhagen. Partitur.
    [15]p. 27 x 32½ cm.
For male quartet and chorus, unaccompanied.
Pasted on title-page is an autograph letter of Rungenhagen to the actor Beschort to whom the composition is dedicated, dated B[erlin] 30. Oktober 1836.   LIBRARY OF CONGRESS

Russell, Henry, 1812-1900
1579. "The chain I gave." A ballad . . . Henry Russell.
    [2]p. 18 x 23 cm.
Song with piano accpt.   HISTORICAL SOCIETY OF PENNSYLVANIA

Russell, William, 1777-1813
1580. Anthem. Hear, o Thou shepherd of Israel.
    11 p. 32½ x 25 cm.

MEMORIAL LIBRARY OF MUSIC, STANFORD UNIVERSITY

Sacchini, Antonio Maria Gasparo, 1734-1786
1581. [Fragment of an orchestral score]
    [2]p. 30½ x 21½ cm.
Former owners: Luigi Cherubini, Julian Marshall.

LIBRARY OF CONGRESS

Sachs, Melchior Ernst, 1843-1917
1582. Totenklage der Goten von Louise Hitz. Op. 15. Für zweistimmigen Männerchor mit kleinern Orchester componirt von M. E. Sachs. Op. 15.
    23 p. 34 x 26½ cm.
Full score.   LIBRARY OF CONGRESS

Sahla, Richard, 1855-1931
1583. Wiegenlied. Richard Sahla . . .
    [1]p. 31 x 24 cm.
Song with piano accpt.
First line: Schliesst, mein Kind, die blanken Augen.
Published as no. 1 of his *Vier Lieder nach Gedichten von M. Grosse* in 1925 by Ries und Erler in Berlin   LIBRARY OF CONGRESS

Saint-Saëns, (Charles) Camille, 1835-1921

1584. [A deux]
       [2]p. 27 x 35 cm.
       Canon for two women's voices, without text.
       At end: C. Saint-Saëns. 1909.
       Published in the *Supplément* to the *Revue musicale*, 15 Sept.-
          1 Oct. 1909, where the first line is: Quand un ami me seconde.
                                        LIBRARY OF CONGRESS

1585. ... Caprice brilliant pour piano et violon. ... C. Saint-Saëns.
          1 leaf, 20 p. 35½ x 27 cm.
       Dedicated to Arthur Gambry.
       Apparently unpublished.
       At end: 3 7bre 1859. C. Saint-Saëns.   SIBLEY MUSICAL LIBRARY

1586. Guitare. Victor Hugo.
          [4]p. 37 x 25 cm.
       Song with piano accpt.
       First line: Comment, disaient-ils.
       Dedicated to Augusta Holmès.
       Composed in 1851.
       Published in 1870 by Choudens in Paris.
       Facsimile of p. 1 in Van Patten, *Catalogue*, p. 231.
                   MEMORIAL LIBRARY OF MUSIC, STANFORD UNIVERSITY

1587. [Symphony, no. 3, op. 78, C major]
          Troisième symphonie en ut mineur. op. 78.
          [3]p. 28½ x 38½ cm.
       Sketches.   LIBRARY OF CONGRESS

1588. Tantum ergo. Soprano, mezzo-soprano et alto (Trio avec choeur
          ad libitum).
          [4]p. 35½ x 27 cm.
       Score (with organ accpt.)
                   MEMORIAL LIBRARY OF MUSIC, STANFORD UNIVERSITY

1589. Victoire! Paul Fournier. Camille Saint-Saëns.
          [3]p. 35½ x 27 cm.
       Song with piano accpt.
       First line: Le voici donc, le jour de la victoire.
       At end: pour Mlle. Demougeot. C. Saint-Saëns.
       Published in 1918 by A. Durand et Cie. in Paris.
                                        NEWBERRY LIBRARY

Salieri, Antonio, 1750-1825

1590. [Chi vuol gustare]
          [2]p. 22 x 29 cm.
       Followed by a two-part song, cancelled: *Combien ces six saucisses-ci?*
                                        LIBRARY OF CONGRESS

Salieri, Antonio—*continued*

1591. Il genio degli stati veneti all'entrata delle truppe austriache in Venezia l'anno 1798. Sonetto del signor abate Cesarotti . . . posto in musica dal signor Antonio Salieri.
[5]p. 22 x 30 cm.
Song with piano accpt.
First line: Larva di libertà. NEW YORK PUBLIC LIBRARY

1592. Picciole composizioni di me Ant. Salieri . . .
[8]p. 23½ x 31½ cm.
Contents.—Song with piano accpt. *Pensieri funesti.—Canone a 2 voci.* "Ein Leben voller Wonnetage."—*Duettino* (unaccompanied). "Son pien di giubilo." LIBRARY OF CONGRESS

1593. Piccolo terzetto composto il giorno 25 sett. 1814, celebrandosi in Liechtenthal il compimento del primo secolo, che fu fabbricato il sacro tempio detto in lingua tedesca, Die XIII Nothelfer. Musica di me Ant. Salieri . . .
[1]p. 23 x 30 cm.
For men's voices, unaccompanied.
First line: Ora fa un secolo.
Former owners: Edward Speyer, Julian Marshall.
LIBRARY OF CONGRESS

1594. Lo spirito di contradizione.
[2]p. 22 x 29 cm.
Trio for soprano, tenor and bass, unaccompanied.
On p. 2 an unaccompanied duet for bass voices: *Amabile signora vivete.*
Former owners: Alexander W. Thayer, Edward Speyer.
LIBRARY OF CONGRESS

1595. Terzetti. Nel giardino di Werring-Gasse. 1 lug. 1819.
[2]p. 22½ x 29 cm.
For 3 voices unaccompanied.
Contents.—*Mentre dormiamo i fomenti.—Canone à* 3: "Horchet leise der himmlischen Töne." MR. CARL H. TOLLEFSEN

See also Schubert, Franz, 1797-1828
[Counterpoint exercises]

Sandby, Herman, 1881-
1596. Agnete and the Merman. Danish folksong by Herman Sandby.
[4]p. 35 x 27 cm.
Song with piano accpt.
First line: Agnete was standing on the lonely strand.
Former owner: David Bispham. NEW YORK PUBLIC LIBRARY

1597. The flight of the moon. Words by Oscar Wilde, song by Herman
    Sandby.
    [5]p. 35 x 27 cm.
    Song with piano accpt.
    First line: To outer senses there is peace.
    Former owner: Horatio Connell.
    UNIVERSITY OF PENNSYLVANIA LIBRARY

1598. In July. Words by Harvey Watts. Song by Herman Sandby.
    [4]p. 35 x 27 cm.
    Song with piano accpt.
    First line: The sun shines through a yellow haze.
    Former owner: Horatio Connell.
    UNIVERSITY OF PENNSYLVANIA LIBRARY

1599. . . . "Roselil." Chanson danoise. Song with piano accompaniment
    by Herman Sandby.
    [4]p. 35 x 27 cm.
    First line: Roselil and her mother were sitting.
    Former owner: David Bispham.   NEW YORK PUBLIC LIBRARY

Sarasate [y Navascues], Pablo [Martín Melíton] de, 1844-1908

1600. . . . Zigeunerweisen pour violon avec accompagnement d'orchestre
    ou de piano composées par Pablo de Sarasate. Op. 20.
    [1], 10 p. 33½ x 24½ cm.
    Reduction for violin and piano.
    Published in 1877 by B. Senff in Leipzig.
    Former owner: Joseph Muller.   NEW YORK PUBLIC LIBRARY

1601. . . . Zortzico pour violon avec accompagnement de piano. Pablo
    de Sarasate. Op. 42.
    [7]p. 35 x 27 cm.
    At end: Biarritz 29 juin 99 Sarasate.
    Former owner: Joseph Muller.   NEW YORK PUBLIC LIBRARY

Satie, Erik Alfred Leslie, 1866-1925

1602. Sept toutes petites danses pour le "Piège de Méduse." Erik Satie.
    5, [3]p. 35 x 27 cm.
    Full score.
    Published in 1929 by J. & W. Chester in London.
    Former owners: Mr. and Mrs. Robert Woods Bliss.
    HARVARD UNIVERSITY, DUMBARTON OAKS

Sauret, Emile, 1852-1920

1603. . . . Farfalla. Pour violon et piano. Emile Sauret.
    1 leaf, 17 p. 34½ x 26½ cm.
    At end: Berlin 30 Octobre 1907.
    Dedicated to Arthur Hartmann.   SIBLEY MUSICAL LIBRARY

Sauret, Emile—*continued*

1604. . . . Six morceaux de salon pour violon avec piano par Emile
    Sauret. Op. 71.
    1 leaf, 49 p. 36 x 27 cm.
    Published in 1921 by Carl Fischer in New York.

Scarlatti, Alessandro, 1660-1725

1605. La sposa de cantici. Oratorio à 4 con stromti per la festa della
    Assunzione di M.V. con suoi nuovi aggiunti del sig. Alesso.
    Scarlatti.
    1 leaf, 219 p. 21 x 27 cm.
    Full score.
    Facsimile of title-page in Van Patten, *Catalogue,* p. 235.

Schenck, Johann Baptist, 1753-1836

1606. . . . Canon für 3 Stimmen. Joh. Schenck, den 7ten April 1822.
    1 leaf. 11 x 17½ cm.
    First line: Viel Wesen mag ich nicht.
    Former owner: Alfred Bovet de Valentigny.

Schmidt, Johann Philipp Samuel, 1779-1853

1607. Ouverture zur Oper Der Kyffhäuser Berg.
    [23]p. 25 x 30 cm.
    Full score.
    At end: Berlin 9 März 1817. J.P.S.

1608. Rinaldo, Cantate von Göthe für eine Altstimme und mit Chor
    und Orchester-Begleitung in Musik gesetzt von J. P. Schmidt.
    Clavierauszug vom Componisten.
    [41]p. 27 x 31 cm.

Schmitt, Florent, 1870-

1609. [O triste était mon âme]
    Romance sans paroles. Paul Verlaine. (Florent Schmitt.)
    1 leaf, [6]p. 35 x 27 cm.
    Song with piano accpt.
    Published as op. 55, no. 1 in 1912 by S. Chapelier in Paris.

Schneider, (Johann Christian) Friedrich, 1786-1853

1610. Der Dessauer Marsch als Ouverture für das ganze Orchestre [!]
    componirt von Fr. Schneider. 50tes Werk. Partitur.
    [34]p. 24 x 33 cm.

1611. Fest Ouverture von Friedrich Schneider. Op. 45.
    [32]p. 23 x 30½ cm.
    Full score.

1612. [Concerto, string quartet]
Konzert für Streichquartett und Orchester nach dem Concerto grosso Op. 6 no. 7 von G. F. Händel in freier Umgestaltung von Ärnold Schönberg. Angefangen etwa 20. V. 33.
46 leaves. 34 x 51½ cm.
Tissues; music on recto only.
At end: Arcachon. 16. VI. 33.   G. SCHIRMER

1613. Die glückliche Hand. Drama mit Musik. Op. 18.
1 leaf, 28 p. 38 x 37 cm.
Short score.
On p. 1: Angefangen: Freitag 9 September 1910.
At end: 18. XI. 1913. Arnold Schönberg.
First performed October 14, 1924 in Vienna.   LIBRARY OF CONGRESS

1614. Pierrot lunair [!]
[2], 38 p. 29 x 37½ and 34½ x 36½ cm.
Full score.
Text by Albert Giraud.
On p. 1: Angefangen 12/3/1912.
Most sections are dated and appear in a different order from that of the published score.
Published as op. 21 in 1914 by Universal Edition in Vienna.
LIBRARY OF CONGRESS, WHITTALL FOUNDATION

1615. [Quartet, strings, no. 2, op. 10, F sharp minor]
. . . II. Quartett für 2 Violinen, Viola u. Violoncell von Arnold, Schönberg.
1 leaf, 45 p. 34½ x 27 cm.
Score.
The 3rd and 4th movements have voice parts to texts by Stefan George, *Litanei* and *Entrückung*.
Published in 1910 by the composer (later Universal Edition) in Vienna.   LIBRARY OF CONGRESS, WHITTALL FOUNDATION

1616. [Quartet, strings, no. 3, op. 30]
III. Streichquartett, op. 30. Arnold Schönberg.
35 leaves. 26½ x 34½ cm.
Score, music on recto of each leaf.
At end: Arnold Schönberg. 8 III. 1927.
Published in 1927 by Universal Edition in Vienna.
Dedicated to Mrs. E. S. Coolidge.
LIBRARY OF CONGRESS, COOLIDGE FOUNDATION

1617. [Quartet, strings, no. 4, op. 37]
28 leaves. 24½ x 35 cm.
Score, music on recto of each leaf.
Published in 1939 by G. Schirmer in New York.
Dedicated to Mrs. E. S. Coolidge.
LIBRARY OF CONGRESS, COOLIDGE FOUNDATION

Schönberg, Arnold—*continued*

1618. [Serenade für Klarinette, Bassklarinette, Mandoline, Gitarre, Geige, Bratsche, Violoncell und eine Baritonstimme (4. Satz: Sonett von Petrarca.) Op. 24]
 47 p. 21½ x 35 cm. and 26 x 34 cm.
First draft, last movement unfinished.
Many dates, running from 27.IX.21 to 10. IV.23.
Published in 1924 by Wilhelm Hansen in Copenhagen.
Former owner: Norbert Schwarzmann. LIBRARY OF CONGRESS

1619. Verklärte Nacht von Richard Dehmel für sechs Streich-Instrumente.
 39, [8]p. 35 x 27 cm.
Score.
On p. 39: Fine I/XII/99.
Published as op. 4 in 1904 by Drei Lilien Verlag in Berlin.
  LIBRARY OF CONGRESS, WHITTALL FOUNDATION

Schreker, Franz, 1878-1934

1620. Irrelohe, Oper in 3 Aufzügen von Franz Schreker. Manuscript-Skizze.
 [202]p. 35 x 27 cm.
Piano-vocal score.
At foot of title-page: Paul Bekker überreicht vom Komponisten. 6. IX. 23. Charlottenburg.
First performed March 27, 1924 at Cologne. LIBRARY OF CONGRESS

Schubert, Ferdinand, 1794-1859

1621. Verjüngung. Wien, 17 Apr. 1839. Ferd. Schubert mpria.
 [2]p. 25½ x 33 cm.
Song with piano accpt.
First line: Über Berg und Thal getragen. MR. FRANZ ROEHN

Schubert, Franz (Peter), 1797-1828

The numbers at the end of the bracketed titles refer to the serial numbers in Otto Erich Deutsch's *Schubert, Thematic catalogue of all his works,* London, 1951.

1622. [Abendständchen. An Lina. D. 265]
 Abendständchen. An Lina. den 23. August 1815.
 [2]p. 23½ x 31½ cm.
Song with piano accpt.
Text by Baumberg.
First line: Sei sanft wie ihre Seele.
Published in his Werke, series XX, no. 125.
Former owners: Marie Leins, Jerome Stonborough.
On p. 2 his *Cora an die Sonne.*
  LIBRARY OF CONGRESS, WHITTALL FOUNDATION

Schubert, Franz (Peter)—*continued*

1623. [Abschied von der Harfe. D. 406]
    Abschied von der Harfe. Salis. März 1816. Franz Schubert mpria.
        [2]p. 23½ x 31 cm.
    Song with piano accpt.
    First line: Noch einmal tön, o Harfe.
    Published in 1860 by C. A. Spina in Vienna (with his *Wehmut*).
    Werke, series XX, no. 208.
    On p. 2 his *Wehmut*.
    Former owner: Wilhelm Heyer (catalogue, vol. IV, no. 230).
                                    MRS. MARY LOUISE ZIMBALIST

1624. [Am Fenster, op. 105, no. 3. D. 878]
    Am Fenster von J. G. Seidl. März 1826. Frz Schubert mpria.
        [8]p. 25½ x 32 cm.
    Song with piano accpt.
    First line: Ihr lieben Mauern hold und traut.
    Published as no. 3 of *Vier Gedichte von J. G. Seidl* in 1828 by
        Joseph Czerny in Vienna.
    Werke, series XX, no. 492.
    On p. 5-8 an incomplete autograph of his *Sehnsucht* [D. 879].
    Former owner: Hermine Wittgenstein.
                        LIBRARY OF CONGRESS, WHITTALL FOUNDATION

1625. [Am See. D. 746]
    Am See, von Bruchmann.
        [2]p. 23½ x 30 cm.
    Song with piano accpt.
    First line: In des Sees Wogenspiele.
    Published as no. 2 of his *Nachlass*, Lieferung 9, in 1831 by A. Dia-
        belli & Co. in Vienna.
    Werke, series XX, no. 422.
    Former owner: Hugo Neuburger.   MR. WALTER SLEZAK

1626. [An den Mond in einer Herbstnacht. D. 614]
    An den Mond in einer Herbstnacht. Gedicht von Aloys Schreiber.
        Frz. Schubert mpria. Aprill 1818.
        [11]p. 22 x 30 cm.
    Song with piano accpt.
    First line: Freundlich ist dein Antlitz.
    Published as no. 2 of his *Nachlass*, Lieferung 18, in 1832 by A. Dia-
        belli & Co. in Vienna.
    Werke, series XX, no. 337.   MR. CHARLES L. MORLEY

1627. [An die untergehende Sonne, op. 44. D. 457]
    An die untergehende Sonne. July 1816.
        p. 2 of his *Pflicht und Liebe*.
    Fragment of a song with piano accpt. (17 bars).
    First line: Sonne, du sinkst.
    Text by Kosegarten.

Schubert, Franz (Peter)—*continued*

Published in 1827 by A. Diabelli & Co. in Vienna.
Werke, series XX, no. 237 (the complete version of May, 1817).
Former owner: Alexander W. Thayer.   MR. ARTURO TOSCANINI

1628.   [Auf dem Strom, op. 119. D. 943]
Auf dem Strom von Rellstab. März 1828 Frz. Schubert mpria.
[11]p. 24 x 31 cm.
Song with piano and horn accpt.
First line: Nimm die letzten Abschiedsküsse.
Published in 1829 by M. J. Leidesdorf in Vienna.
Werke, series XX, no. 568.
Former owner: George B. Weston.   HARVARD UNIVERSITY LIBRARY

1629.   [Auf den Tod einer Nachtigall. D. 399]
Auf den Tod einer Nachtigall. 13 May 1816.
p. 2-3 of his *Frühlingslied*.
Song with piano accpt.
Text by Hölty.
First line: Sie ist dahin, die Mayenlieder tönte.
Published in 1895 in his Werke, series XX, no. 218.
LIBRARY OF CONGRESS

1630.   [Auguste jam coelestium. D. 488]
Duett-Arie. Oct. 1816. Franz Schubert mpria.
[20]p. 24½ x 32 cm.
Full score (soprano and tenor and orchestra).
Published in 1888 in his Werke, series XIV, no. 10.
Former owner: Hermine Wittgenstein.
LIBRARY OF CONGRESS, WHITTALL FOUNDATION

1631.   [Die Blumensprache, op. 173, no. 5. D. 519]
Die Blumensprache.
p. 3-7 of his *Schlaflied*.
Song with piano accpt.
Text by Eduard Platner.
First line: Es deuten die Blumen.
Published in 1867 by C. A. Spina in Vienna.
Werke, series XX, no. 299.
Former owner: Countess Rosa Almásy.   SIBLEY MUSICAL LIBRARY

1632.   [Cora an die Sonne. D. 263]
Cora an die Sonne. den 22. aug. 1815.
p. 2 of his *Abendständchen*.
Song with piano accpt.
Text by Baumberg.
First line: Nach so vielen trüben Tagen.
Published as no. 3 of his *Nachlass*, Lieferung 42, ca. 1848 by
A. Diabelli & Co. in Vienna.

Schubert, Franz (Peter)—*continued*

Werke, series XX, no. 123.
Former owners: Marie Leins, Jerome Stonborough.

1633. [Counterpoint exercises. D. 25]
Den 18 Juny 1812 den Kontrapunkt angefangen. 1. Gattung.
[8]p. 23 x 32 cm.
Four cantus firmi by J. J. Fux, the bass in the hand of Schubert's
teacher, Salieri.
Unpublished.
Former owner: Max Friedländer. MR. FRANZ ROEHN

1634. [Das war ich. D. 164]
Das war ich. Gedicht von Körner. Den 26. März [1]815. Frz.
Schubert mpria.
[2]p. 23 x 31 cm.
Song with piano accpt.
First line: Jüngst träumte mir.
Published as no. 2 of his *Nachlass*, Lieferung 39, ca. 1842 by
A. Diabelli & Co. in Vienna.
Werke, series XX, no. 56.
On p. 2 a fragment of his *Liebesrausch*. HEINEMAN FOUNDATION

1635. [Deutsche Tänze. D. 820]
Deutsche. Frz. Schubert mpria. Oct. 1824.
[4]p. 23 x 32 cm.
Six dances for piano 2 hands.
Published in 1931 by Universal Edition in Vienna; not in his Werke.
Former owners: Countess Karoline Esterházy, Countesses Wilhel-
mine and Melanie Almásy, Hermann Graedener.
MR. GEORGE A. STEINBACH

1636. [Deutscher, op. 9, no. 2, A flat major. D. 365, no. 2]
Deutscher von Franz Schubert mpria.
[1]p. 23½ x 31½ cm.
At end: Aufgeschrieben für mein Kaffe-, Wein- und Punschbrüderl
Anselm Hüttenbrenner, weltberühmten Compositeur. Wien den
14 März im Jahre des Herrn 1818 in seiner höchst eigener
Wohnung. Monatlich 30 fl. W.W.
Familiarly known as the *Trauer-Walzer*.
Published as no. 2 of *Original-Tänze für das Pianoforte* in 1821 by
Cappi & Diabelli in Vienna.
Werke, series XII, no. 1 (no. 2).
Former owner: Hermine Wittgenstein.

1637. [Dithyrambe. D. 47]
[4]p. 24 x 31 cm.
Sketch for an unpublished setting for tenor solo and mixed

Schubert, Franz (Peter)—*continued*

    chorus of Schiller's poem *Der Besuch,* written in ink over a pencil copy of the *Minuetto* from Mozart's *Jupiter Symphony* [K. 550].

    Former owner: Max Friedländer.   GALERIE ST. ETIENNE

1638. [Einsamkeit. D. 620]

    Einsamkeit von Mayrhofer. Juny 1822. Frz. Schubert mpria. [20]p. 23 x 32 cm.

    Song with piano accpt.

    First line: Gib mir die Fülle der Einsamkeit.

    Published as Lieferung 32 of his *Nachlass,* ca. 1841, by A. Diabelli & Co. in Vienna.

    Werke, series XX, no. 339.

    Former owner: Jerome Stonborough.

          LIBRARY OF CONGRESS, WHITTALL FOUNDATION

1639. [Erlkönig, op. 1. D. 328b]

    Erlkönig. FS.

    [10]p. 30½ x 22 cm.

    Song with piano accpt.

    Text by Goethe.

    First line: Wer reitet so spät.

    Published (in this version) in 1895 in his Werke, series XX, no. 178b.

    At end: Franz Schuberts Handschrift der gefeierten Künstlerin Clara Wieck überreicht von Schuberts Freunde B. Randhartinger. Wien den 15 Jänner 1838.

    See the summary of J. Braunstein's unpublished account of this ms. in *New York Times,* July 14, 1946.

    Facsimile of one page in *Notes,* VI (1949-50), 206.

          HEINEMAN FOUNDATION

1640. [Die Erscheinung, op. 108, no. 3. D. 229]

    Die Erscheinung. Kosegarten. den 7 July 1815. Frz. Schubert. [2]p. 23½ x 30½ cm.

    Song with piano accpt.

    First line: Ich lag auf grünen Matten.

    Published in 1824 in vol. 2 of their *Album musical* by Sauer & Leidesdorf in Vienna.

    Werke, series XX, no. 92.

    On p. 2 his *Von Ida.*   WALTER SCHATZKI

1641. [Fantasia, piano, op. 15, C major (Wanderer-Fantaisie). D. 760]

    Fantaisie pour le pianoforte composée et dédiée à monsieur Emm. Noble de Liebenberg de Zsittin par François Schubert mpria. 1 leaf, 24 p. 23½ x 31 cm.

    Caption title: *Fantasia. Nov. 1822. Frz. Schubert mpria.*

    Published in 1823 by Cappi & Diabelli in Vienna.

    Werke, series XI, no. 1.

    Former owner: Max Friedländer.   DR. FRANK BLACK

Schubert, Franz (Peter)—*continued*

1642.   [Fantasia, piano 4 hands, no. 3, C minor. D. 48]
  Grande sonate à quatre mains composée par François Schubert
   comp. 1814.
  [27]p. 23 x 31 cm.
The first version, without the fugue.
Published as *Grosse Sonate* in 1871 by J. P. Gotthard in Vienna.
Werke, series IX, no. 32.
Former owners: Albert Stadler, Jerome Stonborough.
The catalogue of the Whittall Collection notes that the authenticity
 of this ms. is open to question.
          LIBRARY OF CONGRESS, WHITTALL FOUNDATION

1643.   [Die Forelle, op. 32. D. 550e]
  Die Forelle von Schubart. Frz. Schubert mpria. Oct. 1821.
  [2]p. 23 x 32 cm.
Song with piano accpt.
First line: In einem Bächlein helle.
Published ca. 1828 by A. Diabelli & Co. in Vienna.
This version differs from the four in the Werke (series XX, no.
 327 a-d) in having a piano introduction of 5 bars.
Facsimile of p. 1 in *Report of the Librarian of Congress*, 1941-42,
 after p. 122. Complete facsimile in *Library of Congress Quarterly
 Journal*, VI, no. 4 (August 1949), 4-6.
Former owners: Freiherr von Stiebar, Johann Latzelsberger, Maria
 Jagla, Jerome Stonborough.
          LIBRARY OF CONGRESS, WHITTALL FOUNDATION

1644.   [Fragment aus dem Aeschylus. D. 450a]
  Aus dem Aeschylus. Juny 1816. Franz Schubert mpria.
  [4]p. 32 x 23 cm.
Song with piano accpt.
Translation by Mayrhofer from *The Eumenides*.
First line: So wird der Mann, der sonder Zwang gerecht ist.
Published in this version in 1895 in his Werke, series XX, no. 236a.
On p. 3 a *Duetto* for violins, cancelled.
Former owner: Max Friedländer.   MR. FRANZ ROEHN

1645.   [Freude der Kinderjahre. D. 455]
  Freude der Kinderjahre. July 1816. Frz. Schubert mpria.
  [2]p. 23½ x 30½ cm.
Song with piano accpt.
Text by F. von Köpken.
First line: Freude, die im frühen Lenze.
Published as no. 35 of *Schubert Album*, Band VII, in 1887 by
 C. F. Peters in Leipzig.
Werke, series XX, no. 240.
On p. 2 his *Grablied auf einen Soldaten*.
Former owner: Max Friedländer.   SIBLEY MUSICAL LIBRARY

Schubert, Franz (Peter)—*continued*

1646. [Die frühe Liebe. D. 430]
  Die frühe Liebe. Hölty. May 1816.
  p. 2 of his *Minnelied.*
 Song with piano accpt.
 First line: Schon im bunten Knabenkleide.
 Published in 1895 in his Werke, series XX, no. 222.
GALERIE ST. ETIENNE

1647. [Frühlingslied. D. 398]
  Frühlingslied. den 13 May 1816. Frz. Schubert.
  [4]p. 31 x 24 cm.
 Song with piano accpt.
 First line: Die Luft ist blau, das Tal ist grün.
 Published as no. 39 of *Schubert Album,* Band VII, in 1887 by C. F.
  Peters in Leipzig.
 Werke, series XX, no. 217.
 Followed by his *Auf den Tod einer Nachtigall, Die Knabenzeit*
  and *Winterlied.*   LIBRARY OF CONGRESS

1648. [Frühlingslied. D. 709]
  parts. 29½ x 23 cm.
 For 2 tenors and 2 basses, unaccompanied.
 2nd bass part lacking.
 Text by Schober.
 First line: Schmücket die Locken.
 Published in 1891 in his Werke, series XVI, no. 31, with title
  Frühlingsgesang.
 Former owner: Max Friedländer.   MR. FRANZ ROEHN

1649. [Der Geistertanz. D. 116]
  Der Geistertanz. den 14. Oct. [1]814. Frz. Schubert.
  [2]p. 24 x 31 cm.
 Fragment of song with piano accpt.
 Text by Matthisson.
 First line: Die bretterne Kammer der Toten erbebt.
 Published as no. 2 of his *Nachlass,* Lieferung 31, ca. 1840, by
  A. Diabelli & Co. in Vienna.
 Werke, series XX, no. 29.
 Former owner: Wilhelm Heyer (catalogue, vol. IV, no. 228).
BOSTON PUBLIC LIBRARY

1650. [Gesang der Geister über den Wassern. D. 705]
  Gesang der Geister über den Wassern. Göthe. Dez. 1820. Frz.
   Schubert mpria.
  [8]p. 23½ x 29½ cm.
 A second sketch, in C sharp minor, for 2 tenors, 2 basses and piano,
  for his op. 167 (D. 714). The piano part is incomplete.
 Published in 1897 in his Werke, series XXI, no. 34.
 Former owner: Julius Epstein.
MEMORIAL LIBRARY OF MUSIC, STANFORD UNIVERSITY

Schubert, Franz (Peter)—*continued*

1651.　[Grablied auf einen Soldaten. D. 454]
　　　Grablied auf einen Soldaten. July 1816. Frz. Schubert mpria.
　　　p. 2 of his *Freude der Kinderjahre*.
　　Song with piano accpt.
　　Text by Schubart.
　　First line: Zieh hin, du braver Krieger.
　　Published as no. 6 of *40 Lieder* in 1872 by J. P. Gotthard in Vienna.
　　Werke, series XX, no. 239.　　　　　SIBLEY MUSICAL LIBRARY

1652.　[Grenzen der Menschheit. D. 716]
　　　Grenzen der Menschheit. Göthe. März 1821. Frz. Schubert mpria.
　　　[5]p. 24 x 31 cm.
　　Song with piano accpt.
　　First line: Wenn der uralte heilige Vater.
　　Published as no. 1 of his *Nachlass,* Lieferung 14, in 1832 by
　　　A. Diabelli & Co. in Vienna.
　　Werke, series XX, no. 393.
　　Former owner: Max Friedländer.　　　MR. FRANZ ROEHN

1653.　[Gruppe aus dem Tartarus. D. 396]
　　　Gruppe aus dem Tartarus. Schiller. März 1816. Frz. Schubert
　　　mpria.
　　　[2]p. 31 x 24 cm.
　　Fragment (first 14 bars) of a song with piano accpt., entirely dif-
　　　ferent from the familiar version of 1817 (D. 583).
　　Unpublished.
　　On p. 2 a fragment of his *Sonatina,* op. 137, no. 1.
　　　　　　　　　　　　　　　NEWBERRY LIBRARY

1654.　[Hagars Klage. D. 5]
　　　Hagars Klage in Musick gesetzt von Franz Schubert den 30.
　　　März 1811.
　　　17 p. 23 x 32½ cm.
　　Song with piano accpt.
　　Text by Schücking.
　　First line: Hier am Hügel heissen Sandes.
　　Published in 1894 in his Werke, series XX, no. 1.
　　Former owner: Albert Cranz.　　　GALERIE ST. ETIENNE

1655.　[Herrn Joseph Spaun. D. 749]
　　　Herrn Joseph Spaun Assessor in Linz. Jänner 1822. Frz. Schubert
　　　mpria.
　　　[8]p. 13 x 18½ cm.
　　Song with piano accpt.
　　Text by Matthäus von Collin.
　　First line: Und nimmer schreibst du?
　　Published as Lieferung 46 of his *Nachlass,* ca. 1848, by A. Diabelli

Schubert, Franz (Peter)—*continued*

& Co. in Vienna, with title: *Epistel von Matth. von Collin an den Assessor Joseph von Spaun in Linz; musikalischer Schwank* . . .
Werke, series XX, no. 588.
Former owner: Max Friedländer.   MR. WALTER SLEZAK

1656. [Der Hochzeitsbraten, op. 104. D. 930]
Der Hochzeitsbraten von Schober. Op. 104. Nov. 1827. Frz. Schubert mpria.
[24]p. 24 x 32½ cm.
Terzett for soprano, tenor and bass with piano accpt.
First line: Ach, liebes Herz, ach Theobald.
Published in 1829 by A. Diabelli & Co. in Vienna.
Werke, series XIX, no. 2.
Former owner: Albert Cranz.   GALERIE ST. ETIENNE

1657. [Hoffnung. D. 295b]
[2]p. 24½ x 31 cm.
Song with piano accpt., second version.
First line: Schaff, das Tagwerk meiner Hände.
This version published in 1895 in his Werke, series XX, no. 175b.
On p. 2 the end of his *Thekla.*
Former owners: Dr. Eduard Schneider, Jerome Stonborough.
LIBRARY OF CONGRESS, WHITTALL FOUNDATION

1658. [Impromptus, piano, op. 90. D. 899]
[23]p. 24 x 32 cm.
Published in 1827 by Tobias Haslinger in Vienna.
Werke, series XI, no. 2.   DR. FELIX OPPENHEIM

1659. [Jägerlied. D. 204]
2 Stim. u. 2 Hörner. Jägerlied. Körner. Franz Schubert mpria.
Half of one leaf. 11½ x 30½ cm.
No. 4 of his *Fünf Duette für zwei Singstimmen oder zwei Waldhörner.*
Published in 1892 in his Werke, series XIX, no. 33.
On verso, sixteen lines of a poem by Hölty in Schubert's hand.
MRS. MARY LOUISE ZIMBALIST

1660. [Der Jüngling und der Tod. D. 545b]
[1]p. 23 x 31 cm.
Fragment (last 11 bars) of song with piano accpt.
Text by Spaun.
Published as no. 18 of *40 Lieder* in 1872 by J. P. Gotthard in Vienna.
Werke, series XX, no. 312b.   MISS ANAHID ISKIAN

1661. [Die Knabenzeit. D. 400]
Die Knabenzeit.
p. 3. of his *Frühlingslied.*
Song with piano accpt.
Text by Hölty.

Schubert, Franz (Peter)—*continued*

First line: Wie glücklich, wem das Knabenleid.
Published in 1895 in his Werke, series XX, no. 219.

1662. [Labetrank der Liebe. D. 302]
Labetrank der Liebe.
[4]p. 11 x 18½ cm.
Song with piano accpt.
Text by Stoll.
First line: Wenn im Spiele leiser Töne.
Published in 1895 in his Werke, series XX, no. 150.
Former owner: Joseph Muller.

1663. [Ländler, nos. 5 and 8. Op. 18. D. 145]
p. 2 of his *Originaltänze,* op. 9.
Published in his *Walzer, Ländler und Ecossoisen für das Piano-forte* in 1823 by Cappi & Diabelli in Vienna.
Werke, series XII, no. 2.

1664. [Lambertine. D. 301]
Lambertine. den 12. Oct. 1815. Franz Schubert mpria.
[4]p. 24 x 31½ cm.
Song with piano accpt.
Text by Stoll.
First line: O Liebe, die mein Herz erfüllt.
Published as no. 2 of Lieferung 36 of his *Nachlass,* ca. 1842, by A. Diabelli & Co. in Vicnna.
Werke, series XX, no. 149.
On p. 4 is a fragment of his *Variations in F major.*
Former owner: Hermine Wittgenstein.

1665. [Leiden der Trennung. D. 509]
Leiden der Trennung. Metastasio. Dec. 1816. Schubert.
[2]p. 24 x 30 cm.
Fragment (first 18 bars) of a song with piano accpt.
Text from Metastasio's *Artaserse,* translated by H. von Collin.
First line: Vom Meere trennt sich die Welle.
Published as no. 32 of *40 Lieder* in 1872 by J. P. Gotthard in Vienna.
Werke, series XX, no. 285.
On p. 2 his *Skolie.*
Former owners: Alexander Posonyi, Dr. Christian A. Herter.

1666. [Liebesrausch. D. 164]
p. 2 of his *Das war ich.*
Last 6 bars, cancelled, of the first version of a song with piano accpt., followed by the 2nd and 3rd stanzas of Körner's text.
Published in *Musik aus aller Welt,* Vienna, January 1928, p. 7.

Schubert, Franz (Peter)—*continued*

1667. [Liebeständelei. D. 206]
   Liebeständeley. Körner. den 26. May 1815. Frz. Schubert mpria.
   [2]p. 23 x 30 cm.
   Song with piano accpt.
   First line: Süsses Liebchen! Komm zu mir.
   Published as no. 11 of his *40 Lieder* in 1872 by J. P. Gotthard in
      Vienna.
   Werke, series XX, no. 75.
   On p. 2 are his *Lützows wilde Jagd* and *Der Morgenstern.*
   Former owner: Hermine Wittgenstein.

1668. [Das Lied im Grünen, op. 115, no. 1. D. 917]
   Das Lied im Grünen. Gedicht von Reil. Juny 1827. Frz. Schubert
      mpria.
   [5]p. 24 x 31½ cm.
   Song with piano accpt.
   First line: In's Grüne, in's Grüne, da lockt uns der Frühling.
   Published as no. 1 of *Drei Gedichte* in 1829 by M. J. Leidesdorf
      in Vienna.
   Werke, series XX, no. 543.
   Facsimile of p. 1 in Van Patten, *Catalogue,* p. 238.
   Former owner: George T. Keating.

1669. [Lützows wilde Jagd. D. 205]
   Lützows wilde Jagd. Körner. für 2 Stimmen oder 2 Waldhörner
      den 26. May 1815. Frz. Schubert mpria.
   p. 2 of his *Liebeständelei.*
   No. 5 of his *Fünf Duette für zwei Singstimmen oder zwei
      Waldhörner.*
   Published in 1892 in his Werke, series XIX, no. 34.
   Former owner: Hermine von Wittgenstein.

1670. [Das Mädchen aus der Fremde. D. 117]
   Das Mädchen aus der Fremde. Schiller. den 16. Oct. 1814. Franz
      Schubert mpria.
   [4]p. 24½ x 32½ cm.
   Song with piano accpt., first version.
   First line: In einem Tal bei armen Hirten.
   Published in 1894 in his Werke, series XX, no. 30.
   Former owner: Max Friedländer.

1671. [Magnificat, C major. D. 486]
   8 parts. 29 x 22½ cm.
   Not all the parts in Schubert's autograph.
   Published in 1888 in his Werke, series XIV, no. 11.
   Former owner: Max Friedländer.

Schubert, Franz (Peter)—*continued*

1672. [Mass, no. 1, F major. D. 105]
 parts (82 leaves). 31½ x 23½ cm.
 Published in 1856 by F. Glöggl & Sohn in Vienna.
 Werke, series XIII, no. 1.
 Former owner: Max Friedländer. MR. FRANZ ROEHN

1673. [Mass, no. 1, F major. D. 105]
 Missa in F. violino IIdo.
 19 p. 31½ x 24 cm.
 Former owner: Dr. Eduard Schneider.
 MRS. MARY LOUISE ZIMBALIST

1674. [Mass, no. 4, op. 48, C major. D. 452]
 Missa in C dur. July 1818. Franz Schubert mpria für Herrn
 Holzer.
 [40]p. 23 x 30 cm.
 Full score.
 Published (parts) in 1825 by A. Diabelli & Co. in Vienna.
 Werke, series XIII, no. 4.
 Former owners: Carl Pichler, Hermine Wittgenstein.
 LIBRARY OF CONGRESS, WHITTALL FOUNDATION

1675. [Minnelied. D. 429]
 Minnelied. Hölty. May 1816.
 [2]p. 31½ x 24 cm.
 Song with piano accpt.
 First line: Holder klingt der Vogelsang.
 Published as no. 3 of his *Nachgelassene Lieder* in 1885 by C. F.
 Peters in Leipzig.
 Werke, series XX, no. 221.
 On p. 2 his *Die frühe Liebe*. GALERIE ST. ETIENNE

1676. [Der Morgenstern. D. 203]
 Der Morgenstern. Körner. für 2 Stimmen oder 2 Waldhörner.
 den 26. May 1816. Frz. Schubert mpria.
 p. 2 of his *Liebeständelei*.
 No. 3 of his *Fünf Duette für zwei Singstimmen oder zwei Wald-
 hörner*.
 Published in 1892 in his Werke, series XIX, no. 32.
 Former owner: Hermine Wittgenstein.
 LIBRARY OF CONGRESS, WHITTALL FOUNDATION

1677. [Nähe des Geliebten, op. 5, no. 2. D. 162b]
 Nähe des Geliebten. Göthe. Den 27. Februar 1815. Frz. Schubert
 mpria.
 [2]p. 23½ x 30 cm.
 Song with piano accpt., second version.
 First line: Ich denke dein, wenn mir der Sonne Schimmer.
 Published in 1821 by Cappi & Diabelli in Vienna.

Schubert, Franz (Peter)—*continued*

Werke, series XX, no. 49b.
On p. 2 his *Sängers Morgenlied.*
Former owner: Dr. Wagener. DR. ARTHUR DREY

1678. [Original-Tänze, piano, op. 9, nos. 6-7. D. 365, 6-7]
[2]p. 22 x 29 cm.
Published in 1821 by Cappi & Diabelli in Vienna.
Werke, series XII, no. 1, nos. 6-7.
On p. 2 two of his *Ländler.* MR. JOHN BASS

1679. [Pflicht und Liebe. D. 467]
Pflicht und Liebe. Gotter. August 1816. Franz Schubert mpria.
[2]p. 24 x 31½ cm.
Song with piano accpt., last bar lacking.
First line: Du, der ewig um mich trauert.
Published as no. 17 of his *Nachgelassene Lieder* in 1885 by C. F.
Peters in Leipzg.
Werke, series XX, no. 593.
Former owner: Alexander W. Thayer.
On p. 2 his *An die untergehende Sonne.* MR. ARTURO TOSCANINI

1680. [Polonaise, piano four hands. D. 618A]
Polonaise. July 1818. Frz. Schubert mpria.
[4]p. 24 x 32 cm.
Sketches, incomplete, for an unpublished composition. There are
also drafts of the *Polonaises,* op. 75, nos. 2 and 4, and the theme
of the *Variations,* op. 10. In each case only the treble of the
primo part is given.
Former owner: Otto Dresel.
HARVARD UNIVERSITY, ISHAM MEMORIAL LIBRARY

1681. [Quintet, violins, violas and violoncello, C minor. D. 8]
P-a-r-t-i-t-u-r-a. Ouverture puor [!] le quintetto. Gewidmet meinem
Bruder Ferdinand del sig. N Schubert N den 29 Juny 1811.
Score (1 leaf, [18]p.) and 5 parts. 23½ x 32 cm.
Parts dated 12 July 1811.
Unpublished.
Former owner: Albert Cranz. GALERIE ST. ETIENNE

1682. [Rondo, violin and piano, op. 70, B minor. D. 895]
Rondo. Oct. 1826. Frz. Schubert ...
[27]p. 25 x 32 cm.
Published as *Rondeau brillant* in 1827 by Artaria & Co. in Vienna.
Werke, series VIII, no. 1.
Facsimile of one page in *Notes,* VII (1949-50), 207.
HEINEMAN FOUNDATION

1683. [Salve Regina, op. 153. D. 676]
Salve Regina. op. 153. Nov. 1819. Frz. Schubert.
[14]p. 23 x 31 cm.
Score (soprano solo and string orchestra).

Schubert, Franz (Peter)—*continued*

Published as *Drittes Offertorium* (parts) ca. 1843 by A. Diabelli
& Co. in Vienna.
Werke, series XIV, no. 3.
Former owner: William H. Cummings (catalogue, no. 177)

1684. [Sängers Morgenlied. D. 163]
        p. 2 of his *Nähe des Geliebten.*
        Song with piano accpt., first version.
        Text by Körner.
        First line: Süsses Licht! Aus goldenen Pforten.
        Published in 1894 in his Werke, series XX, no. 50.
        Former owner: Dr. Wagener.

1685. [Schlachtlied, op. 151. D. 912]
        Fragment aus der 1ten Scizze des Doppelchores "Schlachtlied"
        (von Klopstock). Op. 151.
        [2]p. 23 x 28 cm.
        Title not in Schubert's hand.
        Published as *Schlachtlied, Gedicht von Klopstock, für 8 Männer-
        stimmen* ca. 1843 by A. Diabelli & Co. in Vienna.
        Werke, series XVI, no. 28.

1686. [Schlaflied, op. 24, no. 2. D. 527]
        Abendlied von F. Mayrhofer.
        [7]p. 22 x 29 cm.
        Song with piano accpt.
        First line: Es mahnt der Wald.
        Published in 1823 by Sauer & Leidesdorf in Vienna.
        Werke, series XX, no. 298.
        On p. 3-7 his *Die Blumensprache.*
        Former owner: Countess Rosa Almásy.

1687. [Die Sehnsucht, op. 39. D. 636a]
        Die Sehnsucht, Gedicht von Friedrich von Schiller für eine
        Bass-Stimme mit Begleitung des Pianoforte in Musik gesetzt
        von Franz Schubert mpria.
        [8]p. 24½ x 31½ cm.
        The first version of the second setting of this song.
        First line: Ach, aus dieses Tales Gründen.
        Published in 1895 in his Werke, series XX, no. 357a.
        Former owners: Adalbert Rotter (received from the composer April
        24, 1824); Hermine Wittgenstein.

1688. [Sehnsucht, op. 105, no. 4. D. 879]
        p. 5-8 of his *Am Fenster.*
        Song with piano accpt., lacking last 18 bars.
        First line: Die Scheibe friert.

Schubert, Franz (Peter)—*continued*

Published as no. 4 of *Vier Gedichte von J. G. Seidl* in 1828 by Joseph Czerny in Vienna.
Werke, series XX, no. 493.
Former owner: Hermine Wittgenstein.

1689. [Skolie. D. 507]
Skolie. Dec. 1816. Frz. Schubert mpria.
p. 2 of his *Leiden der Trennung.*
Song with piano accpt.
Text by Matthisson.
First line: Mädchen entsiegelten, Brüder, die Flaschen.
Published in 1895 in his Werke, series XX, no. 283.
Former owners: Alexander Posonyi, Dr. Christian A. Herter.

1690. [Sonatina, violin and piano, op. 137, no. 1, D major. D. 384]
p. 2 of his *Gruppe aus dem Tartarus.*
The last 6 bars of the sonatina, in a slightly different version.

1691. [Sonatina, violin and piano, op. 137, no. 2, A minor. D. 385]
Sonata II pour le pianoforte et violon. März 1816. Franz Schubert mpria.
32 p. 11 x 18½ cm.
Last movement lacking.
Published in 1836 by A. Diabelli & Co. in Vienna.
Werke, series VIII, no. 3.

1692. [Ständchen, op. 135. D. 921]
Chor mit Alt Solo. July 1827. Frz. Schubert mpria.
10 p. 24 x 31 cm.
Score (4-part women's chorus and piano) of the second version.
Text by Grillparzer.
First line: Zögernd leise.
Published ca. 1838 by A. Diabelli & Co. in Vienna.
Former owner: Max Friedländer.

1693. [Symphony, no. 5, B flat major. D. 485]
[5]p. 30 x 24 cm.
Fragment of the 1st movement of the composer's reduction for piano 4 hands.
The published arrangement for piano 4 hands (C. F. Peters, 1870) is not by Schubert, but by Hugo Ulrich.
Facsimile of one page in Parke-Bernet sale catalogue, 318, no. 489.
Former owner: Hugo Riesenfeld.

1694. [Tantum ergo, C major. D. 460]
      Tantum ergo . . . August 1816. Franz Schubert mpria.
      [4]p. 23½ x 30½ cm.
   Full score (chorus, organ and orchestra).
   Dedicated to M. Holzer.
   Published in 1888 in his Werke, series XIV, no. 7.
   Former owner: Hermine Wittgenstein.
                   LIBRARY OF CONGRESS, WHITTALL FOUNDATION

1695. [Thekla, op. 88, no. 2. D. 595]
      p. 2 of his *Hoffnung.*
   Song with piano accpt., second half only.
   Text by Schiller.
   Published in 1827 by Thaddäus Weigl in Vienna.
   Former owners: Dr. Eduard Schneider, Jerome Stonborough.
                   LIBRARY OF CONGRESS, WHITTALL FOUNDATION

1696. [Totengräber-Weise. D. 869]
      Todtengräber-Weise von Schlechta.
      [7]p. 25 x 32 cm.
   Song with piano accpt.
   First line: Nicht so düster und so bleich.
   Published as no. 3 of Lieferung 15 of his *Nachlass,* in 1832 by
      A. Diabelli & Co. in Vienna.
   Werke, series XX, no. 496.
   Former owner: Jerome Stonborough.
                   LIBRARY OF CONGRESS, WHITTALL FOUNDATION

1697. [Um Mitternacht, op. 88, no. 3. D. 862]
      Um Mitternacht. Dec. 1825. Frz. Schubert mpria.
      [4]p. 22½ x 31½ cm.
   Song with piano accpt., incomplete (lacks last 13 bars) and com-
      pletely cancelled.
   Text by Ernest Schulze.
   First line: Keine Stimme hör ich schallen.
   Published in 1827 by Thaddäus Weigl in Vienna.
   Werke, series XX, no. 499.
   Former owner: Hermine Wittgenstein.
                   LIBRARY OF CONGRESS, WHITTALL FOUNDATION

1698. [Variations, piano, F major. D. 156]
      on p. 4 of his *Lambertine.*
   Theme and 11 bars of the 2nd variation, completely cancelled.
   Published in 1887 by Weinberger & Hofbauer in Vienna.
   Werke, series XI, no. 6.
   Former owner: Hermine Wittgenstein.
                   LIBRARY OF CONGRESS, WHITTALL FOUNDATION

Schubert, Franz (Peter)—*continued*

1699. [Variations, piano 4 hands, op. 10, E minor. D. 624]
    [2]p. 21½ x 27½ cm.
    Fragment containing part of the 2nd, all of the 3rd, and part of the
    4th variation.
    Published as *Variationen über ein französisches Lied* in 1822 by
    Cappi & Diabelli in Vienna.
    Werke, series IX, no. 15.   SIBLEY MUSICAL LIBRARY

1700. [Variations, piano 4 hands, op. 10, E minor. D. 624]
    [2]p. 21½ x 28½ cm.
    Fragment of the last variation, no. 8, Più moto, tempo di marcia.
    The identification was made by Mr. Maurice J. E. Browne.
    Former owners: Gustav Oberlaender, George R. Siedenburg.
                                              DR. HAROLD T. HYMAN

1701. [Vergissmeinnicht. D. 792]
    Vergissmeinnicht, Gedicht von Fr. von Schober. März 1823.
      Frz. Schubert mpria.
    10 p. 24 x 31 cm.
    Song with piano accpt.
    First line: Als der Frühling sich vom Herzen.
    Published as no. 2 of Lieferung 21 of his *Nachlass* in 1833 by
    A. Diabelli & Co. in Vienna.
    Werke, series XX, no. 430.   HEINEMAN FOUNDATION

1702. [Viola, op. 123. D. 786]
    Viola. Gedichtet von Schober. März 1823. Franz Schubert mpria.
    [21]p. 23 x 32½ cm.
    Song with piano accpt., the last part in another hand.
    First line: Schneeglöcklein, o Schneeglöcklein.
    Published in 1830 by A. Pennauer in Vienna.
    Former owner: Max Friedländer.   MR. FRANZ ROEHN

1703. [Von Ida. D. 228]
    p. 2 of his *Die Erscheinung.*
    Song with piano accpt.
    Text by Kosegarten.
    First line: Der Morgen blüht, der Osten glüht.
    Published in 1894 in his Werke, series XX, no. 91.
                                              MR. WALTER SCHATZKI

1704. [Wehmut. D. 404]
    Die Herbstnacht. Salis. März 1816. Franz Schubert mpria.
    p. 2 of his *Abschied von der Harfe.*
    Song with piano accpt., rough draft.
    First line: Mit leisen Harfentönen.
    Published in 1860 by C. A. Spina in Vienna.
    Werke, series XX, no. 200.
    Former owner: Wilhelm Heyer (catalogue, vol. IV, no. 230).
                                    MRS. MARY LOUISE ZIMBALIST

Schubert, Franz (Peter)—*continued*

1705. [Winterlied. D. 401]
    Winterlied.
    p. 4 of his *Frühlingslied.*
    Song with piano accpt.
    Text by Hölty.
    First line: Keine Blumen blühn.
    Published in 1895 in his Werke, series XX, no. 220.
LIBRARY OF CONGRESS

1706. [Die Zauberharfe, op. 26. D. 644]
    Die Zauberharfe. Ouverture.
    1 leaf, 18 p. 23½ x 31½ cm.
    Full score [?]
    Published in 1867 by C. A. Spina in Vienna.
    Perhaps the *Overture* to Act III, since the autograph score of the
    Overture to Act I is in the Paris Conservatoire.
MEMORIAL LIBRARY OF MUSIC, STANFORD UNIVERSITY

1707. [Die Zauberharfe, op. 26. D. 644]
    Zauberharfe. VII.
    [2]p. 24 x 28 cm.
    Fragment of full score, cancelled.
    Former owner: Anselm Hüttenbrenner.   MR. GREGOR PIATIGORSKY

Schumann, Clara (Josephine), 1819-1896

1708. [Cadenzas for the first and last movements of Mozart's piano con-
    certo in D minor (K. 466)]
    2 leaves. 20½ x 27 cm.
    In the cadenza for the first movement the composer has used mate-
    rial from the cadenza by Brahms for the same concerto.
    Former owner: Jerome Stonborough.
LIBRARY OF CONGRESS, WHITTALL FOUNDATION

1709. [Cadenzas for the first and last movements of Mozart's piano con-
    certo in D minor (K. 466)]
    2 leaves. 25 x 31½ cm.
    The cadenza for the first movement appears to be a variant of the
    one in the preceding entry, but the cadenza for the last movement
    is a different piece from the foregoing counterpart.
    Former owners: Friederike Sauermann, Jerome Stonborough.
LIBRARY OF CONGRESS, WHITTALL FOUNDATION

Schumann, Robert Alexander, 1810-1856
    [Albumblätter. Op. 124]
    see his *Kinderscenen.* Op. 15

1710. Auf dem Rhein von K. Immermann.
    [2]p. 31½ x 23½ cm.
    Song with piano accpt.

Schumann, Robert Alexander—*continued*

First line: Auf deinem Grunde haben sie.
At end: d. 29 Juni 1840.
Published in 1842 as no. 4 of op. 51, *Lieder und Gesänge*, by C. F. Whistling in Leipzig.
Werke, series XIII, vol. 2, no. 38.   MR. GREGOR PIATIGORSKY

1711. [Fantasiestücke, piano, op. 12, no. 1]
Des Abends.
[2]p. 15 x 25½ cm.
At end: Am 18 August 1837 seinem lieben Becker. Robert Schumann.
Many variants from the first edition.
Published in 1837 by Breitkopf & Härtel in Leipzig.
Werke, series VII, vol. 2, no. 12.   HEINEMAN FOUNDATION

1712. [Fantasiestücke, piano, op. 111]
[4]p. 34 x 26½ cm.
Complete version of no. 3 (C minor) on p. 2-3 and cancelled sketches for no. 2 (A flat major) on p. 1 and 4.
Published in 1851 by C. F. Peters in Leipzig.
Werke, series VII, vol. 6, no. 34.   NEWBERRY LIBRARY

1713. [Fantasiestücke, piano and strings, op. 88]
Phantasiestücke für Pianoforte, Violine und Violoncell componiert . . . von R. S.
Score (31 p.) and 2 parts. 33 x 26 cm.
Corrections and additions throughout.
Dedicated to Frau Sophie Petersen.
Published in 1842 by Fr. Kistner in Leipzig.
Werke, series V, vol. 2, no. 6.   THE ERNEST SCHELLING COLLECTION

1714. Sechs Gedichte von N. Lenau, und Requiem, altkatholisches Gedicht, für eine Singstimme mit Begleitung des Pianoforte, componirt von Robert Schumann, op. 90. Dresden, im August 1850.
[19]p. 32 x 24 cm.
Title-page and part of the music in Schumann's hand.
Published in 1850 by Fr. Kistner in Leipzig.
Werke, series XIII, vol. 3, no. 24.   LIBRARY OF CONGRESS

1715. Herzeleid (T. Ullrich).
[2]p. 30 x 23 cm.
Song with piano accpt.
First line: Die Weiden lassen matt die Zweigen hangen.
On p. 2 unidentified sketches.
Published in 1852 as no. 1 of op. 107, *Sechs Gesänge*, by C. Luckhardt in Kassel.
Werke, series XIII, vol. 4, no. 29, 1.
Former owner: Dr. Christian A. Herter.   NEW YORK PUBLIC LIBRARY

Schumann, Robert Alexander—*continued*

1716. [Ich grolle nicht]
       [1]p. 31 x 26 cm.
       Song with piano accpt.
       Text by Heine.
       Unpublished; a completely different setting from op. 48, no. 7.
                                                MR. CARL H. TOLLEFSEN

1717. [Jägerlied]
       No. 3. Jägerlied (von E. Möricke). R. Schumann. Op. 59.
       [2]p. 30 x 23 cm.
       For 4-part mixed chorus unaccompanied.
       First line: Zierlich ist des Vogels Tritt.
       Published as no. 3 of his *Vier Gesänge für Sopran, Alt, Tenor und
         Bariton* in 1846 by G. Heinze in Leipzig.
       Werke, series XII, no. 2.
       Former owner: Max Friedländer.   MR. FRANZ ROEHN

1718. [Kinderscenen, piano, op. 15]
       [2]p. 28 x 34 cm.
       Sketches for no. 9 (*Ritter vom Steckenpferd*) and no. 6 (*Wichtige
         Begebenheit*) and for his *Albumblätter,* op. 124, no. 7 (*Ländler*)
         and no. 18 (*Botschaft*).   LIBRARY OF CONGRESS

1719. [Lieder-Album für die Jugend, op. 79]
       [8]p. 22½ x 28 cm.
       Fair copy of nos. 14 (*Marienwürmchen*), 24 (*Er ist's*), 29 (*Lied der
         Mignon*) and 27 (*Schneeglöckchen*).
       These songs are respectively nos. 13, 23, 28 and 26 in the first
         edition.
       Published in 1849 by Breitkopf & Härtel in Leipzig.
       Werke, series XIII, vol. 3, no. 20.
       Former owners: Livia Frege, Mrs. Mary Louise Zimbalist.
                                             CURTIS INSTITUTE OF MUSIC

1720. Nachtlied von F. Hebbel. Für Chor und Orch. . . .
       [5]p. 33½ x 27 cm.
       Sketch.
       At end: d. 7 Nov. 1849.
       Published as op. 108 in 1849 by N. Simrock in Bonn.
       Werke, series IX, vol. 3, no. 7.   LIBRARY OF CONGRESS

1721. [Quartets, strings, op. 41]
       III Quartette für 2 Violinen, Viola und Violoncello componirt
         von Robert Schumann. Juni und Juli 1842 . . .
       3 vols. 30 x 23 cm.
       Score.
       On fly-leaf: Meiner lieben Klara dargebracht am 13ten Septem-
         ber 1842.
       On cover: Herrn Raimund Härtel zur Erinnerung. R. Sch. Leipzig,
         den 19 November 1846.

Schumann, Robert Alexander—*continued*

Separate title-page for each quartet.

Dated at the end of each quartet: den 24sten Juni 1842 in Leipzig beendigt, Johannistag, Robert Schumann; 5 Juli 1842 Lpz. Rob. Schumann; Leipzig den 22sten Juli 1842 Robert Schumann.

Published in 1842 (parts) and 1848 (score) by Breitkopf & Härtel in Leipzig.

Werke, series IV.

Former owner: Oscar Bondy. MR. RUDOLF F. KALLIR

1722. [Symphony, no. 1, op. 38, B flat major]

Frühlingssymphonie. 23-26 Januar 1841. Leipzig. 1. Frühlingsbeginn; 2. Abend; 3. Frohe Gespielen; 4. Voller Frühling. 212 p. 29½ x 22 cm.

Original pencil sketches and full score.

p. 159-174, containing the beginning of the *Finale*, not in Schumann's hand.

Two leaves laid in contain the first version of the *Trio II*, later added to the *Scherzo*.

The sketches occupy p. 1-20; the full score begins on p. 23.

On p. 23: 27 Januar 1841. *Frühlingssymphonie*.

At end of first movement: 4 Februar 41. At beginning of 2nd movement: 6 Februar 41. At end of 3rd movement: 13 Februar 41. At end of work: Beendigt am 20sten Februar 1841. Leipzig. Robert Schumann.

On p. 111 six bars of a sketch for mixed chorus unaccompanied of a *Psalm*: Herr, Herr, hast du mich ganz verlassen?

Published in 1841 (parts) and 1853 (score) by Breitkopf & Härtel in Leipzig.

Werke, series I, vol. 1.

Facsimile of p. 23 in the Report of the Librarian of Congress, 1927, opp. p. 126, and in the catalogue of the Heyer Collection, vol. IV, plate 41, with a detailed description of the ms. (p. 342-348).

Former owners: Clara Schumann, Hermann Levi, Wilhelm Heyer (Catalogue, vol. IV, no. 640). LIBRARY OF CONGRESS

1723. Zum Anfang (Rückert).

[3]p. 30 x 23 cm.

For 4-part men's chorus unaccompanied.

First line: Mache deinem Meister Ehre.

The text is from Rückert's *Selbstschau* in his collection *Pantheon*.

Apparently unpublished. NEW YORK PUBLIC LIBRARY

1724. [Drei zweistimmige Lieder. Op. 43]

Wenn ich ein Vöglein wär; Herbstlied von Mahlmann; Schön Blümlein von Reinick. Drei zweistimmige Lieder mit Begleitung des Pianoforte von Robert Schumann. Op. 43.

1 leaf, 10 p. 27 x 34 cm.

Published in 1840 by N. Simrock in Bonn.

Schumann, Robert Alexander—*continued*

Werke, series X, vol. 1, no. 2.
Former owner: George T. Keating.

Schweizer, Leopold

1725. 2 Contratanzi per il violino primo, violino 2do, clarinetto e violone.
Schweizer mpria.
[3]p. 21 x 31 cm.
Score.
At end: Fine den 6ten Januar 1796.
Former owner: Alois Fuchs.

Scott, Cyril (Meir), 1879-

1726. [The ballad of Fair Helen]
Fair Helen of Kirconnel.
10 p. 35 x 27 cm.
Song with piano accpt.
First line: I wish I were where Helen lies.
Published in 1925 by Elkin & Co. in London.
Former owner: David Bispham.

1727. Fantasia for viola & pianoforte. N.B. Some of this work has been
embodied in my concerto for violin & orchestra.
[1], 11 p. 35½ x 27 cm.
Dedicated to Lionel Tertis.

Serrao, Paolo, 1830-1907

1728. Ouverture sullo Stabat del Pergolesi di Paolo Serrao.
1 leaf, 31 p. 23½ x 30 cm.
Full score of an overture based on themes from Pergolesi's *Stabat
Mater*.
Former owner: Natale Gallini (catalogue, no. 57).

Servais, Adrien François, 1807-1866

1729. Concerto en la mineur pour le violoncelle avec accompagnement
d'orchestre ou piano, composé par F. Servais.
[4]p. 31 x 24 cm.
Fragment of score for violoncello and piano.
Published in this form in 1887 by Schott Frères in Brussels.
Former owner: Hubert F. Kufferath.

Variations brillantes et concertantes pour violon et violoncelle . . .
See under Ghys, Joseph, 1801-1848

1730. "Oh, my luve's like a red red rose" by R. Burns. Set to music by
       Cecil J. Sharp.
       [4]p. 30 x 24 cm.
       Song with piano accpt.
       Former owner: David Bispham.   NEW YORK PUBLIC LIBRARY

Shaw, George Bernard, 1856-1950

1731. [Ah, love, I lack thy kisses]
       2 leaves. 35 x 26½ cm.
       Song with piano accpt.
       Text by Caroline Radford.
       Dated: September 1884.   NEW YORK PUBLIC LIBRARY

1732. How she comes, by Caroline Radford.
       [3]p. 35 x 26½ cm.
       Song with piano accpt.
       First line: She comes through the meadow yonder.
       At end: G.B.S. March 1884.   NEW YORK PUBLIC LIBRARY

Shield, William, 1748-1829

1733. [The lass for a sailor]
       [4]p. 24½ x 31 cm.
       Full score of a song with orchestra accpt., but lacking text except
       for first line as given above.
       On p. 3, two songs with piano accpt. without text. On p. 4 piano-
       vocal score (without text) of first 30 bars of Caspar's aria in
       Weber's *Der Freischütz*: Hier im ird'schen Jammertal.
       Former owners: Joseph Alfred Novello, Thomas Pickering.
                                            LIBRARY OF CONGRESS

1734. The post captain.
       [4]p. 30½ x 24½ cm.
       Song with piano accpt.
       First line: When Steerwell heard me first impart.
                   MEMORIAL LIBRARY OF MUSIC, STANFORD UNIVERSITY

1735. The pretty little heart.
       [3]p. 23½ x 29 cm.
       Song with orchestra accpt.
       First line: I've a pretty little heart.
       Former owner: William H. Cummings (catalogue, no. 179).
                                            LIBRARY OF CONGRESS

1736. The pretty little heart.
       [5]p. 24½ x 29 cm.
       Song with piano accpt., a reduction of the preceding number.
       Former owner: William H. Cummings (catalogue, no. 179).
                                            LIBRARY OF CONGRESS

Shostakovich, Dmitrii Dmitrievich, 1906-

1737. [Lady Macbeth of Mtsensk, or Katerina Izmailova]
55-58 p. 36 x 24 cm.
Fragment of piano-vocal score.
Signed and dated at end: 13 X 1935.

Sibelius, Jean, 1865-

1738. Aallottaret. Eine Tondichtung für grosses Orchester. Comp. von
Jean Sibelius. Op. 73 . . .
[3], 45 p. 36½ x 27 cm.
Full score.
The original version of the work, published in revised form as *Die
Okeaniden* in 1915 by Breitkopf & Härtel in Leipzig.

1739. . . . Svanehvit (Aug. Strindberg). Musiken af Jean Sibelius . . .
41 p. 35½ x 27 cm.
Full score of the incidental music to the play.
Published in 1909 by A. M. Schlesinger in Berlin.

1740. Teodora (Bertel Gripenberg). Jean Sibelius.
1 leaf, 12 p. 34 x 27½ cm.
Song with piano accpt.
First line: Det frasar af silke, det strålar af rubinen.
Published as no. 2 of op. 35, in 1910, by Breitkopf & Härtel in
Leipzig.
Facsimile of p. 1-2 in Van Patten, *Catalogue*, p. 245.

Simon, James, 1880-ca. 1941

1741. Legende für Streichquartett in 3 Sätzen. James Simon.
28 p. 33½ x 26 cm.
Score.
Dedicated to Mrs. E. S. Coolidge, Berlin, September 1930.

Sinding, Christian, 1856-1941

1742. . . . Hymnus for organ.
12 p. 34 x 27 cm.
Dedicated to George Eastman.

Sinigaglia, Leone, 1868-1944

1743. Les pâquerettes. (Rollinat).
4 p. 32 x 25 ½ cm.
Song with piano accpt.
First line: Les pâquerettes sont en deuil.
Former owner: Hugo Riesenfeld.

Sitt, Hans, 1850-1922

1744. Festmarsch componirt zur 50jähriger Jubelfeier des Gustav Adolf Vereins von Hans Sitt. Partitur.
1 leaf, 41 p. 34 x 27 cm.
Dated and signed on title-page: Leipzig den 26 Aug. 1882, Hans Sitt, and Leipzig den 4 September 1882.
Former owner: Joseph Muller. NEW YORK PUBLIC LIBRARY

1745. . . . Ouverture zu "Macbeth" für grosses Orchester von Hans Sitt. Partitur. Breslau den 14. März 1871. Hans Sitt.
[1], 62 p. 34 x 27 cm. NEW YORK PUBLIC LIBRARY

1746. Sinfonie für Orchester von Hans Sitt. Partitur.
1 leaf, 243 p. 32 x 28 cm.
On p. 1: 11. Juni 1879. Hans Sitt.
At end: Fine. Lugano Treiano den 14. October 1881. Hans Sitt.
NEW YORK PUBLIC LIBRARY

Smart, Henry Thomas, 1813-1879

1747. Fare thee well. Henry Smart. 1832.
[4]p. 16 x 21 cm.
Song with piano accpt.
First line: Fare thee well and if forever. BOSTON PUBLIC LIBRARY

1748. Serenade. Henry Smart. 1832.
3 p. 16 x 20 cm.
Song with piano accpt.
First line: The star is in the west, my love. BOSTON PUBLIC LIBRARY

Smetana, Bedřich, 1824-1884

1749. Polka No. 2. I Heft. Op. 12. Fr. Smetana.
[4]p. 24½ x 34 cm.
For piano 2 hands.
Composed in 1861. Published as *Souvenir de Bohême en forme de polkas,* op. 12, no. 2 in 1913 by Universal Edition in Vienna.
MR. RUDOLF F. KALLIR

Smith, John Stafford, ca. 1750-1836

1750. [Anthems, motetts, songs, pieces for the harpsichord, catches, &c. by John Blaithwaite, George Holmes (A song on the birth-day of Lady Crew, 1702), Raphael Courtevil, Frescobaldi, Dowland, Scarlatti, Corelli, Parsley, Martin Smith, John Stafford Smith, &c.]
Title from a printed slip on inside front cover, with note apparently in the hand of W. H. Cummings: This volume from the Rimbault sale has evidently been in the possession of John Stafford Smith, a large portion being in his hand and bearing his signature. Many of the pieces are in the autograph of George Holmes.
The compositions of J. S. Smith listed in the index are: *Trio—*

Smith, John Stafford—*continued*

> Fountains that warble; *Catch*—The uproar's begun; *Catch*—Oh, mother; *Round*—Birds and green holly.
>
> At back of volume and in inverted order are the compositions of George Holmes: *Song*—Appear ye nymphs (with flute accpt.); *Air*—Gentle shepherds; *Duo*—Call your jocund; *Chorus*—All celebrate; *Song*—Bring on thou glorious sun; *A song on the Birth Day of Right Honble Lady Carew* by Mr. George Holmes.
>
> Former owners: Edward F. Rimbault, William H. Cummings (catalogue, no. 22).   LIBRARY OF CONGRESS

1751. Glee.

> [6]p. 30 x 24 cm.
>
> Quartet for men's voices, unaccompanied.
>
> First line: In vain we fill the sparkling bowl.
>
> At end: J. S. S. 1796.
>
> Not published in his five collections of glees, etc.
>
>   LIBRARY OF CONGRESS

Solle, Friedrich, 1806-1884

1752. Die Heimath von Albert Träger. Compon. von Fr. Solle.

> [4]p. 36 x 22 cm.
>
> Song with piano accpt.
>
> First line: Wenn du noch eine Heimath hast.
>
> With an added part for horn.
>
> Former owner: The Royal Collection, Lisbon.
>
>   LIBRARY OF CONGRESS

Sołtys, *count* Charles

1753. Polonaise concertante pour violon avec accompagnement de grande [!] orchestre composée par le comte Charles Soltys, amateur. Oeuvre IIme.

> [13]p. 31 x 23 cm.
>
> Violin part only.
>
> At end: da dedicarsi a me Nicolo Paganini. Varsovia il 17 giugno 1829.   NEW YORK PUBLIC LIBRARY

Somervell, *Sir* Arthur, 1863-1937

1754. Two conversations about Bach for two violins with accompaniment for pianoforte. Written by Arthur Somervell.

> 1 leaf, [7]p. 34½ x 27 cm.
>
> Inscribed to A. M. K., September 1919.
>
>   MEMORIAL LIBRARY OF MUSIC, STANFORD UNIVERSITY

1755. . . . Love me not for comely grace. Song, old English, anon. Composed by Arthur Somervell.

> 1 leaf, [5]p. 35 x 27 cm.
>
> Song with piano accpt.
>
> Former owner: David Bispham.   NEW YORK PUBLIC LIBRARY

1756.　. . . O my queen. Song, written by Mark H. Collet, set to music by Arthur Somervell.
[4]p. 35 x 27 cm.
Song with piano accpt.
First line: Gracious smiles unsought and granted.
Former owner: David Bispham.　　NEW YORK PUBLIC LIBRARY

1757.　. . . Young sir Guyon. Ballad written by Rev. Stopford Brooke, set to music by Arthur Somervell.
1 leaf, [5]p. 35 x 27 cm.
Song with piano accpt.
First line: Young Sir Guyon proudly said.
Former owner: David Bispham.　　NEW YORK PUBLIC LIBRARY

Sorabji, Kaikhosru, 1895-

1758.　Fantaisie espagnole:—Kaikhosru Sorabji. (1919). (Piano solo).
23 p. 22½ x 32½ cm.
At end: 5. iii. XIX.
Published in 1922 by London & Continental Music Publishing Co. in London.　　LIBRARY OF CONGRESS

1759.　[Sonata, piano, no. 1]
Sonata. Piano. Kaikhosru Sorabji (1919).
1 leaf, 42 p. 18 x 28 cm.
At end: Finis. 5.viii.McMXIX. Kaikhosru Sorabji.
Published in 1921 by London & Continental Music Publishing Co. in London.　　LIBRARY OF CONGRESS

1760.　[Sonata, piano, no. 2]
Sonata seconda. For piano. Kaikhosru Sorabji . . .
3 leaves, 49 p. 22½ x 31 cm.
At end: Fin:. 11.25':45" P.M. 24. Dec. 1920.
Published in 1923 by F. & B. Goodwin in London.

　　LIBRARY OF CONGRESS

1761.　[Sonata, piano, no. 3]
Kaikhosru Sorabji. Panornos—Feb. 1922—(Trinakria) . . . Completed 5.5.MCMXXIII.
1 leaf, 75, [1]p. 27½ x 35½ cm.
Published in 1924 by J. Curwen and Sons in London.
　　LIBRARY OF CONGRESS

1762.　Symphony for organ. Kaikhosru Sorabji. MCMXXIV.
81 p. 28 x 35½ cm.
At end: 8.20 P.M. 17.XII.XXXV.
Published in 1925 by J. Curwen and Sons in London.
　　LIBRARY OF CONGRESS

1763.　Valse fantaisie. Piano solo. Kaikhosru:—MCMXXV . . .
1 leaf, 16 p. 28½ x 35 cm.
At end: Finis 17.4.25. 4.15 P.M.　　LIBRARY OF CONGRESS

Speranza, Alessandro, 1728-1797

1764. [Mass, soprano, alto and organ]
12 p. 21½ x 28 cm.
Score of the *Kyrie, Gloria* and *Agnus* only.
Former owner: Natale Gallini (catalogue, no. 5).

MEMORIAL LIBRARY OF MUSIC, STANFORD UNIVERSITY

Speyer, Wilhelm, 1790-1878

1765. [Vois-tu sur l'élément mobile?]
[4]p. 22 x 29 cm.
Song with piano accpt.
On p. 1: 2 December 1840.

LIBRARY OF CONGRESS

Spohr, Ludwig, 1784-1859

1766. [Alruna, die Eulenkönigin]
Alruna, romantische Oper in 3 Aufzügen.
3 leaves, 493 p. 22 x 34 cm.
Full score.
This opera, composed in 1808, was never performed and has not
been published except for the Overture (as op. 21 by André in
Offenbach). See E. Schmitz, "Louis Spohr's Jugendoper Alruna,"
Zeitschrift der internationalen Musikgesellschaft, XIII (1911-12),
293-99.
For another holograph score of *Alruna,* see H. Glenewinkel, "Ver-
zeichnis des musikalischen Nachlasses von L. Spohr," *Archiv für
Musikwissenschaft,* I (1918-19), 432-36.
Former owner: Alois Fuchs.

BOSTON PUBLIC LIBRARY

1767. [Faust]
[2]p. 20 x 34 cm.
Sketch in piano-vocal score of the recitative in Act III, scene 3,
beginning: [Die letzte—ja, sie soll's ge]wesen seyn.
Former owner: Carl Pollitz.

YALE UNIVERSITY LIBRARY, SPECK COLLECTION

1768. Glockenklänge. Louis Spohr im Januar 1850.
[2]p. 34 x 27 cm.
Song with piano accpt.
First line: Sanft ertönen Morgenglocken.
Published by Ed. Bote & G. Bock in Berlin. LIBRARY OF CONGRESS

1769. Des Heilands letzte Stunden. Oratorium in zwei Theilen, gedichtet
von Friedrich Rochlitz, in Musick gesetzt von Louis Spohr.
Partitur.
2 vols. (2 leaves, 205, 142 p.) 25 x 35 cm.
Full score.
At end: Ende des Oratoriums. Cassel, im Januar 1835.
p. 133-140 contain trombone parts.

Spohr, Ludwig—*continued*

First performed Good Friday, 1835 in Kassel.
Only the piano-vocal score has been published.

LIBRARY OF CONGRESS

1770. Pot-pourri pour le violon sur deux thèmes de Mozart . . . par
Louis Spohr.
1 leaf, 14 p. 37½ x 26½ cm.
Dedicated to Count Tomasini.

MEMORIAL LIBRARY OF MUSIC, STANFORD UNIVERSITY

1771. Rätselhaft. Frühlingslied für Tenorstimme mit vierhändiger Piano-
forte-Begleitung in Musik gesetzt von Louis Spohr. Cassel im
Februar 1841.
[7]p. 28 x 38 cm.
Song with piano accpt.
First line: Der Frühling ist herangekommen.
Text by Dräxler-Manfred.
Published as no. 1 in *Die deutsche Sängerhalle*.

LIBRARY OF CONGRESS

Spontini, Gasparo Luigi Pacifico, 1774-1851

1772. [Agnes von Hohenstaufen]
Partition lre d'Agnes v. Hohenstaufen. Erster [-dritter] Act.
Primitif.
[672]p. 35 x 25½ cm.
Full score of the version performed at the Royal Opera House,
Berlin, June 12, 1829.
Incomplete, act 1 consisting almost entirely of fragments, acts 2
and 3 showing less important gaps. With the ms. are included
the score of several numbers from the original version of act 1,
as separately performed on May 28, 1827, a number of partly
identified fragments and sketches (some for the definitive version
of 1837), and a declaration by the composer, dated 1838, regard-
ing the differences between the primitive and definitive versions.

LIBRARY OF CONGRESS

1773. [Agnes von Hohenstaufen]
Feuille déchirée de ma partition d'Agnes von Hohenstaufen.
7 juillet 1837. Spontini.
[2]p. 22½ x 34 cm.   LIBRARY OF CONGRESS

1774. [Fernand Cortez]
[18]p. 34½ x 25 cm.
Fragment of the full score of no. 12, beginning: Guerrier que
l'aveugle fortune.   MRS. EUGENE ALLEN NOBLE

1775. Mignon's Lied. Kennst du das Land, etc., mit Begleitung des
Pianoforte componirt . . . von Spontini. 24ten Januar, 1830.
1 leaf, [6]p. 34 x 25½ cm.
Text by Goethe.

Spontini, Gasparo Luigi Pacifico—*continued*

Dedicated to Frau Generalin von Witzleben.
Published in 1830 by T. Trautwein in Berlin.
Former owners: Gustav Oberlaender, George T. Keating.
MEMORIAL LIBRARY OF MUSIC, STANFORD UNIVERSITY

1776. [La principessa d'Amalfi]
    [342]p. 23 x 29½ cm.
    Full score of Act I.   BROUDE BROTHERS

1777. Romance, written for and dedicated à Madame Bonaparte, com-
    posed in 1803.
    [3]p. 34 x 25½ cm.
    Song with piano accpt.
    First line: Un oiseau tout fier des leçons.
    The music is followed by a note explaining the reasons for copying
    this song and offering it to the wife of General von Witzleben,
    in Berlin, May 10, 1830.   LIBRARY OF CONGRESS

Stanford, *Sir* Charles Villiers, 1852-1924

1778. [Concerto, piano, no. 2, op. 126, C minor]
    2nd concerto for pianoforte and orchestra. C. V. Stanford, op. 216.
    1 leaf, 169 p. 34½ x 27 cm.
    Full score.
    At end: C. V. Stanford. July 28, 1911. London.
    Published in 1916 by Stainer and Bell in London.
YALE UNIVERSITY SCHOOL OF MUSIC

1779. . . . Irish rhapsody no. 5 in G minor for full orchestra composed
    by Charles V. Stanford. Op. 147.
    1 leaf, 38 p. 39 x 29 cm.
    Full score.
    Unpublished.   YALE UNIVERSITY SCHOOL OF MUSIC

Staudigl, Joseph, 1807-1861

1780. [Liebesgedanken beym Wein]
    [2]p. 25 x 30½ cm.
    Song with piano accpt.
    First line: Ich denke dein beim ersten Glas.
    At end: J. Staudigl, London, 24 June 1845.
    On p. 2 another song: *Alles ist mein.*   LIBRARY OF CONGRESS

Stavenhagen, Bernhard, 1862-1914

1781. [Concerto, piano, no. 1, op. 4, B minor]
    . . . Concert für Clavier und Orchester. Bernhard Stavenhagen.
    Op. 4 . . .
    1 leaf, 155 p. 35 x 27 cm.
    Full score.
    Published in 1895 by Ries und Erler in Berlin.
MR. HAROLD HUTCHESON

Stern, Julius, 1820-1883

1782. Divertissement pour le violon, composé par Jules G. Stern. Partition.
Op. 1.
[35]p. 31 x 23 cm.   LIBRARY OF CONGRESS

Stör, Carl, 1814-1889

1783. Peter u. Margarethe. Musik von C. Stör. Partitur.
43 p. 27 x 35 cm.   BOSTON PUBLIC LIBRARY

Stolz, Robert, 1880-

1784. [Der grosse Name, op. 63]
Incidental music of the dramatic work The Great Name. Music
by Robert Stolz.
1 leaf, 28 p. 35 x 27 cm.
Full score.   LIBRARY OF CONGRESS

Storace, Stephen, 1763-1796

1785. [Care donne che bramate]
[4]p. 24½ x 30 cm.
Full score of an aria.   LIBRARY OF CONGRESS

1786. Prigioniera abbandonata. Aria del sigr. Dn. Giacomo Insanguine
detto Monopoli. Stefano Storace Padvoni. 1777.
[16]p. 22 x 29 cm.
Full score.
At head of title: Nel *Adriano in Siria*. Sigra. de Amicis. Nel real
teatro di S. Carlo Napoli 1777.
Former owner: William H. Cummings (catalogue, no. 185).
                                                     LIBRARY OF CONGRESS

Strauss, Johann, 1825-1899

1787. Bei uns z'Haus Walzer, von Johann Strauss (Sohn).
[24]p. 26 x 33 cm.
Full score.
Published as op. 361 by August Cranz in Leipzig.
                                                     LIBRARY OF CONGRESS

1788. [Der lustige Krieg. Waltz: Nur für Natur]
[25]p. 26 x 33 cm.
Full score.
Former owner: Stefan Zweig.   GALERIE ST. ETIENNE

1789. [Der Zigeunerbaron]
9-12 p. 33 x 26 cm.
Fragment of full score from Act 3.   GALERIE ST. ETIENNE

Strauss, Josef, 1827-1870

1790. Irenen Polka française für ein ganzes Orchester von Josef Strauss.
  [5]p. 25½ x 33 cm.
  Full score.
  Published as op. 113 in 1862 by Carl Haslinger in Vienna.
  Former owner: Wilhelm Heyer (catalogue, vol. IV, no. 1566).
  GALERIE ST. ETIENNE

Strauss, Richard, 1864-1949

1791. [Die aegyptische Helena]
  64 p. 8 x 13 cm.
  Sketches.
  Inscription to Gustav Brecher, Garmisch, 24 Juni 1927.
  Facsimile of two pages in *Notes*, VII (1949-50), 209.
  HEINEMAN FOUNDATION

1792. [Die aegyptische Helena]
  [7]p. 25½ x 32 cm.
  Voice part only, with text (the piano part not filled in) of Helena's
    aria in Act I, scene 1, beginning: Ein Feuer brennt, ein Tisch
    ist gedeckt.
  At head of title: Der ersten Helena: Elisabeth zur Erinnerung an
    den 27 März 1926.
  Written for a private performance by Elisabeth Schumann with the
    composer at the piano, two years before the first performance of
    the opera.
  Former owner: Elisabeth Schumann.   CURTIS INSTITUTE OF MUSIC

1793. Einerlei von A. von Arnim.
  p. 4 of his *Schlechtes Wetter*.
  Song with piano accpt.
  First line: Ihr Mund ist stets derselbe.
  At end: Richard Strauss. 24 Juni 1918. Herrn Prof. Dr. Franz
    Muncker zu freundlicher Erinnerung.
  Published as no. 3 of op. 69, *Fünf kleine Lieder,* in 1919 by Adolph
    Fürstner in Berlin.
  MEMORIAL LIBRARY OF MUSIC, STANFORD UNIVERSITY

1794. Fanfare zur Eröffnung der Musikwoche der Stadt Wien Septem-
    ber 1924 von Richard Strauss . . .
  1 leaf, 6 p. 35½ x 27 cm.
  Full score (6 trumpets, 8 horns, 6 trombones, 2 bass tubas, 2
    tympani).
  At end: Garmisch 9 September 1924 . . . Richard Strauss.
  Former owner: David J. Bach.
  Unpublished.   MR. SAMUEL R. WACHTELL

Strauss, Richard—*continued*

1795. [Feuersnot. Op. 50]
Richard Strauss. Skizze zu Konrads Monolog aus Feuersnot.
[4]p. 35½ x 27 cm.
Sketches.
Former owners: Edward Speyer, George T. Keating.
Facsimile of one page in Van Patten, *Catalogue*, p. 253.
MEMORIAL LIBRARY OF MUSIC, STANFORD UNIVERSITY

1796. Geistlicher Maien. Text und Melodie nach dem Mainzer Cantual
von 1605, Bearbeitung von Richard Strauss.
[3]p. 35 x 27 cm.
For men's chorus unaccompanied.
At end: Berlin, 12 November 1905. Richard Strauss.
DR. FRANK BLACK

1797. Guck, guck. Nach Forster II (1540). Bearbeitung von Richard
Strauss.
p. 3-4 of his *Hüt du dich!*
For men's chorus unaccompanied.
At end: Berlin, 14 November, 1905. Richard Strauss
DR. FRANK BLACK

1798. Die heilige drei Könige aus Morgenland (Gedicht von Heinrich
Heine) für eine hohe Singstimme mit Orchesterbegleitung com-
ponirt von Richard Strauss. Op. 56, no. 6 . . .
[2], 12 p. 35 x 27 cm.
Originally written for voice and piano.
At end: Berlin-Charlottenburg 7 Oktober 1906.
Inscription to Willy Levin, Berlin, 10 Januar 1913.
Published in this form in 1906 by Ed. Bote & G. Bock in Berlin.
GALERIE ST. ETIENNE

1799. Hüt du dich! Nach Berg und Newber (ca. 1542). Bearbeitung
von Richard Strauss.
[4]p. 35 x 27 cm.
For men's chorus unaccompanied.
At end: Berlin, 13 November 1905. Richard Strauss.
On p. 3-4 his *Guck, guck*.
DR. FRANK BLACK

1800. "Kling! . . . (Karl Henckell)" Richard Strauss, Op. 48, No. III.
[4]p. 25½ x 32 cm.
Song with piano accpt.
First line: Kling! Meine Seele gibt reinen Ton.
At end: Charlottenburg, 30 September 1900.
Published as no. 3 of op. 48, *Fünf Lieder*, in 1901 by Adolph
Fürstner in Berlin.
Former owner: Wilhelm Heyer (catalogue, vol. IV, no. 1664).
Facsimile of p. 1 *ibid.*, plate LXIV.
LIBRARY OF CONGRESS

Strauss, Richard—*continued*

1801. Zwei Lieder von Richard Strauss.
   6 p. 27 x 36½ cm.
   Songs with piano accpt.
   Contents. — *Die erwachte Rose* (Fr. Sallet). — *Begegnung* (Fr. Gruppe).
   First lines: Die Knospe träumte vom Sonnenschein; Die Trepp' hinunter geschwungen.
   Unpublished.   MRS. CHARLOTTE A. KLEISS

1802. . . . Rothe Rosen, Gedicht von Karl Stieler, componirt von Richard Strauss.
   [3]p. 26½ x 36½ cm.
   Song with piano accpt.
   Dedicated to Fräulein Lotti Speyer.
   At end: 11 September 1883.
   First line: Weisst du die Rose, die du mir gegeben.
   Unpublished.   MRS. CHARLOTTE A. KLEISS

1803. Salome. Richard Strauss.
   [1]p. 35½ x 27 cm.
   First page of the full score.
   At end: Begonnen am 27 November 1904.   MR. ARTURO TOSCANINI

1804. [Schlechtes Wetter]
   H. Heine. Das ist ein schlechtes Wetter.
   [4]p. 36 x 26½ cm.
   Song with piano accpt.
   Published as no. 5 of op. 69, *Fünf kleine Lieder,* in 1919 by Adolph Fürstner in Berlin.
   On p. 2 his *Waldesfahrt* and on p. 4 his *Einerlei.*
               MEMORIAL LIBRARY OF MUSIC, STANFORD UNIVERSITY

1805. Sie wissen's nicht. (Panizza).
   [4]p. 27 x 36 cm.
   Song with piano accpt.
   First line: Es wohnt ein kleines Vögelein.
   Published as no. 5 of op. 49, *Acht Lieder,* in 1902 by Adolph Fürstner in Berlin.
   On p. 3 his *Waldseligkeit.*
   Former owners: Edward Speyer, George T. Keating.
               MEMORIAL LIBRARY OF MUSIC, STANFORD UNIVERSITY

1806. Sinnspruch (Göthe, westöstlicher Divan). Richard Strauss.
   [3]p. 36 x 27½ cm.
   Song with piano accpt.
   First line: Alle Menschen, gross und klein.
   Inscribed to Rudolf Mosse.
   At end: Garmisch, 24. Juni 1919.
   Apparently unpublished.   HEINEMAN FOUNDATION

Strauss, Richard—*continued*

1807. [Waldesfahrt]
> p. 2 of his *Schlechtes Wetter.*
> Song with piano accpt., first draft.
> Text by Heinrich Heine.
> First line: Mein Wagen rollet langsam.
> Published as no. 4 of op. 69, *Fünf kleine Lieder,* in 1919 by Adolph
> Fürstner in Berlin.
>> MEMORIAL LIBRARY OF MUSIC, STANFORD UNIVERSITY

1808. Waldseligkeit.
> p. 3 of his *Sie wissen's nicht.*
> Song with piano accpt.
> Text by Richard Dehmel.
> First line: Der Wald beginnt zu rauschen.
> Published as no. 1 of op. 49, *Acht Lieder,* in 1902 by Adolph
> Fürstner in Berlin.
> Former owners: Edward Speyer, George T. Keating.
>> MEMORIAL LIBRARY OF MUSIC, STANFORD UNIVERSITY

Stravinskiĭ, Igor' Feodorovich, 1882-

1809. Apollon-Musagète. Ballet en deux tableaux. Premier tableau
(Prologue) [-Second tableau]
> 70 p. 36 x 28 cm.
> Full score.
> At end: Nice, le 20 janvier 1928. Igor Strawinsky.
> Commissioned by the Elizabeth Sprague Coolidge Foundation and
> first performed at the Library of Congress, April 27, 1928.
> Published in 1928 by Edition russe de musique in Berlin.
>> LIBRARY OF CONGRESS, COOLIDGE FOUNDATION

1810. Concertino composé pour le quattuor [!] de Flonzaley. Partition
d'ensemble et réduction pour piano à 4 m.
> 1 leaf, [23]p. 32½ x 23 cm.
> Dedicated to André de Caplet. Garches, Oct. 1920.
> At end: I. Strawinsky. Carautec-Garches. juillet-août-septembre.
> Terminé le 24 sept. à Garches.
> Published in 1924 by Wilhelm Hansen in Copenhagen.
>> LIBRARY OF CONGRESS

1811. [Concerto, orchestra ("Dumbarton Oaks")]
> Dumbarton Oaks. 8-5-38. Concerto en mi pour orch. de chambre.
> Igor Strawinsky, 1937-38.
> 109 [i.e. 111]p. 35½ x 27 cm.
> Full score.
> At end: I. Strawinsky, Paris, 29 mars 38.
> Published in 1938 by Schott & Co. in London.
> Former owners: Mr. and Mrs. Robert Woods Bliss.
>> HARVARD UNIVERSITY, DUMBARTON OAKS

Stravīnskiĭ, Igor′ Feodorovīch—*continued*

1812. Concerto pour piano et orchestre d'harmonie . . .
   1 leaf, 95 p. 35 x 26½ cm.
   Full score.
   At end: Igor Strawinsky. Biarritz. 21 août 1924.
   Dedicated to Mme. Natalie Koussevitzki, 1931.
   Published in 1926 by Russischer Musikverlag in Paris and Berlin.

1813. [Concerto, violin, D major]
   Violin-Concerto in D. I. Stravinsky 1931.
   1 leaf, [91]p. 26 x 35 cm.
   Full score.
   Each movement paged separately.
   At end: Igor Stravinsky. Voreppe (Isère) la Vezonnière 13 25
   sept. 1931.
   Published in 1931 by B. Schott's Söhne in Mainz.

1814. [Mavra]
   Igor Stravinsky. Mavra, opera-bouffa en un acte, texte d'après
   une nouvelle de Alexandre Pouchkine par Boris Kokhno.
   1 leaf, 129 p. 26½ x 35 cm.
   Full score.
   Title-page in Russian and French.
   First performed in public June 2, 1922 in Paris.

1815. Persephone, mélodrame en trois parties, texte d'André Gide. Mu-
   sique d'Igor Stravinsky. Partition d'orchestre.
   1 leaf, 226 p. 40 x 29 cm.
   Full score.
   At end: Igor Stravinsky. Paris le 24 janv. 1934.
   Published in 1934 by Édition russe de musique in Berlin.

1816. Souvenir d'une marche boche.
   [7]p. 14 x 20½ cm.
   For piano 2 hands.
   At end: Igor Strawinsky. Morges 1 Sept. 1915.
   Unpublished.
   Former owner: Nicholas Nabokoff.

1817. Symphonie de psaumes; musique composée par Igor Stravinsky.
   Manuscrit de la partition d'orchestre . . . Dédicace: Cette symphonie composée à la gloire de Dieu est dédiée au "Boston Symphonie Orchestra" à l'occasion du cinquantenaire de son existence.
   Igor Stravinsky. 1930.
   1 leaf, [60]p. 55 x 24½ cm.
   Each movement separately paged.

Stravīnskiĭ, Igor' Feodorovīch—*continued*

At end: Igor Stravinsky. Nice 1930.
Published in 1931 by Édition russe de musique in Berlin.

BOSTON SYMPHONY ORCHESTRA

Strimer, Joseph, 1881-

1818.   Horovod (Round dance with singing) by Joseph Strimer . . .
1 leaf, [5]p. 30½ x 23 cm.
For 4-part mixed chorus unaccompanied, Russian text.

LIBRARY OF CONGRESS

Stuntz, Joseph Hartmann, 1793-1859

1819.   Cantata posta in musica del mro. J. H. Stuntz. 1822. Manoscritto.
[91]p. 23½ x 30½ cm.
Full score (for mixed chorus and orchestra).   LIBRARY OF CONGRESS

Süssmayr, Franz Xaver, 1766-1803

1820.   [Der Spiegel von Arkadien]
[28]p. 22½ x 31 cm.
Full score of a soprano aria composed for the debut of Pauline
Anna Milder-Hauptmann in this opera in Vienna in 1803.
Former owners: Alois Fuchs, Ferdinand Simon Gassner, William
Pole.   MEMORIAL LIBRARY OF MUSIC, STANFORD UNIVERSITY

Sullivan, *Sir* Arthur Seymour, 1842-1900

1821.   [The foresters]
[83]p. 27 x 34 cm.
Full score (omitting voice parts) of the incidental music to the play.
Text by Tennyson.
First performed March 17, 1892, at Daly's Theatre in New York.
Note on p. 1: Copy no. 3 complete without voice parts.
Former owner: George T. Keating.

MEMORIAL LIBRARY OF MUSIC, STANFORD UNIVERSITY

1822.   [The foresters]
[82]p. 28 x 35 cm.
Full score, as in preceding number.
Former owners: Ada Rehan, Augustin Daly, Mrs. D. S. Blossom.

WESTERN RESERVE UNIVERSITY LIBRARY

1823.   An idyll for the violoncello composed . . . by Arthur Sullivan.
31 July 1865.
1 leaf, [2]p. 36½ x 26 cm.
Dedicated to Col. P. Paget (Farnham).

MEMORIAL LIBRARY OF MUSIC, STANFORD UNIVERSITY

1824.   Sing unto the Lord. A. Sullivan.
[6]p. 30 x 24½ cm.
For 4-part mixed chorus and piano or organ accpt.
A marginal note on p. 1 reads: This anthem in the handwriting of

Sullivan, *Sir Arthur Seymour—continued*

> Arthur Sullivan was composed by him when a boy in the choir of the Chapel Royal and given by him to me. William H. Cummings.

Former owner: William H. Cummings (catalogue, no. 187).

1825. [Trial by Jury]
[4]p. 34 x 39 cm.
Sketches for practically the whole work, although in many respects the final version differs from them.

Szántó, Theodor, 1877-1934

1826. . . . Nuits blanches pour petit orchestre . . . Théodore Szántó, Paris 1931. Partition d'orchestre.
1 leaf, 7 p. 36 x 27½ cm.
Dedicated to Mrs. E. S. Coolidge.
On p. 1: Théodore Szántó. Paris, 1924-25.

1827. . . . Suite choréographique pour quatuor à cordes (4 pièces). Théodore Szántó.
1 leaf, 10 p. 34 x 27 cm.
Score.
Dedicated to Mrs. E. S. Coolidge.
First movement signed and dated: Th. Szántó, Paris, 1929.

Tailleferre, Germaine, 1892-

1828. [Allegro for piano]
[6]p. 36 x 26½ cm.
Dedicated to Jane Mortier.
On cover: St. Jean de Luz, Oct. 1920.

Tansa, Leopold

1829. Quartett in H moll für 2 Violinen, Viola und Bass von L. Tansa, mpria.
[43]p. 23 x 31 cm.
Score.
At end: Fine. Tansa mpria im 8br 1828.
Former owner: Alois Fuchs.

Tansman, Alexandre, 1897-

1830. Burlesque.
[3]p. 35 x 26 cm.
For piano 2 hands.

1831. Mazurka N 2 (p. piano). Alexandre Tansman . . .
[2]p. 35 x 27 cm.
Published by Max Eschig in Paris.

1832. [Quartet, strings, no. 2]
... IIme quatuor à cordes. Alexandre Tansman (1922).
23 p. 35 x 27 cm.
Score.
Published in 1924 by Sénart in Paris.   LEAGUE OF COMPOSERS

1833. ... Serenade (N 3) for orchestra. Alexandre Tansman.
[13]p. 54 x 34 cm.
Full score.
Dedicated to Mrs. E. S. Coolidge.
At end: Alexandre Tansman. June-July 1943, Hollywood, Cal.
LIBRARY OF CONGRESS, COOLIDCE FOUNDATION

1834. ... Sonata n. 4 p. piano. A. Tansman. Premières esquisses.
[10]p. 35½ x 27½ cm.
On margin of p. 1: Mrs. Elizabeth Sprague Coolidge birthday
sonata, Oct. 30—1941.
LIBRARY OF CONGRESS, COOLIDGE FOUNDATION

1835. ... Sonata no. 4 for piano. Alexandre Tansman.
[8]p. 35½ x 27½ cm.
First version.
At end: Alexandre Tansman. New York. September 1941.
LIBRARY OF CONGRESS, COOLIDGE FOUNDATION

1836. ... Sonata n. 4 pour piano. Alexandre Tansman.
[13]p. 35 x 27 cm.
Revised version.
On p. 12: New York, Sept. 1941.
Published in 1942 by Associated Music Publishers in New York.
LIBRARY OF CONGRESS, COOLIDGE FOUNDATION

1837. ... Symphonie en ré. Symphony in d (N 5). 1942 ...
30 p. 54 x 34 cm.
Full score.
At end: Alexandre Tansman. Hollywood. 3 juillet 1942.
LIBRARY OF CONGRESS

1838. ... "Triptyque" pour quatuor (ou orchestre) à cordes. ...
1 leaf, 15 p. 35 x 27 cm.
Score.
Dedicated to Mrs. E. S. Coolidge.
At end: Alexandre Tansman. Paris. IX-XII-1930.
Published in 1931 by Max Eschig in Paris.
LIBRARY OF CONGRESS, COOLIDGE FOUNDATION

Taubert, (Karl Gottfried) Wilhelm, 1811-1891

1839. Abendreihn (Wilhelm Müller). Wilhelm Taubert.
[3]p. 29½ x 23 cm.
Song with piano accpt.
First line: Guten Abend, lieber Mondenschein.
LIBRARY OF CONGRESS

1840. [Tutti frutti, nos. 1-2]
      [10]p. 26½ x 34 cm.
  Tempo di marcia and *Polacca,* for piano 2 hands.
  Published as nos. 1 and 2 of *Tutti frutti, collection de morceaux brillants et non difficiles pour pianoforte* in 1836 by T. Trautwein in Berlin.
  Former owner: Joseph Muller.   NEW YORK PUBLIC LIBRARY

Tausig, Karl, 1841-1871

1841. Liszt, Franz, 1811-1886.
      ... Tasso, lamento e trionfo; symphonische Dichtung von Franz Liszt, für Clavier gesetzt von Carl Tausig.
      6 leaves. 34 x 27 cm.
  Dedicated to Eduard Lassen.
  Incomplete; lacks last 11 bars.   LIBRARY OF CONGRESS

Taylor, Samuel Coleridge-, 1875-1912

1842. Genevieve.
      [5]p. 34 x 27 cm.
  Song with piano accpt.
  Text by the composer.
  First line: Maid of my love, sweet Genevieve.
  Unpublished.
  Former owner: Julian Edwards.
    NEW YORK PUBLIC LIBRARY, MUSIC LIBRARY

1843. Hiawatha's wedding-feast. A cantata for tenor solo, chorus and orchestra. The words written by H. W. Longfellow. The music composed by S. Coleridge-Taylor. Full score.
      [1], 207 p. 35 x 27 cm.
  Published in 1898 by Novello & Co. in London.
    BOSTON PUBLIC LIBRARY

1844. If I could love thee. Song. S. Coleridge-Taylor.
      [5]p. 34 x 27 cm.
  Song with piano accpt.
  Text by Louise Alston Burleigh.
  Published in 1905 by William Maxwell Music Co. in New York.
  Former owner: Julian Edwards.
    NEW YORK PUBLIC LIBRARY, MUSIC LIBRARY

1845. If I could love thee. Song. S. Coleridge-Taylor.
      1 leaf, [4]p. 30 x 24 cm.   MR. ARTHUR BILLINGS HUNT

1846. "Keep me from sinkin' down." Traditional negro melody transcribed for violin and orchestra by S. Coleridge-Taylor.
      1 leaf, [10]p. 36 x 27 cm.
  Full score.
  Unpublished.   YALE UNIVERSITY SCHOOL OF MUSIC

Taylor, Samuel Coleridge- —*continued*

1847. Love's passing.
       [4]p. 34 x 27 cm.
       Song with piano accpt.
       Text by Louise Alston Burleigh.
       First line: The cricket sings in the nearby wood.
       Unpublished.
       Former owner: Julian Edwards.
                                    NEW YORK PUBLIC LIBRARY, MUSIC LIBRARY

1848. "Red o' the dawn (Dramatic ballad for voice & orchestra). Alfred
       Noyes.
       [12]p. 35 x 27 cm.
       Reduction for voice and piano.
       Published as op. 81, no. 2, by Boosey and Co. in London.
                                                  NEW YORK PUBLIC LIBRARY

1849. The violet bank. S. Coleridge-Taylor.
       [5]p. 34 x 27 cm.
       Song with piano accpt.
       Text by "Darling."
       First line: I know a bank where the violets grow.
       Unpublished.
       Former owner: Julian Edwards.
                                    NEW YORK PUBLIC LIBRARY, MUSIC LIBRARY

1850. A vision. Song. S. Coleridge-Taylor.
       [4]p. 34 x 27 cm.
       Text by Louise Alston Burleigh.
       Song with piano accpt.
       First line: My wildest dream is just to touch thy hand.
       At end: S. C. T. Jan. 16 1905.
       Published in 1905 by William Maxwell Music Co. in New York.
       Former owner: Julian Edwards.
                                    NEW YORK PUBLIC LIBRARY, MUSIC LIBRARY

Tchaikovsky, Peter Ilyitch
see Chaikovskii, Petr Il'ich, 1840-1893

Tertis, Lionel, 1876-

1851. Variations on the passacaglia of Handel (from suite no. 7) for
       two violas. Lionel Tertis . . . March 1935.
       1 leaf, 11p. 36 x 27 cm.
       Dedicated to Mrs. E. S. Coolidge.
                                    LIBRARY OF CONGRESS, COOLIDGE FOUNDATION

Thalberg, Sigismund, 1812-1871

1852. Cristina di Svezia, tragedia lirica del cav. Felice Romani, posta in
       musica da S. Thalberg, da rappresentarsi nell' I. R. Teatro di
       Corte a Porta Carinzia la primavera 1855.

Thalberg, Sigismund—*continued*

    2 v. (250, 212 p.) 35½ x 27 cm.
Full score of the Prologue and Act 2.
First performed June 3, 1855 at the Kärntnertor Theater in Vienna.
LIBRARY OF CONGRESS

1853. Weber, Karl Maria (Friedrich Ernst, Freiherr) von, 1786-1826.
    [Der Freischütz]
    Duo. "Freyschütz" de Weber.
    5p. 27 x 35 cm.
Arranged for piano by Thalberg.
At end: S. Thalberg, Paris, mars 1853.
From Act 2 (Schelm, halt' fest).   LIBRARY OF CONGRESS

1854. Pollacca.
    1 leaf. 23½ x 30½ cm.
For piano.
At end: S. Thalberg. Zur Erinnerung an die Rauch Matinées.
    Frankfurt, 11ten Januar 1841.
Former owner: Edward Speyer.   LIBRARY OF CONGRESS

1855. Romance sans paroles pour le piano à quatre mains par S. Thalberg.
    [3]p. 27 x 35 cm.
Published by M. Schlesinger in Paris.
Former owner: Joseph Muller.   NEW YORK PUBLIC LIBRARY

Thomas, Charles Louis Ambroise, 1811-1896

1856. [Hamlet]
    [12]p. 32 x 27 cm.
Full score (?) of Act 2, scene 2, no. 12: O mortelle offense.
MEMORIAL LIBRARY OF MUSIC, STANFORD UNIVERSITY

1857. [Hamlet]
    [36]p. 32 x 27 cm.
Full score(?) of Act 3, scene between Hamlet and his mother.
MEMORIAL LIBRARY OF MUSIC, STANFORD UNIVERSITY

1858. [Le songe d'une nuit d'été]
    7 p. 35 x 27 cm.
Full score of the final duet of Act 2.
MEMORIAL LIBRARY OF MUSIC, STANFORD UNIVERSITY

1859. [La tempête. Ballet fantastique]
    9 p. 35½ x 27 cm.
Piano reduction of the *Introduction* to Act 2, tableau 3 (*Sommeil de Mirande*).
MEMORIAL LIBRARY OF MUSIC, STANFORD UNIVERSITY

1860. [Waltz, piano, D sharp minor]
    Valse.
    [4]p. 35 x 26½ cm.
MEMORIAL LIBRARY OF MUSIC, STANFORD UNIVERSITY

Toch, Ernest, 1887-

1861. Streichquartett op. 28 "auf den Namen 'Bass'" komp. 1921-22.
score (1 leaf, 47 p.) and parts. 32½ x 26 cm.
Published in 1923 by Tischer & Jagenberg in Cologne.

MR. JOHN BASS

Tomášek, Jan Václav, 1774-1850

1862. An mein theueres Vaterland von Carl Victor Hausgirg, für zwei
Tenore und zwei Bässe componirt von Wenzel Johann Toma-
schek.
[7]p. 21½ x 17½ cm.
First line: O schönes, wunderreiches Land. LIBRARY OF CONGRESS

Tosti, *Sir* Francesco Paolo, 1846-1916

1863. Home again! Song without words, by F. Paolo Tosti. London,
October 1896.
1 leaf, 9 p. 30 x 24 cm.
For piano. CURTIS INSTITUTE OF MUSIC

1864. La serenata del beduino. Parole di F. B. Torricelli dall' inglese di
Bayard Taylor. Musica di Fsco. Paolo Tosti.
[4]p. 27 x 38 cm.
Song with piano accpt. BOSTON PUBLIC LIBRARY

1865. T'amo ancora. Valzer-cantabile. Parole del Vittorio Bacci. Musica
di Francesco Paolo Tosti. Ancona 10 agosto 71.
[9]p. 27 x 37 cm.
Song with piano accpt.
Former owner: Mrs. A. M. Ticknor.
Published by Ricordi & Co. in Milan. BOSTON PUBLIC LIBRARY

Tours, Berthold, 1838-1897

1866. . . . Far from my heavenly home. Sacred song, words by the Rev.
H. F. Lyte, music by Berthold Tours.
6 p. 34 x 26½ cm.
Song with piano accpt.
At end: London September 1888. Berthold Tours.
Published in 1888 by Beal & Co. in London.
Bound with this is an autograph arrangement of the same song as
an anthem for 4 voices, with organ accpt. It is a fragment (50
bars) and the organ part is not filled in.
Former owner: Stephen Decatur Smith.
UNIVERSITY OF PENNSYLVANIA LIBRARY

Tremblay, Amédée

1867. Suite de quatre pièces pour grand orgue par Amédée Tremblay . . .
[24]p. 31½ x 24 cm.
Published in 1924 by J. Fischer & Bro. in New York.
LIBRARY OF CONGRESS

Tschaikowsky, Peter Iljitsch
see Chaikovskiĭ, Petr Il'ich, 1840-1893

Uray, (Ernst) Ludwig, 1906-
1868.   Suite für Violine und Klavier.
Score (26 p.) and part. 33 x 26 cm.
Dedicated to Mrs. E. S. Coolidge.
A second autograph score and part.
LIBRARY OF CONGRESS, COOLIDGE FOUNDATION

Vaccai, Nicola, 1790-1848
1869.   Dunque sia ver degg'io abbandonar.
[4]p. 21 x 32 cm.
Full score of a recitative.   THE PIERPONT MORGAN LIBRARY

1870.   Improperi per l'adorazione della S. Croce.
[4]p. 22 x 29 cm.
For 4-part chorus and organ.   THE PIERPONT MORGAN LIBRARY

Van Lier, Bertus, 1906-
1871.   Sonatina no. 2. Piano solo. Bertus van Lier.
10 p. 34 x 24 cm.   NEW YORK PUBLIC LIBRARY, MUSIC LIBRARY

Verdi, (Fortunio) Giuseppe (Francesco), 1813-1901
1872.   [Falstaff]
[2]p. 39½ x 27½ cm.
First draft of the beginning of Act I, scene 1: O la, tutti i servi.
MR. WALTER TOSCANINI

1873.   Gesù mori.
[6]p. 23½ x 29 cm.
Sketches for four sacred vocal duets with organ accpt.
Contents.—*Gesù mori.*—No. 24. *Volgi, Dei, volgi a me il tuo figlio.*—
No. 27. *L'alt' impresa è già computa.*—No. 28. *Jesus autem emissa
voce expiravit.*
Former owner: Ricardo Doego.   LIBRARY OF CONGRESS

1874.   Scala enigmatica armonizzata à quattro voci.
[5]p. 15 x 27 cm.
A setting of the *Ave Maria* for 4-part mixed chorus.
The word *parti* replaced by *voci,* and *Ave Maria* cancelled in the
title.
Published as *Ave Maria,* no. 1 of *Quattro pezzi sacri* in 1898 by
G. Ricordi in Milan.   MR. ARTURO TOSCANINI

Viardot-García, (Michelle) Pauline, 1821-1910
1875.   Etoile du soir.
[1]p. 22½ x 27 cm.
Song with piano accpt.

Viardot-García, (Michelle) Pauline—*continued*

First line: Etoile, belle étoile.
At end: Pauline Garcia. Francfort le 18 août 1838.

1876. Der Gärtner. Lied von Mörike, Musik von Pauline Viardot . . .
[3]p. 35 x 27 cm.
Song with piano accpt.
First line: Auf ihrem Leibrösslein.
Published by Ries & Erler in Berlin.
Former owner: Joseph Muller.

1877. [Vocalises and cadenzas for various opera arias]
23 numbered leaves. 12½ x 19½ cm.
Written for Frau Gertrud Seeger-Engel.

Vieuxtemps, Henri, 1820-1881

1878. Duo concertant sur les thèmes de Don Juan de Mozart [op. 20]
[27]p. 32½ x 24 cm.
For violin and piano.
Former owner: Arthur F. Hill.

1879. [Fantaisie-Caprice, violin and orchestra]
[71]p. 32 x 24½ cm.
Full score.
At end: Fini St. Petersbourg ce 21 février 1840. H. Vieuxtemps.
Published ca. 1841 by B. Schott's Söhne in Mainz.
Facsimile of last 3 pages in J. T. Radoux, *Vieuxtemps, sa vie, ses
oeuvres.*
Inscribed to Jean Radoux, Paris, July 1, 1870.

Vogel, Vladimir Rudolfovich, 1896-

1880. "Losung!" ("Devise")·. . . von Wladimir Vogel. Strasbourg 1934 . . .
23 p. 34 x 27 cm.
Full score (brass and percussion).

Vogl, Johann Michael, 1768-1840

1881. Der Rattenfänger von Göthe.
[5]p. 25½ x 31 cm.
Song with piano accpt.
First line: Ich bin der wohlbekannte Sänger.
Published by August Cranz in Hamburg.
Former owner: Max Friedländer.

Vogler, Georg Joseph, Abt, 1749-1814

1882. Benedictus.
[8]p. 23 x 30½ cm.
Score (solo voice and string orchestra).
At end: 29 7br [1801] G. V.
Former owner: Alfred Bovet de Valentigny.

Vogler, Georg Joseph, Abt—*continued*

1883. ... Divertissement von Abt Vogler.
79 leaves. 20 x 34 cm.
Full scores of 30 short compositions.   LIBRARY OF CONGRESS

Vranken, Josef, 1870-1948

1884. Missa pro defunctis. Von einfacher Orgelbegleitung versehen durch
P. J. Jos. Vrancken.
[20]p. 34 x 25 cm.
Publisher's note says: Gregorian Requiem (Vatican version) harmonized by P. J. Jos. Vrancken ...
Published in 1909 by J. Fischer & Bro. in New York.
LIBRARY OF CONGRESS

1885. Missa festiva. P. J. Jos. Vranken op. 36.
[25]p. 33½ x 25 cm.
For soprano, tenor and bass with organ accpt.
Published in 1908 by J. Fischer & Bro. in New York.
LIBRARY OF CONGRESS

Volkmann, (Friedrich) Robert, 1815-1883

1886. Die Bekehrte von Göthe, für Sopran mit Clavierbegleitung componirt von Robert Volkmann.
[1], 6 p. 32½ x 26 cm.
Song with piano accpt.
First line: Bei dem Glanz der Abendröthe.
Published as op. 54 ca. 1867 by B. Schott's Söhne in Mainz.
YALE UNIVERSITY LIBRARY, SPECK COLLECTION

Wagner, Ernst David, 1806-1883

1887. Hymnus componirt von E. D. Wagner. Berlin den 2. Juni 1837. Partitura.
[22]p. 33 x 26 cm.
For 4-part chorus and orchestra.
Former owner: Franz Commer.   BOSTON PUBLIC LIBRARY

1888. Lied "Sie sollen ihn nicht haben" von Nic. Becker für eine Singstimme mit Begleitung des Pianoforte componirt von E. D. Wagner. Berlin d. 3. Decbr. 1840.
[3]p. 34 x 27 cm.
Caption title: *Lied. Der deutsche Rhein.*   LIBRARY OF CONGRESS

Wagner, Richard, 1813-1883

1889. Les adieux de Marie Stuart. Paroles de Béranger. Musique par Richard Wagner.
1 leaf, [10]p. 34 x 26 cm.
Song with piano accpt.
First line: Adieu, charmant pays de France.
Composed in 1840; published in 1914 in his Werke, vol. XV, no. 10.
Former owner: Doris Gras.
MEMORIAL LIBRARY OF MUSIC, STANFORD UNIVERSITY

Wagner, Richard—*continued*

1890. [Albumblatt, piano, C major]
      In das Album der Fürstin M. (1861) Richard Wagner.
      [2]p. 30 x 24 cm.
      Written for Pauline Metternich.
      Published in 1871 by E. W. Fritzsch in Leipzig.
      Facsimile of p. 1 in Parke-Bernet sale catalogue 318, no. 570.
      Former owner: Hugo Riesenfeld.   PRIVATE COLLECTOR

1891. Attente (Victor Hugo). Paris, 1839.
      [3]p. 33½ x 25 cm.
      Song with piano accpt.
      First line: Monte, écureuil, monte au grand chêne.
      Published as supplement to *Europa, Chronik der gebildeten Welt*,
      in 1842, Band I, after p. 368.
      Werke, vol. XV, no. 13 (date of composition incorrectly given as
      1840).
      Bound with his *Der Tannenbaum*.   HEINEMAN FOUNDATION

1892. "Dors mon enfant!" (namenloser Dichter). Paris, 1839.
      [3]p. 33½ x 25 cm.
      Song with piano accpt.
      First line: Dors entre mes bras, enfant plein de charmes.
      Published as supplement to *Europa, Chronik der gebildeten Welt*,
      in 1841, Band III, after p. 144.
      Werke, Band XV, no. 11 (date of composition incorrectly given as
      1840).
      Bound with his *Der Tannenbaum*.   HEINEMAN FOUNDATION

1893. [Eine Faust-Ouvertüre]
      [2]p. 36 x 27 cm.
      Sketch for piano.   YALE UNIVERSITY LIBRARY, SPECK COLLECTION

1894. [Die Feen]
      Scene u. Arie. Ada, Farganza u. Zemira treten auf.
      [6]p. 34 x 28½ cm. and orchestral parts.
      Reduction for voice and piano of the 2nd act terzett beginning: "O
      grausame" and of Ada's scene and aria, "Weh mir, so nah' die
      fürchterliche Stunde."
      Corresponds almost exactly to p. 191-206 in the piano-vocal score.
      At end: Leipzig. Richard Wagner.
      Former owners: J. A. Tichatschek, Mrs. Mary Burrell (catalogue,
      no. 45, 2), Mrs. Mary Louise Zimbalist.
                                          CURTIS INSTITUTE OF MUSIC

1895. [Die Feen]
      Scene u. Arie aus der Oper die Feen von Richard W.
      [6]p. 23 x 31½ cm.
      Voice part only, with cues.

Music substantially the same as the preceding ms., with text partially changed.

Former owners: Mrs. Mary Burrell (catalogue, no. 45, 3), Mrs. Mary Louise Zimbalist.   CURTIS INSTITUTE OF MUSIC

1896.   Festmarsch.
33 p. 35 x 27 cm.
Full score.
Marginal notes in the hand of Theodore Thomas.
Published as *Grosser Festmarsch zur Eröffnung der hundertjähriger Gedenkenfeier der Unabhängigkeits-Erklärung der Vereinigten Staaten von Nordamerika* in 1876 by B. Schott's Söhne in Mainz.
Werke, vol. XVIII, no. 4.
Former owner: Theodore Thomas.   NEWBERRY LIBRARY

1897.   [Der fliegende Holländer]
[2]p. 36 x 26½ cm.
Incomplete sketch, in piano-vocal score, of the duet in Act II, scene 2, beginning: [Erik]: ... spricht? [Senta]: Wie? Zweifelst du an meinen Herzen?
Facsimile in *Musical Quarterly*, XIX (1933), 29.
    LIBRARY OF CONGRESS

1898.   [Der fliegende Holländer]
[2]p. 25 x 27 cm.
Sketches for Act I, the duet between the Holländer and Daland, and instrumental interludes.
Former owner: Joseph Muller.   NEW YORK PUBLIC LIBRARY

1899.   [Der fliegende Holländer. Senta's ballad]
Ballade.
[5]p. 35 x 27 cm.
Full score of the first 29 bars, with French text, and in A minor instead of G minor.
Former owner: E. W. Rietz (many notes in his hand, and dated 1842).   NEW YORK PUBLIC LIBRARY

1900.   [Der fliegende Holländer. Senta's ballad]
[20]p. 35 x 26½ cm.
Full score, beginning 11 bars before the ballad, and ending with Erik's exclamation, "Senta!"
Former owners: J. A. Tichatschek, Mrs. Mary Burrell (catalogue, no. 113), Mrs. Mary Louise Zimbalist.
    CURTIS INSTITUTE OF MUSIC

1901.   [Der fliegende Holländer. Senta's ballad]
[1]p. 33 x 24½ cm.
Short score of an introduction and ending to the ballad, both differing from the published score. The vocal cue indicates that the 3rd stanza had not yet been written.
Former owners: Natalie Planer, Mrs. Mary Burrell (catalogue, no. 114), Mrs. Mary Louise Zimbalist.   CURTIS INSTITUTE OF MUSIC

1902. [Fugue, F major]
[3]p. 24 x 33 cm.
Written on 4 staves without indication of instrumentation.
Published by Edgar Istel, "Eine Doppelfuge von der Hand Wagners," *Die Musik*, Jg. 114 (1912), Heft 19, p. 27-41.
Former owners: Karl Friedrich Weitzmann, Jerome Stonborough.
LIBRARY OF CONGRESS, WHITTALL FOUNDATION

1903. [Götterdämmerung]
Zur Widmung.
[1]p. 35 x 25 cm.
A setting of 16 lines of Brünnhilde's farewell in Act III, scene 3, belonging to the passage which Wagner discarded. The passage begins: Verging wie Hauch der Götter Geschlecht.
LIBRARY OF CONGRESS

1904. [Götterdämmerung. Vorspiel]
[2]p. 35 x 25 cm.
Sketches for the Norns' scene and for Brünnhilde's farewell to Siegfried.
Former owner: Jerome Stonborough.
LIBRARY OF CONGRESS, WHITTALL FOUNDATION

1905. [Götterdämmerung. Vorspiel]
[1]p. 34 x 25½ cm.
First page of the full score; ink somewhat blurred and discarded.
Dated: 1 Mai 1873. Bayreuth.
Former owner: George R. Siedenburg.
MR. R. THORNTON WILSON, JR.

1906. [Die Hochzeit]
Fragment einer unvollendeten Oper: Die Hochzeit von Richard Wagner. Dem Würzburger Musikverein zum Andenken verehrt. (Introduction: Chor und Septett).
2 leaves, 36 p. 31 x 24½ cm.
Full score.
At end: Würzburg, den 1sten März 1833. Richard Wagner.
Published in 1912 in his Werke, vol. 12.
Former owners: Musikverein, Würzburg; Mrs. Mary Burrell, Mrs. Mary Louise Zimbalist.   CURTIS INSTITUTE OF MUSIC

1907. Gluck, Christoph Willibald, Ritter von, 1714-1787.
[Iphigénie en Aulide]
[39]p. 34 x 27 cm.
Revisions and additions, in full score, for Wagner's version of Gluck's opera, as performed at Dresden, February 22, 1847.
12 p. are inserted in Wagner's copy of the full score, the rest are laid in at the end. They include a new close to the 2nd act and to the last act. In addition, nearly 200 p. of the printed score bear notes or revisions in Wagner's hand.

An abbreviated piano-vocal score of Wagner's version, edited by Hans von Bülow, was published in 1859 by Breitkopf & Härtel in Leipzig.

Former owners: Mrs. Mary Burrell (catalogue, no. 164), Mrs. Mary Louise Zimbalist.   CURTIS INSTITUTE OF MUSIC

1908.   Haydn, (Franz) Joseph, 1732-1809.
  [Symphony, no. 104, D minor]
  Joseph Haydn's Sinfonien. Partitur. Zweite Sinfonie (D moll). Richard Wagner. Leipzig 1831.
  1 leaf, 111 p. 24 x 16 cm.
  Former owners: J. V. Hamm, F. R. Halsey.
                    HENRY E. HUNTINGTON LIBRARY

1909.   [Kraftliedchen]
  [1]p. 20½ x 16½ cm.
  Song; melody only without accompaniment.
  First line: Der Worte viel sind gemacht.
  Written to Louis Kraft, owner of the Hotel de Prusse in Leipzig, April 22, 1871.
  This ms. is in pencil; a fair copy in ink accompanies it.
  Published October 14, 1877 in the *Wiener Illustrierte Zeitung,* and April 1, 1883 in the *Monthly Musical Record.*
  Former owners: Mrs. Mary Burrell (catalogue, no. 477), Mrs. Mary Louise Zimbalist.   CURTIS INSTITUTE OF MUSIC

1910.   [Das Liebesmahl der Apostel]
  Das Gastmahl der Apostel.
  1 leaf, 16 p. 35 x 27 cm.
  The ms. contains three numbers from this work, for men's chorus unaccompanied. No. 1. "Gegrüsst seid, Brüder, in des Herzen Namen."—No. II. *Die Botschaft der Apostel.* "Seid uns gegrüsst, ihr lieben Brüder!"—No. III. *Gebet.* "Allmächt'ger Vater."
  Published in 1843 by Breitkopf & Härtel in Leipzig.
  Werke, vol. XVI, no. 4.   LIBRARY OF CONGRESS

1911.   [Das Liebesverbot]
  [33]p. 35½ x 26½ cm.
  Piano-vocal score of three numbers from the opera.
  Contents.—*Cavatine de Claudio* (a longer version than in the published score).—Trio in Act II.—*Chant de Carneval,* both as duet for 2 pianos and as song for Lucio in Act II.
  French text, not in Wagner's hand.
  Two pages have sketches for *Der fliegende Holländer* and *Rienzi.*
  Former owners: J. A. Tichatschek, Mrs. Mary Burrell (catalogue, no. 47), Mrs. Mary Louise Zimbalist.
                    CURTIS INSTITUTE OF MUSIC

1912. [Lohengrin]
    [2]p. 38½ x 29 cm.
    First sketch for the duet in Act III, scene 2, beginning "[mich zwang dein] Blick zu dienen deiner Huld," and ending "Dass mutvoll ich ein Mühen [trage]."
    On p. 2, sketches for Act III, scene 3, "Mein Gott nun ich lass dich nicht."
    Facsimile in Van Patten, *Catalogue*, p. 275.
    Former owner: George T. Keating.
                      MEMORIAL LIBRARY OF MUSIC, STANFORD UNIVERSITY

1913. [Lohengrin. Vorspiel]
    Violino 1º (1tes Pult) Lohengrin. No. 1.
    [1]p. 33 x 24½ cm.
    Fragment of first violin part (first 21 bars only).
    Former owners: Natalie Planer, Mrs. Mary Burrell (catalogue, no. 157), Mrs. Mary Louise Zimbalist.   CURTIS INSTITUTE OF MUSIC

1914. [Die Meistersinger]
    Die selige Morgentraum-Deutweise.
    [1]p. 38 x 29 cm.
    Vocal part only of three stanzas of Walter's *Preislied* ("Morgenlich leuchtend").
    At end: 24 Dezember 1866. Gedichtet zu Eva's von Stolzing Preise.
    Former owner: Eva Chamberlain Wagner.   MR. ARTURO TOSCANINI

1915. [Die Meistersinger]
    [2]p. 33 x 24½ cm.
    Full score of a concert ending to Walter's song: "Fanget an! So rief der Lenz."
    At end: München, 6 Juli, 1865. R. W.
    Former owner: Mrs. Mary Louise Zimbalist.
                      CURTIS INSTITUTE OF MUSIC

1916. Mignonne (Ronsard). Paris, 1839.
    [3]p. 33½ x 25 cm.
    Song with piano accpt.
    First line: Mignonne, allons voir si la rose.
    Published as supplement to *Europa, Chronik der gebildeten Welt*, in 1842, Band II, after p. 304.
    Werke, series XV, no. 12 (date of composition incorrectly given as 1840).
    Bound with his *Der Tannenbaum*.   HEINEMAN FOUNDATION

1917. Ouverture (D moll). Richard Wagner.
    [38]p. 23½ x 31½ cm.
    Full score of the first version.
    At end: Leipzig den 26ten September 1831.

Wagner, Richard—*continued*

Published in 1926 in his Werke, vol. XX, no. 2.
Former owners: Louis Schindelmeisser, Ernest Pasque, Carl Mein-
ert, Mrs. Mary Burrell (catalogue, no. 41), Mrs. Mary Louise
Zimbalist.   CURTIS INSTITUTE OF MUSIC

1918. Ouverture zu Raupach's "König Enzio" componirt von Richard
       Wagner. Clavierauszug zu 4 Händen.
       [20]p. 34 x 27 cm.
       This reduction for piano 4 hands is unpublished.
       The full score was published in 1907 by Breitkopf & Härtel in
       Leipzig.
       Former owners: Mrs. Mary Burrell (catalogue, no. 44), Mrs. Mary
       Louise Zimbalist.   CURTIS INSTITUTE OF MUSIC

1919. [Parsifal]
       [1]p. 17½ x 26½ cm.
       Lower half of a leaf containing sketches for the *Transformation
       Scene*.
       Former owner: Jerome Stonborough.
                          LIBRARY OF CONGRESS, WHITTALL FOUNDATION

1920. [Parsifal]
       [3]p. 33 x 24 cm.
       An arrangement of the children's and knight's choruses in the Grail
       scene of Act 1 for mixed voices, unaccompanied.
       Arranged for the composer's birthday celebration at Villa Angri,
       Italy, May 22, 1880. The scoring shows the parts were to be
       taken by Fidi and Eva, Soldi, etc., Joh. Plüddemann, Humper-
       dinck, Josef Rubinstein, a girls' chorus and the composer himself.
       Former owners: Blandine von Bülow, Count Gilberto Gravina.
                                            LIBRARY OF CONGRESS

1921. [Das Rheingold]
       [12], 360 p. 35 x 26½ and 19 x 31 cm.
       Short score.
       P. 1-12 contain the prelude and opening bars of scene 1, a fair copy
       in the autograph of Hans Richter. Wagner's autograph begins
       with Alberich's lines in scene 1, "Wie in den Gliedern brunstig."
       The intervening measures between Richter's fair copy and these
       lines are lacking.
       At end: RW 28 Mai 1854.
       Former owners: Karl Klindworth, Kurt Lehman.
                                  LIBRARY OF MR. JOHN H. SCHEIDE

1922. [Das Rheingold]
       [1]p. 19 x 31 cm.
       Full score of a fragment of 10 bars from Scene 1, beginning with
       Flosshilde: "Wie billig am Ende vom Lied" and ending with
       Alberich: "die Dritte, so traut, be[trog sie mich auch]."
       Former owner: Josephine Jacobs.   NEW YORK PUBLIC LIBRARY

1923. [Rienzi]
162 p. 35½ x 26½ cm.
Short score of the complete opera.
Dated at end of overture and at beginning and end of each act.
Overture: Paris 23 octobre 1840.
Act I: Riga den 26 July—7 August 1838; Riga 6 Decemb. 38.
Act II: Riga 6 Februar 1839; Riga 9ten April 1839. Richard Wagner.
Act III: Paris 15 Februar 1840; Fine dell atto 3zo Paris den 7ten
July 1840. Richard Wagner.
Act IV: 10 July 1840; Ende des 4ten Actes. 29ten August 1840.
Act V: Paris. 5 September 1840; Ende der Oper. Paris den 19 Sept.
1840. Richard Wagner.
First performed October 20, 1842 in Dresden.
Former owners: Mrs. Mary Burrell (catalogue, no. 127, 5); Mrs.
Mary Louise Zimbalist.   CURTIS INSTITUTE OF MUSIC

1924. [Rienzi]
Cola Rienzi von Richard Wagner. Riega [!] 1839. Finale des I.
Actes.
[2]p. 36 x 26 cm.
Piano-vocal score of a fragment of no. 4. Begins with the organ
introduction to the hymn: "Erwacht, erwacht, ihr Schläfer nah
und fern," which is complete.
Title in another hand.
Followed by sketches for the finale to Act II, beginning: "O lasst
der Gnade Himmelslicht."
Inscribed to E. W. Rietz, April 7, 1842.
                                   NEW YORK PUBLIC LIBRARY

1925. [Rienzi]
[4]p. 36 x 26 cm.
Short score of a fragment of Act I, beginning: "Rienzi, ha, Rienzi,
hoch."
Former owner: E. W. Rietz.   NEW YORK PUBLIC LIBRARY

1926. [Der Ring der Nibelungen]
1 leaf. 20 x 26½ cm.
Leitmotive arranged as fanfares for brass instruments.
Evidently intended for use at the festival performances in Bayreuth
in 1876.   LIBRARY OF CONGRESS

1927. [Sonata, piano, B flat major]
Sonata in B dur für das Pianoforte von Richard Wagner.
1 leaf, [16]p. 24 x 32 cm.
Published in 1832 by Breitkopf & Härtel in Leipzig.
Former owners: Mrs. Mary Burrell (catalogue, no. 43), Mrs. Mary
Louise Zimbalist.   CURTIS INSTITUTE OF MUSIC

Wagner, Richard—*continued*

1928. [Symphony, C major]
    [14]p. 32 x 24 cm.
Piano reduction of the last three movements.
The full score and the 2nd movement in this version published in
    1911 by Max Brockhaus in Leipzig.
See Edgar Istel, "Richard Wagners C-dur Symphonie," *Neue
    Musik-Zeitung*, Jg 32 (1911), Heft 5, p. 97.
Former owners: Karl Friedrich Weitzmann, Jerome Stonborough.
        LIBRARY OF CONGRESS, WHITTALL FOUNDATION

1929. Der Tannenbaum. (Gedicht von Scheuerlin). Riga, 1838.
    [3]p. 33½ x 25 cm.
Song with piano accpt.
First line: Der Tannenbaum steht schweigend.
Published as supplement to *Europa, Chronik der gebildeten Welt*,
    in 1839, Band IV, after p. 260.
Werke, series XV, no. 8.
Bound with this are three other songs: *Dors, mon enfant; Attente;*
    and *Mignonne*.   HEINEMAN FOUNDATION

1930. [Tannhäuser]
    Kompositions-Skizzen zu Tannhäuser . . .
    1 leaf, [128]p. 33½ x 26½ cm.
Short score of the complete opera, with the exception of the overture.
Dated at beginning and end of each act.
Act I: Dresden, November, 1843; R. W. Dresden, 27 Jan. 1844.
Act II: Fischer's Weinberg b. Dresden. 7 Sept. 1844; 15 October.
Act III: Dresden, 19 Dec. 44; Richard Wagner. Sonntag, 29 Decem-
    ber 1844.
Inscribed to Gustav Schmidt, Zürich, 26 Febr. 1855.
p. 123-28 contain an alternative close to the opera, dated 30 April
    1847.
First performed October 19, 1845, at Dresden.
Werke, vol. III.
Former owners: Gustav Schmidt, Mrs. Mary Burrell (catalogue,
    no. 143), Mrs. Mary Louise Zimbalist.
        CURTIS INSTITUTE OF MUSIC

1931. [Tannhäuser. Overture]
    [2]p. 33 x 25 cm.
Bass trombone and ophicleide part.
Former owners: Natalie Planer, Mrs. Mary Burrell (catalogue, no.
    144), Mrs. Mary Louise Zimbalist.   CURTIS INSTITUTE OF MUSIC

1932. [Tristan und Isolde]
    [2]p. 17½ x 27 cm.
Piano reduction of the first 19 bars of the *Prelude* to Act I.
On p. 2, various phrases from Act I in piano-vocal score.
Former owner: Josephine Jacobs.   NEW YORK PUBLIC LIBRARY

Wagner, Richard—*continued*

1933. Die Walküre. Wotan's Abschied und Feuerzauber. Herr Simons. R. W. [5]p. 35 x 27 cm.
Short score.
Prepared for Carl Simons, who sang it at a Munich court concert December 11, 1864, with Wagner conducting.
Contains variants from the published score.
HEINEMAN FOUNDATION

Waldteufel, Emil, 1837-1915

1934. Dans les champs.
[4]p. 27 x 35½ cm.
For piano.
At end: Compiègne ce 30 novembre 1868. Emile Waldteufel.
Dedicated to Baron Tristan Lambert.
Published as *Dans les champs, polka-mazurka*, op. 125, by A. Durand in Paris. GALERIE ST. ETIENNE

Walker, Ernest, 1870-1949

1935. . . . "From the upland to the sea" by William Morris set to music for baritone, piano and string quartet by Ernest Walker . . . April, 1894.
[18]p. 36 x 24 cm.
Full score.
First line: Shall we wake one morn at spring.
Unpublished.
Former owner: David Bispham. NEW YORK PUBLIC LIBRARY

Wallace, William Vincent, 1812-1865

1936. A fireside song. Words by H. F. Chorley, composed by Vincent Wallace.
[8]p. 30 x 24½ cm.
Song with piano accpt.
First line: When the children are asleep.
Dedication to Vincent Novello, with a note in his hand, January 17, 1849. MEMORIAL LIBRARY OF MUSIC, STANFORD UNIVERSITY

1937. The star of love. Serenade.
6 leaves. 27 x 35 cm.
Full score (voice and orchestra).
Published by Edwin Ashdown in London. BOSTON PUBLIC LIBRARY

Warner, H[arry] Waldo, 1876-

1938. Suite (Trio) for pianoforte, violin & violoncello. Apr. 1921 to June, 1921 . . .
84 p. 36 x 27½ cm.
Score.

Warner, H[arry] Waldo—*continued*

Dedicated to Mrs. E. S. Coolidge.
Awarded the Chamber Music Prize, Berkshire Festival, 1921.
Published in 1923 by G. Ricordi & Co. in London.

LIBRARY OF CONGRESS, COOLIDGE FOUNDATION

Webb, T. Henry

1939. The world's wanderers. Song for mezzo-soprano. Words by Shelley.
T. H. Webb.
[4]p. 27 x 16½ cm.
First line: Tell me, thou star.
At end: Leipzig, May 1894.   BOSTON PUBLIC LIBRARY

Webbe, Samuel, 1740-1816

1940. Collect for the 16th. Sunday after Trinity.
[3]p. 24 x 30 cm.
Unaccompanied sacred 4-part song for mixed voices.
First line: O Lord we beseech thee.
At end: Saml. Webbe. Feby. 1812 at the request of his Friend Mr.
Joseph Smith.   LIBRARY OF CONGRESS

1941. Collect for the 10th. Sunday after Trinity.
[3]p. 24 x 30 cm.
Sacred 4-part song for mixed voices with organ accpt.
First line: Let thy merciful ears, O Lord.
At end: Saml. Webbe Jany. 1812. At the request of his friend Mr.
Jos: Smith.   LIBRARY OF CONGRESS

Weber, Carl Maria (Friedrich Ernst), *Freiherr* von, 1786-1826

The numbers at the end of the bracketed titles refer to the serial numbers
in the thematic catalogue of F. W. Jähns, *C. M. v. Weber in seinen
Werken*, Berlin, 1871.

1942. Canone à tre.
[1]p. 10 x 16½ cm.
First line: Wenn du im Arm der Liebe.
At end: Salzburg den 8ten Juli 1802 ... C. M. v. Weber.
Not in Jähns thematic catalogue, and dated earlier than the earliest
compositions therein.
Former owner: Gustav Oberlaender.   PRIVATE COLLECTOR

1943. [Concerto, clarinet, no. 1, op. 73, F minor. Jähns 114]
Gran concerto per il clarinetto principale composto all uso [dell
signore Enrico Baermann] di Carlo Maria de Weber. Monaco,
Majo 1811.
85 p. 22 x 29 cm.
Full score.
Published in 1822 by A. M. Schlesinger in Berlin.
Former owners: Heinrich Baermann, Hermine Wittgenstein.

LIBRARY OF CONGRESS, WHITTALL FOUNDATION

Weber, Carl Maria (Friedrich Ernst), *Freiherr* von—*continued*

1944. [Grand duo concertant, op. 48. Jähns 204]
Grand duo concertant. Op. 48 pour clarinette e pianoforte composée de Charles Marie de Weber.
14 p. 20 x 24 cm.
Score.
At end: München d. 6. July 1815.
The autograph was unknown to Jähns, who dated the composition 1816.
Published in 1817 by A. M. Schlesinger in Berlin.
Former owner: Jerome Stonborough.
LIBRARY OF CONGRESS, WHITTALL FOUNDATION

1945. [Lieder und Gesänge, op. 66. Jähns 48, 66, 134, 213, 217, 238]
Lieder und Gesänge mit Begleitung des Pianoforte. Musik von Carl Maria von Weber. Op. 66. 15tes Liederheft.
[13]p. 24 x 33 cm.
Contents.—*Das Veilchen im Thale* (217)—*Rosen im Haare* (238)—*Ich denke dein* (48)—*Lebensansicht* (134)—*Die Lethe des Lebens* (66)—*Wunsch und Entsagung* (213).
Published in 1819 by A. M. Schlesinger in Berlin.
Former owner: George T. Keating.
MEMORIAL LIBRARY OF MUSIC, STANFORD UNIVERSITY

1946. [Lützow's wilde Jagd. Op. 42, no. 2. Jähns 168]
Lützow's wilde Jagd. Chor. Tonna, d. 13 Sept. 1814.
[2]p. 22 x 28 cm.
For 4-part men's chorus, unaccompanied (text lacking).
Followed by his *Schwertlied*, op. 42, no. 6 [Jähns 169].
Text of both songs from Theodor Körner's *Leyer und Schwert*.
Published in 1815 by A. M. Schlesinger in Berlin.
MR. CARL H. TOLLEFSEN

1947. [Oberon. Jähns 306]
49 p. 23½ x 31½ cm.
Piano-vocal score of Act II.
Former owner: George T. Keating.
MEMORIAL LIBRARY OF MUSIC, STANFORD UNIVERSITY

1948. [Oberon. Preghiera. Jähns 306, 12A]
Preghiera. Act the second. After the storm.
[2]p. 24 x 30 cm.
Piano-vocal score of Huon's aria, "Ruler of this awful hour," followed by first 14 bars of Fatima's aria, no. 16, "O Araby."
The *Preghiera*, composed after the rest of the score for the singer Braham two days before the first performance, is Weber's last composition.
LIBRARY OF CONGRESS

[Schwertlied, op. 42, no. 6. Jähns 169]
See his *Lützow's wilde Jagd*

Weber, Carl Maria (Friedrich Ernst), *Freiherr* von—*continued*

1949. [Silvana. Jähns 87]
[2]p. 24½ x 30½ cm.
Sketch for no. 8, beginning: "Sie schläft, nun fort aus diesem Haÿn . . ."
On p. 2 a sketch: *Kleiner Tusch von 20 Trompetten. Geblasen am 15. October 1806 in C vermischt mit einigen Mittelsezen von zwey schlecht geblasenen Flöte doucen.* (Jähns 47A, there published complete.)
Former owner: William H. Cummings (catalogue, no. 196).
LIBRARY OF CONGRESS

1950. [Variations, piano, op. 28. Jähns 141]
[Romance "à peine au sortir de l'enfance etc." de l'opéra Joseph de Méhul varié pour le pianoforte]
[2]p. 25 x 33 cm.
Fragment.
Former owner: Max Friedländer.
MR. JOHN BASS

1951. [Variations, violoncello and orchestra, Jähns 94]
Variationen für das Violoncell für seinen Freund Alexander von Dusch componirt von Carl Marie von Weber.
1 leaf, 25 p. 23 x 31½ cm.
Full score.
At end: In 8 Stunden vollendet. Mannheim 28. May 1810.
Former owners: O. A. Schulz, A. H. von Kurtz.
Published ca. 1814 by the Bureau de Musique in Leipzig.
LIBRARY OF CONGRESS, WHITTALL FOUNDATION

Webern, Anton von, 1883-1945

1952. [Quartet, strings, op. 28]
Streichquartett, op. 28. Partitur.
1 leaf. 56 p. 15 x 27 cm.
Dedicated to Mrs. E. S. Coolidge.
Published in 1939 by Boosey and Hawkes in London.
LIBRARY OF CONGRESS, COOLIDGE FOUNDATION

1953. . . . Sechs Lieder nach Gedichten von Georg Trakl, für eine Singstimme, Klarinette, Bass-Klarinette, Geige u. Violoncello. Op. 14. Klavierauszug.
1 leaf, 13 p. 21 x 35 cm.
Contents.—*Die Sonne.—Abendland I-III.—Nachts.—Gefangenen Amsel.*
Published in 1924 by Universal Edition in Vienna.
MR. RICHARD WINTER

Weigl, Joseph, 1766-1846

1954. Sei arie e sei duetti del sig. Giuseppe Weigl . . . no. 1. La lontananza.
[4]p. 23 x 31 cm.
Song with piano accpt.

Weigl, Joseph—*continued*

First line: Richiesi al rio che mormora.
Former owners: Alexander W. Thayer, Edward Speyer.

Weiner, Leo, 1883-

1955. [Quartet, strings, no. 2, op. 13, F sharp minor]
 . . . Quatuor à cordes. Partition. Ecoutez!
 46 p. 35 x 27 cm.
 Dedicated to Mrs. E. S. Coolidge.
 Awarded the prize at the Berkshire Music Festival in 1922.
 Published in 1924 by F. Bárd in Budapest.

1956. [Quartet, strings, no. 3, op. 23, G major]
 . . . String quartet no. 3 (G-dur). (Pastorale, Fantasia e Fuga)
 Op. 23. Score.
 32 p. 34 x 26½ cm.
 At end: Budapest, 27 Jul. 1938.

Weitzmann, Karl Friedrich, 1808-1880

1957. Mignon in Engelskleidern v. Göthe, comp. v. C. Weitzmann.
 [7]p. 8½ x 10½ cm.
 Song with piano accpt.
 First line: So lasst mich scheinen.
 Apparently unpublished.

Wellesz, Egon, 1885-

1958. Alkestis. Op. 35. Handlung in einem Aufzuge mit freier Benut-
 zung des Dramas von Hugo von Hofmannsthal . . .
 2 leaves, 169 p. 50½ x 34 cm.
 Full score.
 At end: 8 Uhr. Altaussee. Beendet 15. Juli Samstag. 1923.
 First performed March 20, 1924, at Mannheim.

1959. [Quartet, strings, no. 5, op. 60]
 37 [i.e. 38]p. 31 x 25 cm.
 Score.
 On p. 1: Egon Wellesz op. 60. 1943.
 At end: 9. I.1944.
 Published in 1948 by Schott & Co. in London.

Wesley, Charles, 1757-1834

1960. Anthem for four voices. Collect for the twenty 2d Sunday after
 Trinity. Composed by C: Wesley . . . London, Feby. 28th.
 An-Dom. 1812.
 1 leaf, [3]p. 29 x 23½ cm.

At end: London C.W. Feby. 28th. An. Dom. 1812. Composed for Joseph Smith Esqre.

First line: Lord, Lord, we beseech Thee.   LIBRARY OF CONGRESS

1961. Anthem for four voices composed for Joseph Smith Esqre by Charles Wesley . . .

1 leaf, 7 p. 29 x 24½ cm.

Collect for the second Sunday after Easter.

First line: Almighty God, who has given Thine only Son.

Published by Bland and Weller in London.   LIBRARY OF CONGRESS

1962. [Collection of anthems]

76 leaves. 41 x 29 cm.

A collection of 28 pieces, nearly all dated between 1775 and 1803.

Former owner: William K. Bixby.   HENRY E. HUNTINGTON LIBRARY

Wesley, Samuel, 1766-1837

1963. [Deus majestatis intonuit]

29 p. 30 x 24 cm.

Score for double chorus and strings.

At end: S. Wesley Septr 26. 1799.

Former owner: William H. Cummings (catalogue, no. 200).

LIBRARY OF CONGRESS

1964. Fuga. Composed by Saml. Wesley.

[3]p. 30 x 24 cm.

For organ, in C major.

Followed on p. 2-3 by an unnamed fugue in D major.

Former owner: William H. Cummings (catalogue, no. 200).

LIBRARY OF CONGRESS

1965. In festo Transfigurationis D. N. Jesu Christe. (Ad offertorium). Sam Wesley.

[4]p. 30 x 24 cm.

Sacred song with piano accpt.

First line: Gloria et honore coronasti eum Domine.

Former owners: Vincent Novello, Musical Antiquarian Society, William H. Cummings (catalogue, no. 200).

LIBRARY OF CONGRESS

1966. [Life is a jest]

The words of the following glee are a translation of a distich which is probably to be found in the Anthologia Graeca, but which S.W. met with in the title page of a well-known humorous work denominated "Crazy Tales." . . .

[4]p. 30½ x 24 cm.

For four voices unaccompanied.

At end: S. Wesley, Jan. 17, 1807.

Former owner: William H. Cummings (catalogue, no. 199).

LIBRARY OF CONGRESS

Wesley, Samuel—*continued*

1967. O Lord God most holy (a 4 voci). A verse from the burial service by
Samuel Wesley . . . 1800.
[3]p. 3 x 24 cm.
For four-part chorus unaccompanied. BOSTON PUBLIC LIBRARY

1968. Boyce, William, 1710-1779.
Peleus and Thetis. A mask written by Lord Lansdowne. Set to
music by Dr. Wm. Boyce. Performed before the Philharmonic
Society.
2 leaves, 80 p. 23 x 30 cm.
The masque, composed in 1734, was introduced in Boyce's altered
version of *The Merchant of Venice* as *The Jew of Venice* in
London in 1749.
Unpublished.
Former owner: William H. Cummings (catalogue, no. 339).
LIBRARY OF CONGRESS

1969. A voluntary for the organ by Samuel Wesley.
[8]p. 30 x 24 cm.
Former owner: William H. Cummings (catalogue, no. 200).
LIBRARY OF CONGRESS

White, Felix (Harold), 1884-1945

1970. The Nymph's complaint for the death of her Fawn. Poem for oboe
(or violin), viola and piano after Andrew Marvell. Felix White.
1 leaf, 13 p. 36 x 28 cm.
Score.
Carnegie Award, 1922.
Published in 1922 by Stainer and Bell in London.
LIBRARY OF CONGRESS

Widor, Charles Marie (Jean Albert), 1844-1937

1971. [Concerto, violoncello, op. 41, E minor]
Concerto de violoncelle. Op. 41.
155 p. 34 x 26 cm.
Full score.
At end: 13 août 77.
Published in 1882 by J. Hamelle in Paris. BOSTON PUBLIC LIBRARY

1972. [Maître Ambros]
[4]p. 35½ x 27 cm.
Fragment of full score, from Act I, scene 3, Nella's aria.
LIBRARY OF CONGRESS

Wieniawski, Henri, 1835-1880

1973. Le carnaval russe; improvisations et variations humoristiques sur l'air national russe populaire "Poulicy mostovoj" pour le violon avec accompagnement de piano, composées . . . par Henri Wieniawski. Op. 11.
   2 leaves, 11 p. 25 x 33 cm.
   Published by Fr. Kistner in Leipzig.
   Former owner: Joseph Muller.   NEW YORK PUBLIC LIBRARY

Wildschut, Clara

1974. Sonate voor viool en piano . . .
   1 leaf, 20 p. 34 x 25 cm. and part.
   Dedicated to Mrs. E. S. Coolidge.
   At end: Sept. 1926.   LIBRARY OF CONGRESS, COOLIDGE FOUNDATION

Willmers, Heinrich Rudolf, 1821-1878

1975. Lied ohne Worte.
   [2]p. 20 x 25 cm.
   For piano.
   At end: . . . R. Willmers, Dresden, d. 22ten Nov. 1838.
   Former owner: Joseph Muller.   NEW YORK PUBLIC LIBRARY

Wilm, Nicolai von, 1834-1911

1976. Humoreske. N. v. Wilm, op. 47, no. 2.
   [7]p. 33 x 26 cm.
   For piano.
   Inscribed to Arthur Smolian, Wiesbaden, 30 Nov. 1890.
   Published by Ries & Erler in Berlin.   LIBRARY OF CONGRESS

1977. Romance. N. v. Wilm, op. 47, nr. 1.
   [6]p. 33 x 26 cm.
   For piano.
   Inscribed to Arthur Smolian, Wiesbaden, 30 Nov. 1890.
   Published by Ries & Erler in Berlin.   LIBRARY OF CONGRESS

Winter, Peter von, 1745-1825

1978. Thema di Caraffa, variazioni di Winter.
   [26]p. 19½ x 24 cm.
   Full score of aria, *O cara memoria,* with variations.
                                           LIBRARY OF CONGRESS

Wolf, Hugo, 1860-1903

1979. Anakreon's Grab.
   [2]p. 34 x 26 cm.
   Song with piano accpt.
   Text by Goethe.
   First line: Wo die Rose hier blüht.
   Published as no. 29 of his *Gedichte von Goethe* in 1890 by Lacom in Vienna.   MR. RUDOLF F. KALLIR

1980. [Der Corregidor]
    [2]p. 34½ x 27 cm.
    Fragment of full score, from Act I, scene 1, beginning: Nachbar:
    Habt Ihr schon einmal berechnet.
                 MEMORIAL LIBRARY OF MUSIC, STANFORD UNIVERSITY

1981. [Gesegnet sei, durch den die Welt entstund]
    [2]p. 35 x 26½ cm.
    Song with piano accpt.
    A Roman numeral III cancelled and 4 substituted.
    Published as no. 4 of his *Italienisches Liederbuch* in 1892 by
    B. Schott's Söhne in Mainz.   MR. RUDOLF F. KALLIR

1982. Lied des transferierten Zettel (aus dem Sommernachtstraum)
    comp. 1889. Hugo Wolf.
    [2]p. 34 x 25 cm.
    Song with piano accpt.
    Text by Shakespeare (Bottom's song in *Midsummer Night's Dream*).
    First line: Die Schwalbe die den Sommer bringt.
    Published as no. 2 of *Vier Gedichte nach Heine, Shakespeare und
    Lord Byron* in 1897 by K. F. Heckel in Mannheim.
                         MR. SAMUEL R. ROSENBAUM

1983. [Man sagt mir, deine Mutter woll' es nicht]
    Italienisches Liederbuch. Hugo Wolf.
    [2]p. 34 x 26 cm.
    Song with piano accpt.
    Published as no. 21 of his *Italienisches Liederbuch* in 1892 by
    B. Schott's Söhne in Mainz.   MR. RUDOLF F. KALLIR

1984. [Manuel Venegas]
    [2]p. 34 x 26½ cm.
    Sketches to the unfinished opera.
    Former owner: Hugo Becker.   WALTER SCHATZKI

1985. Mausfallen-Sprüchlein (Ed. Mörike). Maierling, 18 Juni 882.
    [4]p. 34 x 26 cm.
    Song with piano accpt.
    First line: Kleine Gäste, kleines Haus.
    On p. 4 of his *Zur Ruh! zur Ruh!*   MR. RUDOLF F. KALLIR
    Published as no. 6 of *Sechs Lieder für eine Frauenstimme* in 1888
    by E. Wetzler in Vienna.

1986. Pena d'amor.
    [4]p. 32½ x 25 cm.
    Song with piano accpt., Italian and German text.
    First line: Ein Himmelssegen ist deine Schönheit.
    German title and composer's signature have been erased.
    Said to be an Italian composition or an imitation of one, designed
    to confuse the composer's friends.

Wolf, Hugo—*continued*

On p. 4 are sketches for a song, beginning: . . . liebt mich, er liebt mich nicht. This is, however, not from Goethe's *Faust*, as erroneously stated in Van Patten, *Catalogue*.

MEMORIAL LIBRARY OF MUSIC, STANFORD UNIVERSITY

1987. [Seemanns Abschied. Hugo Wolf. no. 20.
[4]p. 34½ x 26 cm.
Song with piano accpt.
First line: Ade, mein Schatz, du möchst mich nicht.
Published as no. 20 of Heft V of *Gedichte von Eichendorff* in 1889 by Lacon in Vienna. LIBRARY OF CONGRESS

1988. [Selig, ihr Blinden]
Italienisches Liederbuch. 5. Hugo Wolf,
[2]p. 34 x 26½ cm.
Song with piano accpt.
Published as no. 5 of his *Italienisches Liederbuch* in 1892 by B. Schott's Söhne in Mainz. MR. EMIL HIRSCH

1989. [Sonne der Schlummerlosen]
3. Sonne der Schlummerlosen . . . (Lord Byron). comp. 1896. Hugo Wolf.
[2]p. 34 x 26½ cm.
Song with piano accpt.
First line as above, a translation of "Sun of the sleepless, melancholy star," from the *Hebrew Melodies*.
Published as no. 3 of *Vier Gedichte nach Heine, Shakespeare und Lord Byron* in 1897 by K. F. Heckel in Mannheim.
Former owner: George T. Keating.
MEMORIAL LIBRARY OF MUSIC, STANFORD UNIVERSITY

1990. [Ein Ständchen euch zu bringen]
Italienisches Liederbuch. Hugo Wolf.
[3]p. 35 x 27 cm.
Song with piano accpt.
Published as no. 22 of his *Italienisches Liederbuch* in 1892 by B. Schott's Söhne in Mainz. LIBRARY OF CONGRESS

1991. Wo wird einst (H. Heine). comp. 1888. Hugo Wolf.
[2]p. 34 x 26½ cm.
Song with piano accpt.
Published as no. 1 of *Vier Gedichte nach Heine, Shakespeare und Lord Byron* in 1897 by K. F. Heckel in Mannheim.
Former owner: Mrs. R. S. Knapp. MISS LOTTE LEHMANN

1992. [Zur Ruh! zur Ruh!]
p. 4 of his *Mausfallen-Sprüchlein*.
Song with piano accpt.
Text by Kerner.
Published as no. 6 of *Sechs Gedichte von Scheffel, Mörike, Goethe und Kerner* in 1888 by E. Wetzler in Vienna.
MR. RUDOLF F. KALLIR

Woollett, Henri Edouard, 1864-1936

1993. [Octet, oboe, clarinet, saxophone, string quartet and double bass]
Octuor.
95 p. 34½ x 25 cm.
Score.
Former owner: Mrs. R. J. Hall.

1994. Sibéria. H. Woollett. Juillet 1909.
1 leaf, [9]p. 27 x 35 cm.
Reduction for saxophone and piano of his symphonic poem for alto
saxophone and orchestra.
Dedicated to Mrs. R. J. Hall, the former owner.

Worgan, John, ca. 1724-1790

1995. An ode from the Spectator, no. 465, set to music by Mr. John
Worgan, M.B. 1759.
[1], 25 p. 23½ x 28½ cm.
For voices and figured bass.
Text by Joseph Addison.
First line: The spacious firmament on high.

Yradier, Sebastián, 1809-1865

1996. La calesera, canción andaluza con acompañamiento de piano com-
puesta . . . por . . . Yradier. Letra de Sr. Bolignes.
[4]p. 29 x 23 cm.
First line: Ya suenen las campaniles.
Published by Sassetti & Co. in Lisbon.

Ysaÿe, Eugène, 1858-1931

1997. [Concerto, violin, op. 3, B minor]
Concerto en si mineur. 1re partie. E.Y. Berlin, 1880-81.
30, 6 p. 35 x 27 cm.
Reduction for violin and piano.
Followed by 6 p. of sketches.
Unpublished.

1998. [Concerto, violin, D minor]
Final du concerto en ré. E.Y. Berlin 1881.
3-24 p. 35 x 27 cm.
First 2 p. lacking.
Reduction for violin and piano.
Unpublished.

1999. [Concerto, violin, E major]
Finale.
27 leaves. 35 x 27 cm.
Reduction for violin and piano.

The *finale* (17 p.) is followed by an *Autre finale* (8 p.) and by 28 p. of sketches.

The *Autre finale* is dated Paris 8bre fin 1884.

Unpublished.   MR. LOUIS PERSINGER

2000.   Exil.

10 p. 31 x 23 cm.

Score (3 violins and viola).

At end: E. Ysaye. exil! tourmente. désespoir. 1917 New York.

Published as op. 25 by Editions Ysaÿe in Brussels.

MR. LOUIS PERSINGER

2001.   [Fantaisie, violin and orchestra, op. 32]

. . . Deuxième divertimento pour violon principal et orchestre par Eugène Ysaye. Réduction de piano par l'auteur.

25 p. 35 x 27 cm.

At end: E.Y. Zoute, mai 1925 (2d version).

Published in 1927 by Editions Ysaÿe in Brussels.

MR. LOUIS PERSINGER

2002.   [Petit poème romantique, op. 14a]

Aux enfants. Petit poème romantique pour le violon avec accompagnement du piano ou d'orchestre réduit composé par Eugène Ysaye.

20 p. 30 x 27 cm.

Full score.

At end: Composé à Ste. Marie en Ardennes (Sept. 1901) orchestré pour Gabri: New York (avril 1920). E. Ysaye.

Unpublished.   MR. LOUIS PERSINGER

2003.   [Sonata, violin solo, op. 27, no. 3, D minor]

. . . 3ème sonate pour le violon seul par Eugène Ysaye.

5 p. 31 x 23 cm.

Caption title: Ballade.

Dedicated to Georges Enesco.

Published in 1924 by Editions Ysaÿe in Brussels.

MR. LOUIS PERSINGER

2004.   [Sonata, violin solo, op. 27, no. 2, A minor]

. . . 4ème [!] sonate pour le violon seul par Eugene Ysaye . . .

[8]p. 31 x 23 cm.

At end: E.Y. juillet 1923 La Zoute.

Dedicated to Jacques Thibaud.

Published in 1924 by Editions Ysaÿe in Brussels.

MR. LOUIS PERSINGER

2005.   [Sonata, violin solo, op. 27, no. 6, E major]

. . . 6ème sonate.

[7]p. 31 x 23 cm.

At end: E. Ysaye. Zoute, mai 1924.

Ysaÿe, Eugène—*continued*

Dedicated to Manuel Quiroga.
Published in 1924 by Editions Ysaÿe in Brussels.

MR. LOUIS PERSINGER

Ysaÿe, Théophile, 1865-1918

2006. Le cygne. Esquisse symphonique . . . op. 15.
1 leaf, 29 p. 40 x 30 cm.
Full score.
Published in 1907 by G. Schirmer in New York.   G. SCHIRMER

Zachau, Friedrich Wilhelm, 1663-1721

2007. Fantasia . . .
[5]p. 33½ x 20½ cm.
For organ.   MEMORIAL LIBRARY OF MUSIC, STANFORD UNIVERSITY

Zelter, Karl Friedrich, 1758-1832

2008. An Mignon.
[2]p. 26½ x 33 cm.
Song with piano accpt.
Text by Goethe.
First line: Über Thal und Fluss getragen.
Published with this melody but a different accompaniment in his
Zwölf Lieder, Berlin, 1801.
On p. 2 his *Wonne der Wehmuth*.

YALE UNIVERSITY LIBRARY, SPECK COLLECTION

2009. Wonne der Wehmuth.
p. 2 of his *An Mignon*.
Song with piano accpt.
Text by Goethe.
First line: Trocknet nicht.
Apparently unpublished in this setting.

YALE UNIVERSITY LIBRARY, SPECK COLLECTION

Zingarelli, Nicola Antonio, 1752-1837

2010. Lucido eccelso nume. Preghiera. Del sigr. Nicolo Zingarelli.
209-216 p. 22 x 30 cm.
Score for voice and strings.
At head of title: Firenze autunno 1794.
The aria is preceded by the recitative: *Infelice zamoro Alzira.*

LIBRARY OF CONGRESS

Zingarelli, Nicola Antonio—*continued*

2011. Romeo e Giulietta, opera tragica in trè atti posta in musica dal sig. Nicola Zingarelli con cambiamenti di alcuni pezzi e variazioni aggiunte, fatte dal sig. Girolamo Crescentini in ossequio della nobile donna la sig. marchesa Douglas de Clydesdale.
2 v. (306, 307 p.) 22 x 28 cm.
Full score.
Performed in 1796 at the Teatro della Scala in Milan.
From the Hamilton Palace Collection.

FOLGER SHAKESPEARE LIBRARY

2012. [Songs for one, two or three voices with accpt. of strings]
[7]p. 23 x 29 cm.
Score.
Contents.—*Sento l'amaro pianto.—Sotto i presenti colpi.—Veder l'orrenda morte.—Tolto di croce il Figlio.*

THE PIERPONT MORGAN LIBRARY

2013. Varie messe proprie in canto gregoriano.
16 p. 22½ x 29 cm.
Contents.—*Missa de B[eata] V[irgi]ne.—Missa duplex.—Missa paschalis.—Missa angelorum.—Missa dominicalis.—Missa in Adventu.—Credo cardinalis.*
Facsimile of p. 3 in Abbiati, *Storia della musica*, III, 320.
Former owner: Natale Gallini (catalogue, no. 14).

MEMORIAL LIBRARY OF MUSIC, STANFORD UNIVERSITY

Zopf, Hermann, 1826-1883

2014. Deutschlands Auferstehung. Nationalcantate für Männerstimmen u. Orchester.
[56]p. 34 x 25½ cm.
Full score, with piano reduction below.   BOSTON PUBLIC LIBRARY

Zuccalmaglio, Anton Wilhelm Florentin von, 1803-1869

2015. Kinderlied. Sandmännchen.
[2]p. 17 x 21 cm.
Song with piano accpt.
Text by the composer.
First line: Die Blümelein sie schlafen.
Zuccalmaglio took the melody from the old hymn, *Zu Bethlehem geboren*; Brahms in turn used this song for his *Sandmännchen*, no. 4 of his *Volkskinderlieder*.
Former owner: Max Friedländer.   MR. FRANZ ROEHN

Zumsteeg, Johann Rudolf, 1760-1802

2016. Klage. Zumsteeg.
[2]p. 24 x 30 cm.
Song with piano accpt.
Text by Hölty.

Zumsteeg, Johann Rudolf—*continued*

First line: Dein Silber schien durch Eichengrün.
Published as no. 29 of Heft 5 of his *Kleine Balladen und Lieder*
ca. 1803 by Breitkopf & Härtel in Leipzig.
On p. 2 another song: *Gestern liebt' ich, heute leid' ich.*
Former owner: Max Friedländer. MR. FRANZ ROEHN

2017. Das tartarische Gesez, eine Oper in zweÿ Aufzügen, in Musik
gesezt von Zumsteeg.
[228]p. 29 x 35 cm.
Full score.
Text by Friedrich Wilhelm Gotter. LIBRARY OF CONGRESS

LIST OF PRESENT OWNERS

Dealers' names are marked with an asterisk.

Estate of Béla Bartók (Victor Bator, Administrator, 30 East 72nd St., New York 21, N. Y.). Nos. 94-101, 103-66, 168-98.

Mr. John Bass, 275 Central Park West, New York 24, N. Y. Nos. 366, 378, 933, 1220, 1663, 1678, 1693, 1861, 1950.

*Walter R. Benjamin, 18 East 77th St., New York 21, N. Y. Nos. 244, 835, 1105, 1205, 1408.

*Pierre Bérès, 6 West 56th St., New York 19, N. Y. Nos. 1001, 1454.

*H. Bittner & Co., 67 West 55th St., New York 19, N. Y. No. 1336.

Mr. Frank Black, National Broadcasting Co., Rockefeller Center, New York 20, N. Y. Nos. 375, 707, 1641, 1796-97, 1799.

Boston Public Library, Copley Square, Boston 17, Massachusetts. Nos. 12, 25-26, 30, 66-92, 253, 271, 274-75, 284, 286, 315-16, 326, 333, 611, 628, 721, 723-25, 741-43, 748, 766, 769, 791, 797, 820, 822-26, 851, 882, 885, 908, 912, 952, 958, 992, 1013-14, 1035, 1037, 1041, 1061, 1128, 1135, 1198-1202, 1281, 1321, 1323, 1351, 1355, 1362, 1415, 1421, 1559, 1607-08, 1610-11, 1649, 1737, 1747-48, 1766, 1783, 1829-30, 1843, 1864-65, 1887, 1937, 1939, 1967, 1971, 1996, 2014.

Boston Symphony Orchestra, Symphony Hall, Boston 15, Massachusetts. Nos. 962, 982, 1390, 1448, 1561, 1817.

*Broude Brothers, 56 West 45th St., New York 19, N. Y. Nos. 403, 927, 1224, 1776.

Mr. Storm Bull, 603 Spruce St., Boulder, Colorado. No. 872.

Mr. Adolf Busch, 49 East 96th St., New York 29, N. Y. No. 389.

Chicago Symphony Orchestra, 220 South Michigan Ave., Chicago 4, Illinois. Nos. 1020, 1240, 1250.

Curtis Institute of Music, Rittenhouse Square, Philadelphia 3, Pennsylvania. Nos. 19, 1071, 1102, 1288, 1312-20, 1719, 1792, 1863, 1894-95, 1900-01, 1906-07, 1909, 1911, 1913, 1915, 1917-18, 1923, 1927, 1930-31.

Mr. George Darmstadt, 926 Lucile Ave., Los Angeles 26, California. No. 237.

Dartmouth College Library, Hanover, New Hampshire. No. 833.

Mrs. Meyer Davis, Sorrento, Maine. Nos. 422, 1067.

Mr. Wilhelm Dieterle, 22368 Fairview Acres, Canoga Park, California. No. 1692.

Mr. Arnold Dresden, 606 Elm Ave., Swarthmore, Pennsylvania. No. 722.

Dr. Arthur Drey, 355 Riverside Drive, New York 25, N. Y. Nos. 1677, 1684.

Mr. Henry S. Drinker, 249 Merion Road, Merion, Pennsylvania. No. 384.

The Folger Shakespeare Library, 201 East Capitol St. N.W., Washington, 3, D. C. Nos. 15, 479, 487, 720, 730-31, 909-11, 913, 1006, 1225, 1256, 1325, 1452, 1573, 1995, 2011.

The Free Library of Philadelphia, Logan Square, Philadelphia 3, Pennsylvania. No. 999.

*Galerie St. Etienne, 46 West 57th St., New York 19, N. Y. Nos. 356, 843, 1292, 1332, 1637, 1646, 1654, 1675, 1681, 1788-90, 1798, 1881, 1934.

Isabella Stewart Gardner Museum, Fenway Court, Boston 15, Massachusetts. Nos. 776, 828-29, 849, 1058, 1572.

Mr. Alexander Ginn, Gates Mills, Ohio. No. 799.

Mr. Wallace Goodrich, Manchester, Massachusetts, No. 708.

*Ernest E. Gottlieb, 450 North Beverly Drive, Beverly Hills, California. No. 1266.

*Paul Gottschalk, Inc., 21 Pearl St., New York 4, N. Y. Nos. 1083, 1290, 1298.

Harvard University, Dumbarton Oaks Research Library, 1703 32nd St. N.W., Washington 7, D. C. Nos. 553, 1099, 1602, 1811.

Harvard University, Isham Memorial Library, Cambridge 38, Massachusetts. Nos. 809, 811, 1680.

Harvard University Library, Cambridge 38, Massachusetts. Nos. 35, 56-57, 211, 261-62, 453, 490-91, 538, 733, 778, 919, 1026, 1552, 1574, 1628.

Mr. Emil Heermann, 3632 Victoria Lane, Cincinnati, Ohio. No. 245.

Miss Yrsa Hein, 114 East 85th St., New York 28, N. Y. Nos. 1095, 1267, 1685.

The Heineman Foundation for Research, Educational, Charitable, and Scientific Purposes, Inc., New York, N. Y. Nos. 22, 48, 214, 340, 542, 552, 934, 1211, 1223, 1270, 1289, 1294, 1302, 1634, 1639, 1666, 1682, 1701, 1711, 1791, 1806, 1891-92, 1916, 1929, 1933.

Miss Daisy Wood Hildreth, Pacific Institute of Fine Arts, Seattle, Washington. No. 892.

*Emil Hirsch, 558 Madison Avenue, New York 22, N. Y. No. 1988.

Hispanic Society of America Library, Broadway, between 155th and 156th Sts., New York 32, N. Y. No. 860.

The Historical Society of Pennsylvania, 1300 Locust St., Philadelphia 7, Pennsylvania. Nos. 488, 1434, 1579.

*The House of Books, 2 West 56th St., New York 19, N. Y. No. 1259.

Mr. Arthur Billings Hunt, Ridgefield, Connecticut. No. 1845.

Henry E. Huntington Library and Art Gallery, 1151 Oxford Road, San Marino 9, California. Nos. 204, 248, 850, 855, 857, 1094, 1212-13, 1555, 1962.

Mr. Harold Hutcheson, Lake Forest College, Lake Forest, Illinois. Nos. 231, 1781.

Dr. Harold T. Hyman, Pipersville, Pennsylvania. No. 1700.

Miss Anahid Iskian, 6 West 56th St., New York 19, N. Y. No. 1660.

*Walter J. Johnson, 125 East 23rd St., New York 10, N. Y. No. 923.

Mrs. William Powell Jones, Gates Mills, Ohio. No. 1208.

Mr. Werner Josten, 95 Round Hill, Northampton, Massachusetts. No. 406.

Mr. Rudolf F. Kallir, 285 Riverside Drive, New York 25, N. Y. Nos. 32, 43, 243, 272, 371-72, 442, 559, 841, 978, 1029, 1215, 1235, 1280, 1449, 1721, 1749, 1879, 1979, 1981, 1983, 1985, 1992.

Mrs. Charlotte A. Kleiss, 2336 N.W. Everett St., Portland 10, Oregon. Nos. 932, 1801-02.

Mr. Louis Krasner, Syracuse University, Syracuse 10, New York. Nos. 210, 265, 1219.

Mr. Hans Lange, Albuquerque, New Mexico. No. 1021.

The League of Composers, 130 West 56th St., New York 19, N. Y. Nos. 522, 1187, 1242-43, 1357, 1832, 1880.

Miss Lotte Lehmann, Hope Branch Park, Santa Barbara, California. No. 1991.

The Library of Congress, Washington 25, D. C. Nos. 2-4, 7, 9-11, 14, 16-17, 20-21, 23-24, 31, 34, 37, 45, 47, 51, 53, 55, 58-59, 61-62, 64-65, 93, 201, 203, 206-07, 209, 215, 225, 241, 251-52, 254-57, 260, 263-64, 266-68, 277, 280-81, 283, 288-89, 291-92, 296, 308-09, 311, 313-14, 322, 327-28, 330-32, 334, 350, 358, 362, 364, 383, 423-25, 437, 439-41, 443, 445-52, 454-68, 470, 472-78, 480-84, 486, 492-508, 513, 515-17, 529-32, 535, 539, 548, 554, 560-67, 571-82, 584-89, 608-09, 612, 614-15, 617-23, 625-26, 629-30, 636, 641, 645, 649-59, 661-79, 681-97, 703, 706, 716-17, 719, 729, 735-38, 749-50, 767, 770, 775, 777, 779, 783-85, 789, 795, 800, 805, 810, 814-15, 817-19, 821, 834, 844, 853-54, 862-63, 870, 874, 876-81, 883-84, 889, 895, 897-98, 900, 902-07, 920, 929, 937-41, 944, 947, 950-51, 954-56, 959-60, 963, 969, 974, 984-87, 989-90, 993, 997, 1004-05, 1007-08, 1010, 1015-19, 1022-23, 1028, 1031-32, 1038, 1040, 1049, 1052-57, 1059, 1062-63, 1065-66, 1068-70, 1074, 1077, 1081, 1084-86, 1091, 1093, 1096-98, 1101, 1103-04, 1106, 1109, 1113-14, 1116-17, 1119, 1123-24, 1127, 1131-34, 1138, 1146, 1158, 1165, 1175-76, 1189, 1196, 1203, 1210, 1230, 1234, 1236, 1246-47, 1258, 1263, 1279, 1287, 1307-08, 1310-11, 1322, 1326-30, 1333-35, 1338, 1340, 1344-45, 1349, 1353-54, 1356, 1360-61, 1363, 1365-67, 1372-78, 1380, 1384-85, 1387, 1391-92, 1394, 1396, 1399, 1400-07, 1411-12, 1416-20, 1422-27, 1431-32, 1435-36, 1438-40, 1442-45, 1451, 1455, 1458, 1460-1537, 1544, 1548, 1551, 1554, 1556, 1563-66, 1568, 1571, 1575-76, 1578, 1581-84, 1587, 1590, 1592-94, 1604, 1606, 1613, 1618, 1620, 1629, 1647, 1661, 1683, 1705, 1714, 1718, 1720, 1722, 1727, 1729, 1733, 1735-36, 1739, 1750-52, 1758-63, 1765, 1768-69, 1771-73, 1777, 1782-85, 1788, 1797, 1800, 1810, 1816, 1818-19, 1824-25, 1828, 1831, 1837, 1839, 1841, 1852-54, 1862, 1867, 1873, 1875, 1877, 1882-85, 1888, 1897, 1903, 1910, 1920, 1926, 1940-41, 1948-49, 1954, 1956, 1958, 1960-61, 1963-66, 1968-70, 1972, 1976-78, 1987, 1990, 2010, 2017.

The Library of Congress, The Elizabeth Sprague Coolidge Foundation, Washington 25, D. C. Nos. 13, 167, 199, 202, 205, 208, 276, 293, 295, 323, 427-34, 436, 485, 519, 521, 523-27, 541, 568-70, 610, 702, 705, 744, 790, 802, 816, 847-48, 901, 946, 961, 976-77, 981, 991, 995-96, 1044, 1115, 1129, 1159-64, 1166-72, 1180-81, 1187, 1241, 1244-45, 1248-49, 1253, 1358, 1364, 1368-71, 1389, 1413, 1446-47, 1450, 1539-40, 1543, 1545, 1556, 1562, 1616-17, 1741, 1809, 1826-27, 1833-36, 1838, 1851, 1868, 1938, 1952, 1955, 1959, 1974.

List of Present Owners—*continued*

The Library of Congress, Serge Koussevitzky Music Foundation, Washington 25, D. C. Nos. 102, 435, 728, 866-67, 979, 1173, 1233, 1251, 1560.

The Library of Congress, The Gertrude Clarke Whittall Foundation, Washington 25, D. C. Nos. 38, 220, 226-27, 229, 233-34, 335-38, 341, 343-48, 351-55, 357, 359-61, 365, 367-70, 373, 376-77, 380, 382, 385, 387-88, 390-92, 394-95, 397-99, 401-02, 404-05, 407, 409-10, 413-20, 921, 926, 930-31, 1207, 1209, 1217-18, 1221, 1228-29, 1268, 1272, 1283, 1293, 1297, 1301, 1430, 1614-15, 1619, 1622, 1624, 1630, 1632, 1636, 1638, 1642-43, 1657, 1664, 1667, 1669, 1674, 1676, 1687-88, 1691, 1694-96, 1697-98, 1708-09, 1902, 1904, 1919, 1928, 1943-44, 1951.

Dr. Ludwig Loewenstein, 125 East 72nd St., New York 21, N. Y. Nos. 412, 1079.

Mr. John G. McCullough, 128 Christopher St., New York 14, N. Y. No. 36.

Memorial Library of Music, Stanford University, Stanford, California. Nos. 6, 8, 18, 27, 44, 52, 60, 63, 200, 219, 228, 242, 258, 273, 282, 285, 287, 307, 312, 318-19, 321, 324-25, 400, 408, 421, 426, 438, 512, 518, 520, 528, 533-34, 536-37, 544, 551, 556-57, 583, 616, 624, 631, 637, 646, 698, 709, 727, 734, 739-40, 745, 747, 780, 787, 792-94, 796, 801, 803, 827, 832, 836, 838, 840, 842, 852, 859, 869, 873, 886-88, 891, 894, 896, 899, 922, 957, 964-67, 980, 998, 1000, 1045, 1050, 1087, 1118, 1122, 1136-37, 1148-50, 1179, 1182, 1184-86, 1191, 1193, 1197, 1206, 1216, 1227, 1232, 1237, 1239, 1252, 1257, 1260-62, 1265, 1271, 1276, 1278, 1284, 1291, 1324, 1331, 1337, 1339, 1343, 1346, 1359, 1379, 1382-83, 1393, 1396, 1410, 1414, 1428-29, 1453, 1456, 1542, 1546, 1550, 1553, 1569-70, 1580, 1586, 1588, 1605, 1609, 1650, 1668, 1706, 1724, 1728, 1734, 1740, 1743, 1754, 1764, 1770, 1775, 1793, 1795, 1804-05, 1807-08, 1820-21, 1823, 1856-60, 1878, 1889, 1912, 1936, 1945, 1947, 1980, 1986, 1989, 2007, 2013.

Mrs. Etelka Freund Milch, 1511 Park Road N.W., Washington, D. C. No. 349.

The Pierpont Morgan Library, 29 East 36th St., New York 16, N. Y. Nos. 236, 540, 858, 917, 1549, 1558, 1869-70, 2012.

*Charles L. Morley, 25 East 83rd St., New York 28, N. Y. Nos. 1626, 1670.

Mrs. Marion Sanderson Nall, Tarrytown, New York. Nos. 1180, 1190, 1192, 1194-95.

The National Orchestral Association, Inc., 113 West 57th St., New York 19, N. Y. No. 1304.

New England Conservatory of Music, 290 Huntington Ave., Boston 15, Massachusetts. Nos. 510-11, 640, 644, 732, 807-08, 1177, 1264, 1993-94.

The New York Public Library, Fifth Ave. and 42nd St., New York 18, N. Y. Nos. 5, 28-29, 39, 217, 224, 239-40, 329, 444, 509, 514, 555, 613, 660, 700, 713-14, 726, 746, 781, 786, 788, 806, 812, 830-31, 871, 893, 918, 928, 935, 942-43, 945, 949, 953, 968, 970-72, 975, 1002, 1011, 1024-25, 1033-34, 1036, 1039, 1110-11, 1125, 1130, 1174, 1178, 1254, 1286, 1296, 1300, 1303, 1341-42, 1347-48, 1350, 1386, 1409, 1433,

1437, 1441, 1457, 1459, 1547, 1591, 1596, 1599-1601, 1662, 1665, 1689, 1715, 1723, 1725-26, 1730-32, 1744-46, 1753, 1755-57, 1840, 1842, 1844, 1847-50, 1855, 1876, 1898-99, 1922, 1924-25, 1932, 1935, 1973, 1975.

The New York Public Library, Music Library, 121 East 58th St., New York 22, N. Y. Nos. 1009, 1842, 1844, 1847, 1849-50, 1871.

The Newberry Library, 60 West Walton St., Chicago 10, Illinois. Nos. 54, 411, 550, 856, 1076, 1238, 1273-75, 1589, 1653, 1690, 1712, 1896.

Mrs. Eugene Allen Noble, Providence, Rhode Island. Nos. 90, 230, 249, 489, 699, 988, 1222, 1538, 1774.

Mr. Felix Oppenheim, University of Delaware, Newark, Delaware. No. 1658.

Peabody Conservatory of Music, Baltimore 2, Maryland. No. 212.

Mr. Louis Persinger, 340 Riverside Drive, New York 25, N. Y. Nos. 1997-2005.

Mr. Gregor Piatigorsky, 400 South Bundy Drive, Los Angeles, California. Nos. 247, 363, 543, 549, 632-33, 643, 647-48, 771, 774, 925, 1075, 1305, 1706, 1710.

Miss Lily Pons, 10 Gracie Square, New York 28, N. Y. No. 638.

Private collectors. Nos. 40-42, 238, 339, 342, 374, 386, 393, 396, 1277, 1890, 1942.

Mr. Franz Roehn, 2270 La Granada Drive, Hollywood 28, California. Nos. 50, 216, 270, 813, 1621, 1633, 1644, 1648, 1652, 1671-72, 1702, 1717, 2015-16.

Mr. Kenneth Rose, 2006 18th Ave. South, Nashville 4, Tennessee. No. 213.

Mrs. Walter T. Rosen, Katonah, New York. No. 1080.

*The Rosenbach Company, 322 East 57th St., New York 22, N. Y. Nos. 837, 1092.

Mr. Beryl Rubinstein, 2195 St. James Parkway, Cleveland, Ohio. No. 1567.

Mrs. Marie Salabert, 154 Elmwood Ave., Hawthorne, New York. Nos. 712, 890.

*Walter Schatzki, 57 East 56th St., New York 22, N. Y. Nos. 1003, 1100, 1640, 1703, 1984.

The John H. Scheide Library, Titusville, Pennsylvania. Nos. 232, 1921.

The Ernest Schelling Collection, 863 Park Avenue, New York 21, N. Y. Nos. 545, 861, 1713.

G. Schirmer, Inc., 3 East 43rd St., New York 17, N. Y. Nos. 864-65, 868, 1612, 2006.

Mr. Ernst Schneider, 498 West End Ave., New York 24, N. Y. Nos. 751-765.

Mr. Rudolf Serkin, Brattleboro, Vermont. No. 379.

Sibley Musical Library, Eastman School of Music, 44 Swan St., Rochester 4, New York. Nos. 223, 278-79, 381, 469, 471, 635, 642, 772-73, 839, 845-46, 924, 948, 1030, 1051, 1078, 1082, 1089, 1295, 1309, 1398, 1577, 1585, 1603, 1631, 1645, 1651, 1686, 1699, 1742.

Mr. Walter Slezak, 1520 West Laurel Ave., Los Angeles 46, California. Nos. 222, 1625.

Mr. George E. Steinbach, 407 Central Park West, New York 25, N. Y. No. 1635.

Mr. Igor Stravinsky, 1260 North Wetherly Drive, Hollywood 46, California. Nos. 1812-15.

Mr. Alfred J. Swan, 519 Walnut Lane, Swarthmore, Pennsylvania. Nos. 600-07, 1042.

Estate of Frank A. Taft, Montclair, New Jersey. Nos. 33, 1027.

Mr. Carl H. Tollefsen, 946 President St., Brooklyn, N. Y. Nos. 250, 320, 704, 711, 1204, 1595, 1716, 1946.

Mr. Arturo Toscanini, 254th St. and Independence Ave., New York 71, N. Y. Nos. 221, 235, 259, 317, 558, 634, 639, 701, 710, 718, 1183, 1214, 1627, 1679, 1803, 1874, 1914.

Mr. Walter Toscanini, 254th St. and Independence Ave., New York 71, N. Y. Nos. 259, 1872.

University of California Library, Berkeley 4, California. Nos. 297-306.

University of California at Los Angeles, William Andrews Clark Memorial Library, 2205 West Adams Boulevard, Los Angeles 18, California. Nos. 680, 798, 875, 1157.

University of Michigan, General Library, Ann Arbor, Michigan. No. 973.

University of Pennsylvania Library, Philadelphia 4, Pennsylvania. Nos. 1, 768, 1395, 1597-98, 1866.

Mr. Nathan Van Patten, P. O. Box 1768, Stanford, California. No. 310.

Dr. Hermann Vollmer, 25 Central Park West, New York 23, N. Y. No. 1285.

Mr. Samuel R. Wachtell, 1 Cedar St., New York 4, N. Y. No. 1794.

Mrs. Alma Mahler Werfel, 610 North Bedford Drive, Beverly Hills, California. Nos. 269, 1139-45, 1147, 1151-56.

Western Reserve University Library, 11111 Euclid Ave., Cleveland 6, Ohio. Nos. 1231, 1822.

*E. Weyhe, 794 Lexington Avenue, New York 21, N. Y. Nos. 1282, 1299, 1306, 1557.

Mr. R. Thornton Wilson, Jr., 1 Sutton Place South, New York 22, N. Y. No. 1905.

Mr. Richard Winter, 590 Fort Washington Ave., New York 33, N. Y. No. 1953.

Yale University Library, William A. Speck Collection of Goetheana, New Haven, Connecticut. Nos. 218, 1088, 1120-21, 1226, 1381, 1388, 1767, 1886, 1893, 1957, 2008-09.

Yale University School of Music, New Haven, Connecticut. Nos. 49, 782, 1738, 1778-79, 1846.

Mr. Christian Zabriskie, 960 Park Ave., New York 28, N. Y. Nos. 246, 546.

Mrs. Mary Louise Zimbalist, 1816 DeLancey Place, Philadelphia 3, Pennsylvania. Nos. 46, 1623, 1659, 1673, 1704.

Albert, Mrs. Charles. No. 213.
Albrecht, Otto E. Nos. 513, 530.
Alcott, John. No. 1353.
Almásy, Countess Rosa. Nos. 1631, 1686.
Almásy, Countesses Wilhelmine and Melanie. No. 1635.
Alsager, Herr. No. 210.
Amerling, Franz. Nos. 229, 933.
Anastasi, Antonietta Pozzoni. No. 259.
André, August. Nos. 1270, 1273-74, 1305.
André, Carl August. Nos. 1278, 1291.
André, Jean Baptiste. No. 1272.
André, Johann. Nos. 1269, 1304.
André, Julius. Nos. 1281, 1289, 1304.
Appold, Herr. No. 1297.
Arnoldsen, H. Oskar. No. 875.
Artaria, August. Nos. 220, 917.
Artaria, Domenico. No. 219.
Ayrton, William. No. 932.

Bach, David J. No. 1794.
Bach, Johann Christian. No. 49.
Baermann, Heinrich. No. 1943.
Bagannhevoff, Nicolai. No. 1284.
Balassa, Ottilie von. Nos. 335, 341, 359-61, 365, 385, 391-92, 394-95, 407, 413-14, 418-19.
Balling, Frau Michael. Nos. 383, 393.
Bauer-Lechner, Natalie. Nos. 1148-49.
Beauchêne, Alfred de. No. 954.
Becker, Hugo. No. 1984.
Becker, Jean. No. 423.
Beckman, Francis J. L., archbishop of Dubuque. No. 550.
Bekker, Paul. Nos. 1029-30, 1620.

Bethge, Frau Lisbeth. Nos. 804, 808.
Betti, Adelson. No. 1394.
Bispham, David. Nos. 945, 949, 971-72, 975, 1024, 1254, 1596, 1599, 1726, 1730, 1755-57, 1935.
Bixby, William K. No. 1962.
Bliss, Lillie. No. 39.
Bliss, Mr. and Mrs. Robert Woods. Nos. 553, 1099, 1602, 1811.
Blossom, Mrs. D. S. No. 1822.
Bondy, Oscar. Nos. 225, 379, 389, 404-05, 926, 1301, 1721.
Bottée de Toulmon, A. Nos. 475-78, 1284.
Bovet de Valentigny, Alfred. Nos. 44, 1606, 1882.
Brahms, Johannes. No. 933.
Brancour, René. No. 771.
Brecher, Gustav. No. 1791.
Breidenstein, Marie. No. 1098.
Breitkopf und Härtel. Nos. 40-42, 403, 927, 1224.
Brown, W. J. No. 984.
Buckingham, Katherine, duchess of. No. 820.
Bülow, Blandine von. No. 1920.
Bülow, Hans von. Nos. 398, 1087-88.
Burrell, Mrs. Mary. Nos. 1894-95, 1900-01, 1906-07, 1909, 1911, 1913, 1915, 1917-18, 1923, 1927, 1930-31.

Calmann-Lévy, Mme. Robert. No. 1305.
Calvocoressi, Michel D. No. 60.
Carozzi, Mrs. G. N. No. 1360.
Chapman, Nellie. No. 1193.
Chauvot, Eugénie. No. 800.
Cherubini, Luigi. Nos. 59, 1581.
Christ, Viktor. No. 443.
Clinton, earl of Lincoln. No. 25.

Cohen, Harriet. No. 203.
Commer, Franz. No. 1887.
Connell, Horatio. Nos. 1597-98.
Cramer, T. B. No. 2.
Cumberland, Gerald. No. 899.
Cranz, Albert. Nos. 1654, 1656, 1681.
Cummings, William H. Nos. 2, 20, 23, 34, 51, 58, 62, 93, 201, 264, 277, 280, 282-83, 289, 330, 332, 612, 614, 617-18, 629, 784, 870, 895, 920, 938, 984-87, 1005, 1116-17, 1131-34, 1236, 1344, 1353, 1391-92, 1396, 1398, 1554, 1683, 1735-36, 1750, 1786, 1824, 1949, 1963-66, 1968-69.
Czerny, Carl. No. 246.

Daly, Augustin. No. 1822.
Damrosch, Walter. No. 239.
Darmstadt, George. No. 1098.
Davis, Mrs. Meyer. No. 396.
Dehn, Siegfried W. No. 53.
Demidov, Anatol. Nos. 7, 10-11, 314, 539, 716.
Déséglise, Victor. No. 1454.
Devrient, Frau Therese. No. 1211.
Doego, Riccardo. No. 1873.
Dohn, A. W. No. 53.
Dolgorouki, prince. No. 787.
Dragonetti, Domenico. No. 821.
Dresel, Otto. No. 1680.
Drexel, Anthony J. No. 329.
Drexel, Joseph W. Nos. 613, 1296.

Edwards, Julian. Nos. 1842, 1844, 1847, 1849-50.
Engel, Carl. No. 1356.
Epstein, Julius. Nos. 48, 1650.
Eschborn, Natalia Frassini. No. 1283.
Esterházy, countess Karoline. No. 1635.

Farinelli, Carlo Broschi. No. 1054.
Fischer, George. No. 818.
Foote, Arthur. No. 948.

Franck, Major von. No. 1265.
Frege, Livia. No. 1719.
Friedberg, Carl. No. 239.
Friedländer, Max. Nos. 50, 216, 219, 238, 270, 339, 792, 813, 924, 1126, 1633, 1637, 1641, 1644-45, 1648, 1652, 1655, 1670-72, 1692, 1702, 1717, 1881, 1950, 2015-16.
Fuchs, Alois. Nos. 2, 29, 43, 815, 837, 1284, 1367 (?), 1725, 1766, 1820, 1829.
Fuchs-Seligmann, G. No. 1302.

Gabrilowitsch, Ossip. Nos. 1046-48.
Gaebler, Hans T. No. 856.
Gallini, Natale. Nos. 200, 324, 518, 528, 556, 709, 734, 780, 793, 827, 1179, 1184, 1197, 1232, 1260, 1337, 1339, 1346, 1359, 1379, 1382, 1409-10, 1456, 1542, 1728, 1764, 2013.
Gassner, Ferdinand Simon. No. 1820.
Georges, Alexandre. No. 800.
Ginn, Frank H. Nos. 2108, 1567.
Gloetzner, Anton. No. 609.
Göpfart, Carl. No. 1107.
Goodwin, W. No. 21.
Gorke, Manfred. No. 52.
Gras, Doris. No. 1889.
Grassnick, F. A. No. 1272.
Gravina, count Gilberto. No. 1920.
Grell, Eduard August. No. 1027.

Hall, Mrs. R. J. Nos. 510-11, 644, 732, 1255, 1264, 1993-94.
Halsey, F. R. No. 1908.
Hamilton Palace Collection. No. 2011.
Hamm, J. V. No. 1908.
Harrison, Mrs. Benjamin. No. 810.
Hartmann, Arthur. Nos. 642, 839, 1309.
Hase, Helmut von. No. 356.
Haslinger, Tobias. No. 215.
Hayes, Philip. No. 896.
Heckmann, Robert. No. 1258.

Heineman, Dannie N. No. 926.
Helbig, princess. No. 1257.
Henkel, H. No. 61.
Henschel, sir George. No. 375.
Herter, Dr. Christian A. Nos. 39, 240, 893, 935, 1286, 1300, 1665, 1689, 1715.
Heyer, Wilhelm. Nos. 486, 538, 815, 1049-50, 1072, 1294, 1722, 1790, 1800.
Heymann, Karl. No. 1099.
Hill, Arthur F. Nos. 318-19, 787, 1397, 1878.
Hiller, Ferdinand. No. 227.
Hodges, George. No. 331.
Holmes, John. No. 201.
Hopkinson, Francis. No. 768.
Horn, Frau Conrat. No. 48.
Hubermann, Bronislaw. Nos. 221, 235.
Hüttenbrenner, Anselm. No. 1707.

Israel, Mrs. Tillie. No. 215.

Jacobs, Josephine. Nos. 1922, 1932.
Jacobson, Marguerite. No. 1359.
Jähns, F. W. No. 1223.
Jagla, Maria. No. 1643.
Jahn, Otto. Nos. 1279, 1302.
Jefferys, Charles. No. 1117.
Joachim, Joseph. Nos. 229, 350, 1272.
Jones, H. V. No. 1212.
Jordan, Eben B. No. 640.
Joseffy, Rafael. Nos. 719, 729, 1065-66, 1069-70, 1077, 1081, 1085, 1091, 1097, 1101, 1104, 1106, 1109.

Kaffka, Johann Nepomuk. No. 922.
Kahanowicz, Alexander C. Grzy-mala Turzanski. No. 550.
Katenn, M. No. 220.
Keating, George T. Nos. 44, 228, 400, 408, 421, 544, 551, 646, 740, 745, 801, 803, 838, 894, 1087, 1122, 1193, 1216, 1239, 1265, 1278, 1284, 1550, 1570, 1668, 1724, 1775, 1795, 1805, 1808, 1821, 1912, 1945, 1947, 1989.
Kiesewetter, R. G. No. 1367.
Klindworth, Karl. No. 1921.
Knapp, Mrs. R. S. No. 1991.
Koetschau, J. No. 49.
Koester, K. No. 423.
Korgaeff, Serge. No. 833.
Krause, Martin. Nos. 1087-88.
Kreisler, Fritz. Nos. 350, 535.
Krug, Siegfried. No. 49.
Kufferath, Hubert F. Nos. 483-84, 1729.
Kurtz, A. H. von. No. 1951.

Laforge, Frank. No. 638.
Lambert, Alexander. Nos. 217, 1002.
Latzelsberger, Johann. No. 1643.
Lehman, Kurt. No. 1921.
Leins, Marie. Nos. 1622, 1632.
Leschetizky, Mme. Essipof. No. 546.
Leschetizky, Theodor. No. 246.
Levi, Hermann. No. 1722.
Levin, Willy, No. 1798.
Liebig, Carl. No. 1303.
Liebeskind, Joseph. No. 923.
Lind, Jenny. No. 1293.
Lipinski, C. No. 1137.
Livingston, Mrs. Luther. No. 278.
Locker-Lampson, Frederick. Nos. 39, 893, 935, 1300.
Lonsdale, C. No. 1547.
Lowell, Amy. No. 211.
Ludwig I, landgrave of Hessen-Darmstadt. No. 1297.
Ludwig II, king of Bavaria. No. 1304.
Lux, Mary Sefton Thomas. No. 340.

Malchair, G. No. 896.
Manuscript Society of New York. Nos. 531, 619.
Marchesi, Blanche. No. 745.
Marie, princess of Schönburg-Erbach von Battenberg. No. 1297.

Marshall, Julian. Nos. 25, 59, 278, 1581, 1593.
Mason, Lowell. No. 1019.
Mazzoni, Signor. No. 1554.
Meinert, Carl. No. 1917.
Mendelssohn-Bartholdy, Felix. Nos. 46, 239.
Menter, Sophie. No. 1096.
Miller, Dayton C. No. 815.
Mortier de Fontaine, H. L. S. No. 220.
Mosse, Rudolf. No. 1806.
Mühlenfeld, L. No. 1206.
Muller, Joseph. Nos. 5, 29, 555, 700, 714, 746, 781, 786, 806, 812, 830-31, 871, 915-16, 942-43, 970, 1033-34, 1036, 1039, 1043, 1060, 1064, 1073, 1130, 1174, 1347-48, 1433, 1437, 1441, 1459, 1600-01, 1662, 1744, 1840, 1855, 1876, 1898, 1973, 1975.
Muller, Robert. No. 786.
Muncker, Dr. Franz. No. 1793.
Musical Antiquarian Society, London. Nos. 329, 1965.
Musikbibliothek Peters, Leipzig. Nos. 1218, 1273-74.
Musikverein, Würzburg. No. 1906.

Nabokoff, Nicholas. No. 1816.
Naue, Johann Friedrich. No. 213.
Nemeczek, Franz. No. 1294.
Neuburger, Hugo. Nos. 222, 1625.
Nikisch, Artur. No. 1100.
Novello, Joseph Alfred. No. 1733.
Novello, Vincent. Nos. 329, 821, 1936, 1965.

Oberlaender, Gustav. Nos. 412, 1122, 1700, 1775, 1942.
Obrist, Aloys. No. 1015.
Ochs, Siegfried. No. 1269.
Ogny, count d'. No. 930.
Osiris, M. No. 890.

Paris, le comte de. No. 891.
Pasque, Ernest. No. 1917.

Peck, M. No. 331.
Pérégally, Adolphe. No. 727.
Petter, Gustav A. No. 1282.
Pichler, Carl. No. 1674.
Pickering, Thomas. No. 1733.
Pigott, George. No. 1353.
Planché, Jules. No. 290.
Planer, Natalie. Nos. 1901, 1913, 1931.
Pole, William. No. 1820.
Pollitz, Carl. No. 1767.
Posonyi, Alexander. Nos. 248, 928, 1049-50, 1665, 1689.
Powell, George E. J. No. 893.

Radiciotti, Giuseppe. No. 1257.
Radoux, Jean. No. 1879.
Randall, Dr., of Dulwich. No. 25.
Rehan, Ada. No. 1822.
Riddle, George. No. 723.
Ries, Ferdinand. No. 932.
Riesenfeld, Hugo. Nos. 28, 439, 509, 660, 788, 923, 1125, 1175, 1259, 1341, 1454, 1693, 1743, 1890.
Rietz, Julius. No. 46.
Rietz, E. W. Nos. 1899, 1924-25.
Rietz, Eduard. No. 1218.
Rimbault, Edward F. No. 1750.
Rinck, J. C. H. No. 1019.
Ritter, Philipp. No. 1297.
Robinson, John. No. 1005.
Rotter, Adalbert. No. 1687.
Royal Collection, Lisbon. Nos. 833, 1023, 1263, 1366, 1455, 1752.
Rudorff, Ernst. No. 38.
Rust, Wilhelm. No. 43.
Ruthardt, Adolf. No. 1107.

Salabert, C. W. No. 890.
Sanderson, Sybil. Nos. 1188, 1190, 1192, 1194-95.
Sauermann, Friederike. No. 1709.
Saunders, William. No. 967.
Scennis, Frédéric de. No. 1110.
Schaffer, Franz J. No. 1275.
Schindelmeisser, Louis. No. 1917.

Schirmer, Gustav. No. 1279.

Schmid, Anton. No. 928.

Schmidt, Gustav. No. 1930.

Schmitt, Herr. No. 1297.

Schmitt, Philipp. No. 1297.

Schneider, Dr. Eduard. Nos. 1657, 1673, 1695.

Scholz, Janos. No. 963.

Schulz, O. A. No. 1951.

Schumann, Clara Wieck. Nos. 409, 1722.

Schumann, Elisabeth. No. 1792.

Schumann, Marie. No. 374.

Schumann, Robert. Nos. 231, 239.

Schwarzmann, Norbert. No. 1618.

Seabury, Mrs. Mortimer A. (Frida Semler). Nos. 266-67.

Seligmann, Heinrich. No. 1302.

Shattuck, Lillian. No. 989.

Siedenburg, George R. Nos. 412, 1079, 1700, 1905.

Sikemeier, Johann. No. 1099.

Smith, Stephen Decatur. No. 1866.

Smolian, Arthur. Nos. 1976-77.

Society of British Musicians, London. No. 21.

Sonneck, Oscar G. Nos. 16, 209.

South, W. C. No. 213.

Speyer, Edward. Nos. 44, 374, 386, 437, 932, 954, 1271, 1593-94, 1795, 1805, 1808, 1854, 1954.

Spitta, Philipp. No. 963.

Stadler, Albert. No. 1642.

Stanford, earl of. No. 25.

Stern, Alfred. No. 1098.

Stiebar, Freiherr von. No. 1643.

Stillfried, Baron. No. 703.

Stonborough, Jerome. Nos. 220, 226, 233, 335-38, 341, 343-48, 352-55, 357, 359-61, 365, 367-70, 373, 376-77, 380, 382, 385, 388, 391-92, 394-95, 398, 401-02, 407, 409-10, 413-20, 936, 1293, 1297, 1622, 1632, 1638, 1642-43, 1657, 1695-96, 1708-09, 1902, 1904, 1919, 1928, 1944.

Streicher, J. B. No. 1293.

Stumpff, J. A. Nos. 39, 232.

Sullivan, Mrs. William A. No. 1.

Sulzbach, Emil. No. 1406.

Sumner, Charles. Nos. 261-62, 919.

Swift, Mrs. Charles H. Nos. 1273-74.

Taneiev, A. S. No. 835.

Taphouse, Thomas W. Nos. 616, 1353.

Tauber, S. No. 933.

Taubert, Wilhelm. No. 1269.

Taylor, baron. No. 1284.

Teschner, G. W. No. 1386.

Thayer, Alexander W. Nos. 1594, 1627, 1679, 1954.

Thomas, Theodore. No. 1896.

Tichatscheck, J. A. Nos. 1894, 1900, 1911.

Ticknor, Mrs. A. M. No. 1865.

Tollefsen, Carl F. No. 1107.

Toscanini, Arturo. No. 1021.

Toscanini, Walter. No. 707.

Vasconcellos, Joachim de. No. 1387.

Viardot-Garcia, Pauline. Nos. 46, 549.

Wagener, Dr. Nos. 1677, 1684.

Wagner, Eva Chamberlain. No. 1914.

Wall, Harry. No. 117.

Wallace, William. No. 965.

Warren, Samuel P. Nos. 649, 1019, 1054, 1279.

Wartel, Mme. No. 917.

Weber, Miroslav, Jr. No. 17.

Weitzmann, Karl Friedrich. Nos. 1902, 1928.

Wendell, Evert J. No. 1574.

Werschinger, C. V. No. 1283.

Weston, George B. Nos. 35, 56-57, 490-91, 538, 733, 1026, 1552, 1628.

Willmott, Ellen A. No. 1265.

Winterberger, Al. No. 1099.

Wittgenstein, Hermine. Nos. 229, 234, 921, 931, 1624, 1630, 1636, 1664, 1667, 1669, 1674, 1676, 1687-88, 1694, 1697-98, 1943.

Wittgenstein, Paul. No. 38.

Wittgenstein family. Nos. 930, 1268-69, 1272.

Woerz, Hans. No. 226.

Wolffheim, Werner. Nos. 37, 57, 474.

Woltmann, Pauline. Nos. 804, 808.

Ysaÿe, Eugène. No. 535.

Zabriskie, Christian. Nos. 45, 1338.

Zimbalist, Mrs. Mary Louise. Nos. 19, 1071, 1288, 1719, 1863, 1894-95, 1900-01, 1906-07, 1909, 1911, 1913, 1915, 1917-18, 1923, 1927, 1930-31.

Zweig, Stefan. No. 1788.

BIBLIOGRAPHY

CRITICAL EDITIONS OF COMPOSERS' WORKS

Bach, J. S. Werke. 61 v. Leipzig: Bach-Gesellschaft, 1851-1926.
—— ——. Reprinted, Ann Arbor: Edwards Bros., 1947.
Beethoven, L. van. Werke. 35 v. Leipzig: Breitkopf & Härtel, 1864-90.
—— ——. Reprinted, Ann Arbor: Edwards Bros., 1949.
Brahms, J. Werke. 26 v. Leipzig: Breitkopf & Härtel, 1926-27.
—— ——. Reprinted, Ann Arbor: Edwards Bros., 1949.
Chopin, F. Werke. 14 v. Leipzig: Breitkopf & Härtel, 1878-1902.
Friedrich des Grossen musikalische Werke. 3 v. in 4. Leipzig: Breitkopf & Härtel, 1889.
Händel, G. F. Werke. 97 v. Leipzig: Breitkopf & Härtel, 1859-94.
Haydn, J. Werke. 11 v. in 10 (no more published). Leipzig: Breitkopf & Härtel, 1907-37.
Lanner, J. Werke. 8 v. Leipzig: Breitkopf & Härtel, 1889-91.
Liszt, F. Musikalische Werke. Leipzig: Breitkopf & Härtel, 1907-   .
Mozart, W. A. Werke. 74 v. Leipzig: Breitkopf & Härtel, 1876-89.
Musorgskii, M. Sämtliche Werke. Moskau: Staatsmusikverlag, 1928-   .
Pergolesi, G. B. Opera omnia. 26 v. in 5. Roma: Gli amici della musica da camera, 1939-43.
Purcell, H. Works. London: Novello, Ewer & Co., 1878-   .
Schubert, F. Werke. 42 v. Leipzig: Breitkopf & Härtel, 1888-97.
Schumann, R. A. Werke. 31 v. Leipzig: Brietkopf & Härtel, 1886-93.
Wagner, R. Musikalische Werke. Leipzig: Breitkopf & Härtel, 1912-   .

BOOKS AND ARTICLES

Abbiati, F. Storia della musica. 5 v. Milano: Fratelli Treves (v. 2-5, Garzanti), 1939-46.
Abraham, G., ed. The music of Tchaikovsky. New York: W. W. Norton & Co., 1946.
Adams, J. Q. "A new song by Robert Jones," *Modern Language Quarterly*, I (1940), 45-48.
Albrecht, O. E. "Adventures and discoveries of a manuscript hunter," *Musical Quarterly*, XXXI (1945), 492-503. Also, as "Erlebnisse und Entdeckungen eines Manuskript-Jägers in USA," *Musica*, II (1948), 129-138.
Beck, G. Darius Milhaud, étude, suivie du catalogue chronologique complet de son oeuvre. Paris: Heugel et Cie., 1949.
Brahms, J. Johannes Brahms im Briefwechsel mit Joseph Joachim, ed. A. Moser. 2 v. Berlin: Deutsche Brahms-Gesellschaft, 1908 (Brahms' Briefwechsel, 5-6).
Campbell, F. C. "Schubert song autographs in the Whittall Collection," *Library of Congress Quarterly Journal*, VI, no. 4 (Aug. 1949), 3-8.
Catalogue of the Burrell Collection of Wagner documents, letters and biographical material. London: Nonpareil Press, 1929.
Catalogue of the famous musical library . . . of the late W. H. Cummings. [London, 1917.]

Bibliography—*continued*

Debussy, C. Correspondance de Claude Debussy et Pierre Louÿs. Paris: J. Corti, 1945.

Debussy, C. "Lettres inédites de Claude Debussy à Eugène Ysaÿe," *Les Annales politiques et littéraires*, August 25, 1933.

Deutsch, O. E. Schubert, thematic catalogue of all his works in chronological order. London: J. M. Dent & Sons, 1951.

Duncan, B. " 'Home, sweet home' ", *University of Rochester Library Bulletin*, IV (1949), 21-25.

Einstein, A. "On certain mss. of Mozart's," *Journal of the American Musicological Society*, I (1948), 13-16.

Engel, C. "Beethoven's Op. 3 an *envoi de Vienne*?," *Musical Quarterly*, XIII (1927), 261-279.

Falck, M. Wilhelm Friedemann Bach, sein Leben und seine Werke, mit thematischem Verzeichnis seiner Kompositionen. Leipzig: C. F. Kahnt, 1913.

Glenewinkel, H. "Verzeichnis des musikalischen Nachlasses von L. Spohr," *Archiv für Musikwissenschaft*, I (1918-19), 432-36.

Grove's dictionary of music and musicians. Supplementary volume. New York: Macmillan Co., 1940. (Catalogue of Liszt's works, by H. Searle, p. 368-402.)

Haas, R. M. Wolfgang Amadeus Mozart. Potsdam: Akademische Verlagsgesellschaft Athenaion, 1933.

Hertzmann, E. "The newly discovered autograph of Beethoven's *Rondo a capriccio*, op. 129," *Musical Quarterly*, XXXII (1946), 171-195.

Hill, R. S. "A mistempered Bach manuscript," *Notes*, VII (1949-50), 377-386.

Hopkinson, C. A bibliography of the musical and literary works of Hector Berlioz . . . [Edinburgh]: Edinburgh Bibliographical Society, 1951.

Istel, E. "Ein Doppelfuge von der Hand Wagners," *Die Musik*, CXIV (1912), Heft 19, p. 27-41.

——. "Richard Wagners C-dur Symphonie," *Neue Musik-Zeitung*, XXXII (1911), Heft 5, p. 97.

Jähns, F. W. Carl Maria von Weber in seinen Werken. Berlin: Schlesinger, 1871.

Jonas, O. "An unknown sketch by Beethoven," *Musical Quarterly*, XXVI (1940), 186-191.

Jurgenson, B. Catalogue thématique des oeuvres de P. Tschaikowsky. Moscou: P. Jurgenson, [1891].

Kallir, R. F. "A Beethoven relic," *Music Review*, IX (1949), 173-177.

Kinsky, G. Die Handschriften von Beethoven's Egmont-Musik. Wien: H. Reichner, 1933.

——. Musikhistorisches Museum von Wilhelm Heyer in Cöln. Katalog. Vierter Band: Musik-Autographen. Cöln: Heyer, 1916.

Köchel, L. Chronologisch-thematisches Verzeichnis sämtlicher Tonwerke Wolfgang Amade Mozarts . . . Dritte Auflage, ed. A. Einstein, mit einem Supplement . . . Ann Arbor: J. W. Edwards, 1947.

Krebs, K. Dittersdorfiana. Berlin: Gebr. Paetel, 1900.

Leo, G. Leonardo Leo . . . Napoli: Melfi & Joele, 1905.

Library of Congress, Music Division. The Elizabeth Sprague Coolidge Foundation. Autograph musical scores in the Coolidge Foundation collection. Washington, 1950.

Mendelssohn-Bartholdy, F. Letters, ed. G. Selden-Goth. New York: Pantheon, 1945.

Bibliography—*continued*

Nottebohm, G. Beethoveniana. Leipzig & Winterthur: J. Rieter-Biedermann, 1872.

Raabe, P. Franz Liszt. 2 v. Stuttgart & Berlin: Cotta, 1931.

Radoux, J. T. Vieuxtemps, sa vie, ses oeuvres. 2nd ed. Liège: A. Bénard, 1893.

Saint-Foix, G. de. "Les symphonies de Clementi," *Rivista musicale italiana*, XXXI (1924), 1-22.

Schmieder, W. Musikerhandschriften in drei Jahrhunderten. Leipzig: Breitkopf & Härtel, 1939.

——. Thematisches Verzeichnis der Werke Johann Sebastian Bachs. Leipzig: Breitkopf & Härtel, 1950.

Schmitz, E. "Louis Spohr's Jugendoper *Alruna*," *Zeitschrift der internationalen Musikgesellschaft*, XIII (1911-12), 293-299.

Sixty-six XVII-XX century Italian music manuscripts from the Natale Gallini collection. New York: Parke-Bernet Galleries, 1949.

Spivacke, H. "A recent gift from Mr. Fritz Kreisler," *Library of Congress Quarterly Journal*, VI, no. 3 (May 1949), 57-62.

Van Patten, N. Catalogue of the Memorial Library of Music, Stanford University. Stanford, California: Stanford University, 1950.

Versteigerung der Musikbibliothek Werner Wolffheim. 2 v. Berlin, 1928-29.

Waters, E. N. "A Brahms manuscript: the *Schicksalslied*," *Library of Congress Quarterly Journal*, III, no. 3 (May 1946), 14-18.

——. Library of Congress, Music Division. The Gertrude Clark Whittall Foundation. Autograph musical scores and autograph letters in the Whittall Foundation collection. Washington, 1951.

——. "Liszt's *Soirées de Vienne*," *Library of Congress Quarterly Journal*, VI, no. 2 (Feb. 1949), 10-19.

——. "The music collection of the Heineman Foundation," *Notes*, VII (1949-50), 181-216.

Wotquenne, A. Thematisches Verzeichnis der Werke C. P. E. Bachs. Leipzig: Breitkopf & Härtel, 1905.

Yale University Library. William A. Speck Collection of Goetheana. Goethe's Works . . . a catalogue . . . ed. C. F. Schreiber. Vol. 1. New Haven: Yale University Press, 1940.

Zavadini, G. Donizetti, vita, musica, epistolario. Bergamo: Istituto italiano d'arti grafiche, 1948.